THE TICHBORNE CLAIMANT

The Tichborne Claimant:
A Victorian Sensation

ROHAN McWILLIAM

hambledon
continuum

Hambledon Continuum is an imprint of Continuum Books

Continuum UK
The Tower Building
11 York Road
London SE1 7NX

Continuum US
80 Maiden Lane
Suite 704
New York, NY 10038

www.continuumbooks.com

First published 2007

British Library Cataloguing-in-Publication Data
A catalogue record for this book is available from the British Library.

ISBN 10: 1–8528–5478–2

Typeset by Benn Linfield
Printed and bound by MPG Books Ltd, Cornwall

Contents

*To my parents
Allen and Charmian McWilliam
and to my aunt
Fay Solomonsz*

Illustrations

Text Illustrations

Plates

Acknowledgements

This book represents a search for the man who launched the greatest *cause-célèbre* of the nineteenth century and who became an unlikely hero for the British working classes. It was written because the standard histories of the Victorian period did not know what to make of it and thus ignored an affair that many people at the time considered one of the most important issues in British public life. Why were so many people desperate to help a butcher become a baronet? Answering that question, I believe, requires the resources of cultural history. The Tichborne cause reveals a mosaic of mentalities and attitudes that we still do not fully understand. In this book I have tried to be true to the remarkable events that unfolded in the law courts of Westminster during the 1870s but I have also sought to reconstruct the mindset of the people who turned the Tichborne case into one of the largest agitations of the age.

The greatest pleasure of completing any book is the opportunity to thank the people and institutions that made it possible. *The Tichborne Claimant* is derived from an earlier D.Phil thesis that I wrote at the University of Sussex where I was privileged enough to be supported by Professor John F. C. Harrison, who has been an inspiration to me ever since my first weeks as an undergraduate. My thanks must also go to my thesis examiners: Alun Howkins (another mentor) and to Asa Briggs. I hope this book reflects some of the lively, creative and interdisciplinary atmosphere that has always characterised Sussex. I was lucky subsequently to join the Institute of Historical Research in the University of London and to learn especially from a remarkable generation of younger scholars that was nourished by its seminars and lively discussion in the tearoom.

The final writing up of the book was made possible by a grant from the Arts and Humanities Research Council and from Anglia Ruskin University, Cambridge. I am extremely grateful to my colleagues: Mary Abbott, Alison Ainley, Clarissa Campbell Orr (who womanfully shouldered additional administrative burdens whilst I was away), Leonardo Castillo, Jonathan Davis, Andrew Flint, Nicholas Goddard, Tony Kirby, Paul McHugh, Theo Schulte, Don Watts and the late David Weigall. This book was researched in libraries and archives all over Britain and the United States. I would particularly like to thank the staff of the British Library (both at St Pancras and Colindale), Georgetown University Library (Washington DC), Hampshire Record Office, Hanley Central Library, the Institute of Historical Research, Leeds District Archives, Leicestershire Record Office, the Library of Congress (Washington DC), the Lilly Library (Indiana University), Lincoln's Inn Library, the London Library, the National Archives, St Marylebone Public Library, Senate House (University of London) Library, Southampton University Library, Sussex University Library, University College London Library and the Warwick Record Office. Gill Arnott, Julie Biddlecombe and Alastair Penfold at Westbury Manor Museum, Fareham, Stella Beddoe at Brighton Museum, John Ross at the Crime Museum, Scotland Yard, Eilagh Rurenga at Riverina Regional Library, Wagga Wagga, and Nicholas Sheetz and Anna T. Zakarija at Georgetown University Library have been especially helpful. I would like to thank Brighton and Hove Museums, the Hampshire County Council Museums and Archives Service, the Potteries Museum and Art Gallery, Stoke on Trent, and an anonymous private collector who have generously allowed me permission to reproduce items in their collections.

Several friends generously took time to read various chapters and improved the book: Mark Hampton, Susie Steinbach, Justine Taylor and James Vernon. A number of people also provided references or Tichborne materials: the late Arthur Brown, Michael Diamond, Roy Palmer, Leslie Shepard and Dorothy Thompson (who kindly sent me copies of a large number of Tichborne ballads she possessed). Michael Roe, author of a wonderful earlier book on the Claimant, has been extremely supportive to me. I would also like to thank the late Mia Woodruff, widow of Douglas Woodruff, another Tichborne historian, whose collection of materials relating to the case are kept at Georgetown University (Washington DC). I am grateful to Anthony Loudon, John Loudon (who kindly allowed me to visit Tichborne House), Shaun Orton and Timothy Radcliffe OP, all of whom have their connections to people described in this book.

At Hambledon Continuum, I am grateful to Martin Sheppard and Tony Morris. Their commitment to their authors and to publishing History is fast becoming a legend within the profession. Martin Sheppard has also proved an exemplary and eagle-eyed editor as well as a source of excellent advice.

This book was made possible by a rich academic dialogue with a lively group of fellow historians and other scholars who have turned its composition into an adventure. What follows is not an exhaustive list but I would like to thank Brenda Assael, Peter Bailey, Logie Barrow, Joseph O. Baylen, Eugenio Biagini, Dympna Callaghan, Malcolm Chase (who first mentioned the Tichborne case to me), Becky Conekin, Matthew Cragoe, Cathy Crawford, Geoffrey Crossick, Hugh Cunningham, Owen Davies, Ian Dyck, Pamela Edwards, James Epstein, Margot Finn, Martin Francis, Anne Goldgar, the late Robert Gray, Simon Gunn, Michelle Hawley, Ian Haywood, Martin Hewitt, Tim Hitchcock, Kali Israel, Louis James, Anne Janowitz, Patrick Joyce, Rod Kedward, Christopher Kent, Marius Kwint, Jon Lawrence, Paul Maloney, Peter Mandler, Norris Saakwa Mante, Saho Matsumoto-Best, Clare Midgely, Lydia Murdoch, David Nash, James Obelkevich, Richard Oliver, Douglas Peers, Roland Quinault, Mick Reed, Lucy Riall, Judith Rowbotham, Deborah Ryan, James Ryan, the late Raphael Samuel, John Seed, John Shepherd, Joe Spence, John Styles, David Sugarman, Keith Surridge, Antony Taylor, Miles Taylor, David Wayne Thomas, F. M. L. Thompson, Susan Thorne, Amanda Vickery, Dror Wahrman, Tim Wales, Judith Walkowitz, Chris Waters, Julie Wheelwright, Sue Wiseman, Eileen Yeo and Stephen Yeo. My friends outside academia have been no less important. I would particularly like to mention John and Jackie Adam, Stephen Bagley, Diana Banks, Gerald Brady, the late Peter DeAth, Simon Frances, Howard Gilbert, Celia Gurowitch, Fiona Hedgcock, Manus Henry, Bernadette Kiernan, Liz Kirby, Chris Law, Gerry McGough, Gordon McWilliam (my radical uncle), Tara McWilliam, Glenn Mitchell, Stephanie Muggivan, Mary O'Dowd, Len and Kay Orton, Becky Parker, Antoine Rizk, Barbara and Adam Simon, Kevin Richmond, Fionualla and Mike Webb, Julia and Dominic Webb and Ralph Wellington. Needless to say, none of the above has any responsibility for the book's faults. All of them helped the book along its way to completion. Thanks also to Ben Hayes, Joanna Kramer and Anya Wilson.

This book is dedicated to my parents and to my aunt. They have always taught that it is vital to be creative, to ask questions, to be passionate about art, Dickens, the Brontes, the films of Jean Cocteau and John Ford, to vote Labour but also, more importantly, to be kind. My nephew and niece, Alex and Saskia, livened up the final part of the project. The final thanks go to Kelly Boyd, the Tennessee-born historian and cinéaste who has become my wife. This book is very much part of a conversation between us (and so is everything I write). At our first meeting, she nonplussed me with the information that, when studying for her MA, she had written a paper on the Tichborne Claimant (this is the only important work on the subject I have been unable to consult). She has since read the manuscript more times than either of us can remember. What follows is a volume about a man who was alleged to be an impostor. There has, however, been nothing false about the care Kelly has brought to the book or the love she has brought to our marriage. I have been blessed.

*When we recall the details of that great romance we marvel to see
what daring truth may freely take in constructing a tale, as compared
with the poor little conservative risks permitted to fiction.
The fiction-artist could achieve no success with the materials
of this splendid Tichborne romance. He would have to drop out
the chief characters; the public would say such people are impossible.
He would have to drop out a number of the most picturesque incidents;
the public would say such things could never happen. And yet
the chief characters did exist, and the incidents did happen.*

Mark Twain

Introduction

It was an unfortunate end. On April Fool's Day 1898, a man died of heart failure at his lodgings in Marylebone. He was penniless and alone – just one of Victorian London's large destitute population. His poverty had forced the woman he normally lived with to find shelter with her mother. In his final days he had lacked money for both food and warmth. The lives and deaths of such paupers are usually anonymous affairs. Yet his passing did not go unremarked; it featured in most national and local newspapers. Publicans in Marylebone clubbed together to pay for his funeral and two undertakers vied for the privilege of burying him. On the day of the funeral, five thousand people attended as he was laid to rest in Paddington Cemetery. From a photograph taken as the coffin passed through the cemetery's gates, we can see the onlookers were men and women of all classes. Perhaps they wanted to pay their respects, or just tell their grandchildren that they had been there. One wreath read 'A Tribute from a Friend of 1873'. The man's grave was unmarked as it was a pauper burial but on his coffin was inscribed the name that he had sought over more than thirty years. For this was a man who had a story to tell. It was a tale that embraced all points on the compass, from the Australian Bush to the backstreets of London, from a darkened hotel room in Paris to the *cordilleras* of Chile. His identity had provoked the greatest guessing game of the Victorian age. In his day, he had been toasted and reviled throughout Britain. Some defended him, many hated him, no one could ignore him. He was the Tichborne Claimant.

In the two decades following the Reform Act of 1867, the best known public figures in Britain were Queen Victoria, Benjamin Disraeli, William Gladstone, W.G. Grace and a fat man who maintained he was a long lost aristocrat. The claimant to the Tichborne inheritance, whether seen as scoundrel, lovable rogue or aggrieved freeborn Englishman, achieved a celebrity that puzzled contemporaries. Who was he? And why did his story dazzle the public imagination from 1867 to 1886? These questions form the basis of this book.

During the 1870s, many people risked ridicule and the loss of reputation to protest their support for a man considered in high society to be an impostor; some sacrificed a great deal of money in the attempt. Still more devoured the latest installments of the (then) longest trials in English legal history as they unfolded in daily newspapers. The case sparked one of the largest political agitations between the defeat of Chartism in 1848 and the rise of socialism in the 1880s and 1890s. Many working-class people saw the Claimant as their champion and believed that if he could only achieve his inheritance, the world would somehow be a better place.

In the forgotten history of an unlikely hero and his movement, we can find not only an extraordinary story but also a glimpse into the popular mind at a moment of transformation. The Tichborne cause was fought over at precisely the moment when modern mass politics and mass culture were beginning to emerge. In these pages, we will see how complex this moment of democratic change really was.

PART ONE

The Man from Wagga Wagga

I

Enter the Claimant

It began with the land. The four white Tuscan columns of Tichborne House look out over 116 acres of parkland, close to the village of Alresford, near Winchester.[1] The River Itchen flows by and forms a fishpond in Tichborne Park. Beyond, the parish of Tichborne (whose population never exceeded four hundred before 1900) was a landscape shaped by fields of wheat and barley, little touched by the changes of Victoria's century. Rebuilt around 1803, Tichborne House was an intimate example of a stately mansion, befitting the Tichbornes' status as part of the minor aristocracy and one of the oldest Hampshire families (the original Tichborne House had been built in the twelfth century). Shortly before he was executed for his involvement in the Babington Plot to assassinate Queen Elizabeth I, Chidiock Tichborne wrote to his wife: 'I am descended from a house, from two hundred years before the Conquest never stained till this my misfortune.'[2] History mattered to the Tichbornes because they were haunted by an ancient heritage that included an unusual story – the Tichborne Dole.

This medieval legacy was a tale of aristocratic feminine charity. In the reign of Henry II, Lady Mabella de Tichborne on her deathbed asked her husband, Sir Roger, to do something for the poor. The unfeeling Sir Roger replied that he would give as much grain to the poor as she could crawl round during the time it took for a torch to burn. The dying woman accepted his offer and, making a superhuman effort, managed to drag herself round twenty-three acres (land still known as 'the Crawls'). Exhausted by her efforts, she died declaring that the corn in the land she had enclosed must be given each year to the poor – otherwise, disaster would come to the house of Tichborne and the male line would end: seven sons would have seven daughters. Her curse was attended to and each year grain was distributed on Lady Day, an event immortalised by a Flemish painter, Gillis von Tilborch, in 1670. His portrait of the Dole, still hanging at Tichborne, remains an abiding emblem of aristocratic paternalism.

With the coming of the Reformation the Tichbornes remained true to the Catholic Church. Thus it was that in 1586 Chidiock Tichborne, an ardent but impractical papist, supported Mary Queen of Scots and joined Antony Babington in his ill-fated attempt to dispatch Elizabeth I. Unfortunately for him, Tichborne had already been pinpointed by Sir Francis Walsingham and the Elizabethan secret service as a possible traitor and was arrested along with the other conspirators before any attempt could be made on the life of the Queen. Musing in the Tower of London on his approaching death, he penned a much anthologised poem:

My prime of youth is but a frost of cares,
My feast of joy is but a dish of pain,
My crop of corn is but a field of tares,
And all my good is but vain hope of gain.
The day is gone and yet I saw no sun,
And now I live, and now my life is done.

The spring is past, and yet it hath not sprung,
The fruit is dead, and yet the leaves are green,
My youth is gone, and yet I am but young,
I saw the world, and yet I was not seen,
My thread is cut, and yet it was not spun,
And now I live, and now my life is done.

I sought my death and found it in my womb,
I lookt for life and saw it was a shade,
I trode the earth and knew it was my tomb,
And now I die, and now I am but made.
The glass is full, and now the glass is run,
And now I live, and now my life is done.

He was only twenty-seven. His body, like that of his fellow assassins, was torn apart with such ferocity that even his intended victim, Elizabeth I, was shocked by the cruelty of their execution. It was Mary of Scotland's complicity in the Babington Plot that shortly led to her own death.

Despite this embarrassment and their continued Recusant status, the Tichbornes prospered and their local influence remained intact. In 1621, James I actually made Benjamin Tichborne a baronet for his services as a courtier. Lady Mabella's curse was not forgotten and the Tichborne Dole continued, but in the late eighteenth century, Sir Henry Tichborne, the seventh baronet, decided that enough was enough. The prospect of free flour annually attracted an army of vagrants to the area; he therefore abandoned the Dole. Unfortunately, as the years went by he could not miss the fact that his eldest son (also called Henry) produced seven daughters and his other sons either remained unmarried or appeared unlikely to have issue. Moreover, part of Tichborne House fell down. If that were not bad enough, Sir Henry was interned at Verdun in 1803 during the Napoleonic Wars. Whilst he was away, his agents demolished what remained of Tichborne House and replaced it with the current building. When he returned to Hampshire, Sir Henry decided to heed Lady Mabella's words and restored the Dole, a custom that persists to the present day.

Unknown to Sir Henry, another calamity was in store for the Tichbornes, one that would unfold as the new century proceeded. Trapped in Verdun with his son, James, Sir Henry had made the acquaintance of Henry Seymour of Knoyle, near Salisbury in Wiltshire. The Seymours traced their descent from the family of Jane Seymour, the third wife of Henry VIII. Henry Seymour's father had been a lover of Madame du Barry, the last mistress of Louis XV. Like the two Tichbornes, Henry Seymour found himself a prisoner of Napoleon at Verdun in 1803. It was here that he fathered a daughter out of wedlock, with Felicité Dailly-Brimont, the illegitimate daughter of the Duc de Bourbon Conti, a cousin of Louis XV. The girl was named Henriette-Felicité and she was brought up a Catholic in a convent, always aware of the stain of illegitimacy. Nevertheless, she was a Bourbon Conti and as such received 450,000 francs when the duke's property was distributed on his death. She instinctively preferred France to England, especially after her father married an Englishwoman in 1817. During her few visits to Knoyle, Henriette was never terribly happy. When she reached the age of twenty-four, Henry Seymour became concerned about finding a husband for her. At this point, he remembered his old friend, James Tichborne, with whom he had been imprisoned and who most presumed was a lifelong bachelor. Although much older than Henriette-Felicité (he was forty-two) and hobbled by a withered leg which made him walk with a limp, he had the advantage of being a Catholic gentleman. Moreover, on meeting the pretty French girl, he conveniently fell in love with her and the pair were married on 1 August 1827.

The Bourbon Contis frowned on the match believing Henriette-Felicité should have married into the French nobility. Perhaps they were right, for the couple soon found that more than age separated them. Quite why the passionate Henriette agreed to marry this bluff, hard-drinking Englishman with whom she had nothing in common is unclear – although her failure as a woman of her class to find an appropriate match by the age of twenty-four suggests it was a decision born of desperation on her part. James Tichborne's prospects were, in fact, not very good. The third son of Sir Henry, he was unlikely to inherit the Tichborne baronetcy whereas, as a Bourbon Conti, Henriette brought with her a not inconsiderable dowry. They quarrelled regularly and James came to bemoan his wife's violent temper. Having married in haste, they were free to repent at leisure.

Hampshire Society frowned on James Tichborne's decision to marry an illegitimate and headstrong Frenchwoman. We should not therefore be surprised that he opted to settle with his wife in Paris. It was here at their home in the Rue de Ferme that James became the only one of Sir Henry's sons to produce a male heir. On 5 January 1829, Henriette gave birth to her first child, Roger Charles Doughty Tichborne.

The Tichbornes would have been unaware of another birth, five years later. The youngest of eight sons was born to a butcher called George Orton on 20 March 1834 and was named Arthur. Wapping High Street, the site of George Orton's shop, could not have provided a greater contrast to the genteel surroundings in which the young Roger Tichborne grew up. Wapping's dark, narrow streets were overshadowed by the London docks. The local population was made up of seafarers and the enormous army of casual labour who served Britain's imperial trade, loading and unloading ships and housing the Empire's produce in the giant warehouses that jostled one another for space along the Thames. The continual arrival of steamships meant that Wapping's inhabitants virtually never slept; the wharves and docks heaved with labour. Next door to George Orton's shop was the house where, it was alleged, the young Horatio Nelson had purchased his uniform before going to sea.[3] To be born in Wapping was to be born without many of life's advantages but with a ticket to the world. Arthur Orton was sent to sea as a cabin boy in 1849, despite having been a sickly child troubled by St Vitus's dance. His ship sailed round the Horn to Valparaiso where he promptly deserted and travelled for a while in Chile. Returning to his father's shop in Wapping, he set to work as a butcher and met a local girl, Mary Ann Loder, who became his sweetheart for a time. By this time there were a number of Orton children working in the butcher's shop. Finding he was not needed, Arthur decided to emigrate to Australia in 1852 at the age of eighteen.

As he grew up in the France of Louis-Philippe, Roger Tichborne was trapped between two parents who could not stand each other. The young

Tichborne House

Roger was infantilised by his mother to an extreme, being forced to wear frocks until he was twelve. He was brought up essentially as a Frenchman. When he later learnt English he always spoke it with a pronounced French accent. Extremely thin, he was a sickly and sensitive boy. Two sisters, Mabella and Alice, were also born but both died in childhood. Another brother, Alfred, however, survived to adulthood. In 1845, at the age of fifteen, Roger travelled to England without Henriette to attend the funeral of his grandfather, Sir Henry Tichborne, the eighth baronet.

There was now a new baronet, Sir Edward Doughty. He had been away from England for much of his life, managing the estates of the Duke of Buckingham in Jamaica. When he returned, he brought with him a young black servant, Andrew Bogle, who was put to work at Tichborne House. Sir Edward had received an inheritance in 1826 from a distant cousin, Elizabeth Doughty, that included an estate at Upton, near Poole in Dorset, and the freehold of a large part of Bloomsbury, including Doughty Street where Charles Dickens lived for a time. The intention was to create a new Doughty line and Edward adopted the new name as a condition of inheritance.[4] He and his wife, the daughter of the ninth Lord Arundell of Wardour, had a daughter called Katherine in 1834.

The Tichborne Dole (based on the painting by Gillis von Tilborch, 1670)

It was at Sir Henry Tichbornes's funeral that James Tichborne decided to regain control of his son Roger from his wife and to make sure that he was brought up as an English gentleman. After talking to Henry Seymour, but without consulting Henriette, he dispatched his son to the leading English Jesuit boarding school, Stonyhurst. Henriette naturally was aggrieved that her son had in effect been stolen from her and blamed both James and the Tichbornes. Roger's tutor was even instructed to go to England and kidnap the boy, but this attempt failed. There was nothing more she could do, so Roger remained at Stonyhurst. Relations between Henriette and the Tichbornes deteriorated further the following year when, one night, she turned up at Tichborne House where Roger and James were staying. On account of the lateness of the hour, Sir Edward Doughty refused her admittance and she was forced to put up at an inn in nearby Alresford. Outraged at this insult to his wife, James Tichborne did not speak to his brother for four years.

At Stonyhurst, Roger acquired greater proficiency in the English language and the manners of the English upper class. He also enjoyed his removal from the embrace of his domineering mother, insisting in his letters to her that he was not the invalid she had always made him out to be. Quite how much he actually learned academically at Stonyhurst would later be a matter of dispute but he certainly took to drinking, smoking and the life of the carefree, aristocratic lout.

When Roger left Stonyhurst in 1848, Henriette purchased a commission for him in the 6th Dragoon Guards (the 'Carabineers') and he spent the period from 1849 to 1852 stationed in Ireland. Although he seems to have coped, life with the Carabineers did not transform his thin frame or remove his nervous twitch. With his strong continental accent, his fellow soldiers often dubbed him 'Frenchy'. He served as a cornet and then as lieutenant. He remained close to his uncle, Sir Edward, and on leave stayed with him at Tichborne, devoting himself to the sports of hunting and fly-fishing. It was here that a romance began to develop between Roger and his first cousin, Katherine Doughty (Sir Edward's daughter). Roger was nineteen and Kate (or, as she was often known, 'Kattie') fifteen.

Unfortunately, both of Kate's parents took exception to the relationship. Whilst they were fond of Roger, they could not help noticing his loose morals. He smoked and drank to excess and on one occasion was spotted reading one of the pornographic novels of Paul de Kock in the chapel at Tichborne. Their daughter could do better. In any case, Roger was Kate's cousin. They placed obstacles in the way of the marriage, and then, in February 1853, Roger was summoned to see Sir Edward and forbidden to see Kate ever again. As he put it in a letter, Roger was 'thunderstruck'. By this time, Sir Edward was close to death and he was persuaded by his daughter to sanction the marriage in three years' time (when Kate would have come of age). The understanding was also that his daughter should feel free to look for someone else she preferred in the meantime. Roger made a vow to the Virgin Mary that if their marriage went ahead he would build a new chapel at Tichborne.

Fuming at the tyranny of the older generation, Roger hoped that he would be able to go with his regiment to India, an ideal place to forget his troubles. When, however, it became clear that the Carabineers were going to stay in England, he decided to cash in his commission to travel in South America. Roger was not alone in viewing this region with excitement. After years of stagnating trade, British merchants had begun to focus on South America, turning some of it into part of Britain's informal empire. After a period of instability that followed independence from Spain, countries such as Chile were moving towards recognisably constitutional forms of government.[5] For gentlemen of Roger Tichborne's ilk, the desire to hunt was also a deep-seated part of their identity. South America promised a relatively untouched wilderness with exciting species of birds and animals that could be returned as trophies for stuffing to adorn the walls of Tichborne. No aristocratic house was complete without its numerous animal trophies, although it was more usual for hunters to look to Africa or Asia for the pursuit of game.[6] Roger had been at Stonyhurst with the son of the naturalist Charles Waterton, whose *Wanderings in South America* with its detailed instructions on 'preserving birds for cabinets of natural history' may have been an inspiration.[7] Before leaving, Roger entrusted a 'sealed packet' to Sir Edward's steward, Vincent Gosford.

On arrival in Valparaiso, Chile, in June 1853, Roger received word that Sir Edward was dead and that his father, James Tichborne, had become the tenth baronet. As the eldest son, Roger was of course heir apparent to the fortune. Henriette moved into Tichborne but hated living there (admiring only its trees) and pestered Sir James to return to Paris.

Roger decided to move on from Valparaiso to Chile's capital, Santiago. Between the two cities, there is a small village called Melipilla. It is unclear whether Roger stayed there or even passed through it but he could have done. Roger then returned to Valparaiso where he rejoined his ship and travelled north to Lima in Peru from where he went inland shooting birds before returning to Santiago (and possibly to Melipilla). Here his valet, John Moore, later a witness for the Tichborne Claimant, fell ill and was forced to return home. It was also at Santiago that Roger sat for two daguerreotype photographs that were sent back to his relatives, providing a key piece of evidence as to what he actually looked like. Clearly slim, he was handsome in a droopy kind of way with a thin moustache resting on his delicate lips.

In January 1854, he crossed the Andes and arrived at Buenos Aires. Writing to his mother, he spoke of the 'wildness and magnificent scenery' that spread out before him on top of the *cordilleras* of the Andes, the like of which he had never seen before.[8] From Buenos Aires, he travelled north to Rio de Janiero. It was then his intention to visit Jamaica and eventually Mexico. At Rio, he found a ship called the *Bella* bound for Kingston, Jamaica. Unfortunately, there was insufficient time for him to arrange a passport but he agreed with the captain of the ship that he should be smuggled on board so as to escape the eye of the authorities. The ship set sail on 20 April 1854 with Roger as its only passenger alongside a cargo of coffee. The *Bella* was never seen again and all on board were assumed to have drowned.

Henriette was understandably distraught about the loss of her eldest son, even though their relations had been strained. She refused to believe that Roger had drowned, despite the discovery of an upturned lifeboat with the

Sir Roger Tichborne

Bella's name on it, suggesting that all on board had perished. About the year 1858, a former sailor, now a vagrant, appeared at Tichborne asking for alms. Together with an old friend of the family, Francis Baigent, Henriette quizzed him insistently about whether he had ever heard of the *Bella*. The sailor volunteered that he had heard that the crew of a ship of that name had ended up in Australia. Her husband urged her to pay no attention to such nonsense but she would not let go of the idea.

In 1862, Sir James Tichborne died. Had Roger been alive, he would have become the eleventh baronet. Instead the title passed to his younger brother,

Alfred. As it turned out, Alfred's life was as brief as his brother's had apparently been and, during the short time he was baronet, he succeeded in bankrupting the estate. His ambition was to build the world's largest yacht (which he would then use to search the world for Roger), a project into which he poured money without success. His family was forced to move out of Tichborne House and lease it. When Alfred died on 22 February 1866, his wife Teresa was pregnant with their only son, Henry Alfred Joseph Tichborne, who became the twelfth baronet.

Now Dowager Lady Tichborne, Henriette longed for Roger's return. Why had he not contacted her? Following the sailor's suggestion that the crew of the *Bella* had ended up in Australia, she placed advertisements for Roger in the *Times* and the world's press in 1863. A reward was offered for information about his whereabouts. Concerning Roger, she stated that he 'would, at the present time, be about thirty-two years of age, is of a delicate constitution, rather tall, with very light brown hair and blue eyes'. She then went on to note that he was the son of Sir James Tichborne and 'is heir to all his estates'. There was no immediate response. Two years later, however, an advertisement in the *Times* placed by Arthur Cubbitt's Missing Friends Agency of Sydney caught her eye. Cubitt specialised in tracing the whereabouts of former convicts and, on being contacted by Henriette, agreed to circulate her advertisement in the Australian press.

At about this time, a man in New South Wales read Mary Elizabeth Braddon's latest sensational bestseller, *Aurora Floyd* (1863). He was struck by the following passage: 'I should think fellows with plenty of money and no brains must have been invented for the good of fellows with plenty of brains and no money, and that's how we continue to help our equilibrium in the universal see-saw.' To commit this sentiment to memory he simplified it slightly and wrote it down in his pocket-book: 'Some men has plenty money and no brains, and some men has plenty brains and no money. Surely men with plenty money and no brains were made for men with plenty brains and no money.' He then signed his name, 'R. C. Tichborne, Bart'.

Australia in the 1860s was a frontier society. With the gradual ending of transportation between 1840 and 1868, much of the land in the east was developed for farming. But what really drew people to Australia was the prospect of gold. Following the discovery of gold in 1851, British and Irish people of all classes were drawn to the country to seek their fortunes. 150,000 immigrants flocked to the goldfields of New South Wales and

Victoria in the 1850s. As with many frontier societies, order frequently broke down and outlawry was rife. If an aristocrat wanted to lose his identity, remove himself from the gaze of his family and descend among the common people, this was the place to do it. It was a land for chancers.

The story of the Tichborne Claimant really commences in 1865 with Mrs Gibbes. She was the wife of William Gibbes, a lawyer in Wagga Wagga, New South Wales, about half way between Sydney and Melbourne on the Murrumbidgee river. The town (whose name comes from the aboriginal and means 'a place of crows') had been founded in the late 1840s and its population in 1865 was only about 700. Wagga Wagga was mainly known as a place to buy and sell livestock.[9] It was Mrs Gibbes who noticed the Dowager's advertisement in a newspaper and it set her thinking. One of her husband's clients was a butcher called Tomas Castro. His business had failed and he was employing Gibbes to declare his bankruptcy. Despite his Spanish name, the butcher's accent marked him out as English. He had just married an illiterate Irish woman called Mary Ann Bryant in the Methodist church at Wagga Wagga. She was a twenty-year-old former domestic servant, who was pregnant with their first child (and had another child from a previous relationship). They lived in poverty. Castro's shop in Garwood Street was no more than a small, wooden shack. In the course of discussions with Gibbes, Castro had casually mentioned some property to which he was entitled in England and then spoke mysteriously about a shipwreck in which he had been involved. In a land of convicts, it was not unusual for men to prefer not to talk in too much detail about their pasts, so Gibbes had not persisted. Mrs Gibbes, on the other hand, put two and two together. Was this not the man whose whereabouts were being sought by a grand aristocratic family back in England? Her husband agreed that appearances could be deceptive and there might be more to this butcher than met the eye.

Gibbes encountered Castro walking down the street and challenged him as to his identity, saying that he knew his real name. Castro at first was reticent but Gibbes noticed that his pipe had the initials 'R.C.T.' scratched into it. 'Shall I say the name?' he offered. Castro protested immediately that he did not want his family to know about his whereabouts. Gibbes would have none of this and persuaded Castro that he should abandon his incognito and reveal himself to the world. After some hesitation, his client agreed to do as Gibbes suggested. This was the moment when Tomas Castro of Wagga Wagga became the Tichborne Claimant or, as he would have put it, Sir Roger Tichborne.

As the putative heir to the Tichborne inheritance, the Claimant represented an investment opportunity. Both Gibbes and Cubitt (who was
contacted about the discovery) had expectations of a lucrative reward for
discovering the eleventh Tichborne baronet. Gibbes took the Claimant and
his family under his wing, paid off his debts and urged him to write home
to his mother. Cubitt in the meantime also informed Henriette that Roger
was alive and well. Anxious to take credit for the successful delivery of her
son, he warned that the Claimant had been engaged 'in a menial capacity'.
The idea of an aristocrat who had disowned luxury and opted to live the life
of an ordinary person would soon capture the public imagination.

In return for his services, Gibbes insisted that the Claimant make out a
will. The Claimant set out details of Tichborne property in the Isle of Wight
(that did not exist) and, even more alarmingly, referred to his mother as
'Hannah Frances'. He wrote to Henriette promising to return home if she
would forward the money: 'Of one thing rest Assured, that although I have
been in a humble condition of Life I have never let any act disgrace you or
my Family. I have been A poor man and nothing worse.' To identify himself,
he mentioned a brown mark on his side and the card case at Brighton.
Although Roger possessed the former, the second reference was obscure (the
Claimant later maintained that he had once lost a large amount of money to
a man who was later involved in a notorious card swindle in Brighton). But
this was enough for Henriette who was mourning the death of her son
Alfred in February 1866. At least her elder son was now coming back.

Once Mary Ann had given birth to a girl, Teresa, in March 1866, it was
time for the Claimant and his family to leave Australia. The Dowager cabled
money for the passage to England but the Claimant by this time had been
able to borrow sufficient funds. He took his family to Sydney and remarried
Mary Ann in the Catholic church at Goulburn in July. She was only able to
sign her name by a mark. Flush with cash, the Claimant put up at the
Metropolitan Hotel, which he tried to buy, grandly proffering a cheque for
£10,000 to be drawn from Drummond's Bank in London. The Tichbornes
did not bank at Drummond's, so the cheque bounced. It was typical of the
Claimant's high spirits at this time that he felt he could get away with this
kind of gesture and the episode shows that there were already enough people
on hand to believe him.

In Sydney were two people who had actually known Roger Tichborne. The
first was Michael Guilfoyle, a former gardener on the Tichborne estates, who
instantly recognised the Claimant as Sir Roger and invited him into his

home. Subsequently, after repeated requests for money by the Claimant, he withdrew his recognition and insisted he was an impostor. More importantly, the Claimant was visited by Andrew Bogle, an old negro servant who had once worked for Sir Edward Doughty and knew Roger well. He had married two women during his time at Tichborne; the first was a nurse to Lady Doughty and the second a local school-mistress. Both had died. Following the death of Sir Edward, he had used a pension from Lady Doughty to retire to Sydney with his two sons, believing, as he was later to say, that the streets were paved with gold. It was one of his sons, a barber, who first heard about the Claimant in Sydney and sent Bogle to meet him. The Claimant saw him in the yard of the Metropolitan Hotel and hailed him, 'Halloo, Bogle, is that you?' According to his own subsequent testimony, Bogle did not immediately recognise the Claimant but, when they went inside, he said to him, 'How much stouter you are got'. About eleven stone two years previously, the Claimant was now some thirteen and a half stone in contrast to Roger's wraithlike figure. His weight, which was his most notable feature, was to increase dramatically over the next few years. At the time, he laughed to Bogle, 'Yes, I am not that tender lad I was when I left Tichborne'.[10] The weight did not prevent Bogle from deciding that this indeed was Sir Edward Doughty's nephew and he became the Claimant's most important witness until the day he died.

But how had Sir Roger Tichborne ended up in Australia? And why had he never bothered to contact his family? On this last point, the Claimant was never to produce a satisfactory answer, leaving it for others to reconstruct his motives or impose their own meanings on his conduct. In order to secure funds, however, the Claimant was forced to make a declaration about his life up to that time. He stated that the *Bella* had indeed been overturned during a storm at sea and that he, with some of the crew, had escaped in a longboat. Fortunately, they were picked up by a passing ship, the *Osprey*, which was bound for Melbourne. Here he assumed the identity of Tomas Castro, a name, he subsequently revealed, that was taken from a man he had met when visiting Melipilla in Chile.

It appears that Henriette herself, after seeing a photograph, had begun to wonder if the Claimant really was Roger. The Claimant responded to her doubts with an illiterate letter: 'Surely my dear Mama you must know my writing. You have cause a deal of truble. But it matters not. Has I have no wish to leave a coountry ware I enjoy such good health I have grown very stout ...' Surprisingly, Henriette was satisfied by this letter; it was time for

The Claimant's Hut

the son to return. The Claimant brought his family with him, as well as Old Bogle, Truth William Butts (the son of the owner of the Metropolitan Hotel, whom he had engaged as his secretary) and Rosina McArthur, the nurse to the Claimant's children. They caught the *Rakaia* which was bound for Panama. On board, the Claimant repeatedly propositioned the nurse and suggested they run off together in Panama for a new life in the United States. A shrewd lady, she turned him down. From Panama, the family sailed to New York, where they stayed for a month before the voyage across the Atlantic. They reached London on Christmas Day 1866.

The Claimant's first task was to find the Dowager. On arrival, however, he discovered that Henriette had returned to Paris. The Claimant deposited his family at Ford's Hotel in Manchester Street where (according to Bogle) the Tichbornes always stayed when in London. That same evening, he performed the act which, more than anything else, was to bring about his downfall. He took a cab to Wapping High Street where he knocked at what had once been the home of the Ortons. No one was in. He then visited the Globe public house nearby, where he asked about their whereabouts. The landlady told him that the Orton parents had died, though she was able to inform him of the location of two of the younger Ortons, Charles and Mary Ann (who was now Mrs Tredgett). To the landlady, Mrs Jackson, he seemed

The Tichborne Claimant (left) and Mary Anne Bryant, the Claimant's wife (right)

fascinated by the street and asked after various locals; he also seemed familiar
with the Globe pub itself. Mrs Jackson's mother then said, 'You must be the
Orton who left some twelve or fourteen years ago and who has not been
heard of since'. The Claimant denied this but said he was a friend of the
family. He also volunteered that he had been in Wapping 'some twelve or
fourteen years ago'. Upon being given the address of Mary Ann Tredgett (at
a lodging house she kept in East India Dock Road), the Claimant went off
to visit her, but no one was in. When he returned the following day, Mrs
Tredgett was still out but he did speak with her sister-in-law, Mrs Pardon.
Adopting the soubriquet of 'W.H. Stephens' (the name of an American
journalist he had met on the ship coming over), he was again asked if he
was the long lost Arthur Orton but replied, 'No, but I am a great friend of
Arthur Orton, who is one of the wealthiest men in the Colony, and I promised him that I would enquire after his sisters'. He then showed Mrs Pardon
a locket containing what he said were photographs of Arthur Orton's wife

Andrew Bogle

and child but which were in fact pictures of his own family. He left a much disputed letter which claimed to be by Arthur Orton and presented 'Mr Stephens' as a friend who had offered to find out how the Ortons of Wapping were. Quite why the Claimant should have carried out such a reckless act is one of the great mysteries of the case.

The Claimant then travelled to Hampshire, where he stayed at the Swan Hotel, Alresford, a short distance from Tichborne. By this time, the family home had been leased to a tenant, Colonel Franklin Lushington, formerly of the Scottish Fusiliers. Edward Rous, the owner of the Swan, was intrigued by his guest's curiosity about the Tichborne estate. The Claimant again employed an assumed name, but rumours had been circulating already in the neighbourhood about the return of Sir Roger. Rous thought he detected a resemblance between the stranger and the late Alfred Tichborne. The Claimant admitted who he was but urged that he did not want people to know about his presence until after he had seen the Dowager. Nevertheless, word immediately began to circulate and the Claimant was approached by the Tichborne family solicitor, Frederick Bowker, whom he rudely rebuffed.

A solicitor, however, was something that the Claimant himself needed. On his return to London, he secured the services of John Holmes, a lawyer who not only took the case but also agreed that the Claimant and his family, currently without funds, could stay at his home in Croydon.

Understandably, the rest of the Tichborne family was hostile to the new arrival, especially as he was a threat to the inheritance of the infant baronet, Alfred's son, Henry. Hostile articles about the Claimant began to appear in the *Pall Mall Gazette* by Matthew Higgins ('Jacob Omnium'). A leading journalist and advocate of administrative reform, Higgins was married to Roger Tichborne's cousin, Emily. It was clear to Holmes that the family was closing ranks against the Claimant. He therefore advised his client to proceed at once to Paris for the all-important meeting with the Dowager and they set off. As a premonition of things to come, a large crowd assembled at London Bridge to see the Claimant, who was already being much discussed in the press. Holmes and his client were accompanied by a Mr Leete, the man who had recommended the services of Holmes to the Claimant during a chance meeting in a railway station. Leete worked for Allsopps brewery, which employed Holmes as a solicitor. This was to be the first connection between the Tichborne cause and the drink interest.

Arriving in Paris, the three put up at the Hôtel de Lille et d'Albion. The following day, 10 January 1867, the Claimant was expected to visit the Dowager in the Place de la Madeleine where she was staying. For the Claimant, this was the key throw of the dice. With Henriette's support, it would be far more difficult for the Tichbornes to act legally against him. Without her, his claim would be over. Henriette sent a message urging him to come. The Claimant, however, was so ill that morning that he could not get out of bed. Clearly, his nerves had got the better of him, although sea-sickness was given as the cause of his indisposition. Message followed message but the Claimant insisted that he could not leave his room. Eventually, the Dowager decided to visit him herself. Entering his room, which was darkened, she found him reclining on a bed with a handkerchief over his face. She walked over to the bedside and removed the handkerchief.

2

Going to Law

The Dowager's recognition was immediate: 'He looks like his father, and his ears look like his uncle's.' We know what the Dowager said because her words were later repeated in court by her servant, John Coyne, who was in the room. She kissed the Claimant and insisted on sending out for the best medical assistance in Paris to promote his recovery. 'Where's your wife and child? What is your little girl's name?' she asked. The Claimant apologised, suggesting that he did not think she would care to see them, but Henriette would have none of this: 'They are yours and, therefore, they are mine; they are dear to me.'

What should we make of Henriette's recognition of the Claimant? Perhaps she was sincere. Perhaps, as many would insist, she was hysterical and eager to recognise anyone as her son. Perhaps the recognition was the understandable reaction to the recent loss of her son, Alfred, the last of her surviving children. Perhaps (more darkly), she knew exactly what she was doing and consequently helped to establish an impostor as a way of getting back at the Tichbornes whom she had always detested. Perhaps, finally, this really was her long lost son, returned from his sojourn in Australia, where he had abandoned the decadence of his aristocratic youth for the humble life of a butcher.

All that mattered for the moment was that Sir Roger Tichborne had returned to claim his inheritance. Holmes wrote to *The Times* announcing the result and persuaded the Dowager to sign a declaration at the British Embassy. Back in Tichborne, bells were rung to celebrate Sir Roger's return. The Claimant stayed with the Dowager for a week and soon recovered his health. But Holmes realised this was unlikely to be the end of the matter. Sir Roger's childhood tutor, the Jesuit Father Chatillon, had visited the Claimant and, on meeting him, turned to Henriette and said, 'He is not your son'. Henriette paid no attention but did agree with Holmes's suggestion that she should return to England to defend the Claimant against the sceptical Tichborne family. She also provided the Claimant with an income of £1,000 a year.

Back in England, the Claimant moved his family to a house called Essex Lodge in Croydon where they could be together and not impose on Holmes's hospitality. Aware of the high standard of proof that might be required in any subsequent trial, the solicitor realised that it was now imperative to build up the number of people who recognised the Claimant (Henriette's recognition might well not be sufficient). His client was therefore dispatched to Hampshire, where he put up at Alresford once more. Francis Baigent, the antiquarian and friend of the Tichbornes, recognised him, as did Edward Hopkins, the family solicitor (now retired), and J.P. Lipscomb, the family doctor. The Claimant also used this opportunity to resume Roger's former life of country sports. Mr Lamb, who sold fishing tackle in Alresford and who had once served the young Roger Tichborne, was struck by the fact that the Claimant asked for the same flies as Roger had done many years before. The Claimant visited Tichborne House where its lessee, Colonel Lushington, was so impressed by the Claimant's knowledge of the property that he became a firm believer in him. Given time, Lushington was even prepared to vacate Tichborne House.[1] Remarkably, the Claimant took as his groom Thomas Carter, who had once been Roger Tichborne's servant in the Carabineers and who recognised him at a meeting. This recognition was then followed by numerous Carabineers who, after encountering the Claimant, were prepared to testify that he was indeed their former fellow officer. James M'Cann, a former private in the Carabineers, visited the Claimant in Croydon and decided he was the man with whom he had served for two years. He subsequently admitted that the Claimant had paid him some money because he was living on a small pension, but it is unclear whether this was a matter of generosity or an attempt to buy his testimony.[2]

Others were not convinced. Henriette's brother, Henry Seymour, on meeting the Claimant, addressed him in French, which he could no longer speak (although, as we have noted, Roger was fluent in the language).[3] After a long period in the Australian Bush, he had apparently forgotten what was his native tongue. The Claimant would later insist that he could not even comprehend letters written in French by himself when young. Seymour was equally appalled when he produced letters containing the handwriting of Roger's father, which he did not recognise.

Even worse was the meeting with the former Katherine Doughty in March 1867. Not long after Roger Tichborne's departure for South America, she had married Joseph Percival Pickford Radcliffe, the scion of another eminent Catholic family. The Radcliffes called on the Claimant in Croydon, together with a cousin, Mrs Townley. Sir Joseph left his wife outside and entered the house with Mrs Townley, who wore a veil to make the Claimant believe she was the former Kate Doughty and thus catch him out. Moreover, Sir Joseph excluded the Dowager, who was at home, from the room in which the conversation was to take place. The real Lady Radcliffe later entered the house and they all spoke for an hour, at the end of which the Radcliffes were simply unsure about the Claimant and requested a further interview. This took place at Holmes's house in Sydenham Road. The Claimant believed Radcliffe would be accompanied by his wife and her mother, Lady Doughty. In fact Sir Joseph came with another Tichborne cousin, Mrs Nangle, who was again made out to be Lady Radcliffe. The Claimant was asked if he recognised Mrs Nangle. He did not and, on being asked by her if he spoke French, could only manage a paltry 'oui, madame'. The interview broke down there and then with denunciations of the Claimant as a fake. The Claimant for his part was furious at being subjected to a second imposture.

He had more luck elsewhere. On 18 May 1867, he was recognised by Anthony Wright Biddulph, a distant cousin of the Tichbornes, who became the only member of the family to accept his claim. A country squire devoted to hunting and shooting, Biddulph was to become an important leader in the Tichborne agitation. Initially, he had assumed the Claimant to be an impostor, but he was struck on talking to him by his knowledge of Biddulph's pipe collection, which persuaded him that he was the real thing. He and his wife became godparents when the Claimant's new son, Roger, was christened in the chapel at Tichborne. Biddulph (who had not known Sir Roger well) was not put off by the Claimant's lack of education or literacy because, as he pointed out, Roger was not a well-educated person. He later said:

> I could point out several English gentlemen who would not pass muster as English gentlemen any better than he does. They are men apparently no better than farmers, and I would place Tichborne among that class. I have heard of persons called English gentlemen who were so illiterate in conversation that you would take them to be nothing better than pig-jobbers.[4]

The Tichborne case exposed the poor level of education that prevailed among some members of the aristocracy.

Elite support also came in the form of Horace Pitt-Rivers (Lord Rivers) who believed in the Claimant because 'he thought he could tell a gentleman from a butcher'. A familiar figure on the turf, Lord Rivers stuck to the Claimant's cause, providing him with money. James Scott of Rotherfield, a local Justice of the Peace who had known Sir Roger, decided the Claimant was genuine (although his wife took the opposite view). In July, Guildford Onslow, the Liberal MP for Guildford, recognised the Claimant. The Onslows were major property owners in the Guildford area and dominated it politically. Guildford Onslow had known Sir Roger and now became the Claimant's leading supporter, causing much consternation in his own family. Although a sporting gentleman of the sort the Claimant often attracted, Onslow was a sincere believer in the Claimant and did more for him than anyone else.

Such recognitions were remarkable because the Claimant was rapidly gaining weight. At Christmas 1866, he was eighteen stone. Two years later, he was twenty-two stone, and by 1871 he would weigh a full twenty-eight stone four pounds.[5] His fatness became his most noticeable characteristic, a far cry from the wiry Roger Tichborne who had served in the Carabineers. The Claimant's bulk was picked up on in popular iconography. It was as though the new life he had entered into, complete with multi-course meals and fine wines, was written onto his body (which of course it probably was). What is more difficult to assess is the Claimant's accent. There were some suggestions that he spoke the English of Wapping but this was rarely employed against him, although we do know that Roger's French accent had completely disappeared. Perhaps we come closest to hearing his voice when the Attorney-General mocked him later for talking about a 'clerk in Holy Horders'.[6]

The hostility between the Claimant and the Tichbornes continued to increase because he was a threat to the inheritance of the infant baronet, Henry, Roger's nephew. At the same time as Disraeli's Reform Bill was piloted through Parliament, legal action by the Claimant to recover Sir Roger's property began. In June 1867 bills were filed in Chancery based on the Claimant's affidavits. Two actions ensued for the Tichborne and Doughty estates. The following month, the Claimant was examined in Chancery where he demanded that his sister-in-law, Teresa Tichborne (Alfred's widow), abandon the Tichborne estate and hand over all rents and profits to him. The annual rental value of the estates were subsequently valued (in 1874) at £21, 371, including land and properties in Hampshire, Dorset, Buckinghamshire and London. The examination in Chancery was the Claimant's opportunity to set forth what had happened to him during the time he had been away.

He told of how the *Bella* on its fourth day at sea had sprung a leak. The crew escaped in two long boats. Captain Birkett of Liverpool commanded the first boat, whilst he had gone in the second. The boats stayed close together but, after two days, lost sight of each other. For three further days the crew was adrift on the ocean, during which time he was seriously ill. None of his possessions survived the wreck of the *Bella* except the clothes he was wearing. Fortunately, he and the crew were saved by a passing ship, the *Osprey*, bound for Melbourne, Australia, where he was deposited. Although he might have returned to England at this point, there were few ships going to England because gold fever was causing crews to desert. Wandering the streets of Melbourne, he encountered William Foster, a cattle rancher. Impressed by Roger's riding abilities, Foster offered him a job working with horses back at his home in Gippsland. Attracted by the possibility of good hunting and shooting, he travelled with Foster to Boisdale, some three hundred miles from Melbourne. It was at this time that he adopted the name of Castro (after Don Tomas Castro whom he had known at Melipilla in Chile). He worked at the Boisdale and Dargo stations for a number of years before taking up residence in Wagga Wagga.

The Claimant was examined by the Tichborne family's barrister, Chapman Barber. If, as some commentators argue, the Tichborne trials were a cata-logue of legal mismanagement, it really began here.[7] The Claimant's subse-quent prosecutor, Henry Hawkins, who watched the proceedings, believed this would have been the best moment to demolish the Claimant's case, something that would have saved huge amounts in legal expenses that the Tichbornes and the Treasury would later have to bear. Barber's neutral line of questioning, and his tendency inadvertently to feed the Claimant useful pieces of information about Roger's past, meant that this was an opportu-nity missed. Hawkins believed that a more aggressive tone (his stock in trade) would have demolished the Claimant at this early stage.[8]

The matter of the 'sealed packet' that Roger had left behind with the steward, Vincent Gosford, arose. It had been destroyed following Roger's 'death'. The Claimant refused to talk about it in the examination but, shortly afterwards, revealed to Holmes that, before his departure for South America, Katherine Doughty had told him that she feared she was preg-nant. Allegedly, inside the sealed packet was a letter asking Gosford to look after Kate should the pregnancy prove to be true (as well as more mundane instructions about the upkeep of the estates). This was a staggering and scandalous claim which later, when it was expressed in open court, was to remove any chance of the Claimant's cause being considered respectable. Even if he were the genuine article, the Claimant was then a seducer of women, a figure that haunted the Victorian imagination. If he was a fake, he had attempted to blacken the name of a reputable lady of High Society. Even more mystifying, this revelation was completely unnecessary, as it added nothing to his case. The Claimant never played safe, making allegation after allegation with reckless abandon. It would later be suggested that this proved he was the right man. No impostor would come up with such appalling tales unless they were true. The Claimant made his scandalous confession in a written deposition to John Holmes, who decided to keep it secret for the time being. Later, in 1871, the Claimant alleged that he and Katherine Doughty had been married by Father Guidez, the parish priest at Tichborne, in a secret ceremony (which made them both bigamists).

The story began to take on an international dimension once more as letters and agents were dispatched across the globe to procure evidence. Holmes, hungry for anything that could substantiate the claim, asked the Claimant to write to Tomas Castro (whose name he had borrowed) in August 1867. The Castros lived in Melipilla on one of the main roads from Valparaiso to Santiago. A reply eventually came back not from Castro but from his son, Pedro, who explained that his father was now in a lunatic asylum. Pedro Castro had consulted the locals that the Claimant mentioned in his letter but, as subsequent correspondence showed, none could remember Roger Tichborne. They did, however, remember a young English sailor who had jumped ship called 'Arturo Orton'. Melipilla was soon invaded by lawyers from both sides attempting to discover the truth.

Attention also focused on Australia. Dobinson and Geare (solicitors for the Tichborne family) had dispatched an agent, John Mackenzie, to Australia in March 1867 to gather evidence. Mackenzie had an extraordinary piece of luck. It was the Claimant's testimony that, when he landed in Melbourne, following the wreck of the *Bella*, he had found employment with William Foster of the Boisdale cattle station. When Mackenzie arrived in Australia, he discovered that a friend of his was actually married to Foster's widow (now Sara Macalister). For the first time, photographic evidence proved important. On being shown a photograph of the Claimant, she identified him as Arthur Orton, whose name could be found in the Boisdale records. There was no reference to a 'Tomas Castro'. Moreover, Foster's widow had a copy of Orton's illiterate handwriting. Indefatigable in pursuit of his quarry, Mackenzie travelled to Hobart in Tasmania where Orton had originally come from. Here he found Mina Jury, a relative of the Ortons by marriage, who had originally been sent there as a convict. Arthur Orton had failed to repay some money she had leant him, so she was quite happy to provide

Francis Baigent

Mackenzie with Orton's letters as further evidence. In Wagga Wagga, Mackenzie gleaned more key pieces of information. One witness remembered he had been informed by the Claimant that he had learned his skill as a butcher in London. Another crucially recalled that Orton hailed from Wapping.

Mackenzie transmitted this news back to Dobinson and Geare in London. The firm immediately obtained the services of Jonathan Whicher, the leading detective of his time.* His reputation was based on his role in the Constance Kent murder case of 1860. Whicher interviewed the Orton sisters, but they denied that a photograph of the Claimant was a representation of their brother. It subsequently emerged that that they were receiving

---

* The following year, Whicher would be the inspiration for Sergeant Cuff in Wilkie Collins's *The Moonstone* (1868) and therefore the prototype for all great fictional sleuths.

money from the Claimant. So too was Orton's brother Charles, who only changed his testimony that he was unrelated to the Claimant when these payments stopped. The Orton sisters never changed their minds and always insisted the Claimant was not Arthur Orton. Whicher's discoveries were as revealing as those of Mackenzie in Australia. He uncovered the Claimant's visit to Wapping the previous Christmas and interviewed Mary Ann Loder, Arthur Orton's former sweetheart in Wapping. He also found a curious letter that 'Tomas Castro' had penned to James Richardson, a local doctor in April 1865. The Claimant had asked after 'a person called Orton' to whom he had written and received no reply. He had particularly asked after his son, Arthur. The Richardson letter has been employed to try to prove that the Claimant may not have been Orton. If he was Orton, why was he trying to find out about himself?[9] The Claimant always insisted that he knew Orton and that they had worked together in Australia. References to his alleged alter ego were, however, often clouded with occasional suggestions that the two had been involved in a terrible crime. There were hints that it concerned the murder of one 'Ballarat Harry', last seen alive in Orton's hut in Dargo. Thus the Claimant felt he could not speak freely about Orton and did not know his whereabouts. Orton himself was never found.

In March 1868, the worst calamity that could happen to the Claimant occurred. As long as he had Henriette's testimony on his side, it was unlikely that the opposition would risk a long trial. A mother's recognition would have had too strong a hold on the jury's sympathy. On 12 March 1868, however, she died from heart failure.[10] With her demise went the Claimant's regular income and his last chance of a settlement with the Tichborne family. At Henriette's funeral at Tichborne, the Claimant was naturally distraught. There were almost fisticuffs with the Tichbornes when he took his place in the funeral procession as chief mourner.[11] Inspector Whicher was present at the funeral with Mary Ann Loder. When she saw the Claimant, she recognised him as the man she had once known in Wapping and fainted melodramatically into Whicher's arms.

Afterwards, Colonel Lushington organised a meeting of local gentry and other interested parties. This created an annual income of £1,400 for the Claimant, who moved to Alresford, where a small house was procured for him. He took up the life of a country squire, excelling at shooting and fishing. Some felt he must be Sir Roger as such gentlemanly pursuits came naturally to him. Additional funds were not forthcoming, however, as he was prevented by the courts from taking over the Dowager's estate. The

Anthony Biddulph (left) and Henry Tichborne, the Infant Baronet (right)

Claimant then suffered another blow with the death of Edward Hopkins, the family solicitor, a key witness on his behalf.

The Claimant wanted to proceed to law as soon as possible to have his property restored. Any hopes for a speedy trial were dashed when Justice Wilde gave permission in June 1868 for commissions to be dispatched to Chile and Australia to gather evidence. The idea was that the Claimant himself should go and confront the foreign witnesses – a cheaper alternative to paying them all to come over for the trial.

The South American interlude proved yet another remarkable episode in this extraordinary story. The Claimant disembarked at Buenos Aires, to avoid the treacherous passage round Cape Horn, but made no attempt to reach Chile. His small legal team progressed to Valparaiso whilst he spent two months hanging around in Argentina, where he became friendly with the explorer Richard Burton and the poet and travel writer Wilfred Scawen Blunt. Burton and the Claimant became a 'strange, disreputable couple'. Burton and Blunt tended to believe in the Claimant. Blunt had been at Stonyhurst with Roger's younger brother, Alfred, and fancied that the Claimant had similar eyebrows to his childhood friend. He remembered

Alfred as being almost illiterate, so the Claimant's lack of ability in the English language was no surprise. He and Burton were reminded by the Claimant of 'a young man of decent birth gone woefully to seed', a not unfamiliar type, especially among Englishmen abroad.[12] Then, instead of crossing the Andes to join the Chilean commission and confront the witnesses in Melipilla, the Claimant caught a ship back to England. In Chile, it was confirmed that the original Tomas Castro was insane but had been away during the months when Sir Roger Tichborne would have visited Melipilla. When asked, he had indeed never heard of anyone called Tichborne but did remember a young Englishman called 'Arturo', who the town had looked after when he turned up destitute. Other locals had a similar memory.[13]

Holmes in the meantime was becoming more and more astounded by what the Claimant had not revealed to him. He was informed of the Wapping visit and discovered that the Claimant had been paying money to the Ortons. Unless he obtained satisfactory answers, Holmes warned he would have to give up the case.[14] Onslow pleaded with him: 'How do you account if he is Orton his coming back to England into the lion's mouth?'[15] As stunned as anyone by the Claimant's return, Onslow proposed a meeting between the Claimant and his creditors at the Swan Hotel in Alresford. At the meeting, the Claimant said he had returned because of ill-health and the possible threat to his life if he had proceeded to Chile. Indeed, the passengers of the stagecoach he was meant to use had all been murdered by brigands. Few were satisfied by the Claimant's explanation and many creditors withdrew their backing. Holmes resigned as his solicitor. He was owed £5,393 14s. 9d. but saw hardly any of his money again. Onslow and Baigent remained faithful, but the Claimant was now bankrupt.

There was no prospect of the Claimant attending the Australian Commission, which sat through the second half of 1869. Mina Jury, as well as many of the inhabitants of Wagga Wagga, provided evidence. There were some who identified the Claimant as Orton while others suggested that Orton and Castro were two distinct people. A complicating factor was that in Australia, after the end of transportation, men (particularly with a criminal or convict past) were accustomed to changing their names frequently. It transpired that a man called William Cresswell had also employed the name of Arthur Orton.

To obtain funds, the Claimant's new solicitors, Walters and Moojen, launched the Tichborne Bond scheme to raise £100,000. Mortgage debentures were issued at the nominal sum of £100, which the Claimant offered

Guildford Onslow

to repay with interest after coming into his estates. In other words, people could buy shares in him and his inheritance. They were sometimes known as 'Wagga Bonds'.[16] Only £40,000 was raised in this way.[17] Most of the notes in fact only changed hands at £65 and their worth soon declined to between £40 and £50. It was recorded that in Birmingham they were even being offered openly for sale at ten shillings each.[18] The bond scheme was of dubious legality but in tune with the roguish, sporting image the Claimant increasingly presented. It was the first attempt by supporters to develop a relationship between the Claimant and the public.

3

The Courtroom

The Tichborne trials have little status in legal history as usually practised. No precedents or points of law were determined to shape the conduct of future legal practitioners.[1] They were not what the legal profession calls 'leading cases'. They were merely the most talked about and discussed trials of the nineteenth century, as well as two of the longest in the whole of English legal history (before the McLibel action of the 1990s). In the course of them, the Claimant became a popular hero among the working classes. They therefore merit a place in the social history of the law. For his partisans, the case came down to the simple question of whether a poor man obtain justice in a court of law.

If the Tichborne trials were a form of spectacular theatre, then so was the practice of law. It was not unusual for lawyers to consult actors or acting manuals for instruction in the art of pleading.[2] But the theatricality of the courtroom went deeper than this. It was an integral part of the 'public sphere'.[3] As such, the public had the right to attend court and constitute an audience. Many leading Society figures including the Prince and Princess of Wales and Lady Dorothy Nevill attended the trial, which became a fashionable talking point. The Emperor of Brazil even put in an appearance.[4] But the Claimant's audience extended beyond the courtroom to include the readership of the press. Both national and local newspapers in the nineteenth century devoted numerous column inches to detailed trial accounts – something that did not always please the Victorian Bar.[5] The fidelity of newspaper reports was frequently contested, although such reportage was sometimes more accurate than the original transcripts. The lawyers in the Tichborne trials were always aware that they were not simply addressing a packed courtroom but, in effect, the nation at large.

Tichborne became a *cause célèbre*. It is no coincidence that the popularity of newspaper trial accounts coincided with the heyday of the serialised novel. Both forms created communities. Readers found a new identity, based on fascination with the narratives contained in novels or newspapers, that linked them to other individuals and helped constitute that imagined community called 'public opinion'. Just as the Sensation Novel turned its readers into detectives requiring them to guess the dark secrets at the heart of the tale (and prefiguring the detective story), *causes célèbres* required that readers of the press should consider the evidence and become anonymous members of the jury.[6] The high levels of Tichborne literacy (the detailed understanding of often obscure aspects of the case) means that we should see the Tichbornites both as detectives and as aggrieved members of a jury that was not called upon.

The *cause célèbre* was an important part of Victorian culture.[7] Momentum was given to the form by reports from the Divorce Court from 1858 onwards which permitted readers to savour a stream of tawdry and squalid details that would normally have remained private. Excitement and concern about trials was lodged deep in the Victorian psyche. Cases such as the Yelverton trial in 1861 allowed for extensive reporting of bigamy. The Mordaunt divorce case in 1870 provided plenty of delicious copy about the secret lives of the aristocracy when Sir Charles Mordaunt sued his wife for adultery with the Prince of Wales and others.[8] The Tichborne trial needs to be seen in the context of these scandals amongst the elite, which permitted the mid-Victorian press to mix melodrama, sensation and reportage. Legal and literary London were never far apart, as the novel aspired to much the same function as the courtroom. Wilkie Collins was so impressed by the succession of different forms of testimony when attending the trial of the poisoner William Palmer in 1856 that he adopted the technique of multiple voices and narrators for *The Woman in White* (1860).[9] The courtroom was a place where moral and ethical issues could be debated and to some extent resolved; it was a location where claims as to what constituted truth were in conflict. At its worst, the *cause célèbre* made readers into a nation of busybodies fascinated with the misfortunes of others; at its best it produced a public culture that insisted, like Dickens's novels, that we all have a responsibility for each other's welfare – a motivation for Tichbornism.

The case was scheduled for the end of 1870 but was delayed until 1871.[10] The civil trial felt like an elaborate performance not just because of the wigs and robes of its personnel but because it was based on a fiction. The case had ceased to be two suits and had taken the form of an action of ejectment to remove Colonel Lushington from Tichborne House – *Tichborne* v. *Lushington*. The title of the case implied that the Claimant was the plaintiff whereas it was clear when the trial began that he was in fact the defendant. The action of ejectment was based on a legal fiction common in land law.[11] Thus the form of the trial was itself an imposture. There was another profoundly symbolic dimension to the proceedings because they were a contest over landed property. The Claimant wished to obtain the family inheritance and insisted that all rents from the Tichborne estates should come to him. The development of civil law was essentially based around the protection of private property.[12] If possession really is nine-tenths of the law, it is not surprising that nineteenth-century fiction was taken up with struggles over inheritance and that the Tichborne trials laid bare the essentials of power relations in Britain.[13] The aristocracy, the land, the lawyers: they were all here.

English common law makes its claim for authority on a series of judicial precedents that date back to time immemorial. Yet the Tichborne trials took place at a specific moment in the development of legal culture in England. Legal London was based around the Central Criminal Court (the Old Bailey), the courts of Westminster (which handled civil matters) and the network of chambers around the Inns of Court. Elsewhere, the legal system consisted of an elaborate mosaic of courts, assizes and circuits with their messes. To become a barrister, the main qualification was the eating of dinners in one of the Inns of Court. Legal education was something barristers were meant to acquire by watching other lawyers in action and reading the occasional manual. Just as the Tichborne trials were taking place, it was clear that the chaotic and amateurish aspects of legal culture needed reform and rationalisation. The anti-theoretical leaning of English law was being challenged by the increasing interest in the jurisprudence of John Austin. Austin distinguished philosophically between law and morality and supported the codification of law (a move that his supporters believed would bring clarity and sense back to the law, break the stranglehold of fusty, medieval precedents and render the law comprehensible to ordinary people).[14] There were also demands for the reform of the circuit and assize courts, which culminated in the Judicature Acts of 1873-75 that introduced greater centralization and remodelled the court system. From 1872, aspiring barristers had to take an examination, part of the tendency towards professionalisation.[15] The theatre of justice was also changing with the abolition of public executions in 1868.

At the time, the actual impact of these changes was mixed and should not be overestimated. The Inns of Court went unreformed; many in the profession were dismissive of the utility of examinations and the common law resisted demands for codification. The Tichborne trials were essentially part of the pre-professional legal world and took place before the law courts shifted from parliament to the Strand. They involved many of the leading lawyers of the period bound by a culture of special pleading and extrovert advocacy that flourished in both civil and criminal cases. Some barristers were well known as personalities to the public and their skills in opening and closing statements and in cross-examination were very much perform-ances.[16] Criminal trials in particular had taken a more adversarial form after the Prisoner's Counsel Act of 1836 granted the defendant an automatic right to defending counsel.[17] Even before this, the rules of evidence, regarding proof and hearsay as well as the nature of a reliable witness, had also been sharpened.[18] The Tichborne trials in both their civil and criminal forms exhibited the more sophisticated adversarial procedure that characterised the Victorian Bar.

Whilst leading barristers were sometimes well-known figures, the popular reputation of lawyers was generally low and had been since the middle ages.[19] They were often represented as being concerned less with the achievement of truth than the prospect of pocketing a fee. John Austin's notion that the law could be separated from morality was anathema to the popular mind. Legal ethics also left much to be desired. Charles Philips's defence of Courvoisier, the valet who murdered Sir William Russell in 1840, was a case in point. The defendant admitted to Philips during the trial that he was guilty but still expected the lawyer to defend him to the utmost. Philips (already known to some as 'Counsellor O'Garnish') notoriously went on to swear his belief in his client's innocence and attempted to shift the blame for the murder onto a maidservant. None of this helped Courvoisier, who was hanged, but it damaged Philips's reputation and heightened the perception of the legal profession as ethically blind.[20] Moreover, the use of deliberate obscurity and legal fictions left the profession looking like an organised conspiracy against the public. The law was frequently perceived as a cloak behind which the wealthy could hide. Many believed there was one law for the rich and one for the poor. According to a ballad entitled *A Sketch of Roguery* –

> The lawyers do it brown
>   When ever they go to law,
> And if you have ought to do with them
>   Your money they will draw,
> They will take you to the county court,
>   There the matter to decide,
> They will rob you of every screw
>   And humbug you beside.[21]

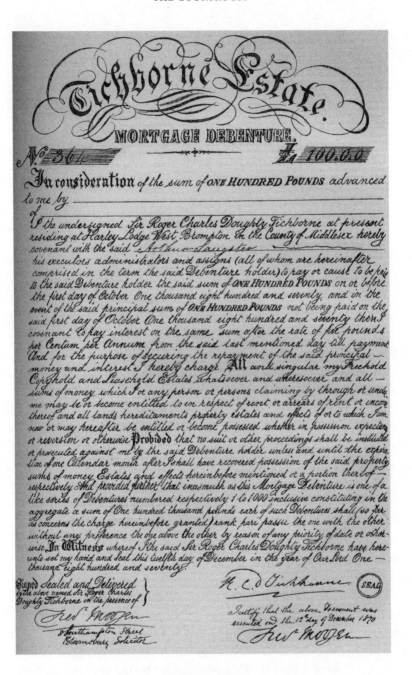

Tichborne Bond

In a song called *Law* sung by W. H. Williams in his entertainment *Wine and Walnuts*, the chorus ran –

> If you're fond of pure vexation,
> And a long procrastination,
> You're just in a situation,
> To enjoy a suit at Law.[22]

A ballad on the *Barnsley Miners Lock Out* was equally cynical:

> Next comes the Lawyer with his wit
>   A clever man they say:
> He advocates the master's cause,
>   And doesn't he make them pay! [23]

Such sentiments can be found elsewhere within Victorian culture, most notably in Charles Dickens's *Bleak House* (1853). Lawyers who, by the very nature of their profession, could just as easily prosecute as defend, transgressed against the longing for integrity in public behaviour. The Tichborne cause traded on this widespread derision for the legal profession.

The Claimant's solicitor engaged the services of Sergeant William Ballantine for the defence. Ballantine was a rakish figure who enjoyed his high status as Serjeant-at-Law because of his oratorical powers. Although he never publicly denounced the Claimant as an impostor, even in his memoirs, he privately considered him to be a 'd – – – – d scoundrel'.[24] In his youth, Ballantine had been an aspiring littéerateur but settled for a career as a barrister. He was well known for his advocacy, especially during the successful prosecution of Franz Muller for murder in 1864 and, later, for his brilliant defence in 1875 of the Gaekwar of Baroda, on a poisoning charge, for which he received £10,000, one of the largest fees ever made at that time by a barrister. Supporting him was a rising legal star, Hardinge Giffard (later Lord Halsbury) who went on to become Disraeli's Solicitor General in 1875 and, later, Lord Chancellor in 1886, but is now best known for the encyclopaedia of English law that bears his name. They were supported by three further counsel and were more than matched by the lawyers employed for the 'defence' (in reality, the prosecution).

This opposing legal team was led by Sir John Duke Coleridge, the Solicitor-General, whose presence increased the feeling that Gladstone's government itself was prosecuting the Claimant (it was not unusual for the Solicitor-General to take private clients). A great nephew of the poet Samuel Taylor Coleridge, Coleridge himself had strong literary leanings. A contributor to the *Edinburgh* and *Quarterly* reviews, he was prepared to take literature into the courtroom; in 1853, he attempted to save a man from execution for murder by reciting long passages from *Othello* (he was unsuccessful).[25] He had been heavily influenced by John Henry Newman as a student at Oxford and became an ardent Tractarian, though he did not follow Newman's example by going over to Rome (unlike his brother, Henry, who became a Jesuit priest and a leading writer on Roman Catholic matters). Coleridge opted for a career in public life that would achieve some distinction. He became a Liberal MP and was active under Gladstone's leadership in the abolition of religious tests at university; he opposed vivisection and supported the disestablishment of the Irish Church and, later, Irish Home Rule. As a lawyer, he made his name in the notorious case of *Saurin* v. *Star* (1869) in which a former nun alleged that she had been imprisoned in a convent by her Mother Superior. The episode was a touchstone for the kind of anti-Catholicism that the Tichborne cause would revive.[26] During the Tichborne trial, Gladstone promoted Coleridge to the post of Attorney-General but he accomplished little in terms of law reform, partly because he was forced to be in court for so long dealing with the Claimant. He in time became Chief Justice of the Common Pleas (1873) and Lord Chief Justice of England (1880), presiding over the notorious case of Dudley and Stephens where two shipwrecked sailors, rescued after a long spell adrift at sea, were put on trial for eating the cabin boy.[27]

Doubts remain over Coleridge's effectiveness in the Tichborne trial. None apply to the next member of his legal team, Henry Hawkins, whose cross-examination combined forensic skill with a probing style that was frequently brutal. One of Hawkins's early memories was glimpsing the corpse of a Captain Swing rioter on the back of a cart; the man had just been hanged at Bedford Gaol for setting a stack of corn on fire.[28] Such a sight at the impressionable age of thirteen did not prevent him in later years from sending plenty of men to the gallows, which is why (after becoming a judge) he came to be known as 'Hanging Hawkins'. Away from the courtroom he was a model sporting gentleman, a regular at the turf and the prize fight. Part of his memoirs were written in the voice of the great love of his life, his dog, Jack. At one point, he was retained to represent the Claimant (which might have changed the course of the trial) but, in the event, he plumped to represent the Tichborne family. Coleridge's position as Solicitor-General meant that he, rather than Hawkins, led the legal team which was also made up of Charles (later Lord) Bowen, who did much of the work, Chapman Barber (who had cross-examined the Claimant in Chancery) and Sir George Honeyman.

The judge was the Chief Justice of the Common Pleas, Sir William Bovill. He was very conscious of the danger of making a mistake, thus bringing on a new trial, and later claimed the strain of conducting the proceedings undermined his health.[29] He was both delighted and wearied by the dignitaries and hangers on from High Society. Fashionable ladies in brightly coloured dresses hovered around the judge occasionally providing him with information about French or Geography.[30]

The Tichborne case lasted from 10 May 1871 to 6 March 1872. During its long passage, the Prince of Wales almost died from typhoid, the reading public first encountered George Eliot's *Middlemarch* and Stanley at last found Doctor Livingstone. The trial's olympian length was caused by the conviction on both sides that they were playing for high stakes. Lawyers for the prosecution and defence each believed their case was all too easy to lose. They therefore adopted the strategy of reviewing and interrogating in depth evidence from all parts of the case. This, of course, happened in most trials. But, as we have seen, this was a complex story drawing on witnesses and events in Australia, South America and elsewhere. As it was, the commencement of the trial was delayed by the siege of Paris, which prevented French witnesses from crossing the Channel. Coleridge complained, in a letter to his father in January 1871, that '*Five* of our best witnesses in the Tichborne case are shut up there. The other side don't know this; and don't you mention it, but we can't go to trial without them.'[31] In retrospect, it is difficult to see the French evidence, whilst important, as crucial. As the trial went on, witness after witness was examined with very little attempt to focus on key parts of the case. Bovill allowed the lawyers to proceed as they wished. Readers of the press found themselves assailed by the surfeit of information. George Eliot attended the Tichborne trial and was struck by Coleridge's address to the jury: 'The digest of evidence which Coleridge gives is one of the best illustrations of the value or valuelessness of testimony that could be given.'[32]

The Tichborne trials cut into the popular imagination because they raised questions about the value of testimony. Witnesses were brought on by Ballantine to insist that the Claimant was genuine. Coleridge and his team would sometimes break down these testimonials in cross-examination but would also advance their case through a counter-narrative based on circumstantial evidence, making clear that the Claimant was a calculating impostor, identifying contradictions in his case (not hard) and reconstructing the life of Arthur Orton, who, they insisted, was in the courtroom before them.[33]

The trial took place in the Court of Common Pleas or, as Ballantine later put it, 'one of those holes situated at Westminster'.[34] The demand for tickets was such that the trial had shortly to be moved to the larger Court of Queens Bench, also part of the Palace of Westminster (located just off Westminster Hall in the law courts designed by Sir John Soane that were demolished in 1883). Perhaps because it was understood that this was likely to be a long affair, on the first day only two members of the jury could be found and therefore proceedings could not commence. On the second day, eleven jurors were eventually dragooned after a lot of difficulty; both sides then agreed to carry on with this number rather than the usual twelve. As it was, the jury (effectively shackled to the courtroom for a year) became the object of popular sympathy and amusement. Six months into the civil trial, a member had to ask Bovill if he could be excused from a fine, as he had been summoned to appear on the jury of another trial. The judge not only agreed but suggested that all the Tichborne jurors should be exempt from jury service for the rest of their lives.[35]

Ballantine opened for the Claimant.[36] Over two days he took the court through the story to date, which he noted had already been heavily aired in public. He built up a sordid picture of Roger's youth. His father was represented as a violent alcoholic who drank every hour of the day (perhaps to explain why a man would want to leave a troubled home, go to the other side of the world and not return). Roger, further, had had little education, had been over fond of smoking and 'associated with those who were not equal to him in rank and who were not likely to benefit his mind'.[37]

Anticipating the Claimant's inability to remember key details from Roger's past, he insisted that his brain had been weakened during those terrible days adrift in the longboat after the wreck of the *Bella*. He also tried to head off the Wapping evidence by insisting that Arthur Orton was a separate person who had been a friend of the Claimant at Dargo and Wagga Wagga ('he was butcher of the butcher type – the butcher type of Wapping').[38] He made the point that the Claimant and his family had been continually followed around by a private detective (presumably Whicher) who had concocted the Orton allegation.[39] He also drew attention to the trustworthiness of the

key witness, Andrew Bogle and, of course, the Dowager. Ballantine had had
an interview with Henriette before she died and insisted that she was of
sound mind and capable of forming a proper judgement. Coleridge, listening,
was unimpressed and confided to his diary that it was 'the poorest opening
I ever heard for a clever man in a great case'. His opinion of Ballantine's
advocacy did not improve, later on noting that it was 'feebleness itself' and
asking 'How has he got his reputation?'[40]

After the reading of affidavits, witnesses for the Claimant were called. A
series of former Carabineers who had once served with the young Roger
Tichborne insisted that he was their former fellow officer. Their testimony had
the merit from the Claimant's point of view of being generally disinterested.
The other main group of witnesses were servants or locals from Tichborne
who had known Roger. Their evidence was frequently treated patronisingly
by opposing counsel, a sure sign of class snobbery. James M'Cann, a former
private who served with Roger in Canterbury and at Clonmel in Ireland,
was the first witness:

> I recognised him from his forehead, head, and ears. His ears I knew
> well by seeing him in bed every morning for two years ... There is
> nothing extraordinarily particular about the ears that I know of, only
> I knew them. (Laughter.) I don't know if I could have recognised him
> from his ears if I had seen nothing else. (Laughter.)[41]

The sound of laughter frequently punctuated the proceedings. Roger's
military tailor, James Greenwood, told of how he decided the Claimant was
the right man by taking his trouser measurement – the length was the same.
He added that 'he is considerably stouter – the only thing left of him is
about his eyes', which was followed by guffaws. The following exchange –
worthy of music hall – also took place between Coleridge and Greenwood:

Coleridge	Who is your clerk?
Greenwood	My sleeping partner.
Coleridge	But who is that?
Greenwood	Why, Mrs Greenwood, of course.[42]

Colonel Norbury, now a Justice of the Peace in Herefordshire, told how he
had not been inclined to believe the Claimant was his former friend until a
three hour interview settled the matter.[43] Major General William Neville

Custance backed up Ballantine by insisting that Roger Tichborne was not well educated.[44] Many remembered Roger's former French accent (which they allowed had now disappeared) or the twitch in his eyebrows, which the Claimant had.

From early on, the case was notable for its disputes over the use of photography as a form of evidence. In Santiago, Roger had posed for two daguerreotype photographs, then a new process (as indeed, to some extent, was photography itself). The court could therefore compare the Claimant's features with those of the undoubted Roger. From the trial account, however, we can see the claims of photography to offer 'reality' or an objective portrait were contested; it appeared that the camera could lie. Mrs Sherstone, the wife of a Carabineer who brought Roger to their home, thought the 1853 daguerreotype was a poor likeness and noted, 'I very seldom see any likeness in photographs unless they are very good'.[45] On the other hand, Sir Edward Doughty's former coachman, Thomas Muston, felt the 1853 photograph had a strong resemblance to the undoubted Roger, whereas, when he was shown a recent photograph of the Claimant, he did not detect any resemblance. It was only when he met the Claimant and noted his twitching eyebrows that he was convinced.[46] Hardinge Giffard noted the drawbacks of photography as evidence because it was prone to manipulation: 'photographers were able to place any face they pleased on any form they pleased. A common form of libel in Paris was to place very well-known faces upon very grotesque bodies.'[47]

The Chile daguerreotype was studied carefully by William Savage, a Winchester photographer, because of concerns about abrasions on the picture. Nevertheless, the portrait did have its uses. Coleridge was able to employ it to demonstrate that Roger Tichborne did not have ear lobes whereas the Claimant did.[48] Comparisons of the thumbs of Roger and the Claimant were made based on the picture. Bovill stopped the trial for two hours so that he could study the photographs intensively. Coleridge was indignant, later telling his father: 'I said – I hope loud enough for him to hear – that there was no objection whatever to the judges learning photography if they didn't learn it in court at the expense to the suitors before them of £200; for it was really that, at least.'[49]

Anthony Biddulph was cross-examined as the only member of the Tichborne family to believe in the Claimant. He told of how the return of Roger Tichborne had been much discussed in Catholic society and that, initially, he considered him to be 'the greatest impostor of modern times'.[50]

Sergeant William Ballantine (top left), *Sir John Duke Coleridge* (top right),
Sir William Bovill (bottom left), *Sir Henry Hawkins* (Bottom right)

As we have seen, he changed his mind on meeting the Claimant, although he admitted that he had known Roger's brother Alfred better: 'Sometimes when he finished his sentences I could have thought it was Alfred talking. There was something peculiar in the way he finished his sentences. It was a drawl that Alfred had.'[51] Again, the Claimant's twitch helped clinch it; this was a family trait that was shared by Roger, Alfred and Robert Tichborne as well as Sir Edward Doughty. Doctor Lipscomb, the family doctor, who also supported the Claimant, was quizzed by Coleridge and revealed the young Roger had been tattooed (though he was unsure with what mark), but was rather vague.

At the end of May, the Claimant went into the witness-box for over a month of examination and cross-examination. On the first day, Bovill complained that he could not hear him and the Claimant was moved nearer. The Claimant was allegedly suffering from the loss of some of his teeth and from a chest infection. He was also so fat that he had difficulty in standing up, so a chair had to be procured for him. Eventually a sounding-board was set up to amplify his voice. Ballantine and Giffard took him through the details of his early life. Thus, on his education:

Giffard	Were you a diligent student?
Claimant	Well, I think I was an idle one. (A laugh.)[52]

Echoing the case made by Ballantine in the opening statement, the marriage of Henriette and James Tichborne was presented as deeply unhappy, driving Roger to leave England. He was asked by Giffard about the 'sealed packet' but declined to reply. The lawyers then took him through the South American episode and the shipwreck. When they moved on to his life in Australia, the Claimant made it clear that he had been a friend of Arthur Orton, whom he had met at Boisdale where they both drove cattle: 'He had rather sharp features and a lengthy face, and he was a large boned man ... He was slightly marked with the small pox. The marks were quite distinct. He was about an inch and a half taller than I am ... He had very large hands and feet.'[53] The two associated with each other over the years after they left Foster's cattle station. Both frequently adopted different names. Orton went by the alias of 'Alfred Smith' whereas the Claimant was variously known as 'Bob' or 'The Foreigner' in addition to 'Tom Castro'. He last saw Orton in June 1866 at Wagga Wagga, where he had confided in him about his inheritance. The subsequent whereabouts of Orton proved impossible to trace.

This was followed by twenty-three days of cross-examination by Coleridge, in what became a formidable battle of wits. Despite his considerable forensic skill, Coleridge realised that he had met his match in the Claimant as they duelled over each detail of the case; hence, he came to develop a curious respect for him even though he considered him 'odious'. At the time, he noted 'a cleverer and more slippery scoundrel I never had to do with in my life'.[54] Coleridge admitted to his diary that his skills at cross-examination were inferior to those of Hawkins and the others.[55] Later, after a hard day's sparring with the Claimant, he confessed: 'I am not fit for this case. I don't understand it and do it badly, but I get the kindest help ever man had from his juniors.'[56] Despite his self-doubt. Coleridge was a combative figure in the courtroom; indeed, it was his effectiveness (expressed through devastating sarcasm) that transformed him into a popular hate figure. Ballantine later said that 'no cross-examination was ever heard in a court of justice which exhibited more labour and industry, or was more successful'.[57] Coleridge would frequently introduce his questions by saying 'would you be surprised to hear?' which became a popular catch-phrase.[58] At times, the encounter with the Claimant descended into knockabout abuse as in these questions about Roger's early life in Paris:

Coleridge   I think you did say that you learned to dance?

Claimant   Yes.

Coleridge   Do you mean to say that you can't recollect the name of any young lady with whom you danced?

Claimant   If I did I would not. I consider it a very impertinent question for you to ask.

Coleridge   Impertinence has no application to me. It has nothing to do with me, except that it is irrelevant to the case before us.

Claimant   But you said that meant to be as insolent as you could.

Coleridge   If such word escaped me, I am very sorry for it.

On another occasion, the Claimant rounded on Coleridge by saying, 'You appear to be very innocent, considering your brother is a Jesuit'.[59] Not only did the judge rebuke him for making an improper observation but Coleridge was subsequently able to point out how odd it was that a supposedly Roman Catholic gentleman should use the word 'Jesuit' as a term of abuse. Coleridge exposed the Claimant's ignorance of anything that

Roger would have been taught at Stonyhurst. There were exchanges like this:

Coleridge	Have you heard of Virgil?
Claimant	Of course I have.
Coleridge	Who is he?
Claimant	I don't know.
Coleridge	Is he a general, or a statesman, or what is he?
Claimant	I told you just now that I totally forget.
Coleridge	Do you know what he wrote about – geography or what?
Claimant	I don't know.
Coleridge	Was he Greek or Latin?
Claimant	I don't know.
Coleridge	Did he write verse or prose?
Claimant	I don't know; my recollection is entirely gone.
Coleridge	Look at that (copy of Virgil produced). What is it? Is it Greek or Latin?
Claimant	It appears to me to be Greek. (Laughter). I can't say.
Coleridge	It is Greek to you, anyhow.

Then there was this exchange:

Coleridge	What is chemistry?
Claimant	It is about chemistry, of course.
Coleridge	I know. History is about history, and so on. I ask you what is it about?
Claimant	About different herbs and poisons, and the substance of medicines.
Coleridge	Do you mean what is in a chemist's shop?
Claimant	I think a dose of it would do you good. (Laughter).[60]

The undoubted highlight of the conflict came on the second day of the cross-examination. Coleridge quizzed him relentlessly about the contents of the sealed packet that Roger had left behind with Vincent Gosford, which was only to be opened in certain circumstances and which had since been destroyed. The Claimant stonewalled, as he often did, refusing to answer, but Coleridge would not let it go:

> *Coleridge*   What is the event you hoped had not happened?
>
> *Claimant*   The confinement of my cousin.
>
> *Coleridge*   Do you mean to swear before the Judge and jury that you
> seduced this lady?
>
> *Claimant*   I most solemnly to my God swear I did. (Sensation.)
>
> *Coleridge*   This lady (pointing to Mrs Radcliffe, who sat by the side of
> her husband, immediately below counsel)?
>
> *Claimant*:   Yes, that lady.[61]

This stunning revelation changed the dynamic of the struggle with the Claimant because it meant that his opponents were not just fighting for the inheritance of the infant baronet but also to vindicate the reputation of Katherine Radcliffe. Almost as bad, the Claimant suggested that, when he was courting Katherine Doughty, he was also making advances to a Miss Hales of Canterbury, although he could not remember her Christian name ('our acquaintance was very short').[62] Coleridge went home that evening and wrote: 'Poor Mrs Radcliffe had the charge made against her, but why should I say "poor"? She behaved nobly, and so as to command admiration from us all.'[63]

The Claimant did not deny the Wapping visit and was combative about the evidence from Australia and Chile:

> *Coleridge*   Would you be surprised to find that Roger Charles Tich-
> borne was never at Melipilla in his life?
>
> *Claimant*   'Tis rather cool for you to tell me so. (Laughter.)
>
> *Coleridge*   Would you be surprised to find it is so?
>
> *Claimant*   I am not surprised to hear you say so. (Laughter.)
>
> *Coleridge*   Would you be surprised to hear that it is a fact?
>
> *Claimant*   Certainly.[64]

On 5 July, after twenty days of cross-examination, Coleridge came up with another startling piece of evidence, the Pittendreigh letters. Mrs Pittendreigh was the wife of a clerk in the offices of Dobinson and Geare, solicitors for the Tichborne family. Coleridge revealed that the Claimant had been in contact with her, offering to pay money for copies of papers relating to the case to which her husband had access. When this correspondence was introduced in court, however, some of the letters were shown to be forgeries. Although the Claimant admitted that he had been in contact with the

Pittendreighs, Coleridge decided not to persist with this line of inquiry and brought the cross-examination to a close. When the Claimant was then re-examined by Ballantine he insisted that it was Mrs Pittendreigh who had approached him, offering information but nothing had come of it. On 7 July, the trial adjourned for the summer recess of four months.

When the case resumed on 7 November, Ballantine continued to call witnesses. A number of witnesses who had been in Melbourne in 1854 were brought in to testify about the *Osprey* and Roger's alleged arrival in Australia, but to little effect; their evidence was unclear. More significant was the testimony of Andrew Bogle. Now white-haired, he had to request the use of a stool for the long examination to which he was subjected. He told of how he had retired to Australia on a pension from the Tichbornes, which had been stopped when he recognised the Claimant. Bogle insisted that the Claimant was genuine. So too did the antiquarian Francis Baigent, who was an old family friend of the Tichbornes. Hawkins examined him for over a week, breaking down his testimony and mocking him relentlessly for his failure to consider any action of the Claimant's suspicious. Hawkins's implication was that Baigent had fed the Claimant information, which he was able to use.

The case resumed again in the new year, with Coleridge's speech for the defence, which lasted for over a month. In an elegant and closely argued argument, he elaborated on the Claimant as 'a conspirator, a perjurer, a forger, an impostor – a villain'.[65] It was incredible to suppose that a noble-minded aristocrat such as the true Sir Roger could be confused with the figure before them: 'The letters of Roger Charles Tichborne are the letters of an educated, high-minded English gentleman ... The letter of this fellow is the letter of a low blackguard: blackguard in thoughts, blackguard in expressions, blackguard in the whole connection.'[66] The Claimant in his view was comparable to Martin Guerre and the other great impostors of history.[67] Coleridge's purpose, however, was to show that the Claimant was not Roger Tichborne rather than to demonstrate that he was Arthur Orton. In particular, he drew attention to the tattoo evidence and the fact that the Claimant had ear lobes unlike the original Roger. The Bogle and Baigent evidence was attacked and he returned to the point that there was no evidence that Roger Tichborne had ever visited Melipilla.

Commencing on his own witnesses, Coleridge brought on Lady Radcliffe first. He asked, 'Was Sir Roger Tichborne ever guilty of taking a liberty with you?', to which she replied 'Never'. She did remember that Roger had a tattoo on his arm. Lord Bellew, Roger's friend from Stonyhurst, was then called. He said that, as a boy, he had tattooed a heart crossed with an anchor on Roger's inner left arm – marks that the Claimant did not possess. Ballantine was suspicious, as this was crucial evidence that should have been introduced earlier. Bellew said that he had not mentioned the tattoos to the family before the previous year because he presumed they knew about it. Alfred Seymour then went into the dock to argue that the Dowager had not known about the tattoo marks and thus presumably had not checked the Claimant's arm when she recognised him.

Many more witnesses were set to appear when, on 4 March (the one hundred and second day of the trial), the foreman rose to say that the jury had heard enough and did not need further evidence. Rather than let the jury come to a verdict, Ballantine played for time by asking to communicate with Giffard, who was away on circuit. The two did not have time to speak and the trial ended two days later. Ballantine complained about the late introduction of the tattoo evidence, which he had not been able to quiz witnesses about. He asked if the jury was making a decision derived from the tattoo evidence alone, but was informed that it was based on all evidence heard so far. Rather than allow the jury to deliberate, Ballantine then went for a non-suit. This archaic legal form meant that his candidate simply abandoned his case. When he heard about it, Giffard thought this was the wrong course of action because, with what looked likely to be a hostile verdict, they could have moved for a new trial by disputing several of Bovill's rulings about evidence. Given the problems of length associated with this case, the two parties might then have decided to abandon proceedings.

Bovill, however, then decided that the jury's statement was a decision in favour of the Tichbornes. This meant the Claimant was guilty of perjury and that a criminal trial should ensue. With Coleridge's agreement, it was decided that the new prosecution would be public (funded by the government). When the news came through, the Claimant was hobnobbing with supporters and Tichborne Bond holders in a West End hotel. Some panicked as they witnessed their investment go down the drain but the Claimant was 'the coolest of cards' when he heard what had happened.[68] He was arrested and, on arrival at Newgate prison, was cheered by the crowd outside.[69] His entry into public life had begun.

4

Stumping the Country

Before the civil trial came to an end, the Royal Alhambra Palace of Varieties (a sumptuous music hall on the site of the modern Odeon Leicester Square) staged its Christmas pantomime, *Harlequin Happy Go Lucky*, with a cast of two hundred. At one point, the character King Hurleyburley exclaims:

> Bring me no more reports! The midnight taper
> In vain I waste over every daily paper.
> They're filled with that exasperating trial.

The Lord Chamberlain tries to comfort him:

> Your Majesty is right – in never heeding it.

But the King replies:

> No, that's the worst of it – I can't help reading it'. [1]

The audience at the Alhambra no doubt felt the same way. The Tichborne case was the talk of the age. Most local as well as national newspapers carried lengthy reports of the trial so that the public could feast on every lipsmacking detail. As it proceeded, the Tichborne trial devoured column inches and turned the Claimant into a celebrity not only in Britain but around the world. The *Era* sighed: 'It must be owned that, exciting as the story is, it becomes rather oppressive, for one can go into no company whatever without being asked to discuss the matter, and to hear reasons why other people are satisfied that the claimant is the right man, or is not, with variations of speculation, which are somewhat wearisome.'[2] The Claimant clearly rejoiced in his own fame. He happily sat for his sculpture at Madame Tussaud's and provided a set of his own clothes for the model. When it was displayed, the desire to see it was such that it was one of the first occasions when a queue extended out of the front doors of the exhibition.[3]

But this was not just a matter of notoriety; the Claimant was transformed during the first trial and its aftermath into a popular hero. Thomas Wright (the artisan recorder of working life and habits who wrote under the name 'the Journeyman Engineer') argued that the Claimant was the 'best-beloved or most-grieved-over personage in the country'.[4] An unknown supporter sent the Claimant twenty guineas as a Christmas box for his children as well as a guinea for Bogle, who had lost his pension from the Tichbornes.[5] There had been nothing like it since the Garibaldi enthusiasm. When the hero of the Risorgimento had visited Britain in April 1864, he was fêted not only by politicians and dignitaries but also by the working classes, who queued for the privilege of cheering him at his public appearances. Women reportedly swooned over him. Staffordshire figurines were struck of the romantic liberator and unifier of Italy. Pubs and a well-known brand of biscuit were named after him. He also indirectly sparked the popular movement that agitated for the extension of the franchise, which bore fruit in the Reform Act of 1867.[6] Garibaldi's cult was the Victorian equivalent of radical chic. The Claimant did not quite become the repository of liberal aspirations that the Italian had been a decade earlier but he did strike a chord with the public, particularly the working classes who were distressed by the outcome of the trial. In an age where earnest citizens championed democracy, temperance, popular education, the human rights of Christian Bulgarians and the disestablishment of the Church of England, Tichbornism constituted the most unlikely of pressure groups. How and why did the Claimant become a figure of fascination and heroism for the Victorian working classes?

In 1872–73 we find the Tichborne cause at its most spontaneous. Support flowered dramatically for the Claimant, expressed in demonstrations, petitions, newspapers, souvenirs and the Claimant's stump campaign. Some of these were no doubt inspired or 'got up' by the Claimant's associates, but they were also rooted in a deep popular concern, particularly about the nature of the law. Although the cause did not present itself as 'political' in 1872–3, the issues it promoted were sufficiently controversial to warrant its suppression.

The Claimant's cause was shaped by the events that immediately succeeded the end of the Civil Trial. Six counsel were engaged for the prosecution in the new criminal proceedings – Coleridge, Hawkins, Serjeant Parry, Charles Bowen, Sir George Honeyman and Sir Thomas Archbold. As the Claimant was too poor to fund his own defence, this government-funded prosecution became a symbol of the Establishment closing ranks to crush him.[7] The question of such an extravagant use of public expenditure became a political issue in itself. Coleridge (who left the prosecuting team) was forced to defend the number of counsel in Parliament by pointing out that the case was unprecedented and therefore there were no rules for its conduct.[8] Within the government, more controversial was the question of expenses needed to obtain witnesses from abroad. Lord Hatherly, the Lord Chancellor, and Robert Lowe, the Chancellor of the Exchequer, objected to the cost. As the Claimant could not afford a comparable amount of money to obtain witnesses, they believed it would appear that the government was prejudiced and an acquittal might ensue. Coleridge felt he was being challenged by people who did not know anything about the matter and was compelled to argue, backed by the whole of the prosecuting team, that this was simply not how the law operated. Witnesses had to be brought from abroad as evidence obtained by a commission could not be heard in a criminal case.[9] This apparent injustice enabled the Claimant to pose as a victim of the government. When a reporter asked him why he had lost the case, the Claimant replied: 'Money'. [10]

The Tichborne cause illustrates the gap between the law's procedures and the popular understanding of them. There was nothing out of keeping in the Crown funding the prosecution. As one paper editorialised, 'The Government had no option but to assume the duty the Court of Common Pleas imposed upon it'.[11] What interests us is that the popular mind refused to recognise this.

When the Claimant was finally released on bail, he was greeted by a crowd that blocked the entrance of the Old Bailey. The journalist W. E. Adams later recalled that the 'butcher of Wapping was much the hero of the hour that it was almost dangerous to doubt the truth of his story'.[12] In June a London merchant was charged with being drunk and disorderly after he was spotted staggering down a street shouting, 'Hurrah for Tichborne. I am one of his friends'.[13] The Claimant's celebrity was such that the tightrope walker Blondin even offered to carry him over Niagara Falls as a stunt. The Claimant replied with understatement and self-knowledge, 'I think I am a little bit too heavy'.[14]

Even before the popular movement in his favour began to gather momentum, the trial elicited great interest and concern at a local level. The case featured in the centres of working-class discussion, the popular debating societies. The Mechanics' Institute in Plymouth listened to a lecture on aspects of the trial that criticised the way that it had been conducted in court. When a member of the audience defended the Tichborne family, he was shouted down by the rest, who all supported the Claimant.[15] In April, a large meeting of the Carlisle Debating Club discussed the question of whether the Claimant was an impostor and resolved by a small majority 'That the gentleman now incarcerated in Newgate is the rightful heir to the Tichborne title and estates'. The debate lasted two and a half hours.[16] On 22 April, a well-attended meeting at the club room of the Ancient Druid's Inn in Nottingham was addressed by Sergeant-Major Marks, a friend of Sir Roger's from the army and a believer in the Claimant. Expressing their sympathy with the man in prison, a committee was formed and many contributions received.[17] A Nottingham local paper noted that the lower classes generally sympathised with the Claimant.[18] Such interest so early on in the affair, before the organised movement had commenced, suggests a degree of spontaneity in popular support for the Claimant. To this extent, Tichborne was a cause *of* the people.

In Birmingham, the Sunday Evening Debating Society that met at the Hope and Anchor Inn discussed current affairs. Although it described itself as a 'meeting of Gentlemen, Tradesmen and Artizans', its membership was mainly working class. In June 1872 the society voted at a badly attended meeting that the Tichborne trial had ended satisfactorily. The majority was 10-1. In September, however, following a visit to the city by the Claimant, the motion 'Is he the person he represents himself to be?' was carried in the affirmative by a majority of 51–23.[19] The location of these debates is telling: the public house.

Around this time a book of cartoons titled *Tichborne Comicalities* was published, just one example of the tide of ephemera that came on to the market to exploit the case. Its woodcuts gently mocked many aspects of the new sensation. One picture showed a group of men gossiping in a tavern:

> This is the Public drinking their malt
> and discussing the case of Tichborne.[20] (see p. 63)

Tichborne was perceived as inseparable from the world of drink. A West Hartlepool reporter, testing the opinion in Mr Gallon's hostelry, found that opinion was very much in favour of the Claimant.[21] This is really our point of entry into the world of Victorian popular culture. The cause was propagated largely through a network of pubs as publicans started to establish defence funds. Edwin Lamb of the Duke of Wellington pub, Bishopsgate, London, offered to receive subscriptions. H. W. Flower of the Red Lion, Harrow Road, urged his fellow traders through the *Morning Advertiser* to put a Tichborne Fund box in their shops: 'I have one on my counter, and

Lord Bellew

the customers and public are responding to it freely. The Licensed Victuallers are a strong body and will not see a man crushed.' J. T. Peacock of the Green Dragon, Doctor's Commons, was already doing just this and claimed that 'Principally by the pence of working men, who express their feelings very strongly as regards the unsatisfactory termination of the last trial, I have collected nearly three pounds in two days'.[22] Publicans often invited the Claimant to dine. Mr Warner of the Welsh Harp in Hendon was impressed by the Claimant's skill at sharpening a carving knife, which proved at the very least that he was a butcher.[23] In Loughborough, the publican of the White Swan Inn had actually served with Roger Tichborne and identified the Claimant as the right man.[24] In time the Claimant would inspire a number of pub names. Loxwood in Surrey and Alford in Sussex both have pubs named 'Sir Roger Tichborne'.

Drink was one of the fault-lines of Victorian society. During the nineteenth century, the public house was deserted by the upper and middle classes, although it was not unusual for rakish swells to slum it in search of low life and to tour metropolitan hostelries. The hotel or restaurant was the more appropriate place for a gentleman to drink once the temperance movement had located the pub as the key site of social disorder. In 1888, the *Licensed Victualler's Gazette* noted sardonically that 'it would be almost the ruin of a barrister's reputation to be seen entering a public house unless it were called a restaurant'.[25] Working-class life was also divided into two cultural spheres by alcohol. The world of temperance, chapel and self-improvement was distinct from the louche world of the pub and the free and easy. Skilled workers (the so-called labour aristocrats) defined their respectability by frequently shunning the pub, leaving it to the less well off and the unrespectable. In 1872, 95 per cent of those charged with drunkenness in Manchester, Liverpool and Leeds were either semi-literate or completely illiterate.[26] Labour aristocrats knew that the bottle led to marital violence, neglected children, the workhouse and an early grave. From the 1830s, the temperance movement became one of the great popular causes of the nineteenth century, advocated by some Chartists amongst others as a crucial element of working-class progress. Disdaining the state's laissez-faire attitude to the drink trade, temperance advocates became inadvertent pioneers of the idea of state intervention, urging the restriction of pub opening hours or even total prohibition. The public house was also suspicious because it was, as the name suggests, 'public'. By contrast, temperance prized the domestic virtues of the home, the hearth and family life. It represented a finger-wagging threat to popular culture.[27]

Despite the temperance offensive, the pub remained the centre of the working-class community and the hub of masculine popular culture. It was the setting for entertainment, sociability, sport, discussion and politics. Employers often paid out wages in pubs or beer shops whilst trade unions and radical clubs used the upstairs room for meetings. Music hall, the great popular entertainment of the period, emerged from the pub in the 1850s. Many pubs had friendly societies or furniture clubs attached – the only sources of social insurance before the welfare state. It was not unusual even for inquests to take place in pubs because they were the only public venues available in many places.[28] The pub could also be a place to discover people of similar views or ethnic background. In Liverpool, for example, Irish nationalism was developed through the pub as a meeting place and source of mutual support.[29]

The pub was a distinctive cultural terrain within which the Tichborne movement was incubated. Although pubs varied according to locality and the social background of patrons, they often offered the only place of luxury frequented by working men and women with their elaborate gaslit lamps, baroque fittings and embossed or stained glass. The barmaid promised a cheap and vivacious but safe form of sensuality.[30] This was a world presided over by the publican. Frequently the acknowledged senior figure in a locality, the publican's social role was complex. He was usually more affluent than his patrons – indeed a middle-class person who lived among the working class. Publicans (like other shopkeepers) often found their role was a stepping-stone to local government as they were the most articulate and best-known figures in a district. Publicans were engaged in the performance of being 'mine host', the loud-mouthed but gracious source of bonhomie who knew all his 'regulars'. This performance was accompanied by a set of beliefs that were conservative but aggressively demotic. Thus it is not surprising that publicans, with their experience of organisation, became the linchpins of Tichbornism. They not only collected money but helped organise the Claimant's campaign.

Consumption of beer and spirits peaked just after the Tichborne agitation began (in the mid-1870s) but this was also the moment when the drink trade had to confront the challenge of temperance.[31] Gladstone's 1872 licensing legislation restricted opening hours and assigned magistrates the sole author-ity for granting licences. The response of brewers and drink retailers in the 1870s was uncoordinated as it lacked the centralised funds and organisation required to function as an effective pressure group until at least the 1880s.[32] The association of temperance with the Liberals propelled many publicans towards Disraeli's Conservative Party, which championed the right of the working man to drink. Although this was a complex process that took place over a long period, publicans became associated with the promotion of Toryism in many districts, fearful that the Liberals would withdraw their licences. In Lancashire, publicans were the backbone of the Tory revival in the early 1870s, assisting with electoral organisation and the promulgation of the view that the Conservatives were the national party whilst the Liberals were puritanical, middle-class busybodies who had no conception of the need for simple pleasures in a life of hardship.[33] It would be incorrect, however, to assume that Tichbornism was simply a form of demotic Toryism; it also had much in common with Liberalism and Radicalism.

Was there a link between the publican advocacy of Tichborne and the licensing crisis of 1872? We should be suspicious of any formal linkages between the two events, which were coincidental. On the other hand, we can uncover some affinities once we look at the deeper cultural terrain. As working men placed their subscriptions to the Tichborne cause in collecting boxes and listened to the muttonchop-whiskered publican extol the virtues of Toryism, they embraced a mentality that privileged the common-sense and decency of the working man and dramatised the way in which his independence was under threat. Working men frequently held that the aristocracy was on the same side as 'the people' whereas the middle classes could not necessarily be trusted. This was a politics of both ends against the middle. What united the aristocracy and the working class was the politics of pleasure. Sporting and fun-loving aristocrats (as exemplified by the Claimant) understood the importance of the people's beer. Pub culture was central to the Tichborne ethos.

The Tichborne case also resonated at the racecourse. At Newmarket, 'the case was all the talk of the hour' amongst the toffs who assembled there.[34] Sporting gentlemen could make wagers for or against the Claimant and his cause never quite escaped the atmosphere of the turf. An object of speculation (in every sense of that word), the Claimant became a horse to be backed. The Claimant was himself not averse to the racecourse, which he frequented on occasion. The turf was patronised by both the aristocracy and the working classes (although some courses remained exclusive), an appropriate place for a man who was imagined as both a toff and a plebeian at the same time. The world of sport, gambling and a belief in pleasures that were disapproved of by middle-class do-gooders provided a background against which the cause could thrive.

Within three weeks of the trial's end, the Claimant launched his 'Appeal to the British Public' from his cell at Newgate. In a letter to the press, he announced:

> Cruelly persecuted as I am, there is but one course that I could see, and that is, to adopt the suggestion so many have made to me, viz. to 'appeal to the British Public' for funds for my defence, and in doing so

I appeal to every British soul who is inspired by a love of justice and fair play, and who is willing to defend the 'weak against the strong'.[35]

Subscriptions were to be sent to William Warren Streeten, a solicitor, and would be acknowledged in the daily papers. The response was startling. From around the country, individual donations poured in and local defence associations were formed.

The idea of a defence fund was familiar to the British people. It had been a sustaining factor within Chartism as a way of obtaining funds for imprisoned leaders such as Joseph Rayner Stephens and Peter M'Douall. The defence fund became the main activity of local Tichborne organisations, along with petitioning and arranging visits by the Claimant. After the Claimant's initial 'Appeal', it seems to have been a relatively spontaneous activity. Both Abraham Anidjah, the Claimant's assistant, and the legal firm of Boddington and Manley later claimed to have originated the idea, but neither could take the credit for the fund's enormous success, as there was little attempt to generate the subscriptions through the mass media.[36] What is striking is the strength of local initiative in the matter. Support was not restricted to the working class but they probably contributed most.

Local committees were formed such as that at the Ancient Druid's Inn, Nottingham.[37] The Claimant's Appeal caused a meeting to be held at Pontypridd in South Wales at which a considerable number of working men were present and a defence fund was formed.[38] Any community meeting point was fair game as a place to collect money. Subscription cards were hawked around factories in Yeovil and shilling subscriptions were got up in several glove factories in the town. Nineteen out of twenty glovers apparently believed in the Claimant.[39] In Leeds, the employees of Messrs J. and C. Boyle, brickmakers, began a weekly subscription on behalf of the Claimant.[40] At Tichborne meetings agents distributed bills soliciting money for the defence fund.[41]

The subscription lists reveal a mosaic of popular attitudes.[42] They indicate that the majority of funds were collected either at work or in pubs: 'Collected by ten servants in one house in Belgravia', 'Seamen of her Majesty's ship 'Valorous'', 'Working men, collected at Havelock Coffee-House', 'One hundred and six Cab-drivers, Great Western Railway, by Mr Goodman', 'A few Boiler makers at Maudesley, Son, and Fields', 'Garibaldi Arms, Eastbourne, per Charles Wadey.' Sometimes subscriptions were collected out of doors: for instance, 'Near Great Eastern Terminus' or 'Collected at the Cattle Market by B. Tree.' The lists present a strong social cross-section from

Lord Rivers and Lady Frankfort de Montmorency through to the night-stokers at the Equitable Gasworks, Pimlico. Subscriptions came in from all over the country, but were mainly from the working class. It is unfortunately impossible to quantify this evidence in any accurate way as so many of the individual contributors remained anonymous. About half of the donations were under a pound and of these few were of more than a shilling, even when groups had banded together to send in a subscription, which suggests that the donors were poor.

The list of occupations given in the subscription lists shows a wide range of proletarian professions: cab drivers, cabinet makers, chair makers, hatters, joiners, metal founders, plasterers, railway workers, saddlers, servants, shoe makers, soldiers, tailors, vellum binders. The cause cut across the working class although the lists suggest a higher representation amongst craft workers, the aristocracy of labour. Casual labour was in any case not so likely to be represented because such workers had less money and were less easy to organise. What is clear from the subscription lists is that, with the exception of the 'Sunderland Defence Fund', subscriptions were not solicited by central-ised organisations in towns but by individuals or small groups. Often these did not indicate themselves by name but adopted soubriquets, which reveal a great deal about popular attitudes to the case.

For instance, one person employed 'Oliver Cromwell' as a name, which suggests an invocation of English republicanism. Similarly, another wrote: 'E. K., who sees this pressure of might against right will help on republicanism – remember the fable of the Lion and the Mouse'. Many presented them-selves in the language engendered by the case: 'Fair Play', 'Fair Play is a jewel', 'Might against Right', 'Strong for the weak' 'Lovers of fair play'. Many chose to classify themselves in terms of their social status: 'T. and B., two working men', 'A few workmen'. One simply called him or herself '*Vox Populi Vox Dei*'. This is in itself a key to the Tichborne cause. Supporters believed that the people instinctively saw the justice of the Claimant's case and believed their assessment should be respected.

The soubriquets reveal other reasons for being concerned about the Claimant: 'One who has faith in a mother's recognition'; 'From a few income-tax payers, who protest against the prostitution of public funds by filling the pockets of six counsel to prosecute in this case'; 'Seven workmen who do not believe the tattoo marks'; 'Anti-tattoo Humbug', 'C. M., no faith in his L.'s Tattooing'; 'Did Lord Bellew dream of the tattoo marks?'; and 'Tattoo marks too late to be true.' The Attorney-General in particular, was

TICHBORNE COMICALITIES.—No. 2.

THIS is the Public drinking their malt,
And discussing the case of Tichborne.

Tichborne Comicalities

abused: 'Three who fear the A. G. has Tattoo on the brain'; 'One who despises the Attorney-General's language'; 'Liberals who protest against C. being A. G. any longer'; and 'One who would like to see the A. G. get the cat.' The ending of the trial was criticised: 'One who regrets the trial so ending as to prevent a full and rightful reply for the Claimant', as well as 'D. P. and C.'s work people who protest at effigy burning.' Some employed a biblical tone: 'Widow's Mite.' There was also an anti-Catholic element: 'An enemy to the Jesuits and their permissive system of lying'; 'R. M. B. who believes the tattooing to be a got-up Popish plot'; and 'One convinced that Jesuit influences have been exercised against the Claimant.' Some reflected the feeling of people already alienated from justice: 'R. Haswell, a sufferer by Common Law' and 'H. Tate, Godalming, who has suffered from false swearing, and therefore feels for Sir Roger.' Finally, there was a sense of class distinction at work, particularly over the tattoo evidence, which, as we have seen, exercised many of the contributors: 'One who thinks no more of a peer than a peasant's word.' These soubriquets therefore give us an insight into the matrix of mentalities that formed the cause. They show the broad sweep of concerns that made people with very little money contribute to the defence fund.

Streeten resigned as trustee of the fund and subscriptions were then to be sent to a Captain Hunt at the offices of the Tichborne Defence Fund at 376 Strand.[43] There were, however, constant complaints about irregularities in the collection of subscriptions. Nothing arrived in November from Millwall, Southampton, Birmingham, Loughborough and other cities, despite the large meetings that had taken place there.[44] 'Publicity' wrote to the *Hampshire Chronicle* demanding a balance sheet. Hunt replied that he was prepared to show this but resigned beforehand.[45] The accounts were never properly presented and it is unclear how much filtered through to the Claimant's defence in the criminal trial.

From his arrival in Britain, the Claimant had found it difficult to get a fair hearing in the press. The *Pall Mall Gazette* was against him from the start. After the non-suit in March, the *Times* considered the verdict a triumph for the defence and approved of the government decision to prosecute, barely masking its own belief that the Claimant was an impostor.[46] This might have been permissible comment had the case not been *sub judice*. The Claimant was right to feel aggrieved. Virtually all the major London and provincial papers took the same line. The *Daily Telegraph*, the *Morning Post*, and the *Daily News* attacked him. The *Saturday Review* considered his to be 'one of the most daring and extraordinary impostures which have ever been brought to light'.[47] The Claimant and his supporters continually denounced the duplicity of the press. The Nottingham Tichborne Committee actually made a bonfire of copies of their local paper, the anti-Claimant *Daily Guardian*.[48] *Reynolds's Newspaper*, which later wholeheartedly supported the Claimant, was initially cautious in its approval of his progress. Only the *Morning Advertiser* supported him outright. From the Claimant's committal to Newgate, the paper sympathised with his plight and wondered aloud whether the witnesses against him had some interest in the property. If the tattoo evidence were true, Bogle would have known about it and informed him accordingly. At first the paper was cautious, but insisted he had a right to a fair trial and gave publicity to the movement as it arose.[49] The *Morning Advertiser* was owned by the Incorporated Society of Licensed Victuallers and appealed to a lower middle-class readership of shopkeepers and publicans. Formerly Liberal, Gladstone's licensing legislation pushed it towards the Conservatives in the 1870s. Unfortunately for the Claimant, its circulation was low and its reputation dubious (it was dismissively known as the *Tiger* or the *Tap-Tub*).[50]

At street level people were inundated with souvenirs, songs, posters, cartoons and pamphlets about the case – what we might call 'Tichborniana'. The number of items suggests that there was a considerable market for these. Inspired by the rejection of the cause by most of the press, two newspapers specifically devoted to Tichborne matters were launched. The *Tichborne Gazette* was the first to appear, proclaiming that 'The want of such a paper has been much felt, and inquiries for it have been innumerable'.[51] Its price, one penny, indicates that it was aimed at a popular audience. Unlike most popular papers, however, which were sold at the weekend, it was published on a Tuesday. It first appeared on 28 May 1872. The paper gave coherence to the nascent movement as it developed through the defence fund and mass meetings. Its editorials insisted, however, it had nothing to do with the organisation of the cause.[52] The paper was wholly given over to Tichborne. The front page was devoted to the expanding subscription list. We can detect in each issue the feel of a movement enlarging itself. The list had a unifying effect through its intention that 'the poor man's penny may appear as well as the rich man's pound'.[53] While criticising the rest of the press for inventing facts about the case, it presented arguments for the Claimant and reports of meetings. It recoiled, however, from some of the 'strong language' of the cause (usually directed against the legal profession) and urged its contributors to desist. The paper also tended to assert the paternalist arguments for the Claimant, arguing he would prove 'to be a good landlord, a kind neighbour, a faithful friend'. The paper was sold at Tichborne meetings amongst other locations.[54]

In June 1872, it was joined by the *Tichborne News and Anti-Oppression Journal: A Weekly Newspaper Advocating Fair Play for Every Man*, a title which sums up the ethos of Tichbornism very well. It was not as long lived as the *Gazette*, running only four months. Its price was also one penny and it was published on Saturdays. Its masthead contained the declaration, 'See not thy brother persecuted'.

Otherwise, the paper was similar in content to the *Gazette* but more strident:

We now unfurl our banner, and the motto is – NO OPPRESSION! AND FAIR PLAY FOR EVERY MAN.[55]

Its scope was larger than the *Gazette*, noting other causes and news with which the Tichborne cause had some affinity. It was first published on 15 June 1872, the day of the anniversary of Magna Carta. The proprietor, George Gilbert, also owned the *Brixton and Clapham Advertiser*. All goods advertised in the paper had London addresses, which implies that the paper was only expected to have a London circulation, although it advertised for agents to sell the paper at Tichborne meetings around the country.

The paper included articles on the legal aspects of the case by William Cobbett, son of the great reformer. A barrister himself, he criticised both the non-suit and the increasing complexity of the law. Other articles concerned miscarriages of justice. For instance, when David Welcome was sentenced to two months for stealing half a pint of beer from his master, the paper cynically commented, 'This is Justice's Justice'.[56] It opposed Sunday Closing – a long-standing working-class issue as Sunday was the only day on which many could shop – and reported the activities of the Agricultural Labourers' Union as well as strikes and lock outs.[57] Its political line was that arbitration should be preferred to strikes (the view of the Trade Union Junta who were endeavouring to make unions both legal and respectable).[58]

Both papers gave coherence and unity to the cause. The *Gazette* was almost certainly stopped by the *sub judice* action (discussed below) but it resurfaced after the criminal trial.

The most dramatic aspect of this phase of the Tichborne affair was the period from May 1872 to March 1873 when the Claimant 'stumped the country' to stir up support for his cause. The Claimant appeared at public venues throughout Britain appealing directly to the public for financial aid and sympathy. Stern critics blanched as the Claimant attracted huge audiences in many cities. He and his associates (particularly Guildford Onslow) delivered lectures and invective about the case. The agitation focused the popular indignation over the Claimant's treatment. It stood up for a 'public opinion' that was offended by the duplicity of the elite and its domination of the cumbersome legal system. After the Claimant visited Newcastle, the *South Durham Herald* wondered whether even a royal visit could generate so much enthusiasm.[59]

The Claimant was not the only public figure on the stump. 1872 was the year when parliamentary politicians began to seriously address the wider public through speeches intended to command a national audience.[60] Politicians had delivered speeches to large audiences before (usually in their own constituencies) but the 1867 Reform Act had introduced a new rhythm into politics and a new electorate to be addressed. The month before the Tichborne campaign began, Benjamin Disraeli spoke to a mass audience in Manchester, making an appeal that assisted his subsequent election victory in 1874. This reflected the wider context to the Tichborne campaign. From the platform to the pulpit, the Victorians loved talk.[61] Theirs was a society in thrall to public discussion. They prized eloquence in the law courts and on the lecturer's rostrum. The 1870s proved a good time for talk. In 1873,

The Claimant on the stump

the American evangelists D. L. Moody and Ira Sankey visited Britain and transfixed audiences with their revivalist message.[62] At the end of the decade, Gladstone made a sensational political comeback with his speeches as part of the Midlothian campaign. The Claimant was not in the same class as a speaker but his lectures were a part of the same culture of public discussion. At the same time, the Victorians distrusted eloquence, particularly the speaker who used fine words to cover up a lack of authenticity. Thomas Carlyle complained about stump oratory:

> Perhaps there is not in Nature a more distracted phantasm than your commonplace eloquent speaker, as he is found on platforms, in parliaments, on Kentucky stumps, at tavern-dinners, in windy, insincere times like ours.[63]

For his critics, the Claimant would have exemplified Carlyle's fears: a stump orator whose trade was deceit. On the other hand, his supporters may have taken comfort from his lack of a smooth tongue. He had no need to flatter his audience because he was the right man.

The prelude to the campaign took place at Alresford on 14 May 1872, where the Claimant attended a demonstration by several thousand locals in his favour.[64] The event was flamboyantly staged. The village was decorated with flags, banners and bunting often of a primitive kind. The Claimant came over in a carriage with a driver in a scarlet satin jacket from Onslow's house at Ropley. Tenants from the estate cheered him as he made his triumphant progress whilst two different bands played 'Auld Lang Syne' and 'Home Sweet Home'. Just outside, a group of labourers removed the horses from the wagon and drew the carriage into town, where a crowd awaited in the courtyard of the Swan Hotel whose new proprietor, Mr Newman, had organised the event. This was a ritual familiar from elections where the heroic candidate was conducted around town. Disraeli had been paraded through Manchester in this manner. Onslow and the Claimant delivered speeches attacking the conduct of the trial and praised workers for coming to their aid. Five days later, several members of the clergy as well as some tenants presented an address to Lady Teresa Tichborne denying that the Claimant had been invited by all tenants and wishing her well. The declaration was immediately rebutted by nineteen tenants who wrote to the *Times* saying that not only were they delighted to receive the Claimant but that they had also invited him.[65]

The Claimant went on to appear all over Britain, from Swansea to Glasgow, from Southsea to Dundee. The meetings usually conformed to a pattern. A defence committee would invite the Claimant and organise a venue for him to speak at. The defence committee would also advertise the meeting in the local press ('Sir Roger is coming') and post handbills all over town. The Claimant would arrive at the local station where hundreds or even thousands would turn up to see him. He would be taken to his hotel and then later to the place where he would speak, usually a town hall. Proceeds from the event went to the defence fund. The Claimant was usually supported by Onslow and others who delivered speeches as well. The evidence employed in the trial (particularly the tattoo evidence) was torn to shreds. It was also not uncommon for a former Carabineer to attend and testify that this was the Sir Roger Tichborne he had once known. Questions would be taken from the audience, although the crowd was often angry if a questioner called the Claimant anything apart from 'Sir Roger' (typical shout from the audience: 'Go it, Roger'). Afterwards the Claimant would return to his hotel, where he would stand on a balcony and address the crowd (frequently made up of those unable to afford tickets for his lecture).

The campaign proper was launched at Bristol on 24 May. A defence fund committee of forty people was already in existence under the chairmanship of H. A. Cross, an accountant and auctioneer. Its members included a J. F. Collins, a publican, as well as a clothes dealer, an outfitter and a commercial traveller.[66] Posters with the message 'Welcome Sir Roger' were plastered round town.[67] The *Western Telegraph* compared the excitement generated by the Claimant's arrival at the station with that of Garibaldi.[68] Between three and four thousand people crowded into Bristol Temple Meads station to catch a glimpse of him. The defence committee had to form a ring around the Claimant to keep the crowd away and drove off speedily before the horses could be taken from the carriage. As it was, a carriage door was ripped from its hinges in the mêlée.

The first meeting was at 8 o'clock in the Broadmead Rooms and was only three-quarters full. Cross, as chairman, opened the proceedings with an appeal that the Claimant, irrespective of whether he was guilty or innocent, should have a fair trial. He went on to criticise the tattoo evidence and urged the importance of the Dowager's recognition, asking 'whether it was just to her memory to say "Oh, she was an imbecile when she swore to her son"'. Resolutions urged the importance of fair play for the Claimant. The abuse of the defence fund by newspapers was denounced. Another member of the defence committee maintained criticism of Coleridge was fair as 'he was a public servant and therefore public property'. One area of struggle between the Tichbornites and the government concerned the term 'public'. If the government was a public body, then its agents could be criticised. It challenged notions of the accountability of the law.

Onslow delivered the main speech, with what became standard, class-based abuse: 'Sir ROGER TICHBORNE, at this moment, would have been in Newgate, and his beautiful children and his wife in the workhouse, if it had not been for the working classes – that noble part of the British public (loud cheers).' The trial itself was elitist: 'The court was filled by the aristocracy, and it was impossible for a working man to obtain admission.' He courted anti-Catholicism: 'the jury accepted the evidence of seventeen witnesses who, with the exception of the two Mr SEYMOURS, were all Jesuits – (laughter, and a voice: 'Shame').' On the incident when Mary Ann

Loder fainted on seeing the Claimant, Onslow drew a laugh by saying: 'Though he had the highest respect for his friend Sir Roger, he did not think he was exactly the sort of figure that a young woman would faint away at.'[69] The Claimant spoke briefly but apologised for being a bad speaker. Resolutions criticised the conduct of the trial and the appointment of six counsel to the prosecution. Seconding the resolution, the publican J. F. Collins used the term 'fair play' twenty times in his speech.

The audience the next day was fuller, perhaps because it was a Saturday night but more probably because the seat prices were halved to 2s. 6d., 1s. and 6d, which attracted a larger working-class audience (with considerable numbers of women). Not only was the house packed but a thousand people were turned away. Onslow alleged that the witnesses for the Tichborne family had been bribed. The meeting was also enlivened by the spectacle of a former servant of the Tichbornes forcing her way to the platform, shaking hands with the Claimant and stating that he was genuine.[70]

Even more successful was the visit to Southampton.[71] The Claimant made a flamboyant entrance on 11 June and addressed a crowd of about 3,000 people in the Church Congress Hall. Facsimiles of a poem presented to him on arrival by its author, William Ellis, were later sold to aid the defence fund, as were colour portraits of the Claimant.[72] The following day, a brass band paraded the streets with a banner displaying the words: 'Welcome, Sir ROGER TICHBORNE, the rightful heir to the Tichborne Estates.' Its route ended at the back of the York Hotel, where a second meeting was held. They placed the banner alongside another that proclaimed 'Thou shalt not bear false witness against thy neighbour', an example of the biblical line that the cause often took. The local defence fund clearly had a greater social mix than at Bristol. It included several dignitaries, including Alderman Tucker (who chaired both meetings) and Councillors Pearce and Purkiss, but also Mr Fasham, formerly of the Royal Engineers, who described himself as a 'working man'.

Onslow made great play of the affidavit of Dr Massey Wheeler, who had sworn that he knew both Castro and Orton in Australia, a testimony that was bolstered by Wheeler's status as a gentleman, as opposed to the more proletarian witnesses the Claimant usually attracted. Onslow was quite capable of flattering the 'nobility' of the working class whilst maintaining firm distinctions on the basis of rank. The Claimant attacked the Pittendreigh letters and the Attorney-General, upon which there was a shout of 'Give it to him hot'. This partly explains the appeal of the meetings – a delight in hearing major institutions of the state attacked.[73] A petition, complaining about the use of public money to crush the Claimant, signed by 3700 inhabitants of the town, was later presented to Parliament by Southampton's MP, W. Cowper Temple.[74]

The meeting was also notable for the first appearance of George Whalley on the Tichborne platform. It was perhaps inevitable that Whalley should take up a cause that was becoming increasingly tinged with anti-Catholicism, for he was one of the most notorious ultra-Protestants in the House of Commons. He explained in Parliament, however, that the reason for his involvement was the proximity of some of his property to Tichborne.[75] George Hammond Whalley was the Liberal MP for Peterborough. Along with Charles Newdegate, he was the leading anti-Catholic of his day and was perceived by many as a ridiculous figure obsessed with conspiracy theories about Jesuits.[76] It was a rare parliamentary speech of his that was not interrupted by shouts of 'Order' from the Speaker to still the laughter and derision of other MPs. *Punch*, by no means pro-Catholic, found his activities fanatical and waged a long campaign against him.[77] The parliamentary journalist Henry Lucy referred to him as 'poor, half-cracked Mr Whalley' and Disraeli considered him absurd.[78] Whalley's devotion to the Protestant cause was such that he came within striking distance of arguing that Christianity had been a British invention in the first place. He believed many of the original apostles escaped Roman persecution by fleeing to Britain – a cradle of liberty even then.[79] Whalley's contribution was to develop the anti-Catholic dimension of the Tichborne cause. He later complained that 'Roman Catholic influence was at work in every village, in every town, in the press and elsewhere, joining the hell-hounds'.[80] Whalley viewed the Claimant as a freeborn Englishman whose cause drew on the radical tradition:

the Claimant has descended from the highest circle of society to the 'refreshing cold' of the lowest depths, and had come thence braced and invigorated to assert a right as sacred for Englishmen as that which JOHN HAMPDEN, his (Mr WHALLEY's) ancestor, had asserted.[81]

At one meeting, Whalley told his audience that the working men in his constituency were 'all ... for Tichborne'. When he asked one about this, he was informed that it was 'Because ... they call him such bad names'.[82] Popular opinion was apparently outraged by the unfairness of the law. A friend of Sir Arthur Underhill's quizzed his gardener, who took a great interest in the case about why he supported the Claimant. He replied: 'Well, Sir, I reckon they'm werry 'ard and so be they judges, and then, zur, the 'ardest of all be they counts. Oh, they be werry 'ard on 'im.' Underhill realised 'The good man had mistaken the counts for prejudiced foreign noblemen'[83]

Publicans often took the lead in inviting the Claimant. His speech at Dewsbury came about because local publicans decided to organise the meeting. It was accompanied by a banquet at which a publican from Dawgreen presided.[84] Similarly, the Tichborne committee in Newcastle was presided over by the publican of the Express Inn.[85] The *Birmingham Daily Post* employed this association with drink to dispute the popular base of the Tichborne movement after the Claimant had spoken in the town hall:

> There was a 'committee' of course – nothing is easier than to manufacture a committee – but it had no appointment from anybody outside itself, nor was anything 'committed' to it – the whole business was self-contained; incubated in the 'bars' of public-houses, conducted by publicans or their intimate friends, and made conducive mainly to the mighty interests of 'drink'.[86]

Local Tichborne committees were sometimes concerned about the respectability of the movement. In Grimsby, the local committee insisted that the Claimant speak in the town hall as it felt it was beneath Sir Roger's dignity to address the public in the local music hall.[87] This did not prove to be a problem elsewhere. The Claimant appeared in music halls in Swansea, Sheffield and London amongst other places, though not as part of the normal entertainment. In such cases, the manager agreed to the loan of the premises (sometimes cancelling a performance) in exchange for a share of the takings. At Liverpool, the Claimant appeared in the theatre normally presenting Newsome's Circus.[88]

Although generally successful, the Claimant's lectures did not always sell out. Many of those who supported him could not afford tickets. Even when the Claimant spoke on the bowling green at Caistor, spectators still had to pay to hear him.[89] The most democratic aspect of his tour was his arrival at each railway station, because this allowed anyone to view him. His procession from train to hotel became a form of street theatre in which he was cheered (and sometimes abused) by the crowd. Indoors it was different. The arrangement of most Victorian theatres (including the auditoriums of town halls) expressed the gradations of the nineteenth-century class system. It is significant that the gallery or balcony in theatres (containing the cheapest seats) were usually packed; the more expensive seats frequently had gaps, which reveals the class composition of Tichbornism. Overall, the majority of those who attended were working class although it was not unusual for many middle-class spectators to turn up. At the Grimsby Town Hall, tickets cost three shillings, two shillings and one shilling whilst the cheapest seats went for sixpence. 1,070 people attended and the house was almost full; only the two shilling seats were empty, implying that spectators were either middle class (wanting to maintain their distance from those below) or solidly working class.[90] When the Claimant spoke at the Royal Amphitheatre in Liverpool, it was noted that '"Sir Roger" appeared to be the most popular with the "gods" who densely crowded the gallery'.[91]

The purchase of a ticket to a Tichborne event (even if proceeds did go to the defence fund) did not imply commitment to the cause. Many came simply to enjoy the spectacle. Some heckled, though trouble-makers were usually thrown out and most were loud in their cheers for the Claimant. Press reports suggest that a fair number of women attended. At the Nottingham's Mechanics Hall, the ladies present seemed 'idolotrously fond of the Claimant' and some cried 'poor thing' when he spoke about his plight.[92]

Local papers were often aghast at the vulgarity of the Tichborne spectacle and disdained the class of the Claimant's supporters. The *Newcastle Weekly Chronicle* was shocked that working men could demean themselves by dragging the Claimant's carriage through the streets of the city, evidence of the 'prevailing infatuation' with the 'adventurer'. The paper recalled that the millenarian prophetess Joanna Southcott had had many local supporters.[93] The *South Durham Herald* wearily opined: 'Somehow the *hoi-polloi* have marked "Sir Roger" for their own. Without exactly knowing why, the crowd idolizes the man ... '[94] A Nottingham paper adopted a similar line:

> There is a vulgar interest in the creature, on which he knows how to trade successfully, just as there is about anyone who has outraged all laws of society. People flock round the Claimant just as they used to go to executions, or anywhere else in which there is a direct appeal to morbid sentiment. But we refer now to ... those who debate about his wrongs in tap-rooms, and indulge in maudlin eloquence about 'right' and 'might' ... Those who cheer Sir Roger in the conviction that he is at once a hero in achievement and a martyr to the law, offer in themselves a strange study, to the interest of which the socialist will not be

insensible. His friends are chiefly those of the lowest orders – people who take up a theory without examining its basis lest they should acquire a leaning the other way.[95]

The Tichborne movement was hardly an example of class struggle that Karl Marx would have approved of. However, the Tichborne spectacle allowed for many middle-class expressions of disdain for the lower orders.

The content of the meetings was similar and the speeches did not vary much from one event to another. As one would expect from an MP, Onslow was adept as a speaker. But the person people most wanted to hear was the Claimant. His accent excited a lot of comment. Many journalists suggested that he had a cockney accent. A Birmingham reporter found that he spoke 'with a marked cockney accent and with his h's in what printers call "pie"' while the *South Durham Herald* found: 'He drops his g's and misplaces his h's. He puts the emphasis in long words just where the Londoner bred east of Temple Bar would put it.'[96]

The report following the Claimant's speech in Birkenhead near the end of his tour gives us an even closer approximation of his voice:

> There was an unmistakeable cockney accent running through the whole of it, and the mispronunciation of words gave rise to some amusement. 'Oil' was pronounced 'hoil', 'get' was called 'git', 'beans' was read 'be ans', and 'catched' 'ketched'.[97]

The Claimant usually insisted that he was not asking spectators to believe he was Sir Roger Tichborne but that he should have the right to a fair trial. The meetings were distinctive for the abuse directed at the judiciary and the legal profession. Why was so much public money being employed to prosecute an English gentleman when real villains (corrupt bankers and others) got off scot free? Was this not an infringement of English justice, the basic liberties enshrined in Magna Carta?[98] Coleridge was abused because he allegedly only cared about his fees.[99] In Cardiff, the Claimant noted: 'I have no doubt … lawyers can do a great many things; they frequently make black appear white – (laughter) – but more frequently, I am sorry to say, they make white appear black.'[100] The press was also abused. At one meeting, the Claimant complained that reporters did not bother to note down what he said, leading to abuse against the press from the audience and 'such language that is generally to be heard in a 'penny gaff' (cheap theatre) in London'.[101]

In Darlington, he attacked the editor of the *Northern Echo* for his scurrilous articles. When a man in the audience was identified as the editor, he had to be protected by the police. In a case of mistaken identity, the man declaimed, 'Ah's not t'editor, and ah's nowt to de wi'd!'[102]

The most significant symbol of the rapport between the Claimant and the working classes occurred on Saturday 6 July in Millwall in London's East End. Thousands assembled in holiday spirit from Poplar, Stepney, Blackwall, the Isle of Dogs and Wapping, Arthur Orton's former stamping ground. The crowd convened at the Market House Tavern in Poplar. The area was decorated with flags and banners suggesting local pride – 'Welcome Sir Roger to the East End'. Most shops were closed for the occasion. For an afternoon at least, the Claimant appeared to rule the East End. The cheers for him were almost incessant along the route of the procession.

The crowd led by the Tower Hamlets Artillery Band and the Millwall Musical Volunteers marched to a field lent by a Mr Bradshaw. According to the *Morning Advertiser*, Garibaldi did not attract a more numerous crowd than the Claimant. Five thousand people, 'mainly of the artisan class' walked with him. It was a symbolic occasion as the Claimant was seen as daring to show his face near Wapping. If he were Orton, would he dare enter the vicinity where many locals might recognise him? The willingness of the Claimant to stick his head in the lion's mouth was further proof of his identity. At the meeting a resolution insisting that the Claimant was genuine was unanimously carried.[103]

Unlike the other meetings, the Millwall event was exclusively proletarian in composition. Both the committee and the audience was working class. Out of deference to them, the Claimant suggested that the chairman of the local defence fund, W. D. Hipperson, a working man, should chair the meeting. The organisation of the meeting had caused acrimony. Abraham Anidjah, acting as campaign manager, had decided that the Claimant would not attend open-air meetings and persuaded the proprietor of the Eastern Hall, Limehouse, to give him free use of the hall as well as a donation to the defence fund. Hipperson, however, went ahead with the Millwall meeting and abused Anidjah when he addressed the crowd.[104]

It was about this time that Anidjah's involvement with the cause came to an end. He was a cigar merchant who lived in the Strand. Anidjah had called upon the Claimant in Newgate Prison and offered to get up a defence fund as well as organise meetings.[105] He then came to an agreement with Onslow that he should arrange for the provision of carriages, banners and posters.

For this, he would receive expenses, 5 per cent of the gross receipts and £10 for each successful meeting. It was Anidjah who came up with the idea of arranging a carriage and four horses at the stations to meet the Claimant. Anidjah asked Onslow to ratify the agreement in writing. Onslow did so but would not hand the document over. As a result, Anidjah had him summonsed to Bow Street Magistrates Court in August. Onslow's lawyer accused Anidjah of appropriating demonstration funds. Anidjah himself complained that he had lost hundreds of pounds through his involvement in the affair. The case was dismissed as the magistrate ruled that he had no jurisdiction over a private letter.[106]

Relations with Anidjah worsened. At a meeting in Birmingham on 27 August, he sat in an orchestra seat and tried to make a speech about his involvement with the case. He was already known in the area, as he possessed a small furniture shop in New Street. When he began to criticise the Claimant, he was shouted down, even though he protested his belief in his identity and that he had been providing him with £10 a week to live on. The Chairman told the audience, 'I am proud to introduce to you ... a most unworthy descendant of Old Father Abraham, Mr Anidjah, the Jew, I believe'. Anidjah did not secure a hearing.[107] Later the same month, the Claimant used Edward Napper, the pugilist he employed to protect him, to bar Anidjah's entry to a meeting in the Cambridge Music Hall in the East End. Napper threatened to throw him over the bannister.[108] Anidjah had him summonsed to Worship Street Police Court, where Justice Bushby decided that there was no evidence to suggest that the threats were the result of instructions from the Claimant. He did, however, make Napper enter his own recognisance at £40 as well as two sureties to keep the peace. As the Claimant was present, the court was crowded.[109]

Supporters of the Claimant were very quick to deny the impression that there was a kind of unseen hand behind the meetings. The firm of Boddington and Manley, the solicitors looking after the defence fund, criticised the idea that the meetings were organised by a 'professional and paid agent, and were not the voluntary efforts of gentlemen in the respective towns'.[110] Whalley insisted that 'the object was not ... to get up' meetings, but to regulate and control such as might 'originate as the genuine and spontaneous offspring of public opinion.'[111]

There was a strong atmosphere of show business in all the Claimant's meetings. At the Liverpool Amphitheatre, the meeting was addressed by Professor Anderson, 'The Wizard of the North', a conjurer with a national reputation.[112] He was notable for taking valuable objects from the audience, shooting them out of a pistol and then producing them from inside a candle.[113] Anderson endowed the movement with additional glamour. He also appeared with the Claimant at the Oxford Music Hall, attesting that he had known both Orton and Castro at Castlemain in Australia in 1859.[114]

Coleridge had complained to Gladstone in June that he had 'been made the subject of constant & scurrilous attacks from the Defendant himself, & from a Mr Onslow who goes about with him; & who spares neither witnesses nor judge, nor jury nor counsel in his scandalous speeches'.[115] It would seem likely that the prosecution from that time forth was looking for an opportunity to suppress the slanderous accusations of the movement.

Nothing happened until 11 December when Onslow, Whalley and the Claimant appeared at the St James's Hall, Piccadilly. The speeches were very much in the usual style. As chairman, Whalley asked the audience 'whether there is not a great conspiracy, the greatest, I believe, which has ever been known to the law; and further, that you do believe that the law of England is unequal to cope duly with and to expose and punish that conspiracy except by the aid and support of the watchful eye of the public'. Onslow complained about the conduct of the trial, about the Pittendreigh letters and the fact that the jury had not heard all the evidence. The next day, Whalley went further:

> It has been said there was a conspiracy. He had no doubt there was ... the Attorney-General and the Government were attempting to prosecute under a penal Act a man whom they knew was innocent of the charges made against him. The object was to keep the large Tichborne estates in the hands of the ARUNDELL family – a family which they all knew was influential in certain sections of English society.[116]

After this, both Onslow and Whalley were summonsed to appear on 20 January 1873 before the Lord Chief Justice for contempt of court. Hawkins made the application to summons the two MPs but made allowances for the Claimant and maintained that he hoped he would receive a fair trial.[117] Ironically, this fringe trial and the one that followed it had far more effect on the legal system than the more famous Tichborne trials. It was established in particular that a case was *sub judice* from the moment the defendant was committed for trial, rather than from the beginning of the trial itself. Sir John Karslake, acting for Onslow, tried to argue that the case was not *sub judice* at all, the criminal trial not having started, but was immediately quashed by the Judge, Alexander Cockburn.

In the trial, Karslake apologetically claimed that Onslow was not trying to pervert justice but was merely trying to balance out the prejudice that existed against the Claimant. Such was the only honourable course, having promised the Dowager before her death that he would never desert her son. He explained that it had not occurred to Onslow that he was attacking the character of witnesses in the trial and that he had never meant to obstruct the legal process. He therefore guaranteed that Onslow would attend no more public meetings. Digby Seymour, for Whalley, claimed that his client was not trying to influence the trial but simply to support the defence fund. Cockburn, however, maintained that both were commenting on a trial that was *sub judice*. He used the following as a test of contempt:

> Suppose that one person was at that meeting who afterwards became a Juryman. Would not that man, having heard a gentleman of position publicly charge witnesses with being guilty of a foul conspiracy, and as having committed perjury, be under the impression that those witnesses, when they came to give their evidence, were not worthy of credit.[118]

Cockburn found them both guilty. He noted that if cases could be discussed in public in this way, it would be open to the other side to behave accordingly. Thus sensational meetings and organised agitations would create 'appeals ... to popular prejudice and passion'.[119]

Present in court was G.B. Skipworth who had chaired the meeting at St James's, Piccadilly. Skipworth was a Justice of the Peace from Caistor in Lincolnshire and had entertained the Claimant at his home when he was speaking at Grimsby. Incensed, he went down that evening to Brighton where he was due to chair a meeting with the Claimant in the Dome and denounced the verdict.[120] The Claimant further condemned the fitness of the Lord Chief Justice to try him, as he had denounced him as an impostor four years before at his club. As a result, both Skipworth and the Claimant were summonsed for contempt of court on January 29 before Justice Blackburn. It was the first case since 1768 when a 'stranger' (one not directly involved with the case) had been tried for contempt of court for slandering a judge.[121]

Skipworth was a passionate and bizarre figure – typical of the kind thrown to the forefront in the case. When the officer came to deliver the summons at his house in Caistor, he threw him out for keeping on his hat indoors.[122]

G. B. Skipworth

In court he appeared, wearing his legal robes, to defend himself. The Claimant also acted for himself, as he said he had not committed a contempt. Skipworth maintained that, far from bringing the law into contempt, he was actually trying to maintain its 'dignity, majesty and integrity'.[123] He insisted that his actions were motivated by his character as an Englishman and as a Christian. For an exhibit, he produced letters, which he was forwarding to the Secretary of the Society for the Propagation of Christian Knowledge about the Tichborne case. They were, he maintained, intended to function as a subscription as they were 'proof of a greater heathenism than any that could be found either abroad or at home'.[124] He wound up by saying that he would rather place himself in the hands of God than in those of Justice Blackburn.

The Claimant started by denying the validity of the proceedings and demanding to be tried by a jury. Blackburn insisted that this was not how contempt cases were tried.[125] The Claimant then questioned the modes of legal procedure that had been used to deal with him up to that time: how he had been incarcerated in Newgate whilst a team of eminent lawyers was assembled against him. He could not even prosecute hostile newspapers, as he did not have the financial means to do so. Blackburn agreed that a passage the Claimant read out from the *Saturday Review* attacking him was 'improper'. The Claimant then explained that he had called the meetings in response to criticism in the press and staked his defence on the right to freedom of speech. Further, he asked why he had not been summonsed before if his utterances constituted contempt.

Making his judgement, Blackburn denied that he was concerned with 'the personal dignity of judges as individuals': rather, he wanted to ensure that a fair trial took place. He justified the summons for contempt as a practice that had existed since the earliest times and used as a precedent the case of Lechmere Charlton, an MP who was imprisoned in 1836 for contempt after he wrote threatening letters to the Master of Chancery during a law suit. Otherwise, Blackburn declined to cite further authorities. He found both men guilty of contempt. Skipworth was fined £500 and given three months' imprisonment. The Claimant was simply bound over for three months with a security of £500. It was considered that he would not be able to raise the money for his defence if a fine was imposed. This may have been an example of the discretionary tactics of the judge. To have fined or even imprisoned the Claimant would have confirmed the image of his pursuit by a merciless judiciary.

In prison, Skipworth maintained the defiant style he had shown in the trial. From Holloway, he issued a poster claiming 'I have done my duty to my God, my conscience, and my country; for that I willingly suffer'.[126] He followed this up with a pamphlet denying that he had ever said anything in Brighton that could be construed as contempt of court and that it was therefore not only illegal to send him to prison but a violation of Magna Carta itself.[127]

The Tichbornites had tapped a weak point in the law because contempt of court was an ambiguous area. The power to summons those allegedly in contempt was crucial in enforcing the authority of the legal system. Derived from Star Chamber, contempt of court had been enlarged in the seventeenth and eighteenth centuries largely to deal with comment in the developing press.[128] Up to the late nineteenth century, there was widespread use of the power to punish comment on civil and criminal proceedings.[129] The main modern authority was the case of *R. v. Almon* (1765) where Justice Wilmot in an undelivered judgement held that a 'stranger' could be punished summarily in a court of common law for libel or slander of a judge. Although it was not cited in the cases against the Claimant and his associates, it formed the background not only for the judgements in these instances but in every similar case in the nineteenth century.[130] Wilmot's judgement assumed that the power was an immemorial practice and Blackstone concurred. The later research of Sir John Fox was to show that this was not so.[131] After the Skipworth trial, the legal critic, W.F. Finlason, noted that the *R. v. Almon* verdict rested on no authorities and was in any case printed posthumously without Wilmot's sanction.[132]

The law of contempt had been controversial throughout the nineteenth century. An Act in 1830 was needed to remedy the situation where persons imprisoned for contempt could effectively be sentenced for life and forgotten. The machinery for the supervision of the Act was improved in 1860 when the Officer of the court was empowered to visit prisons every quarter and interview persons committed for contempt and then report back to the Lord Chancellor.[133] The absence of a jury and the tendency to limit the freedom of the press led to attempts to amend the law of contempt in 1883, 1892, 1894 and 1896.[134]

In making their protest, the Tichbornites had latched onto a real ambiguity in the law. The idea that summary commitment for contempt was sanctioned in common law by immemorial practice was not only disproved both at the time (by Finlason) and by later scholarship, but no contemporary was able to cite any authority before *R. v. Almon* to prove it. Ironically, the two trials themselves became precedents. They established that it was a contempt to state that an accused was either guilty or not guilty and to attack witnesses when a case was *sub judice*.[135] Such assertions remained in contempt regardless of whether they were true or false or if there was little actual risk of prejudicing the trial.[136] In 1899, the case was actually used in the United States to argue that contempt had never been tried by jury.[137]

The Tichborne movement and the Skipworth trial in particular were striking because they challenged the logic on which the law operated. They exposed the law as a theatre of power relationships where it was impossible to tell the truth as the Tichbornites saw it.

After the *sub-judice* trials, the Claimant was unable to hold forth about his problems in the way that he had done. To raise money, he reverted to another staple of the lecture circuit: the narrative of travel exploration. He read aloud an account of his travels in South America and Australia, promising to produce a book on the subject. He was not nearly as effective at this. The *Oswestry Advertiser* described his talk in the town as the 'dreariest recital that ever mortal man was doomed to listen to'.[138] Many in the audience drifted away with boredom. The speech included descriptions of Peruvian cookery and advice about emigration, urging his audience to consider going to Australia: he had nothing to say against the life he had led there, and if he had his life to live over again, he would prefer being a stockman in the Australian colonies to being an earl with £20,000 a year in England.[139] His appeal was one of a nobleman who had descended amongst the common people and been purified by the experience. The Claimant continued to deliver his reminiscences right up to the criminal trial. Audiences were briefed not to ask him questions about his case, as he was threatened with a fine. In Birkenhead, when an audience member tried to ask him about the trial, he was shouted down.[140] The *sub judice* ruling assisted Bill Bailey, the manager of the Canterbury music hall in London. One evening a fat bacon curer from Bermondsey was shown into a box in the theatre. The audience, thinking it was the Claimant, went wild with applause and demanded a speech, refusing to quieten down for the next act. Bailey solved the problem by telling the patrons that the Claimant was forbidden from speaking in public. The bacon curer satisfied the audience by taking a bow and the next act went on.[141]

The Tichborne movement had been in effect suppressed for the time being. Just before the trial began, the Claimant published a letter in the *Daily News* thanking the public for their support over the past year and asked that all outstanding contributions should be sent to Onslow. There was then the question of who would represent the Claimant. Serjeant Ballantine was prepared to take the case on. The Claimant, however, had not been impressed by his advocacy, maintaining that the lawyer had done nothing at all, and refused his services. Several leading barristers were approached but declined. Shortly before the trial began, Lord Rivers, who had raised bail for the Claimant and made himself responsible for his fees, engaged a lawyer who not only accepted the brief but went on to transform the Tichborne cause.

5

The Great Trial at Bar

On 13 February 1850, Policeman 288 was walking his beat in Snowhill, near Clerkenwell, on the fringes of London's East End, when he came across a small crowd. Moving to investigate what had brought them together, he found that the object of their interest was a little boy wretched with tears. A lost child perhaps? The locals' concern, however, ran deeper. They showed the constable some terrible bruises on the boy's back. When the six year old was taken to the police station, it was found that there were red, blue and black stripes all over his body, from head to foot; worse, it appeared from marks on his neck that a person had tried to hang him. Some of the skin on his throat had actually been removed by the pressure of a cord. Even in an age that did not believe in sparing the rod, this was clearly child abuse. The boy was taken to the West London Union and his parent sought. The court that examined the case heard that the boy, whose name was Edward Hyde, was the illegitimate son of his father with whom he lived alone. They slept in the same bed (not unusual at that time) and, when he was good, the man would give him presents. At other times, however, he would beat him for telling lies or not learning his lessons. The brute would flog the half-naked boy or would tie a rope round his neck and squeeze. The court found the man not guilty on the charge of hanging Edward Hyde but guilty of aggravated assault. He served a month in prison. A quarter of a century later, the man would become the Tichborne Claimant's lawyer. He was Edward Kenealy.

Edward Vaughan Hyde Kenealy was the most eccentric product of a profession peopled by eccentrics. He and the Tichborne cause were made for each other. Larger than life, he ignited what was already a tinder box of popular emotions. He was a barrister, poet, critic, part-time prophet and would-be politician who, in all his guises, exhibited signs of melancholic obsession and was often considered to be slightly mad. Tormented by furies of his own devising, he became alienated from all around him, turned inwards and made a religion of his own. As we will see, his tilting against the windmills of the judiciary transformed him into a Victorian Don Quixote.

Born in Cork on 2 July 1819, Kenealy was the son of a shopkeeper. Originally trained as a surgeon, he moved to England, where he entered

Edward Vaughan Kenealy

Gray's Inn to become a barrister and later acquired a Doctorate in Laws from Trinity College, Dublin. Along the way, Kenealy sired his illegitimate son, Edward Hyde, in Ireland and removed him to England when he found the child was being neglected.

Like many lawyers, Kenealy was also inspired by literature. His writing career developed from an acquaintance with the flamboyant Irish littérateur William Maginn, who began to publish him in *Fraser's Magazine*, one of the leading periodicals of the 1830s noted for its swashbuckling Radical Toryism. His poems and criticism also appeared in *Ainsworth's Magazine* and the *Dublin Review*, all reflecting his considerable scholarship and knowledge of classical languages. An admirer of Daniel O'Connell, he contested the seats of Trinity College, Dublin, in 1847, Kinsale in 1848 and Cork the year after on a nationalist Young Ireland platform, but retired before the poll each time. Also in support of Irish nationalism, he became president of the London Davis club and in 1848 found himself defending the Irish rebels, Francis Looney and William Paul Dowling, but lost both cases.

It was at this moment that he was charged with beating his illegitimate son. His practice looked as though it would be damaged when he was imprisoned in 1850. Lord Campbell later consoled him by saying there was no serious stain on his character and indeed Kenealy did not let the embarrassment of the case affect his career. He joined the Oxford Circuit as a barrister in 1851, the year in which he married a sixteen-year-old girl, Elizabeth Nicklin, who was to become the mother of twelve children by him and the one stable force in his life. He built up a reputation for erratic behaviour in court, often criticising the judiciary. In 1856, after participating in the defence team (led by Serjeant Shee) of William Palmer, the poisoner, he was credited with the authorship of the pamphlet *A Letter to the Lord Chief Justice Campbell*, which complained of the latter's conduct of the trial and compared him to Judge Jeffreys.[1] Nothing could be proved, though Campbell felt he should be disbarred.

Kenealy had been a republican in his youth after reading Paine: 'There were occasions when I should see beauty only in socialistic and in communistic theories.' Immersion in Montesquieu and Burke drew him back to monarchical institutions.[2] On the anniversary of the execution of Charles I, Kenealy's diary records that he felt grieved by his martyrdom.[3] He became an admirer of Robert Peel and also of Radical Toryism, applauding Lord Ashley's attack on poverty.[4] But this was an age in which distinctions between political parties (then in an early stage of formation) were not fixed. In the early 1850s, he pursued a political career once more. Disraeli was a friend but Kenealy failed to convert him to Irish nationalism. They fell out over his contribution to Disraeli's paper, the *Press*. His political career in England got no further than it had done in Ireland. He attempted to stand as a Liberal at Stoke in 1862, and in 1868 contested Wednesbury in the General Election, standing as an Independent People's candidate, claiming to love the working man; but the working man did not love him and he came bottom of the poll.[5]

As a lawyer, he was more successful and in 1868 became a Queen's Counsel. Amongst his more notorious cases was the defence of the Fenians Burke and Casey in 1867, a brief he threw up after an attempt was made with explosives to free the prisoners from Clerkenwell prison, and, in 1869, the prosecution in *R. v. Overend and Gurney*, the great financial scandal.

Kenealy was steeped in the Romantic movement. At university, he read Byron, Rousseau and Shelley.[6] Reality existed for him on two levels – in the day to day and in his extravagant imagination, which he escaped into by means of scholarship. He was a Gothic Romanticist who wandered onto the political stage. It is not surprising that he admired Disraeli and the Young England movement, with its chivalrous emphasis on benevolent social feudalism.[7] But Kenealy always managed to be *sui generis*. His writings were long, mystical and obscure, with a frequent tendency to digression. He admitted as much in his novel *Edward Wortley Montagu*:

> I mean to write, not according to rules of art, but in accordance with the humour of the moment, and I shall follow my own whim in preference to that of Aristotle, or any other dead or living critic. Learned reader if thou like it not say so, abandon my book forthwith, but revile me not in the least, for truly I have had enough abuse in my time, and I am now rhinoceros-hided against opinion.[8]

In his writings, he often constructed alter-egos for himself (Barney Brallaghan or E. W. Montagu) but his work usually reflected his feeling of being a stranger in a strange land or a prophet in the wilderness. Being at odds with the world made him see conspiracies everywhere – even Shakespeare's plays were written by someone else, he believed.[9] His insularity took the form of a passionate integrity and dislike of masks and pretence:

> The truth is, civilised society seems to me like a picture of Hell in little ... There is not a man or woman that I meet who is not masked. As in the great carnival, everyone assumes a character which is not his own, so it is in town and cities. The young are caught by externals; they think the dress and the outside represent the inner man; but they wake from their delusion at some period, and find that all is theatrical ... I have ever shunned the sinning crowd – myself perhaps as bad as they – but still I longed to separate from them. I have sought repose in the East and West; in mountains and the wilderness.[10]

This hostility to masks, illusion and theatricality was to prove an important factor in the Tichborne case – it fired Kenealy's denunciations of Establishment hypocrisy. Indeed Kenealy on fire was something to be seen. Bad temper is always an important part of anti-Establishment polemic and in Kenealy's case it was to wreck his legal career. His daughter, Arabella, blamed his irritableness during the trial on diabetes.[11]

Kenealy was born a Catholic but abandoned Catholicism for a religion of his own.[12] It began with his interest in ancient languages but was essentially founded on an obsession with himself. He had little contact with other groups trying to establish 'alternative' forms of religion such as the Owenites or spiritualists, although he did attend at least one séance and was later (mistakenly) associated with theosophy.[13] Many of his beliefs were similar to Christianity, holding that there was one supreme creator god and that everyone who led a moral life would be admitted to heaven.[14] He was a passionate Orientalist, similar in this respect to his contemporary, Sir Richard Burton. His interest in Egyptology emerged from the Victorian belief that it was the oldest civilisation, but he was also obsessed with India. He could read Sanskrit and Hindustani, and dearly wanted to visit the country. On one occasion, he attempted and failed to become Chief Justice of Madras.[15] He became a critic of Empire, condemning the British presence in India and Africa.[16]

Kenealy saw himself as a kind of Victorian Prospero, in touch with a celestial 'Essence' running through the universe. He was a believer in the Naronic cycle – a period of six hundred years during which time the world would be in spiritual darkness until the rise of an inspired messenger.[17] These messengers were of two kinds: messianic (teachers) or cabiric (judges). The line began with Adam and included Jesus, Mohamed and Gengiz Khan. The Twelfth Messenger was known by the Hindus as 'Parasu-Rama' and by Mohamedans as 'Imam Mahidy' but it is quite clear that he was known to the British as 'Edward Kenealy'.[18] According to his follower, Charles Wells Hillyear, a school teacher, 'It was the special mission of the Twelfth Messenger to bring about the re-establishment of a universal monotheism, without the use of militant force.'[19]

This theology was based on a belief in an original sacred text – the Apocalypse – which came from Egypt, 'the crypt of all primeval lore'.[20] The Old Testament was made up of extracts from it but the version that had come down through history was a forgery. Moreover, the Catholic Church had apparently tampered with the Gospels.[21] Fortunately, the truth about the Apocalypse had been revealed to Kenealy, in his role as Twelfth Messenger, and he devoted several long, scholarly and largely incomprehensible texts to an exposition of its contents. He argued that there was a unity via the Apocalypse to all the world religions. Man had existed on Earth for ten thousand years and the perfect monotheistic religion of the Apocalypse was spread through sacred mysteries, which could be found in ancient Greece but also in the practices of freemasons, although he claimed they had lost the 'mystic secret' and substituted fictions derived from Judaism.[22]

It was all very incoherent. The creed of monotheism was really aimed at one person – Kenealy – which explains why he had few followers as a religious leader. The texts in which he expounded his philosophy were long-winded in the extreme, inaccessible and expensive. The creed anyway boiled down to little more than a belief in a supreme creator god who infused his essence into each human being.[23] The significance of the theology was that it accounts for Kenealy's millenarian tone as leader of the Tichborne movement. Kenealy was a fantasist, religious fanatic and egomaniac who by accident found himself involved in the most notorious court case of the century. Unlike his religious writing, he ensured that nothing he said or did thereafter would be obscure.

In taking the Tichborne case, Kenealy set himself an appropriately heroic task. The odds against him were considerable. The brief was enormous and he had to work day and night to master it in time.[24] Against him he faced a talented team under Henry Hawkins, most of whom had been through the civil action and knew the case. As juniors, Kenealy had only Patrick McMahon and later Cooper Wyld. McMahon was the Liberal MP for New Ross, but proved to be little help, as he was rarely in court. The Claimant himself was by and large apathetic during the case and so Kenealy found himself on his own in the *cause célèbre* of the century.

The trial at bar of the Tichborne Claimant was every bit as momentous and controversial as *Tichborne* v. *Lushington*. *Regina* v. *Castro* lasted almost a year, from April 1873 to February 1874, a total of 188 days in court (the earlier civil action had lasted 102 days) and took place in the Court of Queen's Bench. There was no slackening of public interest. Towards the end of the trial, the *Daily News* commented dolefully, 'Life to a good many persons will not seem quite the same when the morning no longer brings the reports of the Tichborne case.'[25] The new trial contained as many surprises as the first. Neither side believed it was assured of victory and so reviewed each piece of evidence in detail. The biggest difference between the two trials was that the Claimant could not be examined. Defendants in criminal trials had been barred from testifying since 1836 (although in practice they were not called as witnesses long before this) as lawyers had taken over the conduct of the trial, creating a culture of adversarial advocacy. This replaced the earlier form of criminal trial where the judge directed the proceedings and counsel (if they attended at all) had virtually no role.[26] Defendants in criminal cases were silent until 1898.[27] The Claimant sat quietly in court, doodling and sketching caricatures of the protagonists, apparently uninterested as Kenealy pressed his case. He presumably lived for the evenings when he took in the London night life. The American novelist Mark Twain (Samuel Clemens), who was fascinated by the case, attended a party thrown by the Claimant during the trial. He discovered the Claimant in evening dress being fawned over by about twenty-five men all of whom came from an elite background (probably the kind of sporting gentlemen whose company he enjoyed). All made a point of calling him 'Sir Roger'. Twain noticed how they emphasised the name over and over 'as if it tasted good'. When he was in Australia, Twain made a point of visiting Wagga Wagga.[28]

The trial at bar was a special sitting of the criminal court (now no longer employed) tried before three judges. It was required because of the expected length of the proceedings. The Claimant had been charged with forgery (for signing the Tichborne Bonds with his alias) but he could not be tried for this, as forgery trials required the jury to be locked up at the end of each day's proceedings. This could involve imprisoning a jury for up to a year. He was therefore tried on the other charge of perjury which was made up of two counts: that he claimed to be Tichborne during the examination in Chancery in 1868, and then did the same thing during the civil trial. Within these counts, he was particularly charged with making up the story of the seduction of Lady Radcliffe.

The trial was presided over by Sir Alexander Cockburn, Chief Justice of the Common Pleas and Lord Chief Justice of England. Cockburn was a distinguished lawyer, scholar and politician. In 1843, he had secured the acquittal of Daniel M'Naghten for murdering Robert Peel's secretary, employing the defence of insanity. The M'Naghten rules (subsequently established by the House of Lords) became the basis for all cases involving the insanity defence. In 1856, he successfully prosecuted the poisoner William Palmer (in which case Kenealy, as we have seen, acted as a junior for the defence). As a Liberal MP he was renowned for his defence in Parliament of Palmerston during the Don Pacifico affair in 1850 and had gone on to take the post of Solicitor-General and then Attorney-General. He subsequently represented Britain during the *Alabama* arbitration (concerning the British construction of a ship for the Confederacy during the American Civil War). Becoming Chief Justice of the Common Pleas in 1856, he presided over many of the great trials of the period. A friend of Dickens (whose readings he often attended), he had a passion for literature and the classics that matched Kenealy's. He lived in Mayfair surrounded by books and wrote articles on hunting. A familiar figure at West End dinner parties, he could be mischievous and crotchety, unafraid to make his views known.[29] This often got him into trouble. Lord Rivers heard rumours circulating in the London clubs

Sir Alexander Cockburn

that Cockburn had promised Mrs Milbank (a friend of Rivers) that he would send the Claimant to prison. Rivers was dissuaded by Kenealy from petitioning Parliament that Cockburn had already made his mind up about the case before it began.[30] Kenealy had formerly been close to Cockburn; he had dedicated his *Poems and Translations* (1864) to him and had actually made him godfather of one of his sons, but the relationship between the two had broken down.

The other two judges in the case were Sir John Mellor and Sir Robert Lush, both stalwarts of Queen's Bench. Mellor was noted for his experience with railway legislation whilst Lush was the author of a standard work on the practice of the Common Law courts published in 1840.[31] They made a smaller contribution than Cockburn but attended the whole of the proceedings (the three judges usually wore blue gowns with mauve silk sleeves and round tippets).[32] Another group to attend the whole trial was the jury, again the object of sympathy, tied to a case that seemed likely to go on forever. The foreman of the jury was Henry Dickins, owner of the shop Dickins and Jones on Regent Street. The jury was less aristocratic than the civil trial jury, being made up of tradesmen and publicans. On the first day, one of the jury was excused as he had actually manufactured collecting boxes for the Tichborne Defence Fund. 'He is in the wrong box now, my Lord', Hawkins dryly retorted.[33] The courtroom was notable for the amount of laughter and comic remarks from the judiciary, which antagonised the humourless Kenealy but sustained the protagonists in a case that would have tried any-one's patience. The trial drew in huge numbers of spectators (more than the court could accommodate) including the great Liberal tribune John Bright, who followed the case closely. Amongst the people trying to obtain tickets was the future Labour leader, George Lansbury, then a boy, who recalled how the 'case which I was fighting to get in to hear ... drove the most unlikely people into a frenzy of partisanship, though no public issues were involved ... But London for years was passionately moved by it'.[34]

There was a brief skirmish before the trial. Kenealy brought an action against the publisher, George Routledge, for issuing a book titled *The Tichborne Romance: Its Matter of Fact and Moral*. The book's criticism of the Claimant breached the *sub-judice* rule but the court declined to take action (in contrast to the treatment of Onslow, Whalley and Skipworth), generating a feeling of unfairness right from the start. Cockburn reaffirmed his intention to take a 'wide' view of contempt, but the trial was to be a constant battleground.[35] The *Times* complained that 'millions have discussed the case day by day, but not a word of criticism must be printed. This, we submit, is a curious and not very satisfactory result of the judicial prerogative'.[36] Henry James Cochrane, the owner of the *Cheltenham Chronicle*, was fined £150 for an article arguing that the Claimant was not Orton but Tichborne. Kenealy complained that the *Times* reports of the trial went beyond summaries, which provoked both the reporter, who was present, to stand up for his own accuracy, and the paper itself to print an editorial making no apology for its criticism.[37] Coleridge (as Attorney-General) did act against Edward Appleyard's anti-Claimant broadsheet, *Arthur Orton's Appeal to the British Public*. Kenealy believed that the broadsheets, which often passed round the jurymen, had a bad effect on them, but also considered that Coleridge's action was a screen to pretend that the law treated all parties equally, even though the hostile press was rarely prosecuted.[38]

A further hindrance to the defence was its lack of funds. The contempt cases had halted the 'stump' campaign and the Tichbornites were forced to resort to other devices. The Claimant appeared at pigeon-shooting matches but, having won a contest at Spennymoor, made a speech about his difficulty in obtaining money and was shortly after prevented from appearing in public in this way.[39] The Grand National Tichborne Picture Company was formed in October. The object of the business was to commemorate the case by commissioning a picture of the trial which would then be copied and sold. The company promised to engage an eminent artist. It sounded innocent enough but its rubric promised 'to devote a portion of the funds of the company to ensure that the trial now pending shall not be brought prematurely to a close before all the persons whose evidence is essential for the full disclosure of all the circumstances of this case shall have appeared before the court'. It was obviously a 'front' for the defence fund. Amongst its subscribers were Whalley and William Quartermaine East, a leading Tichbornite and owner of the Queen's Hotel, St Martin's-le-Grand.[40] What happened to the company is unclear, as is the seriousness of its intention to produce a painting rather than just pocket the money. At about this time, the distinguished artist William Powell Frith declined an offer to paint what he later described as a portrait of the Claimant.[41] Without further support, the Claimant had to continue to write to newspapers to appeal for funds.[42]

When the trial commenced on 23 April 1873, Ballantine's restrained approach to advocacy was replaced by Kenealy's histrionic style.[43] As in any criminal trial, it was incumbent on the prosecution to prove its case (that the Claimant was not Roger Tichborne) beyond reasonable doubt. Ballantine's strategy would have been to suggest that some of the evidence put forward by the prosecution was dubious (this was especially true of the Orton evidence), in the hope of swaying the jury to believe the prosecution's case was not proven.[44] Kenealy instead opted to attempt to prove that his client was Roger Tichborne and also not Arthur Orton. Although this was an unnecessary strategy, it was certainly permissible. Kenealy, however, went beyond all legal etiquette and attacked the Tichborne family and the witnesses and even the judiciary in the trial. All were held by him to be part of a Jesuit-inspired conspiracy. He suggested that witnesses were bribed or immoral and that much of the prosecution's evidence had been forged or manufactured in the Reform Club.[45] He drew attention to the use by the Tichbornes of private detectives (particularly Whicher) and itemised the Pittendreigh letters as examples of the lengths to which the family would go to undermine his client. Perjury had been committed on a grand scale. The trial was continually interrupted as Kenealy wrestled with Cockburn over appropriate lines of questioning and procedure. The judges were compared to Scroggs and Jeffreys (a familiar theme of Kenealy's), two judges who had abused their roles during the Popish Plot (1678–80) and the Bloody Assizes (1685). To invoke these names implied that the judges were not acting as impartial umpires but as prosecution counsel.

The ethics of advocacy and the relationship of a lawyer with his client were a grey area. Should he stop at nothing on his behalf? Henry Brougham, the distinguished lawyer and polymath, had famously pronounced on this matter during the trial of Queen Caroline in 1820:

> an advocate, by the sacred duty which he owes his client, knows, in the discharge of that office, but one person in the world, THAT CLIENT AND NONE OTHER. To save that client by all expedient means, – to protect that client at all hazards and costs to all others, and amongst others to himself, – is the highest and most unquestioned of his duties; and he must not regard the alarm – the suffering – the torment – the destruction — which he may bring upon any other. Nay, separating even the duties of a patriot from those of an advocate and casting them, if need be, to the wind, he must go on reckless of the consequences, if his fate it should unhappily be, to involve his country in confusion for his client's protection![46]

But Brougham's views had never been wholly accepted within the legal profession and Cockburn in 1864 had criticised Brougham when he repeated his remarks at a banquet in the Middle Temple, insisting that a barrister also needed to consider the 'immutable interests of truth and justice'.[47] This was an area within the law that was largely dependent upon custom and on which little guidance could be found in the standard authorities.[48] A contemporary later suggested that Kenealy adopted 'too thorough an acceptance of Lord Brougham's conception of the whole duty of an advocate – to win his client's cause ... by fair means if he could, but if these were not available, then by foul'. Another described him as 'an advocate to Brougham's order'.[49] His fervency of advocacy may have been caused by the fact that he did genuinely seem to believe in the Claimant.[50] The trial turned Kenealy into a national figure.

Much of the first month of the trial was given over to reading evidence from the first trial into the record. The strategy of scrutinising every possible piece of evidence from the long and complex story was retained. Prosecution and defence both tried to make their case by piling up large numbers of witnesses, many of whom were examined in depth. Hawkins opened for the prosecution by making it clear he intended to demonstrate that the Claimant was Arthur Orton. He went over the story, showing how the imposture had been constructed and revealed alarming discrepancies in the Claimant's evidence. For example, the Claimant had given the names of sailors who had been on board the *Bella* when it was lost at sea. He established that these men had not been on the *Bella*, but their names could be found in the crew of the *Middleton*, the ship that had taken the young Arthur Orton from London to Hobart.[51] Not only this but the Orton sisters – Mrs Tredgett and Mrs Jewry – as well as the brother Charles Orton had received money from the Claimant.

The prosecution then went on to call 215 witnesses for the Crown. Many had appeared in *Tichborne* v. *Lushington*. By and large they tended to be grouped according to different parts of the story and (for sake of convenience) that is how they will be treated here. First up were the French witnesses to testify about Roger's childhood. These included several Jesuit priests whom Kenealy suspected of making up evidence.

The Abbé Salis ('a venerable looking ecclesiastic of the old French school', according to *The Times*) had known Roger from his childhood.[52] The Abbé spoke more in sorrow than in anger about the Dowager. She was certainly not insane but, in his view, had fixed ideas. She had apparently promised to reward him if he would publicly accept the Claimant as genuine. After the Abbé refused, she grew cold towards him. The Abbé remembered Roger's tattoo, although he said he had not mentioned it to anyone before coming to London in 1871 for the first trial. Kenealy probed him aggressively about details of the confessional (a traditional Catholic-baiting exercise), even though the Abbé claimed that the young Roger had never confessed to him. The confessional was (and is) one of the great faultlines between Catholicism and Protestantism. For Kenealy (as for other anti-Catholics), it was an object of suspicion, a place where the innocent might be corrupted. The next witness was the Jesuit Alexis Lefèvre who had actually been Roger's confessor. Kenealy asked if Roger had informed him in the confessional that 'he had had connexion with his cousin'. The white-haired cleric replied through an interpreter that 'It would be infamy to disclose it if he had told me in confession but he never said it'. In a characteristically circuitous exchange, Kenealy quizzed Lefèvre about the fifth-century saint Alexis after whom Lefèvre had been named. The saint had left his family to seek God and later returned disguised as a beggar. He lived for years in the family home and no one recognised him. Kenealy clearly believed there was a parallel with the Claimant's homecoming.[53] Lefèvre denied that the Claimant was genuine as did Chatillon, Roger's old tutor. After the trial, Kenealy (who had a particular dislike of the French witnesses) noted that they had all stayed together in the same hotel, implying that it was there that they had concocted their testimony.[54]

Kenealy's obsessive hatred of Catholicism matched George Whalley's, attacking the Jesuit order as the originators of a conspiracy against the Claimant.[55] He also noted the Jesuit doctrine of equivocation – that they were not bound to tell the truth in certain circumstances.[56] Whalley also wrote to *The Times* dividing the witnesses into Roman Catholics, persons of known character (such as officers) and miscellaneous. He alleged that there was a conspiracy by the church, which wanted to retain the Tichborne property in its own possession.[57]

The allegations did not stop there. During the trial, Whalley claimed that Dr Massey Wheeler, who was said to have known both Orton and the Claimant in Australia, had been forced to abandon his testimony because it would endanger his future employment by the government. T. C. W. Murdoch of the Government Emigration Board (which employed Wheeler) retorted that he had not even known Wheeler had any involvement with the case.[58] This criticism of the conspiracy between government and the Church was later developed to the point that after the trial Kenealy could describe them in this way –

Mr GLADSTONE, who was perhaps unconsciously, a perfect catspaw throughout the case, in the hands of Dr MANNING and the priests ... Mr LOWE, a public adventurer to whom place and pay were everything ... the prince of WALES had from the beginning been indoctrinated by the Jesuits around him, with a powerful prejudice against Sir ROGER.[59]

There were witnesses brought over from South America. Tomas Castro (whose name the Claimant had adopted) made the trip but was found to be too ill to provide testimony. Having been in a lunatic asylum, he relapsed when he came to England and could not appear in court. The difficult voyage was a waste of time for the poor man. Arriving with him was Donna Hayley, also of Melipilla. She had a clear memory of the young Arthur Orton, who used to impress locals with stories of how his father was butcher to Queen Victoria. The people of Melipilla looked after him for a year during which time he was received into the Roman Catholic Church. She had no memory of any other Englishman staying in the town. Captain Thomas Oates swore he had seen Roger Tichborne go on board the *Bella* at Rio and told the court the Claimant was not the same man. The barrister Henry Purcell told of how he had gone to Melipilla to assist the Chilean Commission on behalf of the Tichborne family. He had shown the daguerreotype of Roger to locals who did not recognise it. The key Australian witnesses were Mina Jury and Sara Macalister, who both identified the Claimant as Orton.

Things did not get any better for the Claimant when the many witnesses from Wapping were called. Mary Ann Loder once more stated that the defendant was her former sweetheart. Robert Ford Jackson, a master lighterman, and many others who had known Orton in his youth, swore that he was there in the courtroom with them. William Willoughby, an oil man of Wapping High Street, testified that when he met the Claimant he sounded like George Orton, Arthur's father. Kenealy increasingly suggested that these witnesses had been bought. Nevertheless, the Wapping evidence was not as damaging as it might have been because Arthur Orton, when last seen even by his family, had been only eighteen when he sailed for Hobart in 1852. Hawkins did not call the Orton sisters, whose evidence might have been crucial, and later claimed that he believed Kenealy would call them (which did not happen).

When attention returned to Stonyhurst, Lord Bellew, who had allegedly tattooed the young Roger, testified once more. Given that his evidence had brought the first trial to a conclusion, it was clear that Kenealy had to demolish his evidence. Everyone was shocked by what happened next. First of all, he got Bellew to admit his memory of the tattoo was imperfect. It turned out that, when approached by the Tichbornes' solicitor, he was unsure which arm of Roger's he had tattooed or indeed what the tattoo illustrated. Then Kenealy asked him about a Captain Percy Harvey. Bellew was shocked and refused to answer but Kenealy persisted. Cockburn allowed the line of questioning to proceed. Bellew was then forced to admit that not only did he know Captain Harvey, but he knew his wife even better, as he had committed adultery with her. Indeed it transpired that Captain Harvey had actually paid her five pounds to join Bellew in Dublin. Bellew, deflated by this unexpected turn in the questions, admitted that his own wife had left him. Sensational as these sordid revelations were, they were irrelevant to the matter at hand but Kenealy's purpose was to demonstrate that Bellew was immoral and that his evidence could not therefore be trusted. Kenealy (who had received informal information about the *ménage à trois*) was happy to destroy a gentleman's reputation. His puritanism, as we will see, led to continuous performances of outrage at the debauched life of the elite. It made great copy for the newspapers and fed into the anti-aristocratic polemics of the Tichborne movement at large. Back in the courtroom, all that mattered was Bellew's shame.

Hawkins countered the huge number of Carabineers who had testified for the Claimant in the first trial with military witnesses who denied the Claimant was their former fellow officer. Chief among them was Captain Polhill Turner (later MP for Bedford), who presented in evidence a sketch he had once drawn of Roger, which looked nothing like the Claimant. Turner had approached the Claimant as he was leaving the courtroom during *Tichborne* v. *Lushington* and asked if he recognised him. When the Claimant said he did not, someone prompted him by whispering Turner's name into his ear and then the Claimant alleged he knew who he was.

Then there was the Tichborne family. Lady Radcliffe was examined at length in order to rescue her reputation from the Claimant's suggestion that he had seduced her. Kenealy quizzed her about the tattoo marks. She remembered seeing them on one occasion, when Roger rolled up his sleeve to scoop up minnows from the pond in Tichborne Park. Mrs Nangle, Roger's aunt, also recalled the tattoo. The testimony of the family's land agent, Vincent Gosford, was the subject of great interest. He insisted that the contents of the sealed packet was written in his presence and, far from containing instructions about dealing with her pregnancy, contained the promise by Roger to build a chapel to the Virgin Mary. He denied that Roger had any involvement with the Brighton card case. On encountering the Claimant, he was appalled by his ignorance of Roger. Whilst testifying, a letter was delivered to Gosford, which contained threats against him. He presented it to the judges, who were outraged. Kenealy nevertheless tried to turn the tables on him by introducing an irrelevant line of questioning. He suggested that Gosford had helped himself to rent money from the Tichborne estates. Gosford angrily rebutted this suggestion but Kenealy exposed the fact that he had mismanaged his own finances and lost his property. Kenealy's knowledge was almost certainly derived from Bulpett, the Winchester banker and supporter of the Claimant, who had a strong grasp of the financial affairs of the locals (although Bulpett later denied this).

The final key witness for the prosecution was Charles Chabot, a handwriting expert, who was examined in great detail. He had studied letters written by the Claimant, Orton and Roger Tichborne. His view was that the Claimant's handwriting matched that of Orton and did not at all resemble that of the undoubted Roger Tichborne. Kenealy would claim after the trial that the Orton letters had been forged to resemble the handwriting of the Claimant.[60]

After each day's proceedings, Kenealy and the Claimant were cheered as they left Westminster Hall. They had become popular heroes. On 23 September 1873, the crowd got so restive that it broke through the police cordon. Michael Flynn, a labourer, put his foot on the chest of a policeman who had been pushed down by the crowd and shouted, 'That's the way to serve them'. Another man waved his stick in the air and shouted, 'Bravo, Dr Kenealy'. Flynn was sent to prison with one month's hard labour, as he had made a deliberate assault on a police officer.[61] In January, Hawkins was attacked as he left Westminster Hall. A crowd pursued him to his cab, which was nearly turned over, and John Donovan, a young lithographic engraver, shouted 'Here's b– old Hawkins, let's do something with him.' Donovan and three other men, aged between seventeen and twenty-one, were charged with riotous behaviour and using obscene language; the police force was strengthened the following day.[62]

After almost two months of cross-examination, Hawkins brought his witnesses to an end. Kenealy then commenced an olympian speech for the defence before calling his own witnesses. This meandering address lasted from 22 July to 21 August. As he reviewed the evidence, he built up the theme that the young Roger, far from the virtuous gentleman presented by Coleridge in the first trial, was in fact a moral degenerate. He had been corrupted by early exposure to Catholic priests both in Paris and Stonyhurst; his schoolfriend Lord Bellew had similarly become debauched. Nor had Roger learned much at Stonyhurst, explaining the Claimant's ignorance. To prove that the young Roger was a sensualist (by implication, not that different from his client), Kenealy pointed to his reading material. Roger was known to have read the novels of Paul de Kock, some of whose stories were considered pornographic. Ladies had to be removed from the court as Kenealy read out lengthy extracts from *Frère Jacques* and *Sister Anne*, as well as an extract from Moliere's *The Misanthrope*, which Roger also read. He maintained that Roger's home life was deeply unhappy. His father, James Tichborne, was a brute, which would explain why a man who found himself in Australia would not wish to return home but rather to lose himself in the Bush.

The Westminster Tragedy

Kenealy attacked the witnesses against the Claimant as dishonest and part of a conspiracy backed by the Tichborne family. The evidence given by Catholic priests was particularly suspicious. He derided the tattoo evidence for having been introduced so late in the first trial. Suggestions that the Claimant might have discovered information about the Tichbornes through London newspapers taken at the mechanics institute in Wagga Wagga were dismissed because there was no evidence the Claimant went in there. Moreover, the Claimant's pocket book (with the quotation from *Aurora Floyd*), now in the hands of the prosecution, was a forgery. The will that the Claimant made at Wagga Wagga, Kenealy agreed, was full of falsehoods, but this was characteristic of the cavalier way that the aristocracy dealt with money men. He placed huge emphasis on the recognition by the Dowager. When he alleged that Coleridge had not known about the tattoo marks at the commencement of the civil trial, Hawkins angrily objected and an unpleasant confrontation ensued. The judges made Kenealy move on but not before angry words crossed between the barrister and the bench. Kenealy pursued at length a theory that Roger had not been tattooed at all but had been marked with a blue pencil, producing an image on the skin that eventually faded. He dismissed the Wapping evidence, though he agreed his client had been foolish in visiting the place. Moving on to the question of physical characteristics, he noted that the Claimant had a twitch of the eye, a Tichborne characteristic that Roger was known to have possessed. Kenealy pointed out that he had witnessed it in Lady Radcliffe when she was in the witness box. That Orton was known to have a twitch was merely a coincidence. He complained about Chabot's evidence concerning handwriting because the defence did not have the funds to pay for its own expert. This produced the news from Cockburn that the Treasury would pay the expenses of defence witnesses.

Kenealy went on to call these witnesses, a process that lasted from 21 August to 1 December 1873. He rebutted the testimony of Hawkins's Wapping witnesses with figures who had known Orton when he lived in the East End. George Saloway, a sailmaker, denied that the Claimant was his childhood friend whilst John Finnis, a lighterman of Wapping, insisted that Orton had never been known as 'Bullocky Orton' as had been suggested (perhaps to show that Orton was fat). Saloway, it transpired, had been at a meeting in a Wapping pub where the Claimant had invited anyone who knew Orton to come forward and say if he was the same man. Some of the witnesses were pulled apart in the witness box. The evidence of Henry Dunn, a wharf foreman, was so poor that his expenses were disallowed. The same thing happened with some Australian witnesses. Charles Janes, a Hornsey greengrocer, told the court he had known Orton and Castro in Australia and that they were distinct people. He was recalled by the court when the dates he provided for the encounter were shown to be incorrect and Sergeant Parry for the prosecution denounced his testimony as a pack of lies. The same thing happened to Albert Pavis, a Newmarket tout, who alleged he had met the Claimant at Wagga Wagga in 1859, when it was accepted that the Claimant had not moved there till 1861. A Truro hotel keeper, William Philips, denied the two men were the same and claimed Orton had stolen a horse from him when they had both been at the gold diggings in Australia. He maintained that Orton had been tried for the crime but given the benefit of the doubt and released. Orton had been tried under the name of 'Scott', however, which made it easy for Parry to take apart his testimony.

There were many witnesses from Hampshire who swore that the Claimant was Roger. Thomas Lillywhite, a labourer on the Tichborne estate, recalled seeing Roger with his shirtsleeves rolled up grubbing the moor.

The Tug of War

He noticed no tattoo. He could not give any reason, however, why he thought the Claimant was Roger and Parry could not even be bothered to cross-examine him. Worse, the testimony of George Etheridge, the son of a blacksmith at Tichborne, was disallowed because he was drunk. David Pink, a labourer on the Tichborne estate, identified the Claimant as Roger but was then forced to admit he had only met the undoubted Roger twice. When he encountered the Claimant, he asked him if he remembered Pink giving him some tobacco at a hunt. The Claimant said he did and that was enough for Pink.

Bogle took the stand and told how his pension from the Tichbornes had been stopped when he recognised the Claimant. His recognition was based on the Claimant's resemblance to the Tichbornes. He said Roger had no tattoos and insisted that he had not provided the Claimant with information. Various Carabineers testified about the extraordinary knowledge the Claimant possessed of Roger's time in the military. It was brought to the court's attention that Roger's servants, Carter and M'Cann (who had since died), had been living with the Claimant and could have provided him with information. Some Carabineers insisted that Roger had never been tattooed. The evidence shifted back to Australia. A merchant called Benjamin Ward remembered two ships called the *Osprey* in Melbourne when he had been there in 1854. A sailor called James Brown testified that he could remember the *Osprey* in Rio and named as one of its crew a Dane called Jean Luie.

Then, in one of the most remarkable twists of the trial, Kenealy called Jean Luie himself. He was potentially a crucial witness. Luie told the court

Jean Luie

that not only had he been the mate or steward on the *Osprey*, but he remembered how in April 1854 the ship had come across a lifeboat about 500 miles from the coast of Brazil. They picked up six people in the boat including one who was delirious and who Luie identified as the Claimant. The *Osprey* took the rescued men to Melbourne, including the delirious and untattooed 'Mr Rogers', whom Luie nursed back to health. After depositing the crew of the *Bella* in Australia, he had never seen him again until recently when, on travelling through Britain, he heard about the Tichborne case.

Luie's evidence was suspicious. He admitted that he was living with a Mr Pulleyn who had raised money for the defence fund. George Whalley, after being introduced to him, had gone to New York (from where the ship had set out) to check his story. The trial was adjourned for over a fortnight on October 31 so that agents could be dispatched to New York and Luie was told not to leave the country. Henry Purcell was sent over to find if the *Osprey* had ever been in New York. He brought back a number of witnesses. Paul Cornell, a New York customs house official, brought over the boarding book for 1853-54, which showed no record of the *Osprey*. Officials from a number of other American ports revealed they had no record of the *Osprey* either. An American detective called Joseph Hercules de Rosiers testified that he had checked the New York evidence but had found nothing; no one had heard of a Jean Luie. The captain of a ship called the *Osprey*, which had been in New Bedford, Massachusetts, in 1854, was brought to the stand. He claimed he had never had a steward called Jean Luie nor had he ever picked up a shipwrecked crew. On being presented with Luie, he said he did not know him.

Two shipping clerks were brought in who identified Luie as a Captain Sorenson. Luie insisted that he had never seen them before but by now it was clear that there was something wrong with his testimony. Kenealy began his final speech for the defence but it was interrupted by news about Luie. Two wardens from Chatham Prison identified Luie as a man called Lundgren who had only just been released from jail. A string of other witnesses swore the same thing. He had gone by the names of Strom, Landberg, Petersen, Saftsrom and Grundlum. Moreover, he was found to have been in Britain when the *Bella* was lost in 1854. Luie was committed for contempt and perjury. It was an enormous setback for Kenealy, who was forced to admit that the decision to call him was a mistake (although the Claimant apparently told him that he did not know Luie).[63] Captain Brown, who had identified Luie as the mate on the *Osprey*, was later sent to prison for five years. Luie himself went to prison for seven years but later ended up a tax inspector in Sydney.

Kenealy's summing up expressed total confidence that the Claimant was genuine. The speech lasted, with interruptions, from 2 December 1873 to 14 January 1874. He commenced by saying the case was 'THE WORST, THE WICKEDEST AND THE MOST PROFLIGATE PUBLIC PROSECUTION THAT HAS DISGRACED THIS COUNTRY SINCE THE DAYS OF THE STUARTS'.[64] His speech featured the now routine attacks on the judiciary

George Whalley

and the prosecution witnesses. In Kenealy's mind, the Wapping visit proved the Claimant was Tichborne. If he was Orton, would he have done something so foolish? When Kenealy closed on 14 January, the Claimant said to him: 'Doctor, I tender you my very sincere thanks for the very able manner in which you have defended me; and I hope to be able to clear off some of the 600 guineas I am indebted to you.'[65]

Hawkins's summing up for the prosecution was briefer, lasting a mere two weeks. He complained about Kenealy's allegation about the use of bribery and forgery. In his final remarks, he observed that a verdict for the Claimant would be an attack on the character of Lady Radcliffe. During the speech, Whalley was fined for remarks published by the press in which he claimed that, despite everything, Luie's evidence about the *Osprey* was substantially correct. Whalley spent a night in prison until the fine of £250 was paid.

Hopes that the case would now come to an end were disappointed when Cockburn as Lord Chief Justice then embarked on a month-long summary of the evidence. The reason for this elaborate procedure was the belief that at least one juror was undecided. The speech was a tour de force. The future Prime Minister, Herbert Asquith, then a young barrister, later remembered the summing up as 'a masterpiece of its kind'.[66] Cockburn's task was to take the enormous amount of evidence with its fragmented stories that pointed in diverse directions and turn it into a narrative that made sense. His summing up was later published in book form because it provided an orderly digest of the case and presented the case in a form that resembled a novel. Its subsequent publication reminds us that the law is made of story telling. Courts decide how a story should be told. The relationship between law and literature, as we have already seen, is close.[67] Indeed we might view Cockburn's summing up as one of the great sensation novels that so dazzled the mid-Victorian public (such as Wilkie Collins's *The Woman in White* and *The Moonstone*, or Mary Elizabeth Braddon's *Lady Audley's Secret*). Mrs Braddon sent Cockburn a copy of *Aurora Floyd* during the trial so that he could check the Claimant's quotation from it that was in his pocket book. Winningly, Cockburn told the court he had spent some evenings during the trial devouring the novel when he should have been concentrating on the case.[68] Employing the judicial function as an exercise in persuasion was vital because it was possible for a juror to be sensitive to some aspects of the case and deaf to others. Cockburn sorted out how the numerous facts in the case should be approached and arranged. At least two stories had been told (by Hawkins and by Kenealy) and both had power. It was clear that Cockburn favoured the Hawkins version, which is why his speech proved so controversial.

From the beginning, he established that he disdained Kenealy's style of advocacy and all allegations of corruption made against the prosecution and judiciary. He instructed the jury to concentrate on the central question, which was whether the prosecution had proven that the Claimant was not Roger Tichborne. He went through the entire narrative commencing with Roger's youth. He found the Dowager 'selfish and perverse'; worse, she was 'thoroughly and essentially a Frenchwoman'.[69] Cockburn rejected Kenealy's claim that Roger had been particularly dissolute; a familiarity with Paul de Kock did not make the reader immoral.

For him there was no evidence that Roger Tichborne had been at Melipilla in Chile. Moreover, he was not satisfied with the Claimant's account of why he had not at least written home from Australia. Surely Sir Roger would have cared about the feeling of his family? The court did know of one who was indifferent to others: Arthur Orton. He followed the life story of Orton in Wapping, Chile and Australia. He was snobbishly aghast at the idea that Sir Roger Tichborne might have married Mary Ann Bryant:

> We know from his own statement that his wife was a domestic servant, that she was perfectly illiterate, being unable to read or write, and that to the marriage register she affixed only her mark ... I think it right you should consider how far it is likely that Roger Tichborne would have formed such a union ... There is apparently no reason to suppose he had abandoned the intention finally and for ever of returning to his native country and resuming his station. He must have known that if ever he did so the marriage he was forming would create a difficulty, as he could not place his wife in the position which the wife of Roger Tichborne ought to occupy as regards society and intercourse with persons of equal rank and station.[70]

The Lord Chief Justice did accept that the Claimant's wife was blameless in the affair. He also thought it extremely unlikely that a Catholic aristocrat would agree to be married in a dissenting chapel as the Claimant had done. In the marriage register, Castro had given his age as thirty (Orton's age), whereas Roger Tichborne would have been thirty six at the time.

Cockburn was critical of the Wapping visit (why so much concealment?), as well as the revelation that the Claimant had been paying money to the Ortons. Moving on to the tattoo marks, he rebuffed Kenealy's attacks on Lord Bellew's character. Finally, he argued that there were similarities between the defendant's handwriting and Arthur Orton's.

On Saturday 28 February, the final day of the trial, many leading figures of the Bar attended to witness the verdict. Mindful of his place in history, Cockburn declaimed, 'Never was there a trial in England, I believe, since that memorable trial of Charles I which has excited more the attention of Englishmen and the world than this'.[71] He went over the evidence once more and defended himself against charges that he had been one-sided in his conduct of the trial:

> In my opinion, a Judge does not discharge his duty who contents himself with being a mere recipient of the evidence, which he is afterwards to reproduce to the jury without pointing out the facts and the inferences to which they naturally and legitimately give rise.[72]

The law required a unanimous verdict from the twelve jurors. He agreed that, if one juryman should disagree, he had the right to follow his own conviction but then followed by stating that such a person should reflect 'that the one individual is more likely to be wrong than the eleven from whom he differs'.[73] Acknowledging the extraordinary interest that the case aroused, Cockburn also warned the jury against relying on public opinion or making a decision simply to receive the ovations of fellow countrymen.

He then turned his attention to Kenealy saying, 'I have heard language applied to this tribunal which I will undertake to say in the whole course of the annals of the administration of Justice in this country no advocate ever yet thought of addressing to a court'.[74] He objected to Kenealy's habit of making *sotto voce*, abusive remarks under his breath, loud enough for reporters to hear but not loud enough for the judges, who would have punished such insulting behaviour. Then he finished with a remark to the jury that would become infamous:

> I am sure that the verdict you will pronounce will be received on all hands, except by fanatics and fools, as the judgement of twelve men who have brought to the consideration of this great cause the utmost and the most vigilant attention.[75]

He was cheered as he brought the case to a close. Mellor and Lush then supported Cockburn and insisted they had not been one-sided, nor did the criticism of Kenealy mean that relations between the Bench and the Bar were deteriorating.

The jury retired at twelve o'clock. The Claimant sat with Bogle and his solicitor in the centre of the court and looked worried by the presence of three plain-clothes policemen who had not previously attended. Thirty-three minutes later the jury reappeared. It was clear to all in the court what the verdict would be.

The foreman Henry Dickins announced that the jury was agreed and found the Claimant guilty on both charges of perjury. Dickins then read a statement clarifying the verdict:

> We find, first, that the Defendant is not Roger Charles Doughty Tichborne; secondly, we find that the Defendant did not seduce Miss Katherine Doughty, now Lady Radcliffe; and we further believe that there is not the slightest evidence that Roger ever was guilty of undue

familiarity with Miss Katherine Doughty on any occasion whatever. Thirdly, we find that the defendant is Arthur Orton.[76]

The jury also held that 'the charges of bribery, conspiracy and undue influence made against the prosecution in this case are entirely devoid of foundation, and we extremely regret the violent language and demeanour of the leading counsel for the Defendant, and his attacks on the counsel for the prosecution, and on several of the witnesses produced in the cause'.[77] The Claimant quickly scribbled a telegram to John Helsby of Lymington, Hampshire, who was looking after his wife and children. It read: 'All is Lost.'

The Claimant was given two sentences of seven years to run sequentially (in other words, fourteen years). This decision of the court was controversial. Hardinge Giffard always doubted the legitimacy of giving sentences in this way. The Claimant rose and asked to say a few words, but his request was denied. Kenealy then shook hands with him saying, 'Goodbye Sir Roger, I am sorry for you'. This was the last public appearance of the man from Wagga Wagga for a long time. He was taken to Newgate Prison where his possessions were taken from him (a cigar case and some playing cards). He initially retained his own clothes, as no prison uniform was big enough to fit him. The trial was over at last.

The end came before labourers finished work so the crowd outside was not as large as expected.[78] Some 'roughs' uttered threats against the police, but by and large they were well ordered. The *Standard* noted that more than half of the crowd were '"respectable" – They were not Roughs nor labourers, nor even artisans, but *bourgeois* chiefly, and quite a moiety of these were women'. The police, however, feared that if the jury took a long time to deliver their verdict, the 'dregs' might arrive after their long day's work. As it was, some cheered and others hissed when it was announced.[79]

With the trial over, newspapers were at last able to express themselves with complete freedom on the case. Most were united in the belief that justice had been done. The *Standard* opined about the sentence: 'We are only sorry that it is not a more severe one. MARTIN GUERRE, in accordance with the law and sentiment of the day, was hanged; and it is a great pity that the same fate cannot be rewarded to ORTON'.[80] The *Morning Advertiser*, which had supported the Claimant, criticised Cockburn's summing up as alien to the judicial function. It felt it was 'a mighty Niagara of condemnation' and the verdict had not solved anything.[81] Much of the editorialising in the press centred on the question of the trial's length.[82]

It was argued that the lawyers should have concentrated on only a small part of the evidence to save time. James Fitzjames Stephen, the law reformer, wrote several long articles on the case and doubted the wisdom of this. There was no practical alternative to the course taken, although much evidence which counted as hearsay could have been excluded, along with irrelevancies such as the evidence based on the novels of Paul de Kock. He urged stricter enforcement of the rules of evidence and criticised the rule that evidence could not be taken by a commission that met abroad. This would have cut the costs of transporting the witnesses from Australia and South America. He also leaned towards the interrogation of the accused in a criminal case and wanted a stricter code of legal conduct to force witnesses to give evidence, even if it incriminated them.[83]

Working-class opinion on the case was mixed. The *Morning Post* sent a reporter to visit the pubs of Wapping to discern opinion:

> It is true that the praises of Dr 'Kenyly' were still sung, and his bearding of the judges met with special approbation. 'He guv it to 'em proper, he did' was a remark which met with a chorus of assent. But the Claimant's cleverness in 'keeping up the game' so long and in 'gittin' these here Onslows and Whalleys to keep him on the fat of the land these eight years' was extolled in a way which was very significant.[84]

We can glimpse a strong degree of cynicism at a popular level. More direct was the reaction of those who lived close to Lady Radcliffe. In 1875, the Radcliffes were forced to sell their home, Caverswell Castle, near Hanley (a strong Tichborne centre) apparently because of the abuse that Katherine Radcliffe received from many in the neighbourhood every time she left the house. She was also the recipient of a stream of hostile letters.[85]

The trial had several consequences. A False Personation Bill was rushed through Parliament in June and July, receiving no debate during its passage to the statute book (37 & 38 Victoria, c. 36). It laid down that false personation in order to obtain property was a felony, punishable by life imprisonment. At the same time the Tichborne Estates Act of July 1874 provided that the Tichborne trustees would pay the legal costs of the civil trial.

The 1874 General Election took place as the trial was coming to an end. Onslow's advocacy of the Tichborne cause was an embarrassment to many Liberals and he had neglected his constituency in Guildford. He lost the seat to his own cousin, Denzil Onslow, who stood for the Conservatives and his political career was over. The Claimant, meanwhile, was transferred, after a brief stay in Newgate, to Pentonville and later Millbank, Dartmoor and Portsmouth. He appears to have enjoyed his time in jail where he began to lose weight (indeed his prison sentence may have saved his life, given that he had been about twenty-six stone). Supporters who visited him insisted the features of the undoubted Sir Roger Tichborne emerged as he shed his weight. His weight came down to about sixteen stone. In prison he refused to answer to the name of 'Orton' and was usually known as 'Castro'; he also insisted on attending mass and attempted to master French (his inability to speak it had been crucial evidence against him). He was studiously polite but retained the air of one who could expect deference. Many of the warders at Millbank came to believe in him.[86]

With the Claimant in prison, a question remained about Kenealy's conduct. Some considered Cockburn's scolding in his summing up inadequate. The *Pall Mall Gazette* was vociferous in calling for Kenealy's dismissal and the Oxford Mess disbarred him as a member on 2 April, at a meeting of which Kenealy was not even notified.[87] Gray's Inn began a similar inquiry.

Like the earlier contempt cases, this action was predicated on an ambiguity within the law. As we have seen, the duties of an advocate to his client were controversial. Was Brougham right or not? At the end of the trial, the *Law Times* admitted that 'we can see many reasons why the denunciation of a presiding Judge should not be accepted even as evidence against counsel. There may be cases in which it becomes the positive duty of an advocate to resist the control of a Judge, and even to retort upon the Bench'.[88] The paper was not forthcoming in establishing exactly what these cases were but it did urge caution in moving against him. In any case, an inquiry by Gray's Inn was unfair because it reasoned it was neither representative nor eminent enough to decide the fate of a Queen's Counsel. The fitness of Gray's Inn to decide Kenealy's fate was to be taken up within the Tichborne movement, expressed through demands for its abolition.

The Bar's policy towards Kenealy was dependent on highly ambiguous precedents.[89] The *Solicitor's Journal* was wary about the use of this process for contempt of court, considering it 'dangerous and arbitrary' and argued that the Bar should not be so sensitive about the press.[90] There was also a strong point in Kenealy's favour. If he was guilty of contempt, why had he not been punished during the trial itself? It was argued that his punishment simply consisted of Cockburn's denunciation.[91] Therefore, when the Benchers met to judge Kenealy, they considered not his invective during the trial but his editorship of the *Englishman* newspaper (see next chapter). On 1 August, they decided that because of the numerous libels in his paper, Kenealy was unfit to be a member of the society, and he was therefore disbenched. On 2 December, his patent as Queen's Counsel was removed. Stabbed in the back by his own profession, he was the perfect martyr.

6

The Magna Charta Association

The Court of Queen's Bench had decided that the Claimant was not Roger Tichborne and that he was Arthur Orton. This should have been the end of the matter. In the months following the verdict, however, it became clear that much of British public opinion simply refused to see it that way. The Claimant was perceived as an aggrieved working-class man who had failed to obtain justice in a court of law. His lawyer became a martyr and Alexander Cockburn an object of opprobrium. Now that the trial was over there was no problem about the law of contempt. Anything could be said (by either side) and it was.

The verdict gave new life to the Tichborne agitation. Kenealy remade himself from an otherworldly littérateur and barrister into a demagogue. The agitation continued to press for the release of the Claimant but it also began to focus on Kenealy himself. He turned it into something it had not previously been – a political movement. Whilst the agitation between the trials had political implications, few who participated would have considered it more than a single-issue pressure group. Kenealy took this earnest cause and drew with promiscuous abandon from the repertoire of Victorian ideas to fashion an ideology for Tichbornism. Toryism, liberalism and radicalism were all raided. The self-styled people's champion was unembarrassed about taking his clothes from any part of the political wardrobe. He assembled colourful ideas into an elaborate programme for an organisation that would become one of the leading popular movements of its day – the Magna Charta Association. His was a radical people's movement that was drenched in a Baroque mixture of medievalism and chivalry. It was a carnival of cranks, fools and fanatics but it also touched a popular constituency that did not feel represented by the main political parties. Kenealy's revival of the Tichborne cause allows us to explore the mentality of the age.

Barely had the Claimant been sent to Newgate than Kenealy (with no future in the legal profession) proclaimed himself leader of the Tichborne cause. Guildford Onslow (who previously had taken that role) apparently acquiesced. Without his seat in Parliament, Onslow became joint organiser and main trustee of the Kenealy National Testimonial Fund. Another leader came on the scene, T. M. Evans, editor of the *Leicester Evening News*. Evans organised Kenealy's support fund, which was based in Leicester, already a strong centre of Tichborne support and a town with a long history of radicalism.[1] Within weeks, workmen at the Leicester Gas Works had sent in £2 10s.[2] There was concern that, without an income from the law, Kenealy would suffer for his advocacy of the Claimant's cause.

On 25 March, an enormous demonstration of working men took place in Leicester.[3] Its proceedings deserve some attention as they provided a model for many of the future Tichborne meetings and featured many of the themes that would be ritually reiterated when Tichbornites gathered. The meeting took place in the open air at Humberstone Gate in the centre of the town at six o'clock in the evening – about 2,000 were present. The local Tichborne Committee arrived in a wagonette together with a deputation from Nottingham, where Tichbornism was also strong. The focus of the meeting was initially on the wrong done to Kenealy, whose name was on every placard. Walter Perkins admired 'the manliness, the bravery and the ability of Dr Kenealy ... Kenealy pleaded his cause from his very soul'. A Mr Moore drew cheers by quoting the following lines of verse with reference to Kenealy:

> The lion of freedom had come from his den
> We will rally around him again and again.

These lines, a favourite of the Leicester Chartists, had once been applied to the great Chartist leader Feargus O'Connor. The mantle of this kind of radical leadership was thus conferred on Kenealy.[4] T. M. Evans was praised for coming out so openly in support of the former barrister. J. Legg considered him 'Evans Coeur de Lion' or 'Evans the lion-hearted'. The movement's stock in trade was a bombastic combination of manliness and patriotism. It was genuinely moved by Kenealy's integrity in combating the injustice of the legal profession. J. Parker, the chairman, told the spectators that 'They were evincing a similar spirit to that which Dr KENEALY had shown in gathering there that evening'. The shabby treatment of him was strongly condemned. One resolution viewed 'with alarm the doctrine ... that the Judges and Benchers are to proscribe to counsel the line of duty they shall follow'. The whole question of civil liberties was foregrounded with reference to the English Revolution. Mr Dainty thought:

they had not been advancing in the light of freedom's day, but had been receding to the dark ages of Charles I. When their representative, P. A. Taylor, was here, he asked him whether he would support any movement respecting the power of judges with regard to contempt of court; and if he beheld the gathering that night he thought he would alter his opinion.

The quality of justice in the trial was also attacked. Mr Collin proposed a resolution that, without pledging itself as to the identity of the Claimant, nevertheless criticised the 'unusual mode in which the trial was conducted'. He was unimpressed by the Trial at Bar format, complaining that the Claimant had been tried 'by special judges and a special jury (a voice: special thieves) and special counsellors'. Also, he noted 'The verdict had not been in accordance with the majority of the witnesses because the verdict had been declared in favour of the minority'. Leaving aside the question of whether this was an accurate assessment of what had happened at Westminster Hall, Collin's resolution demonstrates an alienation from the contemporary terms of jurisprudence which was a feature of the movement. Mr Godfrey, a 'trades unionist', said that 'no well-conducted trades' union would have been guilty of such an act as the Benchers at Gray's Inn had adopted in reference to Dr Kenealy. Every trade union would cry shame at such an act'. For Perkins, Kenealy stood out from the rest of his profession because he had not '"bled" his client's pockets to the depths that some of the counsel had done'. The law was also connected with the theme of surveillance. Mr Dainty specifically asked 'the working men of England ... What ... they think of the time when a secret police dogged the footsteps of their townsmen who were going to give evidence at the late trial'.

G. B. Skipworth (who had previously been imprisoned for contempt of court) brought the evening to a close by spelling out in vitriolic terms his understanding of the case:

Our Queen and our laws were not fit to be where they were if such a state of things was to prevail and it would be better that that should be swept away, and that they should have something better; he cared not what it was – a Republic or anything else. What was the use of having a mere show – a mere puppet on the throne? If they could not have right and justice they must agitate for an alteration (cheers).

This allusion to republicanism, although it may have chimed with the sensibilities of the locals, was not typical of the rest of the cause which tended at that time to court popular royalism. Kenealy later disowned Skipworth's republicanism.[5] The meeting then dispersed.

On 7 April, 1874 a well-attended public meeting in the Cambridge Hall, off Oxford Street in London, retained an emphasis on the Claimant's fate. It was chaired by Skipworth, who praised Kenealy and took issue with the trial: 'It was sufficient to say that he did not agree in the verdict of the jury, and yet he was not a fool or a fanatic, but a true-hearted Englishman, who wanted to see the administration of the law conducted with dignity and fair play, so that justice might be done to everybody.' He asserted that it was 'the principle of English law that the accused should have the benefit of the doubt; but that principle was entirely ignored at the late trial (hear, hear)'. Like Mr Collin's resolution at Leicester, such an interpretation hinted at an alternative view of law based on fairness and the custom of the community. The meeting ended with a resolution asking that the Queen be petitioned to grant a free pardon to the Claimant 'on the grounds that he had not the benefit of the doubt, which, as an Englishman, he was justly entitled to, from the evidence laid before the Court of Queen's Bench, that he may not be Arthur Orton'.[6] A third meeting followed in Southampton, at which the Claimant's wife appeared, and then a fourth in St James' Hall, Regent's Street, on 18 April.[7] These meetings spoke to the growing popular concern about how R. v. Castro had been conducted.

Kenealy's reaction to the movement against him by Gray's Inn was to remove himself from the legal profession. He founded his own weekly newspaper, the Englishman, just over a month after the end of the trial. The first issue appeared on 11 April 1874 and it became one of the most important radical papers of the 1870s.

The paper had several functions. The first, and most important, was to establish Kenealy as leader of the Tichborne movement. All of the early issues dealt with the injustice of Kenealy's treatment and developed the cult of his personality. He was presented as a brave public figure, full of heroism and integrity. The second function of the paper was to give coherence to the popular movement. Up until the end of the criminal trial, there had been little formal organisation. The few Tichborne societies that existed were those formed to organise visits of the Claimant during the stump campaign. With Kenealy at the helm, the Englishman had the aura of being the official paper of the cause, even though both the Tichborne Gazette and the Tichborne

News briefly resumed publication. Through Kenealy's paper, local Tichborne societies were able to write in as they were formed and the paper was to be instrumental in the greater centralisation he was to introduce.

The paper was presumably set up with Kenealy's own money. From its headquarters in Bouverie Street, off Fleet Street, it appeared every Saturday, price 2d. (cheap enough to be purchased by large sections of the working class). It was sixteen pages in length and concentrated on Tichborne propaganda as well as analysis of the rest of the week's news from a strongly anti-Catholic point of view. There were infrequent illustrations (usually of participants in the trial) and some, though not many, advertisements. Given the paper's longevity (1874–86), it seems reasonable to assume that its profitability depended on the number of copies sold rather than advertising.[8] By September 1875, its average circulation was said to be 70,000, though 'it went up when they had a portrait', according to one of the printer's employees.[9] The number of copies sold probably underestimates the number of people who read it as copies could be passed around.

It was distributed all over the country, usually though newsagents but also through appointed agents. For instance, the *Englishman* stockist in Lincoln was T. Dowd, a coal merchant who had subscribed £20 to the Kenealy Testimonial Fund, regretting at the same time that he had voted for Disraeli (now Prime Minister) in the recent General Election.[10] The reason why these agents existed was that the paper was sometimes difficult to obtain. The newsagent, W. H. Smith, for example, refused to sell it, although this may have been because it did not take papers published on a Saturday. The excuse was that, as they did not return the unsold papers, they would not risk it.[11] This strengthened the paper's conspiratorial conception of society. Smith was advised to:

> avoid playing the part of censor of the press – a hateful character in once free England: a character that our countrymen would not have endured thirty years ago: but slavish principles and Jesuitry since then have made such rapid progress among us, that we seem now content to bear any amount of injustice, and almost any insolence of despotism.[12]

This alleged censorship sometimes prompted supporters to volunteer their services. H. Masters of Aldershot, finding that his local branch of W. H. Smith at the railway station would not stock the paper, wrote in offering to 'work up the sale in this town'.[13] In Shrewsbury, only one newsagent stocked the paper, but apparently had no trouble selling it.[14]

The *Englishman* gave the impression that Kenealy was both owner and editor, which explains why its style had the feel of being part of an older tradition of journalism – that of the campaigning publisher-editor in the Cobbett mould. The internal affairs of the paper are, however, far from clear. It was certainly very much a family affair. Despite the legend on each issue 'Edited by Dr Kenealy QC', Kenealy sometimes bizarrely denied having any formal connection with the paper. The proprietorship was in the name of his son, Maurice, who was about sixteen at the time of the paper's foundation and who became editor. He had previously devilled for his father during the criminal trial.[15] Another son, Ahmed, also performed many of the editorial duties. Most of the articles were unsigned, as was typical of the press at the time. Some of the articles on riddles in the Tichborne case itself were probably written by a journalist, William Alfred Frost, who specialised in difficult questions arising from the affair.[16] The only articles that can otherwise be identified are those signed by Edward Kenealy himself.

Apart from its hostility to the Roman Catholic Church, the paper served as a clearing house not only for the Tichborne movement but also for many 'alternative' or unorthodox political causes such as the anti-Compulsory Vaccination movement, which shared its libertarian vocabulary and was another largely working-class movement. Adults objected to the vaccination of children for smallpox (it was feared that the employment of lymph from another body, whether human or animal, would contaminate and possibly kill children). The state was accused of being despotic in fining parents for non-compliance. Working-class agitators objected on the grounds that that it was 'the only law we have interfering with our bodies'.[17] This issue was not resolved until the introduction of 'conscientious objector' legislation in 1907.

The pages of the *Englishman* in 1874–75 reveal the growth of a popular movement. Virtually every week subscriptions to the Kenealy National Testimonial Fund increased. The movement inherited its format from the previous campaign. People continued to send in donations under pseudonyms: 'A poor widow in the hospital' (again suggesting that the theme of the oppression of the weak and defenceless was a reason for supporting the cause); 'From one who loves the Despised'; 'A Cheshire Admirer of Dr Kenealy'; and 'Right against Might'.[18] From those who did identify themselves, the impression is that working-class support held up: the employees of the Southwark and Vauxhall Waterworks Company, Hampton, subscribed 17s. 6d. Workers at the Atlas Engine Works, St George's, Bristol donated £2 5s.

Servants at Stanstead House sent in 10s. T. Winkles' carpenters in Leicester gave 5s. 3d.[19] Donations came from all over the country, including the Isle of Wight, Finchley, Manchester and Stafford.[20] In August, the journalist Edward Foster (no doubt with some hyperbole) claimed that 'nineteen-twentieths' of the working men of Leeds would vote for Kenealy.[21]

Meetings continued at local level, based around gathering subscriptions for the Kenealy Testimonial Fund. New Tichborne groups were also formed independent of Kenealy, although many employed his name in titling their societies. Whilst Kenealy was later to try and orchestrate the politics of the movement, it is clear that these early meetings were capable of taking on other political causes. For example, the Leicester branch passed a resolution expressing sympathy with the locked out agricultural labourers.[22] Meetings took place in any available public venue from the temperance hall to the pub. In London there were meetings at the Ladbroke Hall in Notting Hill and the Nell Gwynne pub in Fulham. These branches were developing comm-unications with one another. The Chelsea and Fulham branch meeting at the Nell Gwynne included a speaker from the Wandsworth branch.[23]

There was little centralised organisation. The *Englishman* later claimed that 'No external means has ever been resorted to ... Everything that each [Tichborne society] has accomplished has been spontaneous'.[24] There does appear to have been a great deal of spontaneity, as is shown by the diversity of names for societies in 1874: the 'Tichborne Release Association' of Samuel Charles Edward Goss in Shadwell, the 'Tichborne and Kenealy Association' of Leicester and the 'Leeds Tichborne Liberation Society'.[25] Often the organ-isation was so loose as to not have a title at all, although this became less common after the first six months. The presence of one of the participants in the affair at meetings was not unusual. Skipworth often spoke. Onslow chaired the meetings at the Chelsea Eleusis Club (a major radical centre) in July.[26]

In September, the focus of the movement turned from petitioning and raising subscriptions to Kenealy's lecture tour. This resembled the Claimant's stump campaign and became one of the most important platform agita-tions of the period. Organised by T. M. Evans, it was in part a response to popular demand.[27] The first meeting took place in Leicester on 29 September 1874.[28] Kenealy arrived by train to be met by a crowd of two thousand mainly middle-class people (the factories not having closed by that time). He was accompanied by Onslow, John Helsby (who was looking after the Claimant's family) and one of the Claimant's sons. They were greeted by Evans and his wife. Kenealy was given a carriage all to himself to focus attention on him. That evening he addressed a meeting at the Leicester Temperance Hall that was packed, despite the relatively expensive price of the seats. The hall was decorated with banners that related the case to the Bible: 'For we wrestle not with flesh and blood, but against principalities and powers, against the rulers of darkness of this world, against spiritual wickedness in high places'; 'That it may please Thee to bring into the way of truth, all such as have erred or are deceived'; and 'My kinsfolk have failed, and my familiar friends have forgotten me'. This suggests that the cause was interpreted at a local level in religious terms – as a contest over truth. Therefore it was appropriate that the Vicar of Aylestone, Reverend Straton, supported one of the resolutions at the meeting. Also amongst those on the platform were Councillors Goddard and Duxbury, suggesting a continuing degree of respectable patronage.

Onslow was elected to the Chair and gave a speech praising the heroic Kenealy: 'At a late hour he undertook this case ... his mind was a blank with reference to the whole matter.' This chimed with an important aspect of Tichborne beliefs: the desire for integrity. Kenealy was a man who came to the case without any prejudices in the matter (unlike, it was implied, the Tichborne family or the judiciary) and had made his mind up in favour of the Claimant. He summoned up Kenealy's fate in the most emotive way: 'They had all seen that with the Benchers of Gray's Inn a miserable and wicked attempt had been made to take the bread out of Dr Kenealy's mouth, and send his children into starvation, all for the sake of doing duty to his client.' He pointed out that 'Dr Kenealy worked the case at starvation price'. Kenealy then gave a speech recounting the incidents in the trial and created sympathy for the Claimant, whom he described as 'chained to a murderer or a garotter' in prison.

The following evening a second meeting took place in the Temperance Hall aimed at a more popular audience with cheaper seats. The social complexion of the audience can be shown by the efforts of one speaker to flatter his listeners:

He begged to congratulate the working classes of Leicester, of which that meeting might be regarded as a full and fair representation, that notwithstanding the uniform effort of the major portion of the local press to lead you astray into the mazes of prejudice and doubt on the Tichborne case ... you – the bone, sinew and common sense of the community – have shown yourself worthy to uphold the traditions of the town wherein they record how your fathers were always prompt to espouse the cause ... I do not flatter when I say it redounds to your credit, men of Leicester, that while those who profess to mould local thought, and to guide local opinion, have either abdicated their functions, or have not had the courage of their convictions to appear out on a question involving so momentous issues on one side or the other, you have acted independently and chosen to decide for your-selves.

Helsby noted that the Lord Chief Justice 'had asked if it was ever likely that Sir Roger Tichborne would marry a domestic servant. He ... would like to know who the Lord Chief Justice was, that he should insult the domestic servants of England?' He was cheered. The cause thrived on this opposition between the goodness of the people and the snobbery of elites.

Kenealy's speech dealt with the popular movement that he claimed 'would emanate from that great community' and which would make Parliament listen. He also added to the cause a new element. He argued that he had been disbenched from Gray's Inn simply for publishing a newspaper, which was an interference with the liberty of the press. He then went on to con-sider Gray's Inn itself, which he criticised for misusing public money and abandoning 'the honourable traditions of the law' in attempting to crush him. Therefore he recommended that the Leicester petition to Parliament include a prayer that the management of Gray's Inn be replaced and its funds administered for better purposes.

The two meetings were a great success but were ignored by the London press – much to the fury of the *Englishman*.[29] Its pages display a movement trying to be heard when 'official' sources of communication have been closed. One of the regular columns of the paper was titled 'Newspaper Lying'. It argued that the idea of a free press was a delusion and that the *Englishman* stood out for its independence. It later criticised newspapers for ignoring a Tichborne meeting in Nottingham whilst devoting excessive space to the 'accouchement of the Duchess of Edinburgh, which in place of joy brings grief to our working classes; for it means another frightful load of taxation for the support of this new-born prince'. It concluded that 'it is one of the characteristics of Popery and pro-Popery scribblers NEVER to tell the truth'.[30] Leicester set the pattern for future meetings: a meeting with high prices aimed mainly at the middle class and a public meeting, at cheap prices for the working class. The content was usually very similar.

Kenealy defends Self

It was a constant feature of Tichborne meetings that Cockburn's comment about believers in the Claimant being 'fanatics and fools' was reiterated and thrown back at him. The *Englishman* made it clear that crowds in Nottingham (the next stop on the tour) exhibited 'as little of the FOOL and FANATIC as our sober, sensible middle-class and trained operatives ever do'.[31] At a meeting in Leeds (organised by Edward Foster, editor of the pro-Claimant *Yorkshire Independent and People's Advocate*), Onslow wished 'that the Lord Chief Justice could have been present to judge of the "fools and fanatics"' who filled the hall.[32] This inversion of the meaning of Cockburn's original expression – making it a defiant description of Tichborne supporters – was part of the carnivalesque dimension to the case.[33] Kenealy began his speech at the same meeting in this way:

Mr Chairman, Ladies, and Gentlemen, I dare not call you female fanatics and Yorkshire fools, though I have high authority for asserting that anybody who doubts the Lord Chief Justice of England and his asseveration is both a fanatic and a fool. I can only say that if that be true, there are more fanatics and fools in England than I expected to find there; and I should not be at all surprised if, after a very short time, the fanatics and fools were found to be in a tremendous majority of Englishmen, and the wise men in a miserable minority. (Cheers.)[34]

Daniel Parry of Bootle, near Liverpool, wrote to Kenealy promising 'a hearty welcome from the many thousands of fools and fanatics' if Kenealy would visit, which suggests that the inversion was taken up at a local level.[35] The symbolic practice surrounding this became so sophisticated that, at one demonstration, a banner represented it as two 'F's which suggests that people could be counted on to decode its message.[36]

There were meetings at Peterborough, Loughborough, Grantham and Bradford. The petition adopted at Peterborough prayed for the abolition of Gray's Inn, demanding that the Benchers be accountable to the public. It also noted that 'the Benchers spend nearly £1,000 a year for their chapel, which the Benchers of the society, except perhaps two or three, never attend; and while their wine cellars contained twenty-one pipes of port and an unknown quantity of other wines and spirits, they expended only a very moderate annual sum upon the purchase of books for their library'.[37] Thus the popular critique of the law, with its focus on inequality, was dovetailed with the popular critique of aristocratic decadence.

One index of support for the movement is the number of petitions on behalf of the Claimant presented to Parliament. A petitioning movement had commenced in 1872 but it was mainly based around areas that were close to Tichborne or (like Poole) that had some connection to it. After the criminal trial, petitioning burgeoned into an important way of demonstrating support. In 1873, 24,029 people signed petition forms. The number rose to 47,087 in 1874 and peaked a year later at 283,314. The figures remained high over the next two years: 97,593 signatures were recorded in 1876, falling to 25,882 in 1877. The number fell in 1878 to 488, but rose again in 1879 to 14,971. There was little significant petitioning thereafter, but Hampshire in 1882 did manage to raise 4,984 signatures, testifying to the strong local feeling engendered by the cause.[38]

Although petitions came in from all over the country, the figures only suggest the levels of national support. If anything, they probably underestimate it. Some petitions arose from public meetings and contained only one signature (that of the chairman) on the form. The petitioning figures are useful, however, if only because they are one of the few pieces of quantitative material available on the movement. There may have been corruption (false signatures) in their assembly; but the Select Committee on Public Petitions only noted that some names were in the same handwriting on three petitions, one from Greenwich in 1876 and two from Surbiton in 1877. Hampshire and southern coastal towns were always well represented, but there was also a strong showing from the East End of London: Whitechapel, Tower Hamlets, Hackney, Clerkenwell. Collectors of signatures appear to have gone to public places in order to attract signatures.

Petitioning was an important part of political culture during the nineteenth century. It had previously been an informal part of the legal process, but improvement in legal procedures reduced the need for it as a means of redress. The petition therefore came to be preoccupied with matters of public importance rather than with the problems of individuals. Its heyday lasted from the late eighteenth century until 1841, due partly to its effectiveness in promoting radicalism. MPs, when presenting a petition, were allowed to address the House four times, providing a great opportunity to publicise the cause of reform. In 1832, a committee under Sir Robert Peel rationalised the procedure and cut the number of occasions an MP could address the House on a petition to one. Petitioning thereafter declined, although this was partly because people began to use the developing media and political parties. There was, however, a brief resurgence in petitioning from the late 1860s to the mid-1870s and the strength of Tichborne petitioning and its subsequent decline should be seen as part of a national trend in petitioning rather than simply as a straightforward index of Tichborne support.[39] Petitioning was an obvious device for the movement, given that the cause tended to employ older forms of protest. Indeed the use of traditional radical forms such as petitions, stump oratory, or freeborn Englishman imagery in themselves constituted a critique of modernity – the medium was partly the message. Petitioning in any case recommended itself not only because of its historical roots but because of the simplicity of the form. Signatures were easy to collect and represented a direct mobilisation of popular opinion. Petitioning also enabled the signatories to constitute themselves as a larger body – the people – and so was in effect a consciousness-raising exercise.

Most petitions demanded the same thing: the release of the Claimant or the setting up of a Select Commission of Inquiry into the trial. A few came from individuals involved in the case. The Orton sisters sent in a petition asserting that they could prove that the Claimant was not their brother.

Biddulph sent in a petition of twenty-four signatures stating that, as Orton had not come forward, he was either dead or was too frightened to appear in view of some previous misdemeanour.[40]

Whilst the lecture tour was a great success in terms of attendance, there was a need for a follow-up. By September 1874 there were increasing numbers of Tichborne organisations around the country. Some were established after visits of Kenealy but many owed their existence to spontaneous support carried over from the first campaign. In December, after his final disbarring, Kenealy decided to centralise the movement under his own auspices. The *Englishman* was to be the vehicle. He asserted that the action of the Bench 'demonstrates that, in England, Liberty no longer exists, and that independence of action is treated as a crime'. The problem was that England had become a despotism:

> I ask you, therefore, to join me, O Men and Women of England, in forming a National League, to be called
> THE MAGNA CHARTA ASSOCIATION OF GREAT BRITAIN.[41]

It was a typically Kenealyite enterprise, shrouded in medievalist mysticism. To support his actions, Kenealy also invoked the names of Hampden, Milton and Fairfax, showing that he was part of the continuing Victorian interest in the English Revolution.[42] The first aim of the Magna Charta Association was 'to bring back Magna Charta and the Bill of Rights'. The project had the flavour of the atavistic radical movements of the eighteenth century, such as John Wilkes's Society for the Supporters of the Bill of Rights.

The second aim was 'To establish a free and honest Press', of which the *Englishman* was presumably a good example. Kenealy presented a portrait of a dishonest press, which existed only 'to curry favour with everybody who has advertisements to give – Whig, Jew, and Atheist.' This was an outgrowth of the dispute over press coverage that had gone on since the movement began.

Kenealy proposed, thirdly, to send 250 'people's representatives' to Parliament who would derive from the 'middle and the operative class'. With Kenealy as their leader, they would overcome 'class legislation'. They were to be backed up by a fund subscribed by members of the Magna Charta Association. Kenealy also promised to make bribery at an election an act of felony and 'To have a triennial Parliament', both of which were similar to

Chartist demands (although of course the People's Charter sought annual Parliaments).[43] He also supported votes for women, although he did not believe in universal manhood suffrage.

The Association sought 'To abolish the Income Tax Act' and 'To secure a free breakfast table'. This meant the abolition of duties on tea, coffee and sugar, a long-standing concern of the Liberal John Bright.[44] Dislike of indirect taxation was part of an old radical tradition but Kenealy attacked Income Tax as well, equating it with surveillance by the state:

> [It] has made every individual Englishman an absolute slave ... Much better would it be for all of us, as in Eastern Despotisms, that the Government came down when its necessities required it, and demanded a certain sum, than that it should insult us every year, by prying into our means; that it should degrade us, with all our books and accounts, before our neighbours, the Income Tax assessors.

Most workers did not pay income tax at this time. Kenealy coupled these with more apparently conservative demands: 'To support the House of Lords'; and 'To restore the crown to the Queen'. The latter was really part of the older radical discourse whereby the monarch was seen as the defender of the constitution. The former was considered an effective check on despotism. Together, the proposals were an argument in favour of the separation of powers and against excessive centralisation. Finally, Kenealy pledged 'To exclude lawyers from Parliament', although this later came to mean practising lawyers. It was the most obvious reference to his own martyrdom.

What is striking is the emphasis Kenealy placed upon himself. On the subject of the hostile press, he claimed 'All these newspapers are against *me* because I denounce them to you in the language they deserve; because I pull off their masks and show them as they are'. He presented himself as a model of integrity, claiming that there was only one other People's Representative and that was Alexander MacDonald, the Lib/Lab MP who had been elected in 1874, which reveals Kenealy's affinities with radical Liberalism, despite his early Toryism. By the following year he was abusing MacDonald as well as George Potter of the pro-labour newspaper, the *Beehive*.

Kenealy intended that each Tichborne Committee should form the basis of a local Magna Charta Association and transform the organisation into a general political movement: 'It has nothing to do with the TICHBORNE case, or with the KENEALY wrong.' Local committees were instructed to communicate with the *Englishman* office once they were formed. Each member was to subscribe one penny a week, which would become part of a fund to send People's Representatives to Parliament.

This development caused some local problems. For example, most Tichborne societies were the creation of locals who did not always take kindly to their organisation and title being interfered with. Moreover, there was a fear of the cause becoming too 'political'. Mr Burton of the Swindon District Tichborne and Kenealy Association expressed this worry in January 1875:

> some wish to adopt the name of Magna Charta which will at once con-
> stitute us a political section in the nation; but this involves another
> question of most serious importance, and affecting to a great extent
> the success or failure of our Association for whereas there are a great
> many people whose sympathies are with us on behalf of the Claimant
> and his family ... [they] would not, upon any consideration, enter into
> the arena of political controversy.[45]

Though Burton was happy that the new organisation might help gain respect for the cause, the name of his society did not change and the title of 'Magna Charta Association' did not catch on generally until at least February 1875. At a meeting in Lincoln, Kenealy made it clear that he intended the Asso-ciation to become a third party in the land. Less than a month later he said: 'I believe that in ten years, with the Magna Charta Association at my back, I shall make our country prosperous, happy and free.'[46]

In addition to the *Englishman*, Kenealy commenced publication in January 1875 of another periodical – the *Englishman's Magazine*. Published monthly, it was, despite its title, very different from his first paper. No mention was made of the Claimant and the first issue did not even invoke Kenealy's own name. It was devoted to antiquarian and archaeological matters. Each issue included lengthy, detailed articles on learned topics, such as a lecture by Augustus Le Plongeon entitled 'Vestiges of Antiquity' which revealed 'the coincidences that exist between the monuments, customs, religious rites, etc. of the prehistoric inhabitants of America and those in Asia and Egypt'.[47] The paper had no editorial or set of principles but many articles contained the kind of rhetoric that the Tichbornites, and especially Kenealy, were prone to. The first issue featured an article by Ieuan Gryg on the medieval trial by combat. It was part of a series of articles that never materialised, which aimed to show the origins of the modern judicial system, its barristers, inns of court 'and the part which the Roman Catholic priests played, in every age, in these matters'.[48]

The paper ceased publication in December 1875 after only a year, due to lack of support, which suggests the *Englishman* could not have been run at a loss and must have succeeded on volume of sales alone, as there must have been a limit to the amount of money that Kenealy could have pumped into it. On 6 February, 1875, Kenealy began to publish his edition of the criminal trial in weekly instalments. It took five years to complete the series and eventually comprised nine volumes.

Kenealy's entry into the Tichborne affair represented a move away from the relatively spontaneous cause of 1872–73. Instead, Kenealy's aim was to centralise the movement under his control. What is striking is Kenealy's ability to 'read' popular culture. His rhetoric was a loose collection of many of the radical shibboleths of the previous hundred years. The rise in popularity of the cause in the period 1874–75 was in part a testament to his success.

7

The People's Candidate

By the beginning of 1875, Kenealy had decided that he wanted to move from the law courts of Westminster Hall to the House of Commons. He had already attempted to find a parliamentary seat earlier in his career, standing on separate occasions as an Independent or as a Liberal but with a fondness for the more romantic strains of Toryism. Now he was armed with a political programme and a mass movement. The 1867 Reform Act had enlarged the urban electorate to include the more affluent parts of the working classes and the secret ballot had been introduced in 1872. Britain was becoming something like a mass democracy (a status it would not fully achieve until 1928). Supporters of parliamentary reform had had to defend themselves from charges that democracy would lead to demagoguery and the Americanisation of public life (meaning the corruption and machine politics associated with New York's Tammany Hall).[1] The first General Election that took place under the new system (in 1868) put Gladstone and the Liberals in power. Disraeli's flirtation with democracy, however, laid the basis for the Conservative victory of 1874. In the wake of 1867, both main parties realised there was a new electorate to be organised and their political machinery in the constituencies began to improve.[2] With the growth of the new working-class electorate came demands for independent labour representation (in effect the revival of a Chartist aspiration in the 1840s), a call that challenged both parties, but particularly the Liberals. In time these demands for labour representation would divide the Liberals and lead to the formation of the Labour Party.

But there is another story to be told about the years that followed the 1867 Reform Act. Political parties developed their machinery haphazardly as no one knew what to expect of the new electorate. Moreover, there was a deep popular suspicion of the very idea of political parties.[3] A deep strain in political culture continued to believe that MPs should be independent and not subject to the dictates of party. The idea of opposition for its own sake (intrinsic to party politics) had gained only limited acceptance. Kenealy exploited these anxieties.

At the end of 1874, George Melly, one of the MPs for Stoke-Upon-Trent, decided that pressures of business and family required him to resign his seat. The by-election in the Potteries that followed allowed Kenealy to test out the strength of Magna Chartism. At Stoke, Kenealy entered a situation of political chaos. The newly enfranchised electorate was broadly Liberal from a strong nonconformist tradition. The relations between different interest groups in the local party, however, epitomised the contradictory nature of Victorian Liberalism.

The constituency was dominated by an oligarchy of Whig-Liberal manu-facturers who had ensured after 1832 that it had returned two sympathetic Members to Parliament (it was a two-Member constituency).[4] From the late 1850s, however, the ruling group confronted challenges to their domi-nance from radicals, trade unions and temperance reformers. In 1862, they deliberately neglected to inform Samuel Pope, who had stood against the official Liberal candidates on a temperance ticket in 1859, about the selec-tion meeting for candidates so that he would be unable to offer himself as a possible nominee. Even more underhand was the decision to buy off the radical journalist Robert Hartwell (editor of the *Beehive*) in 1868 to prevent him from standing as a working-man's candidate and splitting the vote. Stoke politics became saturated with suspicion which led many Liberal-inclined voters to support the Conservatives. In the late 1860s, working-class confidence was developing with an increase in union membership and encouraged by the local paper, the *Potteries Examiner*. Under the editorship of William Owen, this championed radical Liberal ideas and supported the potters, miners and ironworkers (the main forms of industry in the six towns that formed the constituency).[5] The paper was a powerhouse of popu-lar Lib-Labism. After the 1867 Reform Act swelled the number of voters from 3,446 to 16,204 and with the introduction of the Secret Ballot in 1872, the electorate became increasingly difficult for the Liberals to control. The Liberals George Melly and W. S. Roden had been elected unopposed in 1868 (no Conservative thinking it worthwhile to stand) but it was clear this situ-ation of Whig-Liberal dominance would not continue in the future.

William Owen urged the cause of the Labour Representation League, which stepped up activity in the area and, as a result, Alfred Walton, an architect and spokesman for both the Labour Representation and the National Education Leagues, was chosen as a parliamentary candidate by the leaders of the pottery trade unions.[6] Lloyd Jones of the League and the radical jour-nalist, G.W.M. Reynolds, were also considered.

At the 1874 General Election, George Melly and W. S. Roden stood once more as the Liberal candidates. Melly's seat was unopposed but the challenge

of Walton split the vote for the second seat and the Conservative Robert
Heath was elected. It was a telling testimony to the divisions within the Liberal
interest, although Heath was aided by an improved network of Tory associations and a campaign based on beer. He was supported by many licensed
victuallers alarmed by the temperance concerns of the Liberals.[7]

As a result, William Woodall, the pottery owner and leading Liberal,
decided it would be necessary to conciliate the working-class vote by having
the second candidate nominated by the trade unions. The choice of candidate, however, was crucial and Walton, like Pope, was considered unsuitable
as he was too radical (he was associated with the causes of land nationalisation as well as labour representation). Roden's basis of support was also judged
too insubstantial. Some long-term agreement might have been obtained
had not Melly decided to resign in December 1874, forcing a by-election for
his seat. Unprepared, Woodall decided that there was nothing for it but to
support Walton. Approved on 6 February 1875, Walton's candidacy created
for the first time a real Liberal-Labour alliance. Middle-class Liberals, however, were furious at having Walton thrust upon them.

What there was of the Liberal Party machine had barely adjusted to the
post-Reform age. Although Walton was the candidate of the trade union
leaders (who dominated the local Labour Representation League), it was
unclear whether the latter could deliver the votes of their members. Many
operatives had different attitudes to those of the leadership, opposing temperance, preferring strikes to arbitration, and not always subscribing to the
burial funds and sickness and insurance schemes provided. The Conservatives put forward Henry Davenport (whose middle name, ironically, was
'Tichborne') of the Davenport pottery family, based in Longton.[8] The situation was therefore highly volatile. With the examples of Pope, Hartwell and
Walton, Stoke already had a tradition of independent candidates which
meant that Kenealy did not disrupt the electoral situation as much as he might
have done in a more settled constituency. Given the chaos of inter- and
infra-party strife that existed, Stoke provided the ideal electoral background
for a charismatic and independent figure.

Kenealy already had some links with the district having been a barrister
on the Oxford Circuit (which included Stoke) and having been a possible
candidate in 1862. Rumours that he was going to stand circulated from early
January.[9] The *Staffordshire Sentinel*, local organ of middle-class Liberalism,
mocked these suggestions but it came to pass that a requisition signed by
5,717 people, measuring twenty-eight yards, was made up.[10] Their petition

was presented to Kenealy at the Queen's Hotel, Manchester, while he was on tour and he accepted.[11] With the introduction of the Secret Ballot, it is impossible to define the exact class composition of Kenealy's supporters but the following reconstruction of the election campaign points to some of the motives for voting for him.

Walton's campaign was handicapped by the lack of enthusiasm, which the Liberal oligarchy showed for a man who was foisted upon them. At a Liberal meeting in Stoke on 9 January, Christopher Dickinson, the chairman and leader of the local party, remarked that 'He would not say anything as to Mr Walton being the best candidate; he could not see that he had any special ability or special connection with the district that would make him more likely to efficiently represent the district than some other men'.[12] But he was forced to admit that Walton had polled 5196 votes at the General Election, that he was the choice of the working class and he would support Gladstone in Parliament, which was better than voting for Disraeli. Ten days later, at a meeting at the Hanley Mechanics Institute, the chairman introduced Walton by noting that 'He ... was not going to say that he should have picked Mr Walton out of a row of other men, nor, if he had never been before them on a previous occasion, should he have chosen him on the present occasion'.[13] The following day, another leading Liberal, J. N. Peake, chaired a Walton meeting composed of working men in the covered market at Tunstall. He praised Roden and regretted that he had not come forward for election:

> what should be done under the circumstances? Well, now 5000 men of the borough were of opinion that working men should be represented in Parliament by a working man. ('Hear, hear', and cheers). He did not say he agreed with this, but 5000 men of the borough certainly held that opinion.[14]

Such support delivered through gritted teeth made the Walton campaign seem a mess. The *Staffordshire Sentinel*, representing the Whig magnates, remained equivocal. At first, it hoped that Roden would stand and criticised Walton for his candidature in 1874 and the harm it had done to the Liberals:

> Working men will command public respect and, what is more important, their own self respect, by acting in all public matters as Englishmen, and as Englishmen only. The self-styled 'working man's friend' is in

every instance a self-seeking man, and has his selfish objects in view in the assumption of that patronising title, a title by which every sensible man is insulted.[15]

It also noted that Davenport was a man of great personal standing.[16] During the campaign, the paper therefore seemed to have a pro-Tory bias, noted by the *Potteries Examiner*, its rival, which passionately supported Walton.[17] In the end, the *Sentinel* plumped for Walton, consoling its readers that Walton would at least vote the same way that Melly and Roden had done.[18] Walton was caught up in the awkward relationship between Gladstonian Liberalism (which he professed) and the Whig magnates who usually ran the party at the local level. It was not uncommon for magnates to encourage those over whom they exerted paternalist authority to vote against the Liberals so as to restrain the party when they so wished, as in the 1868-74 period.[19] Part of the problem was Walton's belief in Irish Home Rule. Critics claimed that Walton would dismember the British Empire. Henry Broadhurst (later MP for Stoke) came up on behalf of the Labour Representation League to speak in Walton's favour and Samuel Morley, MP for Bristol, wrote to the *Sentinel* wishing him success.[20] The campaign was not helped, however, by the fact that Walton became too ill to canvass for a time near the conclusion.[21]

Davenport fought an aggressive campaign for the Conservatives, exploiting the divisions among the Liberals. At a meeting in the Burslem Town Hall, Mr Pinder, a local Liberal, actually spoke in support of Davenport:

> In his opinion Mr Walton was not the representative of the Liberal Party. (Applause, and cries of 'Yes he is'). The working class were a very respectable class of people – (A voice: 'Soft Soap') – but he deprecated the idea of working-class representation.[22]

Davenport denied that Walton was the choice of a united Liberal Party and presented himself as a Liberal-minded Conservative, better able to represent Liberal interests than Walton.[23] He said that he would not extend the county franchise to the agricultural labourers (though his mind was not made up), would not abolish primogeniture, the Game Laws or compulsory Sunday closing but would vote to abolish the Contagious Diseases Acts. He would not be drawn on the subject of the Claimant.[24] The Conservatives were able to trade on their developed organisation, holding meetings in their newsrooms and pubs as well as larger venues.[25]

Davenport reacted angrily to one accusation. At Kenealy's meeting in Hanley on 25 January, Liberal supporters distributed a leaflet complaining that Kenealy was a Tory agent who had been put up to split the Liberal vote.[26] At a meeting at Longton, many prominent Tories were seen on the platform with Kenealy and dined with him later at the Portland Arms.[27] Most damning of all, Tory canvassers were reported to be asking people to vote for Kenealy if they would not vote for Davenport.[28] There is no evidence that Kenealy was a Tory plant, but he must have appeared to Davenport's supporters as a useful tool to divide the Liberal vote even more than it had been under Walton. The prominent Tories who fraternised with Kenealy were presumably interested in meeting one of the most famous people in Britain at that time. In any case, it was in Liberal interests to brand Kenealy as the agent of a Tory conspiracy. Walton claimed that Kenealy had been a member of the Conservative Carlton Club and wondered whether he still was.[29] Kenealy was sufficiently stung by the accusation to reply at a meeting in the Stoke Town Hall that he had changed his mind about Disraeli after their earlier friendship.[30] Davenport was also embarrassed and constantly denied the rumoured association.[31]

Kenealy for his part fought a typically flamboyant campaign, the climax to a nine-month triumphal lecture tour, which maintained his notoriety in the eyes of the public. He had already been solicited by Tichbornites to lecture in Stoke before Melly resigned his seat, which explains why his early appearances were in theatres that had already been booked.

Kenealy opened with a talk in the Longton Theatre on 20 January. He and Onslow were accompanied to the theatre by the local borough band. Inside a huge banner was erected on the back of the stage, which read 'May God bless and prosper Sir Roger, and grant him his speedy deliverance upon earth from his persecutions'. Other banners hung from the gallery praised Kenealy and Onslow as 'The only defenders of the people's rights' as well as the ubiquitous 'See the conquering hero comes', derived from Handel's anthem. Kenealy wooed the crowd with his usual speech on the Tichborne case, attacking both the Judge and Jury. He asked the audience to send him to Parliament, which produced 'tremendous cheering, waving of hats, and a voice: We'll send you!' Onslow then spoke whilst Kenealy played to the audience by waving his handkerchief excitedly.[32] By this time, Kenealy was adept in the theatrical skills of demagoguery. He posed as tribune of the people and brought out the pathos of his situation to evoke sympathy. He complained that he and his twelve children had been ruined by Disraeli and that he was being followed by four detectives round the provinces.[33]

Although the Tichborne cause was ignored by the local newspapers, the *Englishman* was sold in the area.[34] Kenealy also established his own local paper for the campaign, the *Potteries People's Paper*.[35] The Kenealyites employed no agents but relied on volunteers to canvass for him. Amongst them was Jack Williams (later a leading member of the Marxist Social Democratic Federation), who travelled to Stoke from London specifically to aid Kenealy. Williams was a working-class agitator who had collected £84 on behalf of the Claimant in his different places of work. He also supported the Irish Land League and the Commons Preservation Society. An enthusiastic member of Kenealy's organisation, he went on to become an associate of William Morris when the poet and artist became a leading socialist.[36]

Kenealy campaigned as an independent 'People's' candidate. Although the Magna Charta Association made much of its dislike of 'party', the campaign in Stoke attempted to give Kenealy a Liberal gloss, which was important given the sympathies of the electorate. He was supported by Onslow, a former Liberal MP, who issued an address on his behalf.[37] 'Principal' wrote to the *Staffordshire Daily Sentinel* asking 'how it is that he [Kenealy] professes to be an independent candidate on one of his placards, and a Liberal candidate on another'.[38]

Amongst local notables, Councillor Thomas Booth of the Hanley Temperance Party gave support.[39] There is some evidence that Kenealy was supported by Francis Wedgwood, the Master Potter of Etruria, part of the great Wedgwood dynasty that dominated the Potteries. Once Kenealy was in Parliament, Fanny Allen (a relative) wrote to her niece, Emma Darwin, 'I hope we may hear no more of him till Frank re-elects him again for the Potteries'.[40] If this is true (and it is the only piece of evidence testifying to this support), Kenealy would have been able to count on Wedgwood's considerable paternalist influence not only in the famous works at Etruria but throughout the district. Francis Wedgwood was the son of Josiah Wedgwood of Maer and had become Master Potter on the latter's death in 1843. He had left the Liberals in 1874 in opposition to Gladstone's foreign policy.[41] Kenealy also spoke at Messrs Worthington's pottery works. Worthington was a local Liberal leader but it is unclear whether he had switched to Kenealy over the Walton dispute or was simply providing him with a forum.[42]

Further respectable support came from the Reverend George Cooke, a Baptist minister in Burslem, who was engaged in selling Bibles and tracts. His influence may be gauged from his claim to have sold 3,000 Bibles, visited 5,000 families, distributed 34,000 tracts, held 230 religious services and induced 300 people to sign the Temperance pledge – all in 1874.[43] He spoke at Kenealy's meetings, as did Edward Bailey, a Wesleyan minister from Tipton, who had been associated with Kenealy since the election at Wednesbury.[44] He later became a prominent Tichbornite. Religious support also came from David Thomas, the Congregationalist minister who edited The *Homilist*, a popular non-denominational periodical devoted to sermons.[45] His review of the *Englishman* in the latter praised Kenealy and was distributed through Stoke as a broadside.[46] In addition, there were addresses from a deputation of working men from Crewe who added to the multi-class nature of his meetings.[47] It was later alleged that this deputation was made up of Tories and that the Crewe Trades Council repudiated them.[48]

The key to Kenealy's success remained his claim to be not only independent but also against political parties. The fact that the Magna Charta Association was meant to provide the basis of a new political party does not seem to have worried him. He told his audience at the People's Music Hall in Hanley on 25 January that 'The days of party ought to be gone by for ever, and efforts should now be made, not for party advancement but for the advancement of Englishmen (Applause)'.[49] Such a message was attractive to an electorate disenchanted with the machinations of the Liberal Party machine. Instead of back room political skullduggery, Kenealy offered himself as untainted by the corruption of the rest. In his election address, reproduced as a poster, he pushed his anti-party line:

> I belong to no Party but to England. The days of Party are gone by with me.
>
> I will support all Measures for the benefit of the people, from whatever side of the House they come. If no such measures are proposed, I will move them myself, and labour with all my might to make them law.

Party was a luxury for the parliamentarians and against the wishes and interests of the people:

> A great Christian country like England, spending £70,000 sterling annually, cannot continue to play at party interminably, while millions of Englishmen and Englishwomen are badly housed, badly fed, and without the pale of genuine civilising influences ... A People's Candidate

should bind himself by no party fetters. What can it be to him from what side good measures come forth? He consults only the Public Benefit. He is not blind to valuable proposals if they come from the Tory side: he willingly accepts any measure of excellence, no matter whence it comes. Party ignores this noble principle. It picks a hole in every project of its adversary; and thus deprives the People of many a good and salutary proposal. I wish to secure the greatest happiness of the greatest number.[50]

For 'Party', he substituted 'Englishness'. He told an audience in the Burslem Town Hall: 'The voice of the nation slept, but it required only a man to summon it from that sleep, and then England would arise in all her glory and ancient grandeur, and would teach those persons in authority that they, the people, were determined to be the masters of England in the future.'[51]

He tapped the culture of independent manliness that the Gladstonian Liberal Party usually managed to call on. He presented himself as a successor to one of the greatest freeborn Englishmen, Oliver Cromwell, who was enjoying a renaissance in popularity: 'Was England made for a few magnates, a few right honourables, or a few Dukes? No. It was made for the people of England, who had not had the land since the time of Oliver Cromwell.' He condemned Speaker Brand's refusal to accept Tichborne petitions and said he would have been executed in Cromwell's time for violating the constitution.[52]

He presented the 'People' as heavily burdened by taxation and praised Joseph Hume, who had fought for retrenchment in government and a reduction in taxation throughout his parliamentary career. The demand for reduced taxation was central to popular Liberalism. Having adopted John Bright's demand for a free breakfast table, Kenealy added a meat dinner table as well.[53] He presented a series of images that expressed a fear of national decline. Englishness, independence and food on the table were potent symbols, which succeeded where more prosaic politics failed.

Kenealy was also capable of talking in a more orthodox way. He contrasted the luxury of the rich with the poverty of the poor:

although Englishman worked harder than any other man in the world, and did his work more skilfully, he was the worst remunerated of any working man on the face of the globe. ('Hear, hear', and applause). These things must be amended and laws must be made for the poor and the rich. (Loud cheers). It was said often that there was one law for the poor and another for the rich, but his opinion was that all laws were made for the rich, and none for the poor. (Cheers). Let them look at the Masters and Servants Act as an example. ('Hear, hear' and applause). If a master broke a contract he was let off with a nominal fine at most, but if a servant broke a contract he must immediately be sent to prison. (Cries of 'Shame'.)[54]

He promised to repeal the Master and Servant Act and, to alleviate poverty, advocated emigration so as to stop too many people being trapped in England and subject to the depression of wages by capitalists.[55] His lecture on temperance that had been published in the February *Englishman's Magazine* also gave him some credibility in the eyes of the temperance group.[56] He promised a Magna Charta Government with himself as Prime Minister.[57]

As usual, his relationship with the press was bad. He condemned the *Staffordshire Sentinel* after trouble over a business letter.[58] R. W. Ship, a journalist on the *Sentinel* at the time, later reminisced about Kenealy's opinion on his paper delivered at a public meeting: 'Thumping the table at which I sat, he forbade his friends to buy the paper, and told them they must not trade with any house who advertised in the *Sentinel*.'[59] In its turn, the *Sentinel* mocked his 'pretentious and ridiculous bombast' and the *Potteries Examiner* labelled him 'the quack doctor'.[60] However, when the *Examiner's* editor, William Owen, a distinguished platform orator, attempted to intervene at one of Kenealy's meetings, he was shouted down. He tried to get three cheers for Walton but only received three for Kenealy. There were shouts of 'How much are you paid to come here?' and he was not allowed to speak.[61] Kenealy's campaign was not always so successful. Victorian elections were often characterised by heckling or even violence. Meetings at Longton and Tunstall were seriously disrupted. Some reports blamed hooligans and others said it was the work of Walton supporters.[62] On the afternoon of 3 February Kenealy addressed a crowd of 250 to 300 people at Lord Granville's pit in Hanley from a wagon that was used as a platform. He wanted to speak to the colliers coming up from the pit after work but they evinced little interest, despite Kenealy's claim to be the working-man's candidate. These reports came from Walton supporters who were there distributing leaflets; the *Englishman* described it as a great triumph.[63]

Apart from invocations of radicalism, Kenealy sought to tap other popular mentalities. Broadsides advertised his cause, representing him as a merry

STOKE ELECTION

HURRAH FOR KENEALY

The People's friend and the Champion of

POOR "SIR. ROGER."

Hurrah for Kenealy: *Stoke Election Ballad*

John Bull. Sending him to Parliament would allow him to destroy government corruption. Kenealy made much of his alleged special relationship with women. He told the crowd at the Deep Pit Bank in Hanley that 'he was sure that whoever had women on his side was sure to be the winner'.[64] A broadside urged:

Come all you married women and do the best you can,
And make your husbands vote for the noble hearted man,
Tell Bob, and Tom, and Bill if they don't do as you say,
They'll have tongue pie for dinner for twelvemonth and a day.[65]

At a meeting at Dale Hall 'a large attendance of most respectable women ... as usual, were foremost in their demonstrations of applause, sympathy and kindly feeling'.[66] Five years later, wives of voters and working girls remained prominent in the campaign that elected Henry Broadhurst as MP for the Potteries.[67]

Although it was not a major part of his campaign, anti-Catholicism featured in some of his statements. On 25 January, he told his audience in the Hanley People's Music Hall that

> He strongly condemned the action of the Government spending a quarter of a million of money over the Tichborne case, and then refusing to hear the application of the letter sorters for an advance of wages. Why, he asked, was this? The reason was because the letter sorters do not belong to the great families of the country, because they do not belong to the great Jesuit order.[68]

There was a local strain of anti-Catholicism perhaps caused by the presence of the Irish, although they were very scattered in the area.[69] Davenport was quizzed at a meeting for his opinion on the inspection of convents.[70] 'An Old Potter' remembered the excitement in the district following the re-establishment of the Catholic hierarchy in 1850. At a Protestant meeting in Tunstall, a strong resolution was passed against Popery and Joseph Capper, a former Chartist, was applauded when he burnt a facsimile of the Pope's Bull.[71] In February 1867, the Rector of Burslem chaired the lectures of William Murphy, a renowned anti-Catholic ranter, in Wolverhampton.[72] Local pottery design often reflected anti-Catholicism. One figure represented a woman with a bag of gold marked £10,000 and a priest offering the veil of dedication. The implication was that the priest wanted her to become a nun simply for her money. Other figures included representations of Thomas Cranmer, Hugh Latimer and Nicholas Ridley, all Protestant martyrs. Another showed 'Protestantism' as a young woman and 'Popery' as a priest with a quotation from the Archbishop of Dublin in 1816: 'Either we must root out the Bible or the Bible will root us out.' There were, however, also figures of Catholic leaders such as Pius IX and Cardinal Manning.[73] It is difficult to quantify how important anti-Catholicism was in 1875 but it may have assisted Kenealy.

All over the country, Tichborne Associations passed resolutions urging the electors of Stoke to vote for Kenealy.[74] The Stoke election was therefore not simply based on local issues but was part of a national campaign. Given the recent extension of the franchise, the *Englishman* published instructions on the mechanics of voting. For example, it emphasised that the elector 'must not place his X in front of, or before the name of the candidate, *but after it*' which suggests it expected to attract working-class electors voting for the first time.[75]

The 1874 General Election had witnessed considerable disorder in the constituency so the police was reinforced by four hundred extra men and two troops of the 12th Lancers, as well as two companies of the 22nd Regiment billeted close by in Newcastle-under-Lyme. As it was, order was generally preserved on polling day (16 February) and they were not needed. Kenealy toured the area in an open carriage accompanied by his wife and Lord Rivers. At Burslem, they were received with great applause as opposed to the mixed reception that the other two candidates got. At Tunstall, there was a carnival-like atmosphere with entertainment featuring a fight between a dog and a red-haired dwarf called Big Enoch, which caused much amusement. Big Enoch was notorious in the area and had even provoked questions in Parliament.[76] When Kenealy arrived, an Irishman shouted 'Let's give him a hoot, boys', but most of the crowd cheered him. Only in Longton was there any disturbance. Roughs attacked anyone of a respectable appearance going to vote: 'Wisps of wet, dirty straw were thrown in his face, his hat knocked off, and, if he retaliated, he was immediately set on by a dozen or more roughs, and severely handled.' This led to stone throwing and one man was knocked insensible. Even the police, who were called in, had initially to retreat under a hail of stones.[77]

Of approximately 19,000 names on the register, 14,000 voted. The result was announced at nine o'clock in the Hanley Town Hall:

Dr E. V. Kenealy	6,110
A. A. Walton	4,168
H. T. Davenport	3,901

Within the hall the result was greeted with hisses but outside there was great cheering. A large number of people dispersed and continued applauding outside Kenealy's committee room and the new Member of Parliament was seen later 'haranguing' a crowd about Magna Charta from one of the bedroom windows of the Queen's Hotel.[78] In celebration, a Kenealy MP mug was manufactured in the district. Elsewhere, a waxwork of the new MP for Stoke was added to Madame Tussaud's.[79]

The result produced a reaction round the country. The day after the election, there was a procession of working men in Gloucester to celebrate Kenealy's victory.[80] The election provoked a debate in the papers about whether the extension of the franchise was a good thing if the new electors were irresponsible enough to vote for a man like Kenealy. 'Stoke', noted The

Times, 'is the kind of borough all the politicians had in their minds during the spirited debates which preceded the last Reform Bill.'[81] *Blackwood's Magazine* considered the result a 'blow to the dignity of the House of Commons'.[82] The *Derby and Chesterfield Reporter* complained that 'a specially working man's constituency cares little for a working man's candidate [Walton]. It is such elections as these that give the impulse to the Conservative reaction'.[83] In Stoke, William Owen, like many advocates of labour, was appalled by the eccentricities of popular opinion. The *Potteries Examiner* considered that the borough had committed 'political suicide'.[84] The *Sentinel* believed the result had harmed the extension of the franchise to the counties by destroying confidence in the working class.[85] The result coincided with the election at Tipperary of John Mitchell, an insurgent who had once been transported for taking part in the 1848 Irish uprising. The *Standard* wondered: 'Are we to despair of household suffrage because it has given us an ex-convict for Tipperary and an ex-barrister for Stoke?' It contented itself, however, that Kenealy in the Commons 'will probably be more harmless than he was on the platform. There is no such institution in the world for the suppression of bores, quacks and public nuisances as that into which he has suicidally thrust himself'. The *Pall Mall Gazette* was of the same opinion.[86]

Most of the accounts blamed the newly enfranchised working men for voting Kenealy into Parliament. *The Times* commented 'In Stoke we decidedly come across the residuum, and rather heavy and thick it seems to be'.[87] It would, however, be as well to be cautious about this. It was convenient for the middle-class press to blame this event on the newly enfranchised, to maintain the belief that the middle classes would not behave in such a way. In fact, many of Kenealy's supporters, as we have seen, were both middle-class and respectable. Attendance at his meetings was not restricted to one class. Furthermore, the indifference of the Hanley colliers implies that his cause did not appeal to all working men. It is difficult to establish with any accuracy the class composition of his electors and their motives because of the new Secret Ballot. The *Sentinel*, however, mentioned the potters and ironworkers who were a large part of the electorate:

> The men who could elect a Kenealy are everywhere regarded as being of the lowest class ... unbiased men of sense everywhere speak of them as being the very residuum which is found more or less in every town but the universal amazement is that in the Potteries it should constitute one third of the voters on the register.[88]

Kenealy probably took votes from all classes and from Liberal and Conservative alike. In a constituency like Stoke, however, the working-class vote bulked large.

Was Kenealy's election a victory for Tichbornism? The evidence points in several directions. There was clearly strong sympathy for Kenealy and the Claimant, and the trial was still fresh in people's minds. On the other hand, the local Liberals were in disarray and the election provided the newly enfranchised the opportunity to vote against the political classes. Another possibility is that Kenealy was elected as a joke or, as the *Sentinel* noted, as a way of getting back at the Lord Chief Justice.[89] Political behaviour at by-elections tends to be different from general elections. Party allegiances become stronger when a whole Parliament is elected. The Stoke by-election did not make any difference to Disraeli's hold on power. Therefore voters could afford to vote for whom they liked at that particular time. Middle-class Liberals could abandon Walton and a third of the Stoke electorate could take a stand on the Tichborne trial. Had Kenealy contested Stoke at a General Election, the results might have been very different.

8

Tichborne Radicalism

Kenealy's election as, in effect, a Tichborne MP marked the peak of the Claimant's movement. The year that followed was filled with activity as he entered Parliament and supporters pushed for the Claimant's release. Petitions to Parliament were signed in greater numbers and demonstrations held all over the country. The Magna Charta Association took its place amongst the metropolitan radical clubs of the 1870s and 1880s. Kenealy hoped it would become a mass organisation capable of giving him real political power. He would accept no rivals in the leadership of the Tichborne movement and during 1875 the cause flourished. Some other radicals were so impressed by its themes and ability to energise the people that they became involved. Ironically, a movement that was in many ways deeply conservative managed to become one of the leading radical causes of the later nineteenth century.

Historians used to assume that after the defeat of Chartism in 1848, radical politics declined until the revival of socialism in the 1880s and then the emergence of independent labour politics. In fact, a lively opposition culture existed on the fringes of mid-Victorian life.[1] The causes varied; proponents of one reform often violently disagreed with supporters of other kinds of social change. There were busybodies and there were practical idealists. Agitators sought to stop their contemporaries drinking or abusing the Lord's Day. Trade unions lobbied for political recognition and labour representation in parliament. Republicans led by Charles Bradlaugh challenged the legitimacy of modern monarchy. Nor was Bradlaugh impressed by organised religion. His *National Reformer* supported secularism, a truly shocking creed in a devoutly religious age. And if that was not enough, Bradlaugh (probably the most significant radical of his time) also promoted birth control. Josephine Butler and the Ladies National Association were at war with Victorian hypocrisy and the double standard of sexuality. They attacked the Contagious Diseases Acts, which permitted the medical inspection of prostitution as a way of preventing the spread of venereal disease amongst soldiers in garrison towns (women, they pointed out, were hypocritically perceived as bearers of disease but not their male clients). Like the anti-Vaccination movement, they believed the state had no right to interfere with individuals in this way. More discretely, feminists such as Millicent Fawcett lobbied parliamentarians for the female franchise. Meanwhile, some (though not many) were becoming aware of a German intellectual who had been toiling in the British Museum. Karl Marx analysed the workings of capitalism and the meaning of history itself. He promoted the International Working Men's Association, the harbinger of a new ideology, socialism. In London's Tottenham Court Road, William Townshend, leader of the Manhood Suffrage League and the Soho O'Brienites (followers of the Chartist Bronterre O'Brien), earnestly promoted socialism and currency reform whilst over in Clerkenwell Green, the Patriotic Club included Irish nationalism amongst its causes. Further away, on Mile End Waste, agitators proclaimed anarchism as the way of the future. London did not have a monopoly on radicalism (much of this could be found elsewhere in the country) but its provision of freethinking bohemian spaces was unique. Somehow a movement to help a working-class man inherit an aristocratic title took its place amongst the radical causes of its day. Radicals such as Bradlaugh and George Potter dis-associated themselves from Kenealy but many had affinities with ideas in the *Englishman* and with the central thrust of the movement, its concern with civil liberties and fairness.[2]

After the optimism of the Stoke campaign, Kenealy's parliamentary career was (almost inevitably) a disappointment. It began in a farcical way with a debate over whether he should be allowed in at all because he had no one to introduce him, as was the custom. Disraeli, however, proposed that the rules be dispensed with in this instance.[3] After this, Kenealy went on to become the most mocked figure in the House of Commons. He almost immediately moved for a commission on the Tichborne trial. He criticised the judges for setting up a 'reign of terror', based much of his argument on the Dowager's recognition and insisted that letters ascribed to Orton in the trial were forgeries. Disraeli and John Bright attacked his use of evidence. In the event, the motion for an inquiry secured only one vote – from Purcell O'Gorman. Kenealy and Whalley had to act as tellers and therefore could not vote.[4] Clearly Parliament would not be easily moved.

In some respects, the vote was the watershed for the Tichborne move-ment. At a local level, it remained strong for the rest of the decade but in Parliament Kenealy was to pursue a lone, maverick course. A year later, his alliance with Whalley was over. The latter upbraided him in the Commons for his bad advocacy and failure to call the Orton sisters (who had denied that the Claimant was their brother) to testify in the trial.[5] Whalley also refused to become President of the Magna Charta Association, claiming that Kenealy's principles 'are in direct opposition to my own'.[6]

Kenealy brought several Magna Charta concerns to the Commons. He twice introduced Bills calling for triennial Parliaments without success and frequently raised issues of legal injustice.[7] Partly spurred on by concern for the Claimant in Dartmoor, Kenealy spoke on prison conditions, arguing that convicts were treated like wild beasts.[8] Despite the importance of the drink interest to the Tichborne cause, he loosely associated himself with, if not temperance, then at least strict regulation of alcohol.[9] He criticised taxes and supported the abolition of the Game Laws.[10] His appearances became infrequent and his arguments contradictory. Over the Royal Titles Bill (to make Queen Victoria Empress of India), he originally 'objected to the title of Empress because it was a despotic one'. Yet two months later, he said that 'He ... wanted to know what harm there was in calling Her Majesty Empress of India? He should like to have had some of the evil results pointed out. He had not heard any'.[11] Kenealy's veneration for monarchy was extremely confused. More consistent with his political line was his opposition to expenditure for royal visits. He failed in his attempt to stop Parliament voting money for the Prince of Wales's visit to India as the Prince was only going in a private capacity.[12] It was not unusual for radicals to attack the wastefulness of public expenditure on ceremonial occasions. Kenealy did not, however, devote a great deal of energy to his parliamentary career. Instead he concentrated on the *Englishman*, his theology and the Tichborne tours. Despite his presence in the Commons, the Tichborne movement remained essentially extra-parliamentary.

After Kenealy's election in February 1875, the Easter Monday demonstration in Hyde Park (which was to become an annual event) was a triumph. *The Times* noted that it had a better turnout than the demonstrations of the Land and Labour League or the movement for the release of the Fenian prisoners.[13] It set the number present at 30,000. There were delegations from the Tichborne Release Associations and Magna Charta Associations. Processions began in Kensal Green, Tooting, Balham, Greenwich, the potteries of West London and Hammersmith – all areas with high working-class populations. *The Times* reporter noted that most of the demonstrators were working men (or 'the lowest class of labourers'), although it claimed 'without the slightest assistance from the Irish element'. The report also noted that there were many 'respectable' people present as well as a few belonging to 'the small tradesman and artisan classes'. This suggests that the Tichborne movement was cross-class, appealing to many sectors of the community but, like a social pyramid, mushrooming out at the working-class level.

At least two of the bands were dressed up – one as Hussars and another in a costume resembling that of the Volunteer force. Banners maintained the usual Tichborne themes: 'I will repay, saieth the Lord', 'Fools and Fanatics' and a portrait of the Lord Chief Justice surrounded by flames. A portrait of Kenealy was titled 'The English Garibaldi'. Kenealy and Onslow spoke. The *Pall Mall Gazette* was dubious about the significance of the meeting, ascribing its high turnout to the fact that it was Easter Monday and an excuse for a good day out, but even so was forced to admit that the Tichborne cause still attracted considerable support.[14] Walter Bagehot was impressed by the turnout and ascribed it to the latent anti-Catholicism of the working class.[15] Kenealy and Onslow went on to address three thousand people at Bristol the following day.[16]

No membership figures for the Tichborne movement exist, which means discussion of support remains impressionistic. Between 1874 and 1886 two hundred and fifty-one Tichborne and Magna Charta organisations came into being. The peak was in 1875, when almost one hundred associations existed at one time. Over one-third of these were concentrated in the London area but membership was truly national, though less strong in Scotland, Ireland and Wales. It was both urban and rural, attracting men and women from all classes but particularly the working class.[17] The movement had clearly lost much of its impetus by 1878 but the longevity of many groups testifies to the obsessive concern of many Tichbornites. Every week during 1875 subscriptions to the Kenealy National Testimonial Fund increased.

Meetings and petitioning continued at local level, based around gathering subscriptions for the Kenealy Testimonial Fund. Meetings took place in any available public venue from the temperance hall to the pub. Many London Magna Charta speakers, including Kenealy, addressed crowds on Mile End Waste (an East End 'speaker's corner' for radicals) at which time the *Englishman* was sold.[18] The reception was usually very good. A South London Magna Chartist claimed that the purpose of the movement was 'to band man and man together for one common good'.[19]

There were further meetings throughout the country. On Easter Monday 1876, the Claimant's wife appeared at a meeting at the Corn Exchange in Ipswich. She was introduced to the meeting as 'Lady Tichborne'. William

Rushbrooke, last of the Ipswich Chartists, took the chair at the well-attended meeting adorned by pictures of the Claimant on the walls.[20]

Local Magna Charta activities proliferated. Many associations mounted their own dramatic and musical entertainments or organised bazaars.[21] In Stoke, a Magna Charta Mutual Defence Association was established for those persecuted for their adherence to the principles of Magna Charta. A Magna Charta Benefit Society (operating like a friendly society) was mooted on several occasions. T. Kimber of Rotherhithe actually established a Magna Charta Benefit Club on principles of mutual assistance: 'First, to render a certain amount of assistance to each other when laid up by sickness, and, secondly, to unite in political agitation for an improvement of our condition while in health.' Each member was to pay 7d. a week to a Sick Club, a penny of which went to the funds of the Magna Charta Association. There was even a scheme in which Magna Chartists would cooperate in growing their own potatoes. In 1886, Sheffield and Nottingham members joined forces to create the Magna Charta Working Men's Patent Producing Society which was intended to aid small investors. None of these projects lasted long but all were attempts to turn Magna Chartism into a way of life.[22]

The movement was strong enough in 1875 for Kenealy to purchase Doughty Hall in Holborn to function as a centre for the movement. Even at this time of relative success, however, the movement had to come to terms with disappointment. It was hoped that Kenealy's son, Ahmed, would repeat his father's victory in Stoke by standing at a by-election. Initially, Ahmed considered Norwich as a seat and began a campaign speaking in favour of triennial parliaments and against state education (which the Liberals had introduced in 1870). He denounced all forms of patronage and sinecures and advocated increased wages for public servants: postmen, telegraph clerks, soldiers, policemen (a possible indication of those he thought might vote for him). Placards were printed both in Conservative and in Liberal colours to draw votes from both sides. The elder Kenealy spoke on his behalf in the city, describing him as someone who was not anti-Liberal or anti-Tory but anxious to represent independent men from all parties.[23] Ahmed, however, withdrew before the election took place. Instead, he opted for Hartlepool in July 1875, offering himself as a 'Working Man's candidate on Independent principles', advocating the Magna Charta programme. He came bottom of the poll with 259 votes. The *Englishman* sourly blamed the defeat on a conspiracy between the two major parties and complained that working men were under the control of 'shams and rogues' like Alexander

MacDonald and George Potter (editor of the *Beehive*). As a result of this remark, Potter sued Kenealy, who maintained disingenuously that he was not the editor of the *Englishman* and that he was referring to another 'George Potter'. The charge was dismissed and Kenealy was cheered as he left the court.[24]

The following year, Ahmed stood at Burnley as an 'Independent People's candidate, prepared to fight the battle of the Middle and Working Classes against the Capitalists who have won power, position and wealth'. Apart from Magna Charta, he emphasised the question of safety in the mines and the folly of giving a grant to the Prince of Wales for his visit to India whilst slums existed at home. Although two thousand came to hear him speak in a factory, he retired before the poll rather than split the Liberal vote and let the Tory in. He never stood for Parliament again. In 1877, Thomas Thomas, secretary of the Grimsby Magna Charta Association, decided to stand at a by-election in the constituency but again retired rather than split the vote in favour of the Tories. It is clear from these two examples that at elections the Tichborne movement was courting the Liberal or Radical vote. It did no good, however, and Edward Kenealy remained the sole Magna Charta MP.[25] Ahmed went on to edit Kenealy's *Staffordshire News* and then became a sub-editor on the *Potteries Examiner*. In 1880, G. B. Skipworth considered contesting North Lincolnshire as an anti-Vaccinator and Tichbornite. The Tichbornite and Radical C. J. Atkinson also considered standing in Clerkenwell in 1884. There were even ludicrous hopes that the Claimant would contest Nottingham in 1880.[26]

Worse was to follow as the movement could barely remain united. One supporter, M. A. Orr, tired at the corruption he perceived, had already left and founded his own short-lived paper, *The True Briton: The Avowed Enemy and Antidote to Dr Kenealy's 'Englishman'*. It lasted for seven issues from April to June 1874. Orr claimed to have been the original publisher of the *Englishman* and to have organised its distribution throughout Britain. He left on discovering that the paper's proprietor, advertised as 'George Hunter, LLD' of Gray's Inn, was in fact Kenealy's son, Maurice. Kenealy was obviously trying to control the paper without appearing to be too closely associated with it.[27]

Kenealy also fell out with Biddulph, who disassociated himself from him, claiming his 'revolutionary principles [were] utterly repugnant to my ideas of order'. He stayed away from all platform demonstrations, though he continued to believe in the Claimant.[28] Another fracture in the movement was caused by a quarrel with T. M. Evans of the *Leicester Evening News*. Evans, who had done a great deal to build up the standing of the movement and Kenealy himself (through publicity and the organisation of the lecture tour), was accused of having purloined funds in 1875.[29] Kenealy recovered most of the money owed but only after Evans had turned his new Tichborne paper, the *Flag of Justice*, into a vehicle to attack him. For this he was disparaged at a Tichborne meeting in Bristol that ritually tore a copy of Evans's newspaper into shreds.[30] Evans was never reconciled to the movement. In November 1876, the Magna Charta Congress was riven by allegations of a conspiracy to get rid of Kenealy. E. W. Bailey and Samuel C. E. Goss were accused of attempting to take over, the plan being hatched with members of the Battersea Magna Charta Association. Bailey, in particular, was accused of attempting to gain control of the *Englishman*. In all, fifteen were expelled.[31] The followers of Bailey formed the short-lived National Magna Charta Association.[32]

At a meeting in Swansea, a new phenomenon began: the barracking of Kenealy and other Tichborne speakers by 'roughs'.[33] It was as though Kenealy had been raised up by the people to mock authority only to be destroyed by them (although violence and disorder at public events and speeches was not unusual in the nineteenth century). In October 1875, when Kenealy was giving a lecture in the Assembly Rooms at North Shields, a fight broke out between his supporters and a group of young men. Several people were hurt after being thrown downstairs. On leaving, Kenealy was attacked by a mob, who tried to beat him with sticks, but he was protected by the police. Six were taken into custody. There was another disturbance the following month when H. B. Harding, the Tichborne lecturer, was addressing the Croydon Tichborne Release Association. Three hundred had paid for admission but the meeting was interrupted by a large group of youths with sticks who tried to get possession of the platform. After a violent fight, the youths were ejected and the lecture continued behind locked doors.[34]

Kenealy's relationship with Stoke also began to deteriorate. He addressed an audience of three thousand constituents in Hanley in May 1875 on the Magna Charta programme. Only half the meeting, however, supported the resolution of confidence in him. A meeting in Stoke a few days later was constantly disturbed by ruffians and there were shouts of 'Give us politics, not abuse'.[35] Touring the constituency in 1877, he received an even more hostile reception. Speaking under the chairmanship of Councillor Booth in Hanley Town Hall, he was received by a mixture of cheers and groans.

When Booth said that Kenealy had 'represented' the borough, there were shouts of 'misrepresented'. When a vote of confidence in Kenealy was moved at the end, less than half the house voted for it and the meeting broke up in disorder. Two days later Kenealy completely failed to get a hearing in Burslem. An assault was made on the platform and he was effectively chased out of town, leaving on the next train. When he addressed an audience in Stoke, crackers were fired and several fights broke out. A man wearing a mask resembling Kenealy held aloft a baggy umbrella. Kenealy had become an object of mockery. Undaunted, he accused the hecklers of being hired by the capitalists and claimed to be a friend of the people. He was forced to leave after fifteen minutes because he could not get a hearing.[36] Speaking in the Potteries six months later, the response was unchanged. Few supported votes of confidence in him and at Stoke he was again heckled all the way to the railway station.[37] Nevertheless, the same month he set up an election fund, dispatched collecting boxes, asked supporters to subscribe a million sixpences for his re-election and established a short-lived local newspaper, the *Staffordshire News*.[38]

Elsewhere, Tichbornites remained very active. In 1875, Edward Kimber, a lawyer from Greenwich, took up the cause of the Claimant. He wrote to Gladstone, his local MP, and challenged him to address a public meeting to prove he acted correctly in advising, when Prime Minister, that the Claimant should be prosecuted. Gladstone denied any responsibility for the case or its outcome.[39] As a solicitor, Kimber addressed many of the problematic issues that the case had raised. In 1879, after becoming solicitor for the Claimant, he obtained a fiat for a writ of error in the case from the Attorney-General. The objection was that it was wrong to make the two seven year sentences run sequentially rather than concurrently, as they were substantially for the same offence. This action was taken independently of Kenealy. The case was not heard until June 1880, when it was dismissed. Kimber embraced the Magna Charta Association informing an audience in the Stepney Temperance Hall in 1875: 'At present, there is a great need of the formation of a new political party. We are practically governed by an oligarchy, and if the Magna Charta Association is successful, then that oligarchy will be destroyed.'[40]

William Cobbett the younger continued to support the Claimant with all the obsessive qualities of the crank. He obtained a writ against the Governor of Millbank Prison on the grounds that the Claimant had been illegally imprisoned. He made a rambling presentation to the court that few could follow. He had only seen the Claimant once but was convinced by 'his quick step, his dark complexion, his resemblance to Tom Sayers' that he was genuine.[41] The court had no trouble siding with the defendant. Cobbett, together with H. B. Harding, also attempted to serve the Governor of Millbank Prison with a writ on the grounds that the Claimant had been illegally detained. The Governor told them if they didn't get out, he'd keep them as well. The pair then tried a further writ maintaining they had been threatened with imprisonment, which was treated (quite properly) with laughter and derision in the court. Harding and Cobbett did not turn up for the hearing so the writ failed.[42]

F. G. Longman, the anti-vaccinator, also took up the cause. He unsuccessfully petitioned the Home Secretary from his home in Clerkenwell that he should receive a deputation about the release of the Claimant. He also wrote to Disraeli about reopening the case without success.[43] Longman later went on to edit his own Tichborne paper, the *Tichborne and People's Ventilator*, at the same time as he was prosecuted for refusing to vaccinate his children.[44]

The *Englishman* continued unchanged, edited by Maurice Kenealy under his father's supervision. Sales figures are not available, though its longevity (1874–86) suggests a solid but unquantifiable bedrock of support. There may have been some falling off from 1875, when it sold 70,000 copies a week, as it had to double its advertising to two pages in August 1876. The content remained the same, rehearsing endlessly Magna Charta themes. It became a clearing house for individualist and anti-statist forms of radicalism. The paper was nostalgic for the face to face relationships of an earlier pre-industrial and pre-urban era before the rise of the anonymous state. In an article entitled 'Dangers of Centralization', it argued that an overworked Parliament was taking over the duties of local government, dating this process from the Poor Law Amendment Act of 1834. It complained that schools, hospitals and workhouses had been taken away from the guardians of the poor and transferred to the Poor Law Commission. In response, Kenealy promised to abolish the workhouse system.[45] 'School Board Tyranny' was condemned, especially the imprisonment of parents too poor to send their children to school.[46] The paper tended to associate the rise of the modern state with the introduction of income tax and Kenealy came to support the Anti-Income Tax League.[47] He declared that he wanted to relieve all persons of taxation, with the exception of landowners and capitalists.

The paper settled on a number of issues, which it considered to be not only against the public interest but also an invasion of privacy and the natural autonomy of the citizen. Apart from school boards and income tax, it condemned the Lunacy Laws, food adulteration, the Contagious Diseases Acts and compulsory vaccination. It was also anti-capitalist in the sense of being against monopolies. This was the language of traditional radicalism and was common to many contemporary groups. For example, in one of her pamphlets against the Contagious Diseases Acts, Josephine Butler claimed that Parliament in passing the offensive legislation had 'invaded and trampled on the liberties of the people'.[48] Tichbornites agreed. Kenealy voted in favour of repealing the legislation in Parliament and his paper condemned it for compelling women to become prostitutes. The *Englishman* also drew attention to the fate of Mrs Percy, who committed suicide rather than be inspected.[49] In the same way it considered compulsory vaccination tyrannous and supported those brought to trial because of their opposition to it.[50]

The *Englishman* supported 'the people' defined as those who were not landowners or large-scale capitalists. The approach was often aggressive and sensationalist:

> This has been the one, sole, and selfish cry of the Mercantile classes, the Manufacturers, the Capitalists, the Stockbrokers – GOLD! GOLD! GOLD! Well, the Gold has come, and with its usual concomitants, Vice, Poverty, Misery.[51]

The paper tended to be ambivalent on labour issues, praising strikes that had been averted. It supported Joseph Arch and his Agricultural Labourers Union as well as the cabmen who were locked out in 1876. On one occasion, Kenealy gave a lecture in aid of the Pontypridd miners. Another time, the *Englishman* received a letter from a miner stating: 'I wish Dr KENEALY were our Leader so that we should not be robbed as we are being robbed.'[52]

Initially, the paper supported Queen Victoria and claimed she was 'in no way answerable for the fearful crime of which Sir Roger was made the unhappy victim'. Many Tichbornites seemed to feel like this. One demonstration in 1878 moved from Trafalgar Square to Buckingham Palace where there were cheers for both the Claimant and the Queen. By this time, however, the *Englishman* was cooling towards the Queen, perhaps because of her lack of support. Kenealy, although never a republican, came to support the reduction of her grant. He may have kept aloof from republicanism because it was dominated by Charles Bradlaugh, to whom he was bitterly hostile. As it was, in 1880, the Magna Charta programme still retained the proposal to 'restore the Crown to the Queen'.[53]

The *Englishman* was never very energetic about the clause in the Magna Charta programme about votes for women, but it did feature a series entitled 'Women at Work' and in 1876 complained:

> There are single women in this country who have ten thousand a year income, and who have consequently the deepest interest in its welfare and in its government, yet who do not possess the right of voting at parliamentary elections, while their coachmen, footmen, boot-cleaners, cobblers, gardeners, and scavengers, who, it may be, can neither write, and who have no more independent judgement than a shoal of herrings, if they happen to be householders or lodgers, are allowed the privilege or the right which is denied to their employers.[54]

The *Englishman* foregrounded the support of women for the Claimant, on one occasion claiming they were more receptive to the word of God.[55]

The paper distanced itself from other political groupings, contrasting attachment to 'party' with its 'patriotism'. Gladstone was attacked on the grounds that he was a slave to the Vatican, despite his anti-Catholicism.[56] It was more ambivalent over the Conservatives, condemning Disraeli's government for having no policies, but later claiming the Tories were 'far truer friends of the working classes than the Whigs'. The paper supported the Conservative Government during the Eastern Crisis of 1877–78.[57]

The large demonstrations continued. There was a strong turnout to escort Kenealy to Westminster for the opening of Parliament in February 1876. *The Times* mocked the event, noting that most people were there in a 'sight-seeing, sight-making spirit'. It also, however, considered the demonstration to be an argument against the extension of the franchise that had taken place in 1867 and thus by implication allowed its significance as a working-class cause.[58] That year's Easter Monday demonstration also attracted a large crowd. Deputations came from largely working-class areas in London. One of the banners showed how the world upside down theme was maintained: 'Would you be surprised to hear we are some of the fools and fanatics of Battersea?' The Edgware Road branch banner presented Kenealy as 'Equity' with the Claimant appealing to Justice. Other banners celebrated Kenealy as 'Yet another Cromwell', whilst another bluntly proclaimed 'Release Tichborne, secure triennial parliaments and the prosperity of the people'.[59]

From the start, Kenealy was unable to achieve the control over the movement he craved and as early as 1875 meetings took place that were not under
his aegis. For example, in July 1875, an open-air meeting was held in Mr
Warren's cricket field in Notting Hill, attended by the social explorer,
Charles Maurice Davies. On arrival, Davies found himself forestalled by a
Tichbornite who wanted him to sign a petition for the Claimant. The
supporter 'had a shiny black frock-coat on, like a well-to-do artisan out for
a holiday'. For Davies, however, 'The presiding genius of the place' was Mrs
Warren, the wife of the owner of the field. She organised the installation of
a greengrocer's cart, which served as a rostrum for the speakers. A table and
chairs were placed on it and another table was placed below the cart for the
Tichborne petition. With the artisan, she attached a scroll to the cart, which
used the words of Psalm 35:11: 'False witnesses did rise up against me. They
laid to my charge things that I knew not.' The makeshift nature of the meeting is important. It was relatively easy to organise and for workmen like
the artisan not only to participate in but to lead. The chairman was a Mr
Saunders who also described himself as a working man. Davies compared
his accent to that of Sam Weller.[60] The speakers were Onslow and the Reverend
Buckingham (a clergyman who had known Orton in the early 1850s and
denied that he was the Claimant). The latter alleged he was being offered
bribes by Jesuits to say the Claimant was Orton. The mood of the meeting
can be shown by the way in which Davies caused 'bad odour' when he jotted
a note in his pocket book and was suspected of being a detective spying on
the meeting. The majority of those present (the *Tichborne Gazette* put the
number at five thousand) seemed unanimous in their support for the
Claimant, although 'there was a good deal of quiet chaff on the outskirts of
the crowd'. Davies felt that it was not the 'monster meeting' it claimed to be
but was impressed by the large number of people the cause had brought
together.[61]

By the middle of 1875, there was considerable dissatisfaction with Kenealy.
It was felt Kenealy was trying to use the Tichborne movement for his own
ends. At best, the Magna Charta principles were a distraction from the release
of the Claimant. It was with this in mind that Anthony Biddulph, the sole
member of the Tichborne family to believe in the Claimant, formed the
Chief Central Tichborne Committee in May 1875.[62] The group harked back
to the Tichborne movement of 1872–73, containing many of the same personnel (including G. B. Skipworth and Lord Rivers) and devoting itself solely
to the Claimant. The group met at the Queen's Hotel, St Martins-le-Grand,

Lord Rivers

owned by Tichbornite, William Quartermaine East. Its strategy contrasted with that of Kenealy's organisation. The aim was to secure by '"quiet, steady, constitutional, but persevering means", Sir Roger's release and his restoration to his rights'. Biddulph insisted that Magna Chartism and Tichbornism were different things and rejected Kenealy's anti-Catholicism. H. B. Harding read the regulations at the first meeting, which insisted that their movement 'avoid all political and religious subjects'. Biddulph's rejection of anti-Catholicism is understandable, as he was a Catholic but Harding's position is more intriguing as he had been an avowed ultra-Protestant who had been involved in opposing Catholic tendencies in the Church of England.[63] The new committee avoided the intemperate language of the other Tichborne petitions and pursued respectability. J. Charles Cox of Belper supported the new committee because: 'I do not believe in mixing up the Tichborne case with a bundle of windy and utterly contradictory political nostrums, some of them Radical, some Tory.'[64] As its organ, the group revived the *Tichborne Gazette*, which had ceased publication in October 1874. It was to 'be conducted in that spirit of order and respect for authority which Sir Roger is well known to have been guided by'. Biddulph became president of the committee and Harding edited the newspaper.[65]

The movement rapidly developed a strongly anti-Kenealy line, rebuking him for his 'selfishness, incapacity as a leader, and positive wickedness as a man'.[66] The *Tichborne Gazette* championed T. M. Evans in the quarrel over the missing funds and incorporated his paper, the *Flag of Justice*. Apart from the *Gazette*, the group's activities were composed of petitioning and the publication of pamphlets. Unfortunately, sales of the *Tichborne Gazette* had dropped by December 1875; the paper had to close and with it went the Chief Central Tichborne Committee, although Biddulph continued to agitate on behalf of the Claimant.

A new initiative emerged the same month with the National Tichborne Release Association. This appears to have been the last vestige of the movement of 1872–73. It was independent of Kenealy, although he was present at its conference in December 1875 at the Philharmonic Hall, Southampton.[67] Its leading figure was G. E. Gray of Southampton, who had looked after the Claimant's children in 1872 and was later an executive member of the Magna Charta Association.[68] Biddulph was persuaded to become a trustee. Gray was devoted to collecting funds, organising petitions and gathering further evidence. Even this movement, however, proved to be fissiparous, despite the relatively uncontentious goal of the Claimant's release. Edward Kimber, the Claimant's solicitor, fell out with the rest over the idea of prosecuting Lady Radcliffe for perjury. Biddulph was more concerned to prosecute the witnesses from Wapping. Kimber was under the instructions of the Claimant's wife but Harding disliked his lack of chivalry in pursuing a vendetta against Lady Radcliffe.[69] The main achievement of the organisation was the publication of a series of Tichborne pamphlets, which appeared throughout 1876. These were all edited by Harding and produced evidence as to the identity of the Claimant.[70]

In 1876–77 attention was directed towards Australia, where it was claimed Arthur Orton had been found. William Cresswell, a lunatic in the Paramatta Asylum, New South Wales, who had lived around Wagga Wagga, claimed to be Orton. Guildford Onslow dedicated himself to bringing him to England and the Claimant in prison, on being shown a photograph of Cresswell, recognised him as his one-time friend. Biddulph, however, remained sceptical. In December 1877, a new organisation with which he was associated, the Provincial Friends of Sir Roger Tichborne, passed a resolution claiming there was no evidence to link Cresswell and Orton.[71] The reason for this was that the Orton sisters (using money subscribed by Tichbornites) had been sent to Australia and had failed to recognise him. The Cresswell question continued to excite many Tichbornites. In 1880, the Midland and Northern Counties Conference of the Magna Charta Association voted to try and bring him over to England.[72]

The resolutions of the Provincial Friends confirmed how divided the movement had become. They concluded that because of the actions of Kenealy, Onslow, Kimber and Quartermaine East further effort in the cause was useless.[73] The organisation also criticised the radicalism of Edward Foster and the *National Independent* (established in Leeds in 1875 as the *Yorkshire Independent*). Foster's paper advocated the Tichborne cause but also featured other radical causes such as land reform, abolition of the Contagious Diseases Acts and compulsory vaccination as well as what were in effect the old demands of the People's Charter. Heavily influenced by the Chartist F. R. Lees, the paper lasted until 1889 and was one of the most important Tichborne newspapers. Many of its concerns resembled Magna Chartism but, characteristically, Kenealy urged supporters to repudiate it.[74] Foster, however, was not the only major radical to support the cause. As important as the coverage in The *Englishman* was the support of *Reynolds's Newspaper*, the most successful radical paper of its day, which came out in favour of the Claimant and presented a favourable impression of the cause to its large working-class readership. The support of *Reynolds's* was a major factor in the longevity of the Tichborne cause.

Kenealy attempted to keep the movement under his own hegemony but was never successful and the cause became a vehicle for other radicals. This is best illustrated through the involvement of John De Morgan with the cause. De Morgan was one of the most notorious radicals of the 1870s yet remains a shadowy figure. He was a popular lecturer, activist and pamphleteer from Ireland whose energy enabled him to briefly make a great impression on radical British politics. In 1871 he was active in the Cork ironworkers strike and was a supporter of Irish nationalism.[75] He was also vice-president of the local society for the repeal of the Compulsory

John De Morgan

Vaccination Acts and established a branch of the militantly secular International Working Men's Association in Cork. The latter led to his ruin, as
he was denounced by both the Protestant and Catholic clergy as a promoter
of atheism. The coachmakers who had originally joined were persuaded to
repudiate all connection with the organisation and the pupils who came to
him for elocution lessons abandoned him.[76]

   Shadowed by the police and without funds, he moved to England where
he promoted republicanism on Teesside and, in December 1872, established
the National Republican Brotherhood, earning the support of the Tichbornite, G. B. Skipworth. His effectiveness in the cause of republicanism, then
at its height, was, however, marred by a falling out with Charles Bradlaugh,

the leader of the movement. The cause of the dispute was over the rival organisation and De Morgan's claim that republicanism was not irreligious, which antagonised Bradlaugh and his atheist followers.[77] He maintained his links with the International, speaking at the Manchester Congress in 1873 in favour of land nationalisation, and earned his living as a popular lecturer addressing audiences in temperance halls and mechanics institutes.[78] He championed the common people against the interfering tentacles of the state. His most notorious intervention was his leadership of the movement against the enclosure of common lands in the 1870s.

The Commoners' movement drew on wide popular support. The attempt by private interests to enclose common land that belonged to the people represented a violation of their rights. Shortly after arriving in London, De Morgan was arrested, along with the radicals, J. P. McDonnell and George Odger, for trying to speak at a republican event in Hyde Park, as all such public meetings were banned. The three were quickly released and became heroes for upholding the rights of the people to assemble in public.[79] In December 1875, De Morgan took up the land question again. When a lord of the manor enclosed part of Hackney Downs, he gathered a large crowd to destroy the fences.[80] The same thing happened six months later on Plumstead Common.

The lords of the manor (the Queen's College, Oxford) had decided to lease Plumstead Common permanently to the military. Two other individuals, William Tongue and Edwin Hughes, had also bought common land from the lords of the manor. On 1 July, De Morgan assembled a group of between two and three hundred supporters.[81] After making a speech about commoners' rights, De Morgan set about pulling down the fence that Hughes had erected. He was arrested and sentenced at Maidstone to one month's imprisonment. His release before the end of the sentence led to a demonstration in his honour on Plumstead Common at which over 20,000 people were present. De Morgan appeared alongside the Tichbornite lawyer, Edward Kimber. The common was later secured for the people when it was purchased by the Metropolitan Board of Works for £9,000. Hence De Morgan could claim a great victory.[82] He had another success the following year preventing the lords of the manor from laying rails over Hunslett Common in Leeds.[83] De Morgan then formed the Commons Protection League and further struggles took place in Banstead, Clapham, Oldham, Putney, Richmond, Stockwell, Walton and Wimbledon.[84]

In addition, De Morgan edited several newspapers. The first was the *People's Advocate and National Vindicator of Right versus Wrong*, which first appeared on 19 June 1875 and was issued weekly. It promised to 'maintain the right of the People to the Franchise, Shorter Parliaments and the payment of members'. Further it demanded 'LAW REFORM: justice to be free to all; magistrates and judges to be elected by the People; labour disputes to be tried by a jury'. It also embraced trade unionism, republicanism, land reform and the anti-vaccination movement.[85] After a dispute with the proprietors, he commenced another paper in 1876 entitled *De Morgan's Monthly*, which he initially edited in jail while serving the sentence for the Plumstead Common riots. In 1877, he used the paper to promote his People's Political Union, which was intended to secure independent working-class representation.[86]

Both of De Morgan's papers gave considerable space to the Tichborne cause. In November 1877, he actually tried to start his own paper, the *Tichbornite*, although it ran for only one issue. Given De Morgan's interests, it was natural that he should become involved with the Tichborne cause and especially with the questions of the law and civil liberties that it raised. The cause was a useful platform as it connected so well with other radical causes. Indeed De Morgan owed his association with the Plumstead dispute to the local Tichborne association, which had asked him to intervene.[87] He proceeded to become one of the most important radicals associated with the Claimant. The day after the verdict, he gave a lecture calling for reform of the law and complained that the judges had no power to inflict two sentences for the same offence.[88] De Morgan's criticisms are an excellent example of the way in which the Tichborne cause brought a radical analysis of the law into focus. He later complained that 'our class-made laws fill our jails with innocent men'.[89]

Thereafter, he was very active in the cause. In 1875, he spoke at a 'Great Indignation Meeting!' on behalf of the Claimant, held outside Barking Road railway station followed by another by Chelsea Suspension Bridge.[90] Well versed in details of the case, De Morgan appears to have been sincere in his support for the Claimant. At a meeting of the Southwark Tichborne Release Association at the Victory pub in Manor Road, he listed the number of questions in the trial that the Claimant had answered truthfully and argued that Lady Radcliffe had lied in court because she was embarrassed about the seduction.[91]

An episode on Wimbledon Common occasioned great controversy. De Morgan called a public meeting on the Common for Sunday 18 July 1875. Sir Henry Peek, the MP for mid-Surrey, decided, however, that the meeting was illegal as it contravened local by-laws. Fortunately, the landlord of the Dox allowed the meeting to be held on land outside his pub. De Morgan spoke for two hours but was later put on trial for 'summoning, holding and attending a public meeting'. Outside the court, the Whitechapel Tichborne Release Association hoisted banners and there were delegations from the Notting Hill and Edgware Road Tichborne Associations. The magistrate decided he was dealing with a bad law and dismissed the case, although he warned against holding another meeting until the law was determined.[92]

Kenealy's attitude to De Morgan's enthusiasm was completely negative.[93] As with T. M. Evans of Leicester and George Whalley, he resented anyone he could not control. Originally, the *People's Advocate*, which devoted at least one of its eight pages to Tichborne, featured items on Magna Charta affairs.[94] However, it included a letter from a Tichbornite who complained, 'The editor of another Tichborne paper once told me that no communication to the *Englishman* that does not further the interest of the Doctor, in addition to supporting the claims of Sir Roger, is welcomed by the editor'.[95] In August 1875, De Morgan tried to attend the Magna Charta Association conference as delegate for Whitechapel but was excluded. Kenealy said he had nothing against De Morgan but would not allow him in for reasons of his own. One delegate left because of the exclusion. The following week, De Morgan was ordered off the premises by Ahmed Kenealy. The Whitechapel Magna Charta Association resolved that Kenealy was not justified in excluding De Morgan and asked that he be given space in the *Englishman*. This did not happen.[96]

De Morgan therefore mounted his own independent campaign in 1877. He launched the short-lived *Tichbornite* in November. He complained that 'Attempts have been made to engraft Political, Social, and Religious views on the Tichborne tree, that the branches have almost weighed down the trunk. We want to cut off these branches, and to place before our readers Tichbornism, pure and simple'. He attributed the numerous splits in the movement to this problem.[97]

Also that year, on April 17, he organised a huge march on the Houses of Parliament to deliver a petition on the Tichborne case. He was informed by the Home Secretary, R. A. Cross, that no one could deliver a petition accompanied by more than ten people. De Morgan was defiant and wrote back saying that the demonstration would take place and warned the police not to come into collision with the people 'for that would be kindling a spark of revolution throughout the country'. Kenealy circulated a notice that the demonstration was illegal and that Magna Charta members should not attend. He compared De Morgan's enterprise to the Gordon Riots of 1780, which had unleashed a disorderly mob on London.[98] As it turned out, the demonstration was quelled by rain.[99] It began in Hyde Park, where De Morgan arrived in a one-horse vehicle and called on the crowd to follow him to Trafalgar Square, where he named a deputation of nine men, including G. B. Skipworth, to proceed with him to Westminster. A large number of police were present but no disorder took place. The Home Secretary agreed to receive the petition, and Whalley took the delegation to the Strangers' Tea Room. It was not the revolution threatened. Considering De Morgan in the tea room, the parliamentary correspondent Henry Lucy commented that it was 'the great and eventful day, which began with menaces and ended with muffins'.[100] R. A. Cross met the De Morgan deputation the following day. De Morgan claimed he had decided to take control of the movement because it was becoming 'too disorderly' as 'the confidence of the public had been shaken in the administration of justice'. Skipworth spoke of the agitation that was sweeping the country, but Cross refused to discuss the merits of the case and the meeting ended.[101]

Two months later, De Morgan was back, convening another Tichborne demonstration in Trafalgar Square. It was badly attended and the band was sent round Charing Cross to try and draw attention to itself. De Morgan promised to bring the government to its knees if something was not done and secured the attendance of one of the Tichborne jury, Charles Dunsby (a hairdresser), who said he had changed his mind.[102] Although the campaign was a damp squib, De Morgan's importance in the movement at this time can be shown by a letter from William Duncan to Onslow in July 1877. Duncan had recently been released from prison, where he had come to know the Claimant. He wrote of the Claimant's miserable condition, subject to constant surveillance, and appealed to Onslow and De Morgan for help. Kenealy was not mentioned.[103]

De Morgan does not appear to have been much concerned with the cause after 1877. Late that year, he was sent to prison on a contempt of court charge during the Hunslett Moor affair. In 1879, he was elected to the Leeds School Board.[104] Not long after, he abandoned Britain for America, where he maintained the cause of Irish nationalism and edited a paper entitled *House and Home*. It claimed to advocate 'the rights of the people against centralisation and monopoly', indicating that his political line remained unchanged.[105] What happened to him thereafter is unclear, although he was later to help the Claimant when he visited America after his release. De

Morgan is significant because he represented an alternative, libertarian Tichbornism to the curious mixture offered by Kenealy.

From 1876 to 1878, foreign policy became the major issue in politics. Like other radical groups, the Tichborne movement was transfixed by the Eastern Question. In itself, this had nothing to do with the Claimant, but it was an issue on which many figures associated with the cause took a stand. An enduring aspect of British foreign policy in the nineteenth century was the determination to resist Russian expansion in the Balkans and the Middle East. This meant supporting the disintegrating Ottoman Empire as a bulwark against Russia. The brutal Turkish suppression of a revolt by Bulgarian nationalists in 1875, however, produced outrage in Britain. Gladstone became the hero of the nonconformist conscience when he denounced what became known as the 'Bulgarian Atrocities'. A large popular movement led by figures such as the journalist W. T. Stead sprang into action in 1876 to denounce Disraeli's failure to act. When the movement staged a demonstration in Hyde Park, the historian Edward Freeman deplored the location because it was associated with the Tichborne cause.[106] The nation was divided over the issue. The situation was transformed in 1877 when Russia declared war on Turkey. Much of public opinion reverted to a pro-Turkish position as Britain hovered on the brink of war with Russia. It was at this moment that a new word entered the English vocabulary to describe the aggressive support for war: 'jingoism'. Some Tichbornites were energetic in the jingo cause but this did not necessarily mean an abandonment of radicalism.

The most significant radical to support the Disraeli line on the Eastern Question was the Scottish journalist Maltman Barry. Barry later became one of the great curiosities of the labour movement – a Tory Marxist.[107] His political position at this time is less easy to define because he was such a shadowy figure who was always suspected of opportunism. In 1871, Barry became the provisional chairman of the newly formed Federal Council of the International Working Men's Association. This enabled him to make the most important political acquaintance of his life, Karl Marx. On the latter's death, he told Eleanor Marx, 'He was more than my master, he was my political maker'. Marx responded to him with genuine warmth, tempered with amused condescension, and provided him with information for newspaper articles. Barry was also a fervent supporter of the Paris Commune and was secretary of the society for the relief and employment of political refugees, which aimed to look after Communards who had left France.

After the departure of John De Morgan, Barry took over the *People's Advocate* in 1876.[108] In its pages, he advocated a radical programme of land nationalisation, republicanism, secular education and law reform as a part of a revolution that would assume physical force proportions unless something was done to ameliorate the condition of the people.[109] He maintained De Morgan's commitment to the Tichborne cause, providing it with publicity. It is, however, difficult to describe him as an avowed Tichbornite and he may have promoted the cause simply because of the number of working-class people who supported it. In any case, his paper only lasted five issues.

He can, nevertheless, be connected to the Tichborne movement because of his extreme Russophobia over the Eastern Question. In this, he was similar to Karl Marx (who, he claimed, taught him 'to be a jingo'). Barry and his mentor were hostile to the Russian intervention in the Balkans and supported Turkish resistance as a defence of liberty. Barry helped popularise Marx's views through his journalism and Marx came to refer to him as his 'factotum'. Barry became in effect the leader of the radical anti-Russian movement. He organised a badly attended a series of London rallies to encourage working-class support for Turkey. The final meeting fell apart in disarray after the platform was overturned by the crowd.

Kenealy and the *Englishman* both managed a complete reversal on the Eastern Question (although it is fair to say that British public opinion did the same thing). In 1875, he claimed that 'Russia is not going to war with us, unless England interferes with the proper, legitimate, and rational designs she has upon Turkey'. In 1877, however, he came out strongly in favour of Disraeli's foreign policy and against the Liberals for encouraging Russia. He defended Turkey over the 'Bulgarian Atrocities'. Russia, he claimed, was in a state of expansion that was a danger to the liberties of Englishmen.[110] In the same way, the *Englishman* in 1876 claimed, 'We desire to see Russia firm in Constantinople for until she gets there we shall never have a chance of peace on earth, or goodwill among men'. Yet two weeks later, it condemned Russia for conspiracy to subvert Turkish power and afterwards did not cease to uphold Turkish territorial integrity.[111]

The anti-Russian line found a response with many Tichbornites. Samuel Charles Edward Goss wrote in the *Englishman* that 'Russia must never hold an inch of Turkish soil'.[112] At a demonstration on 29 December 1877, several Magna Chartists spoke in favour of Maltman Barry and moved resolutions against Russia. These included G. A. Willis, an executive member of the Magna Charta Association. Amongst the societies present were the Chelsea

Tichborne Release Association, the Chelsea Magna Charta Working Men's Club and the Ladies of West Brompton Tichborne Society.[113]

Barry was indefatigable in his agitation, helping disrupt a meeting of the City Neutrality Committee (which advocated peace) in January 1878. He addressed another meeting in the Exeter Hall on 6 February, 1878 when war fever was at its height, which ended with supporters singing 'Rule Britannia' outside the Carlton Club. He had no formal connections, however, with the Conservative Party and criticised what he saw as Disraeli's surrender to Russian claims at the Congress of Berlin when the Eastern Question was temporarily settled after the Russo-Turkish War ended in an armistice.

The Eastern Question continued to excite local Magna Charta groups. In 1880, a Mr Goodman complained to the Marylebone Magna Charta Association that Gladstone had never denounced the Russian atrocities that had been committed.[114] Maltman Barry later became an avowed supporter of the Conservative Party without apparently abandoning his support for labour issues. Like the Tichborne movement, Barry's career shows us that there was no firm distinction between Radicalism and Conservatism in this period.

After the failure of Walton's candidacy in 1875, the Stoke Liberal party was in disarray. By 1880, there were several obvious factions including a Whig group, a labour group, a Tichborne group and a small group devoted to the repeal of the Contagious Diseases Acts.[115] William Woodall and George Melly (whose business problems had eased) became the new candidates, which antagonised those who wanted to see a working-class candidate in Stoke. Henry Broadhurst of the Labour Representation League visited the constituency and claimed there was a good chance for a labour candidate in the area. Melly eventually decided not to stand and it was obvious that a labour candidate should be elected. Alfred Walton was suggested but in the end Henry Broadhurst was nominated by the local trade unions and adopted. As a moderate working-class candidate, he was acceptable to the middle-class leadership. Thus the Liberals were united for the General Election of 1880 in a way that they were not in 1875.

Kenealy took account of this, claiming, in his address to Stoke electors, that he was a 'Liberal of Liberals' and declaring he was 'for every measure – no matter by whom devised – which will promote the welfare, and bring back the freedom, of which the people of England have been robbed since the first Reform Act'. He criticised the Whigs and Liberals for promising a policy of peace, retrenchment and reform when they had led the country into eleven wars since 1835 and had not adopted any measures of reform except the Secret Ballot and the Municipal Corporations Act. He declared himself against Russian aggression and in favour of Home Rule but made only one brief and inconclusive reference to the Claimant.[116]

His relationship with his constituents had deteriorated, despite an active local Magna Charta Association. His campaign did not go well. When he spoke at the Mechanics Institute at Hanley, his speech was disrupted by a group of roughs who put up a poster urging all to vote for Woodall and Broadhurst. Undeterred, Kenealy continued in his usual egocentric style:

> I am born to be a king of men. (Applause, laughter, 'eh, eh', and general disorder, which lasted for some time.) God never created me to be a flunkey of men. (Renewed howls, hisses, and deafening uproar, mingled with a few shouts of 'Order', 'Give him a fair hearing', 'Sit down, now', 'Claptrap', and more stamping of feet.)

Several attempts were made on the platform and there were shouts of 'Down with KENEALY and Toryism'. Kenealy in response claimed the hecklers had been hired by the Liberal Council.[117]

In the General Election, Woodall and Broadhurst won the two seats in the constituency with 12,130 and 11,379 votes respectively. Kenealy came bottom of the poll with only 1091 votes. This was not an unimpressive figure given that the Tichborne trial, which had propelled him into Parliament, had ended six years before.

It was, nevertheless, a bitter defeat for Kenealy. A few days later, on 16 April 1880, he died of heart failure. For the movement, this was a tragedy. The Kingsland branch reported that it put its banner into mourning.[118] Kenealy's body was taken down to Portslade, where he had lived, and was buried in Hangleton churchyard. The ceremony was private with some Magna Charta members in attendance. In typical Kenealy fashion, a great marble tomb was later placed over the grave.

The Christian Spiritualist and sometime follower of Marx, George Sexton, gave a sermon in his honour at St Augustine's Church in Clapham. Many Tichbornites attended. A hymn written by David Thomas (the editor of the *Homilist* and supporter of the *Englishman*) was sung and one of Kenealy's prayers was recited. Sexton's sermon offered no opinion as to the identity of the Claimant but concentrated on Kenealy's religious writings, which he much admired. He suggested that Kenealy had an affinity with spiritualism and felt that Kenealy's fame would live on as a heroic figure and poet. Afterwards, many were weeping.[119] Copies of the sermon were later sold with the intention of devoting profits to the building of a monument to Kenealy.

There is no doubt that Kenealy was a major inspiration to the Tichborne movement. He was its star attraction – a spellbinding and charismatic fabulist. Without his contribution there would have been no *Englishman* and no Magna Charta Association, and the movement might well have faded away by the late 1870s. All independent Tichbornite activities soon floundered without his impetus. He was, however, also the chief impediment to the success of the movement. His insistence on subordinating it to his own influence meant that he was impossible to work with. We have seen how Whalley, T. M. Evans, Biddulph and De Morgan could not find their way into Kenealy's organisation. His closest allies were members of his own family – especially his sons Ahmed and Maurice. He was an eccentric, a self-deceiver and opportunist, but, along with Bradlaugh, the greatest demagogue of the mid-Victorian era. Perhaps he is best seen as a kind of holy fool made king by the crowd to mock authority. George Sexton was right to comment in his memorial sermon:

The crowd makes a demigod today of a man, whom, tomorrow, it will insult and spurn. Dr Kenealy furnished us with one more illustration of this fact. His popularity waned, Stoke rejected him, the flower faded.[120]

9

After Kenealy

The 1880s were a shock decade of change. During the mid-Victorian years, Liberalism appeared to hold all the cards. Many Conservatives even shared its orthodoxies. Laissez faire, free trade and the Gospels were what got the Victorian middle classes out of bed in the morning. Careers should be open to talent. Independence, duty, manliness, self-help, self-restraint and, above all, character were the foundations of the Victorian world view. Britons lived in an age of progress, science and technological advancement – or so many Victorians thought in 1880. That year Disraeli was defeated in the General Election, and Queen Victoria was forced to make Gladstone her Prime Minister once more. The Liberals were back.

But the confident era of Liberal achievement was over. Ahead were years of challenge and doubt in which new ideas emerged and a new synthesis in politics became necessary. Economic competition from Germany and the United States meant that the golden age of the Victorian boom, in which Britain had the world's markets all to itself, was over. In 1882, the occupation of Egypt set off the Scramble for Africa, dismaying those Liberals who were ambivalent about colonial acquisitions. The Liberal Party was itself torn apart by the issue of Irish Home Rule in 1886. In the 1880s, the Victorians also rediscovered the great poverty that existed in the major cities. The terrible conditions of London's East End, where unemployment was endemic, produced Andrew Mearns's pamphlet *The Bitter Cry of Outcast London* (1883), but there were also revelations about poverty elsewhere in the country. The unemployed rioted in Trafalgar Square and went on a wrecking spree smashing West End shops' windows. In 1885, readers of the *Pall Mall Gazette* were appalled by W. T. Stead's sensational series of articles, 'The Maiden Tribute of Modern Babylon', which revealed the extent of child prostitution. The centre of empire appeared to be rotten. As the old order passed, new ideas began to emerge which sought a different role for the state. Previously, many Victorians (although countenancing state intervention in certain areas) felt that state power was the enemy of liberty; indeed it reeked of European despotism. But in 1883 George R. Sims undertook an investigation of London's East End and concluded that state intervention was necessary in order to promote freedom.

Sims was not ahead of his time. Many thinkers and politicians began to promote an increased role for the state. Joseph Chamberlain had paved the way by taking gas and water under municipal control in Birmingham. Henry Hyndman and the polymathic craftsman William Morris proclaimed the new creed of socialism. The Fabian Society also began to construct schemes for state intervention. We should not overestimate the impact of all this. Socialism was a minority interest until well into the twentieth century.

At a modest level, we can detect echoes of this decade of change in the fortunes of the Magna Charta Association. The death of Kenealy proved to be a blessing in disguise. The *Englishman* and the Magna Charta Association, free from his influence, were able to open their doors to other radical groups and political arguments: land reform, republicanism, Irish Home Rule. Independent Tichbornites moved back into the fold but the Magna Charta Association proved attractive to other Radicals as well. Most strikingly, the association helped in the creation of Henry Hyndman's Democratic Federation, which subsequently became the first major organisation in the revival of British socialism (the Social Democratic Federation). It also provided a vehicle for unusual figures such as Georgina Weldon. Despite its flirtation with socialism, the old Radical thrust of the movement was retained.

Kenealy was not the only loss to the movement. George Whalley had died in October 1878 and Lord Rivers just before the General Election on 31 March 1880. Onslow was to die in August 1882. Yet the cause carried on until 1886. Although these years proved to be ones of decline, the continuation of Tichbornism in any form was surprising. In 1884, a parliamentary candidate canvassing in the West Country was surprised to find he was still being asked his opinion about the case.[1]

After Kenealy's death, his wife was elected President of the Magna Charta Association. This was only a courtesy title and she barely played any role in the movement. Captain Morrison, who had been involved with Magna Charta from the beginning, was elected Vice-President and Maurice Kenealy became Financial Secretary.[2] In effect, Maurice became the leader of the movement and its central organiser. He had been the editor of the *Englishman* virtually since its first issue and it was he who encouraged the absorption of other forms of Radicalism.

Few Radical groups in 1880 could boast the national membership of the Magna Charta Association. This disguised underlying problems, however, as local groups were beginning to close and the momentum was going out of the cause. Nevertheless, new ideas began to emerge.

Whilst the elder Kenealy had opposed republicanism, many individuals within the movement did not. Local branches heard speakers who trumpeted their republican credentials during the brief moment when republicanism flourished as an important popular cause.[3] Soon after the death of Kenealy, the *Englishman* began to feature articles denouncing monarchy.[4] It justified republicanism in two ways. First, it appealed to Christianity:

> The true ideal must be looked for in the utterances of the MAN-CHRIST. He was the greatest Republican the world ever saw, or ever will see. All that OWEN or FOURIER dreamed of Socialism, all that philosophers from PLATO to KENEALY have contemplated for the elevation of our race, is found in the teaching of JESUS of Nazareth. The utterances of papists and others who denounce Republicanism as an 'emanation from hell', are flat blasphemies against the Sermon on the Mount.

Things were done differently in the United States:

> What has made America so wonderfully prosperous? Is it not the entire freedom of the individual within the limits of the law? The power of talent and genius to 'make by force its merits known', and claim the homage of men. Letting all forms of Faith make their own way, unaided by the State. Leaving Art, Trade, and Manufactures untrammelled by burdensome taxation.[5]

The *Englishman*'s republicanism was a continuation of its previous political line rather than a break with its past. Monarchy became associated with the interfering state whereas republicanism came to mean not only a country without a monarch but a society with a weak state that guaranteed freedom to all.

The Magna Charta Association had long been a supporter of land reform – a radical cause that threatened to undermine the aristocracy by breaking up estates. The Magna Charta Congress in November 1876 had voted to support an increase of the Land Tax (in the hope that it would allow for the abolition of customs duties on all goods). It also supported the abolition of the Game Laws and a tax on waste land at five shillings an acre.[6] The *Englishman* praised the idea of peasant proprietorship and even quoted John Stuart Mill approvingly on the value of smallholdings. Kenealy himself admired the Land Reform League Association of George Lovett and hoped it would be absorbed into the Magna Charta Association. The League intended to bring all uncultivated land into use and, as a building society, aimed to allot fifteen to twenty acres with comfortable homesteads to all destitute families. Kenealy believed this would end the monopoly in land. The issue became more pressing in the 1880s with the continued agricultural depression and the failure of the Gladstone government to introduce effective land reform.[7] The land question was in many respects the key to the Magna Charta Association's political outlook. It expressed hostility to the landed classes, who not only evaded the Land Tax but also dominated land ownership.[8] Traditional Radicalism was wedded to small-scale capitalism and therefore hostile to any kind of monopoly. Like other Radicals such as Mill and Joseph Chamberlain (and later G. K. Chesterton and Hilaire Belloc), it put its faith in a form of distributism, hoping in an unspecified way to share out the land to all.

The land question was one issue on which it had a great deal in common with Radicals across the board. Its proposals to solve the problem sound almost Marxian: 'The first radical step towards an equal distribution of the profits of labour must be the placing of the ownership of land on a just and equitable basis.' The *Englishman* proclaimed:

That the land of any country is the property of the people who inhabit is too self-evident a proposition to need demonstration. Common sense points out that it is the heritage, the birthright of the whole of the people.[9]

Maurice Kenealy urged the Westminster branch to push for the nationalisation of the land in 1881.[10] He believed the legislation might be introduced with the help of the Irish MPs. Building on the concerns articulated by De Morgan, the *Englishman* featured articles about the threats to common lands. One editorial, 'Open Spaces for the People', expressed fears for Paddington Park.[11] In 1884, the *Englishman* also showed some interest in the ideas of the American reformer Henry George, who advocated a single tax on land rents as a way of redistributing wealth, but it later moved to a more critical stance.[12]

The main issue that concerned Magna Chartists in the early 1880s was Ireland. Kenealy had tended to support Home Rule and the *Englishman* began to encourage Michael Davitt and the Land League.[13] In 1881, Magna Chartists united against Gladstone's Irish Coercion Bill – another issue on which they were able to find common ground with many other Radicals.[14] Local branches all over the country opposed it. The speaker at the Hackney branch denounced the treatment of Parnell whilst the Nottingham branch sent a letter to Gladstone condemning coercion.[15] At the Cumberland Market branch, Mr Williams urged support for the Anti-Coercion League and organised the construction of a new banner displaying verse by Michael Davitt.[16] The Sheffield branch deplored the suspension of the Irish Home Rulers as 'a gross insult to the Irish representatives'. On Mile End Waste, a Magna Charta speaker urged an open air meeting that the government was to be censured.[17]

Magna Chartists were prominent in the Hyde Park demonstration against the Bill in February 1881. The Tower Hamlets branch provided their brass band. Chalcraft of the Magna Charta Association appeared on the platform where the government's Anti Coercion Bill was torn to shreds. The banners were similar in tone to those of the Tichborne demonstrations. It was later claimed by the secretary of the Peckham branch that 'the Magna Charta Association was the only real political association represented, except the Social Democratic (Soho) Society'. He praised the Westminster branch for taking the lead in helping organise the demonstration.[18] The Magna Charta Association convened its own meeting the following Tuesday to protest at coercion and the arrest of Davitt. It was addressed by the MP T. P. O'Connor, as well as F. W. Soutter, editor of the *Radical*. Maurice Kenealy urged that this be the first of successive anti-Coercion meetings. For their work on the Irish cause, the Magna Charta Association gained the respect of other political groups. Charles Garcia, secretary of the King's Cross Radical Club, expressed pleasure that they were working together with Radicals.[19] Ireland continued to be an issue for Magna Chartists. At a Magna Charta demonstration in June 1881, Finlay Finlayson claimed that the Irish Coercion Act might be introduced in England.[20]

In most respects, the anti-statist line of the movement remained intact. Its programme in 1880 urged: 'Fellow Citizens! We call upon you to unite in your thousands, and form a great army to win back Rights which every free-born Briton may claim.'[21] Expounding its clause on education in the Magna Charta programme, the *Englishman* proposed 'To take away from the State all interference or control over Education, which should be in the hands only of Religious Bodies'. It went on to explain:

The State enforces compulsory education *according to its enacted Laws*. It tells the People that, no matter what the body may require to maintain its physical powers, the brain shall be filled with state-appointed food. Now everything which emanates from the State – as Statecraft is – benefits a minority of the people alone, and to the injury of the rest ... We, in ourselves, hold that it is the *Parents* who should be *compelled* to educate their children or have them educated.[22]

The movement continued to examine women's issues and voting rights. It featured articles on women workers upholding the dignity of labour but degenerated into a patronising view of working-class women:

> Their economy in food and clothing is open to the widest improvement ... Large and expensive joints are cooked ... in the most wasteful and expensive fashion, and the very minimum of nutriment is obtained from them.
>
> In thousands of instances, money is spent, or rather wasted, on the Sunday's dinner, that, well laid out, would provide palatable and wholesale nourishment for the week.[23]

There was support for the female franchise in the branches. When the Magna Chartist, Finlay Finlayson, was asked his opinion of the question, he replied 'he could see no possible reason why a woman should not vote the same as a man'.[24]

The elder Kenealy's anti-Catholicism continued but only in a token way. Jesuits were denounced as 'a foe to liberty and progress, an insidious destroyer of domestic peace, a secret promoter of political discord' and there was clear support for ultra-Protestantism at local level.[25] More enduring was the critique of the law. Even after Kenealy's death, the clause excluding practising lawyers from Parliament was retained in the programme. There were denunciations of miscarriages of justice and the association urged the simplification of the laws.

The anti-Irish Coercion movement marked a new phase where the movement became open to other forms of radicalism. The *Englishman* began to advertise other radical club meetings. These included the Battersea Liberal Club, the Chelsea Radical Club, the Chelsea Home Rule Association, the Lambeth Advanced Liberal Association, the Manhood Suffrage League, the National Land League of Great Britain, the North London Secular Society the Peckham Discussion Forum, the Social Democratic Club and the Westminster Liberal Union.[26]

The movement's most significant contribution to radical politics was its assistance in the birth of Henry Hyndman's Democratic Federation. Delegates of the Magna Charta Association and other radical clubs attended a meeting chaired by Hyndman on 19 March 1881 at the Westminster Palace Hotel. The Magna Chartists included Maurice Kenealy, Captain Morrison, Mr Chalcraft of Clerkenwell and Finlay Finlayson, a recent convert. The Democratic Federation was not a socialist organisation at this time (or even a proto-socialist one) but a confederation of advanced radical clubs.[27] The Magna Chartists' intention in attending was to push the cause of land nationalisation. Finlayson argued that no advanced programme would be complete without it and it was duly adopted by the meeting. The resolution of Mr Smith of the Finsbury branch that the Magna Charta clause barring bribery at elections be taken on board was also successful. Magna Chartism thus made a distinctive contribution (although these were standard radical demands). Its standing can be gauged by the fact that the Democratic Federation Conference was organised for the day after the Magna Charta Congress so there would be no conflict.[28]

The *Englishman* viewed the Democratic Federation as having adopted its programme. It published the initial address of the Federation but emphasised its stress on land nationalisation. It differed in interpreting 'working people' as meaning 'all classes who have to labour for their bread' but perceived the Federation as offering a way of cooperating with other radical clubs.[29] There was a two-way relationship here. Henry Hyndman himself likened the programme to that of the Magna Charta Association and, according to Andreas Scheu, actually modelled himself on Kenealy.[30] Hyndman never failed to play the role of the socialist, top-hatted toff. Like Kenealy, he had some associations with Tory radicalism and in a famous episode even sought the dying Disraeli's advice about the creation of the Democratic Federation.[31]

Magna Chartists were much in evidence at the first congress of the Democratic Federation. Chalcraft of Clerkenwell supported Mr Matthews, a former Chartist, in opposing Helen Taylor's resolution in favour of female suffrage as 'It would probably cause great disagreement in the homes of the working men'. Mr Tyler of the Magna Charta Association disagreed and 'pointed out how greatly the Association of which he was a member, was indebted to the efforts of the female, and remarked that the widow of Dr KENEALY was worthily filling the position of President of the Association'. The resolution was carried. Magna Chartists also moved resolutions for

Irish Home Rule, triennial parliaments, equal election expenses and the payment of MPs.[32]

The *Englishman* was apparently genuine in its interest in the new movement. It praised Hyndman's *England for All* and came near to embracing (at least in the abstract) universal male suffrage as well as votes for women.[33] Hyndman and Dr G. B. Clark of the Democratic Federation addressed the Magna Charta Congress in 1881. Hyndman praised the work of Magna Charta in the anti-Coercion movement and its role in the creation of the Federation. Clark, later Liberal and Crofter MP for Caithness, hoped the Association would be able to work for the Federation's proposals 'as well as for the man in prison'. Magna Chartists agreed. Mr Perkins claimed the Association 'was a political association, and they were determined to fight for the interests of the working classes laid down by the late Dr Kenealy as well as for Sir Roger Tichborne'.[34]

Even so there were tensions. When Finlay Finlayson spoke at the first Democratic Federation meeting, there were shouts that supporters 'did not want men with black coats'. At the 1881 Magna Charta Congress, when fears were expressed that association with the Democratic Federation would lead to the demise of Magna Charta, the Congress resolved not to commit any money to the new federation.[35] After this, the relationship between the two organisations was not close. In particular, Magna Chartism had nothing to do with the Social Democratic Federation, as Hyndman's organisation became (with its explicit commitment to socialism), although it did quote verses from the newspaper of its offshoot – the Socialist League's *Commonweal*.[36] The *Englishman* continued to take an interest in other forms of radicalism. In late 1881, it began a series of articles entitled 'An Account of Communism' in which it described the history of the movement. It quoted Karl Marx with approval and discussed Communist philosophy.[37] The paper tended to be positive about socialism:

> Destructive socialism seeks to strike all things down to a level, and is deluded into believing that violence and assassination will deliver the people from the yoke under which they are galled. Constructive socialism seeks to build its way up to a platform which mankind at large may enjoy those benefits that have long been monopolised by the few, and the sole weapon it proposes to use is the consolidated and irresistible will of the people.[38]

1. Roger Charles Doughty Tichborne:
One of the daguerreotypes taken at Santiago in 1853.

2. (Above left) The Tichborne Claimant

3. (Left) The Claimant in 1865

4. (Opposite above) The Claimant in Hampshire, 1868

5. (Opposite below) The Claimant's family

6. (Left) The Dowager Lady Tichborne

7. (Below left) Lady Katherine Radcliffe

8. (Below) The Claimant in 1885

9. (Opposite top) Tichborne plaster figures (image courtesy of Hampshire County Council Museums and Archives Service; the figure of the Dowager is in the Willett Collection, Brighton and Hove Museums, and the remainder come from a private collection).

10. (Opposite below) Tichborne medallion

11. (Above left) Tichborne Staffordshire
    figurine (image courtesy of the
    Potteries Museum and Art Gallery,
    Stoke on Trent)

12. (Top right) Kenealy Jug
    (image courtesy of the Potteries
    Museum and Art Gallery, Stoke on
    Trent)

13. (Above) Randolph Caldecott's terra cotta figures of protagonists in the Tichborne Trial: the Claimant is a turtle, Kenealy a cock and Hawkins a hawk while the judges are owls (image courtesy of Brighton and Hove Museums).

14. The Claimant's funeral.

It later argued that 'the path of legislative progress in England has been for years, and must continue to be, distinctly socialistic' and praised the Education Act as a step in the direction of state socialism, marking a change from its earlier anti-statist position on education.[39] It never, however, committed itself to socialism, urging in its columns the need for a proper definition. In this spirit, it serialised the debate between Charles Bradlaugh and Henry Hyndman on the question 'Will Socialism Benefit the English People?'[40] This was an important moment in the history of the British left: Bradlaugh's individualist form of radicalism was confronted by Hyndman's advocacy of the new socialist doctrines that were gathering momentum. The movement's relative openness to socialism may explain why the socialist and former Chartist Thomas Mottershead chose to attend the Tichborne conference in 1883. He said that he had been opposed to the Claimant but felt that he had now suffered enough and ought to be released.[41]

By 1883, the paper had begun to support Joseph Chamberlain's brand of radicalism, which was in favour of manhood suffrage, equal electoral districts and the payment of MPs. It published articles praising Chamberlain's political stance on Free Land, Free Church and Free Schools as well as housing and agricultural labour. By 1885, however, it was felt that Chamberlain had lost his sense of direction and had not succeeded in changing anything.[42] In this way, all the political alliances that the movement established proved to be only temporary. Although the Magna Charta programme could be constructed so as to suggest an affinity with other forms of radicalism, in the end it remained doggedly independent.

After Edward Kenealy, the strangest Tichbornite was undoubtedly Georgina Weldon, the soprano, spiritualist and social reformer. She came to incarnate a feeling that was central to the Tichbornite imagination.

A standard Victorian fear was not just the paranoia about surveillance but about incarceration. In anti-Catholic propaganda, women were often said to have been kept in convents against their will. This paranoia was exploited in popular pamphlets, which showed how women (portrayed as frail and defenceless) were seduced into surrendering their independence and will power through the confessional. The fear was often twinned with concern about lunatic asylums. By the time of the Lunatics Act of 1845, alienists had established the right to adjudicate in all matters concerning insanity. This represented a real threat to anyone whose views did not conform to an undefined code of normality.[43] Spiritualists and other unorthodox religious groups became targets for incarceration and women, in particular, found themselves in a vulnerable position. In 1849, Louisa Nottidge, a wealthy heiress who had left home to join a millenarian community, was abducted by her mother and confined in an asylum on account of her perceived religious delusions. Nottidge's failing health led to her release, whereupon she not only rejoined the community but sued for wrongful incarceration. At the trial, the Lord Chief Baron ruled that, although the confinement was technically in order, individuals should be free to exercise their own judgement in religious terms as long as they did not harm others. He thus recognised the possibility of wrongful incarceration – a popular fear registered in Wilkie Collins's novel *The Woman in White* (1860) and Charles Reade's *Hard Cash* of 1863.

In the 1870s, when popular spiritualism was at its peak, the medical establishment launched a campaign against it. This was led by Dr Forbes Winslow, who was responsible for the attempted abduction of Georgina Weldon. Mrs Weldon was an extraordinary figure.[44] She had been born into a wealthy family but had married beneath her station. The great passion of her life was music and her singing acquired many admirers, including Arthur Sullivan (she was also Gounod's mistress). She established an orphanage at her home in Tavistock Square where she took children from the streets and brought them up, teaching them musical skills and dressing them in unconventional clothing. She also embraced spiritualism. This was too much for her husband, from whom she had separated. In 1876, he contacted Forbes Winslow on account of his reputation as an anti-spiritualist to organise his wife's committal. Mrs Weldon was saved because Louisa Lowe of the Lunacy Law Reform Association alerted her to the danger and helped her to escape from Tavistock Square before the doctors could get to her.

Mrs Weldon thereafter took up the cause of law reform, complaining about the whole process of incarcerating innocent people. After the Married Woman's Property Act of 1882, she was able to sue her 'abductors' on her own behalf. In doing so, she performed the extraordinary feat of learning enough law to prosecute the case herself in court. The jury twice found against Winslow on the counts of libel and assault, an important blow to medical non-accountability. One consequence of her lawsuits was the reform of the Lunacy Laws between 1888 and 1890. Judicial authority was introduced as a requirement for the detention of a person as a lunatic and restrictions were placed on the opening of private asylums. The medical profession was conciliated by protection 'against vexatious questions where they have acted in good faith'.[45] After her success in the law courts, Mrs

Weldon lost much of the money she had gained by suing virtually everybody who had wronged her. On one occasion, she ended up in prison herself because of a libel case.

It was always likely that she would support the Tichborne Claimant. Her personal history inclined her to sympathise with anyone suspected of wrongful arrest. Her entire campaign (waged with Louisa Lowe) was against unjust surveillance by elites. Lowe wrote a series of pamphlets urging law reform entitled *Quis Custodiet Ipsos Custodes?* – a familiar sentiment to Tichborne supporters. Georgina Weldon was engaged to sing at Covent Garden in 1878 and 1879 and used it as an opportunity to propagandise her cause. She performed concerts at her home, lectured on her plight (rather as the Claimant had done in 1872) and toured the provinces in a play about her experiences entitled *Not Alone*.[46] She employed a clerk called Lever to serve writs for her who was himself a Magna Chartist.[47] Politically, she believed in a kind of socialism as well as female suffrage, although she never worked on behalf of these causes.

Magna Chartists were active in Weldon's defence. Captain Morrison, vice-president of the Magna Charta Association, called a public meeting to protest against her conviction in 1880. At another public meeting, Maurice Kenealy moved a resolution condemning her unjust imprisonment.[48] This was in tune with the movement's belief in Lunacy Law reform. In 1876, the *Englishman* had complained that:

> The easiest way to get rid of an objectionable relative is to pronounce them insane and deal with them accordingly, and it is not a hard task to swear away a person's liberty, if you have money enough, and then to drive them into insanity by basely cruel treatment ... In the sacred names of Liberty, Humanity and Justice, we call for safeguards for the protection of those unhappy ones who are deprived of the power to protect themselves.[49]

It regularly reported cases of people wrongfully imprisoned in lunatic asylums.[50]

Mrs Weldon became a regular correspondent for the *Englishman*, adopting a range of legal issues. She supported the Claimant, observing that the malformation was crucial evidence (see pp. 199–200).[51] Taking up his cause at a meeting of non-Tichbornites in the Clarendon Club, Islington, she said that she had not originally been a believer but that the press reaction had changed her mind.[52] She made her debut in the cause at the annual demonstration in Hyde Park in 1884 and said she was fighting between sixteen and eighteen legal actions and meant to win them all. At about this time, she also became Vice-President of the Magna Charta Association. Her flamboyance made her a useful supporter and journalist for the *Englishman*. She later retired to France but in the mid-1880s drew together a critique of the law and a sense of injustice. As a popular heroine, she epitomised fears of surveillance by the state much as the Tichborne cause did.

By 1882, it was clear that the Magna Charta Association was in trouble. Many local branches had collapsed and leading members had moved on.[53] Only a handful remained committed. In London, Clerkenwell, Tower Hamlets, Hackney, Southwark and Westminster remained strong whilst outside London, Oldham, Stoke, Nottingham, Sheffield and Stalybridge continued to send in reports to the *Englishman*. The Glasgow Central Magna Charta Association petitioned Parliament in 1884 to amend the Prisons Act so that all prisoners could have access to the Bible. The Nottingham branch was active enough in 1885 to memorialise the local mayor to find employment for the poor.[54]

The *Englishman* itself was also in trouble. One letter alleged that most of the working class had not even heard of it.[55] In an editorial of 1882, Maurice Kenealy appealed to readers for money to keep it going. He claimed that 'for some time past the circulation ... has been such that from a business point of view, it has not been worthwhile to issue it', adding that 'a sense of duty alone has urged me ... much to my own personal detriment and loss to carry it on, as I was determined as far as it lay in my power to continue working in the movement'.[56] A circulation fund was created which was successful in that the paper remained in publication for another four years. This was presumably because it was able to trade on the good will of its readers and its owners were extremely dedicated. It had to launch a similar appeal the following year when it complained that advertisers were prejudiced against the paper.[57] One major activity for local activists became the raising of money for the *Englishman*.

From 1882 the divisions between Magna Chartists and independent Tichbornites eased. At the Tichborne conference that year there were many non-Magna Chartist Tichbornites such as G. E. Gray. Biddulph and Skipworth both sent letters of apology but apparently felt no ill will towards a meeting that had had links to the Association.[58] Only William Quartermaine East kept his distance, not wanting to get involved in political questions.[59]

Demonstrations continued on Whit Monday each year, usually starting in the East End and then moving to Trafalgar Square.[60] In 1883, the demonstration began on Clerkenwell Green and included delegations from Cumberland Market, Finsbury, Greenwich, Nottingham, Sheffield and Tower Hamlets. New forms of radicalism can be deduced from the banners. Finsbury demanded the release of the Claimant and triennial parliaments. Another read 'Three Cheers for the Late Dr KENEALY and the Republic'.[61] At the tenth annual demonstration in Hyde Park, on 2 June 1884, every London district was represented by its branch and there were deputations from Leeds, Liverpool, Manchester, Nottingham, Rotherham and Sheffield. The contingents met on Clerkenwell Green for a preliminary meeting and then moved on to Hyde Park, where they were addressed by Georgina Weldon and the Claimant's son, Roger, who thanked all those who had supported his father.[62]

It was the hope of all concerned that the cause would revive after the release from prison of the Claimant. He continued to insist that he was Roger Tichborne.[63] None of the petitions and demonstrations to secure his release succeeded. There were plans for his life after prison, however, including the suggestion that he be provided with a pub – an appropriate gesture.[64] He was released from Pentonville, to which he had been moved, on 11 October 1884. On leaving prison, he was approached by a theatrical agent, who signed him up to appear in circuses. The Claimant remained a great celebrity. He even sat for a new wax model at Madame Tussaud's, which reflected his slimmer figure after his years in prison.[65]

Naturally, it was hoped that his release would provide a boost to the movement. He appeared at the St James's Hall in Piccadilly at the end of the month. The meeting drew the supporters of radical fringe movements attracted to the cause including Georgina Weldon, who sat on the platform with the Claimant, Quartermaine East and Edward Kimber. There were also anti-vaccinators and a group distributing pamphlets claiming that the British race was one of 'the lost ten tribes of Israel'.[66] The Claimant said he 'was not going to trouble them on political or prison affairs but he merely appeared to thank them for the way in which they had supported his cause'. He insisted on the Dowager's recognition and complained that there had been a conspiracy against him. Georgina Weldon, true to form, recommended him to bring as many libel suits as possible. There was a similar meeting two weeks later at the Temperance Hall, Blackfriars. These meetings were intended for serious purposes. Soon afterwards, however, the Claimant appeared at the Varieties Music Hall, Briggate, Leeds, where he was engaged for four nights at £10 a night. He made a short speech between different acts. His supporters were irritated at such lack of dignity, which was the beginning of the trivialisation of his cause that led to its demise.[67] After Leeds, the Claimant went on to speak all over the country although, as a condition of his ticket of leave, he had to report to the local police station wherever he went. He appeared in Dewsbury, Newcastle and Sunderland among other places. At Norwich he played two nights as part of Sanger's Circus. In Edinburgh he was engaged by the manager of Moss's Theatre of Varieties, who placed him near the top of the bill for six nights along with acts such as Professor Buer's celebrated troupe of performing animals and the great foot equilibrist Vallo.[68]

The Tichborne movement now began to collapse very quickly. A meeting at Stoke regretted that the Claimant was talking in towns where no local organisation existed. It proposed a grand campaign to keep 'Sir Roger from the meshes of theatre and music hall proprietors', but the Claimant's solicitor, Edward Kimber, informed the Magna Chartists that the financial terms offered by the music halls, although distasteful, were very good. The Claimant spoke all over the country in 1885.[69]

By the following year, most local groups were disillusioned as the Claimant took no interest in the Magna Charta Association and seemed to have disowned the Tichborne movement. Some, like Jesse Butler on the United Provincial Council, felt that the Claimant appreciated their work but was being shielded from them by his theatrical agents. At almost the same time, the Westminster Magna Charta Association bemoaned his lack of gratitude.[70] This was undoubtedly the saddest phase in the history of the movement. Thomas Hutchinson of Northampton wrote to the *Englishman* to complain that the Claimant 'treats his many noble workers with seeming indifference'. His letter highlights the desperation of the movement:

> if Sir ROGER does not care to encourage the movement – nor help a demonstration, I would say – let us have one in spite of him; and if he never gives a token of gratitude, GOD will smile upon us in proportion to our labours to advance truth, justice and fair play.[71]

A Mr Pescod addressed the Clerkenwell Magna Charta Association on the need to strengthen the movement, 'Tichborne having apparently deserted us'.[72] He was speaking at the same time as the *Englishman* was obliged to close down. It published its last issue on 22 May 1886. The Westminster Magna Charta Association claimed this event was a 'death blow to our cause and the cause of Sir Roger Tichborne'.[73]

All evidence of Magna Charta activities ends with the demise of the *Englishman*. It is unlikely that they continued for much longer. By 1886 there was only a small number of groups, mostly based in London. The release of the Claimant only served to bring about their destruction. Over a century later, the Magna Chartists still sound like lovers spurned.

PART TWO

In Search of The Claimant

10

Spectacle

In the preface to his 1914 play *Androcles and the Lion*, George Bernard Shaw mocked the contradictions in the Bible, including the belief that Jesus could be descended from David but also conceived by the Holy Ghost:

> Such double beliefs are entertained by the human mind without uneasiness or consciousness of the contradiction involved. Many instances might be given: a familiar one to my generation being that of the Tichborne Claimant, whose attempt to pass himself off as a baronet was supported by an association of labourers on the ground that the Tichborne family, in resisting it, were trying to do a labourer out of his rights.[1]

Shaw's views were not out of line with much middle-class opinion. John Ruskin complained in *Fors Clavigera*, 'Just think ... of the flood of human idiotism that spent a couple of years or so of its life in writing, printing and reading the Tichborne trial'. He scorned the 'loathsome thoughts and vulgar inquisitiveness' that Tichborne had thrown up.[2] We ourselves might want to write off the movement, like Shaw, as an example of the contradictoriness or bloodymindedness of popular thought. At best, one might consider it a primitive form of popular politics before the emergence of more sophisticated movements such as socialism. The rationality of Victorian public life was challenged by the pigheaded determination of Tichbornites to promote the Claimant.

The Tichborne case was a major cultural event in Victorian Britain. It mobilised the resources of the media and entertainment industries to create the kind of spectacle on which the nineteenth century thrived. Whether it was a high-wire act at Astley's circus or the tawdry revelations of the divorce courts related through Sunday newspapers, Victorians were in thrall to sensation of all kinds. Modern life promised pleasurable shocks and thrills in the form of Mary Elizabeth Braddon's novels or the damsels in distress on the stage of the Britannia Theatre, Hoxton. The development of city centres provided stages for spectacles about civic pride or imperial greatness.

On the streets, advertising proclaimed the pleasures of consumption. The 1870s does not mark the first moment when the power of images and spectacle shaped everyday life, but Tichbornism was undoubtedly part of a new world of mass communications characterised by the culture of sensation.

The second half of this book explores the relationship of the Claimant to popular culture and to nineteenth-century life in general. It explains why this eccentric lost cause exercised such an impact on the Victorian imagination. Recovering the iconography of the movement will take us through the dustbins of the Victorians to examine souvenirs, bric-à-brac, cartoons, satirical prints, broadside ballads as well as more orthodox sources such as newspapers and trial accounts. Tichborniana enables us to reconstruct the meanings of the cause and probe why the Claimant became a hero for parts of Victorian society.

The man from Wagga Wagga was a shape shifter; he meant different things to different people. Over the period from 1867 to 1886, we find a cluster of representations and performances, some generated by the Claimant himself, some by others. The Claimant became a source of fascination because he lacked a centre. Even the name 'Claimant' was betwixt and between. He was involved in a perpetual guessing game with the Victorian public.

For his supporters, the Claimant was a tragic figure, an Englishman brought down by an aristocratic conspiracy. There was real sadness over his prison sentence. The unfairness of the trial represented the unfairness of life in general. Yet he was also heroic, particularly after he withstood Coleridge's elaborate cross-examination. Nineteenth-century popular culture placed a high premium on the idea of transparency. In popular songs and melodrama, the good are represented as straightforward, whereas the bad are devious. While in many ways there was nothing transparent about the Tichborne Claimant, his supporters felt that his artless self-presentation was a reason to believe in him; he did not dissemble. His very ignorance of Sir Roger's past made him appear truthful (an impostor would have mugged up what he needed to know). In contrast, the Claimant's opponents appeared devious, disguising their conspiracy to retain the Tichborne estates.

The Claimant was also imagined as a sporting gentleman; he was at home with a rifle or a fishing rod. Sports such as hunting and fishing brought elite and working-class people together, joined by the pursuit of pleasure despite the strong anti-aristocratic tradition in popular politics.[3] The best-selling *Reynolds's Newspaper* pursued a vendetta with the aristocracy each week, blaming all social ills on the selfish elite. There was, on the other hand, enormous deference to the aristocracy, particularly in rural areas. The pleasure-loving toff who did not take life too seriously enjoyed great appeal in Victorian Britain. As the Claimant toured the country, music hall audiences were simultaneously being delighted by the performances of George Leybourne as the character 'Champagne Charlie', an aristocratic swell who lived only for the good life.[4] The Claimant was another kind of 'swell'. His love of sport, brandy and the smoking room made him a figure that was easy for ordinary people to identify with. He was the kind of toff who did not mind getting in touch with popular culture. Indeed there was a Falstaffian dimension to the Claimant. In street literature, he was a boozing reprobate who cocked a snook at authority and enjoyed the life of the rich while he had the chance. His was not the mythological Victorian Britain that has come down to us: a world of prudery and respectability.

The lifestyle of the common people is often thought to have been reshaped during the nineteenth century. Out went the bawdy world of rough sports, obscenity, licentiousness, lewdness and bear baiting that had characterised earlier popular life, and was evident on feast days when people coped with lives of dearth and scarcity by letting their hair down and running wild. This kind of popular culture has been dubbed the 'carnivalesque'.[5] The spirit of carnival led by a lord of misrule expressed the wildness of ordinary folk who at festivals (liberally spread through the calendar) celebrated the 'world turned upside down', the brief moments when traditional authority was overturned and could be laughed at. It was a brutal and irreverent culture. In the nineteenth century, however, the tide of Victorianism remade popular culture. Many saints' days and holidays were eliminated and there was a clamp down on unruly behaviour by the new police force. The obscene world of Regency satire, which had employed pornographic imagery to mock the powerful, was driven almost out of existence.[6] Executions, which had been occasions for this irreverent, rough culture of the common people, were withdrawn from the public sphere and took place in prisons after 1868, also terminating a source of popular entertainment.[7] Instead, improving leisure facilities such as mechanics' institutes and libraries were provided for the working classes, a process that has become known as 'rational recreation'.[8] The Tichborne cause suggests that all was not gloom and sober conformity amongst Victorian workers. Instead, it requires us to rethink the idea that the history of popular culture was characterised by a huge disruption imposed by po-faced, middle-class busy-bodies who wanted to secure an industrious and placid workforce. There is at least as much to be said for continuity as change in popular culture. The festival-like atmosphere of the Tichborne campaigns and their connections with the world of drink suggests that popular culture remained untamed. In many ways, Tichborne is an example of something that ought to be a contradiction in terms – the Victorian carnivalesque.

This is not to say that nothing changed. Tichborne should be seen as part of a new world of cheap entertainment in the mid-Victorian era. Rising living standards allowed working people to enjoy the new mass culture – forms of entertainment such as the music hall and Sunday newspapers that spoke the language of the common people but were not produced by them. Instead, everyday life was shaped by entrepreneurs and vendors of cheap pleasures. From the world of the Chartists and subversive forms of popular culture such as the bawdy ballad, we move to the tamer world of the seaside holiday and the Saturday afternoon football match. This was a world based on putting up with life's hardships and trying to have a little fun along the way. Its philosophy was not derived from editorials in radical newspapers (usually unread by most working-class people) but was best expressed in the line of the music hall song, 'A little of what you fancy does you good'.[9] The later nineteenth century witnessed the development of an identity for workers based on fish and chips, love of sport and cheerful jingoism. Even the image of the amiable, working-class cockney, which appears old, was invented in this moment of cultural change from about 1870 onwards – the era of the Tichborne Claimant.[10]

Mass culture (created for the people rather than by them) could be subversive as well as conformist. Music hall, perhaps the most popular of Victorian entertainments, was based around the knowing wink and double entendre, with sexual references carefully inflected for those in the know. It provided urban audiences with a guide to the latest popular fashions: dances, clothes and up-to-date slang that audiences could use to demonstrate their cultural competence.[11] Courtship, alcohol and the battle of the sexes were the great themes of the halls. No wonder reformers disapproved and often tried to close them down. Tichborne expressed the values of this controlled but rumbustious popular culture. We might see Tichborne as a form of music hall in real life. The Claimant's career in the halls (in the stump campaign and his later appearances as a music hall novelty) embodied the Victorian carnivalesque. He was a modern lord of misrule.

The Claimant's appeal challenges the view that Victorian Britain was narrowly defined by the ideal of respectability. According to this, right-thinking

Victorians from middle-class Evangelicals to the labour aristocracy believed in hard work, self-help and the promotion of good character.[12] It was the age of Samuel Smiles' best-selling *Self-Help* (1859). If this view is correct, how can we explain the appeal of a man who was either an impostor or who, if genuine, had proclaimed his seduction of a young woman? How can we explain the appeal of a movement that never wandered far from the world of the pub and music hall (two locations shunned by respectable society)? Eminently respectable labour aristocrats were some of the most active amongst the Claimant's supporters. Many Victorians prided themselves on their belief in progress through hard work, yet they admired the Claimant. Like a nightmare of Samuel Smiles', he was cheered for getting on through doing no work at all. He had not even worked hard at getting his facts straight.

Many Victorians certainly pursued the code of respectability. However, respectability was dependent on context and involved a form of perform-ance.[13] Victorians maintained respectability at work, in church and on the streets but might also enjoy the salacious content of Sunday newspapers or attend a music hall, despite the prostitutes touting for business in the bar. There were appropriate forms of speech and conduct in different areas of life. It was possible to believe in the Claimant's statements about himself whilst not endorsing his seduction of Katherine Doughty. The affair could be enjoyed at the level of gossip and titillation without abandoning respectability (unless you were John Ruskin). The dividing line between respectable and unrespectable culture was extremely thin. Sunday newspapers with their repertoire of scandalous divorces and horrible murders provided a host of abuses that the respectable should not have enjoyed but really did.

The great Victorian hope was to rise through hard work and ability. Music hall songs and routines, however, owned up to the fact that work could often be tiresome and unrewarding. A preferable route to riches was through a lucky windfall.[14] Popular stories continually dealt with people suddenly acquiring inheritances from relatives they did not know they had or winning wagers on horse races (much as a later generation would focus on the Lottery). People were intrigued by the Claimant because he was a butcher who had enjoyed the ultimate lucky windfall. He was a Cinderella figure, a poor man who got to go to the ball.

Another image of the Claimant was that of an Englishman who had been changed by life in the colonies. People were believed to behave differently in colonial settings; there was the possibility of remaking oneself. The empire was a place where white men could become degenerate and abandon their allegedly civilised norms of behaviour. Australia was imagined as a pastoral paradise, a place for possible emigration but also as a land shaped by the convict experience and housing the dangerous classes of Britain and Ireland. The Claimant made out that he had been a figure thrown up by frontier societies – a bandit. If he was Sir Roger, this meant that a member of the aristocracy had become a bushranger. He was always reticent about his Australian years, partly because he may have been involved in the murder of Ballarat Harry. Popular culture often thrives on myths of banditry from Robin Hood to Jesse James.[15] Bandits can be transformed from pariahs to champions of the common people against unjust elites, lovable rogues who steal from the rich to give to the poor. The Claimant could be imagined as a Romantic bandit. He had had the experience of having lived among the common people and could count among his enemies, lawyers – traditional symbols of oppression and henchmen of the rich. Myths such as the Robin Hood stories often made out that bandit heroes were secret members of 'High Society'. This is the key to the problem raised earlier in this chapter by George Bernard Shaw: why should an anti-aristocratic plebeian move- ment be so keen to assist a man in joining the aristocracy? Historically, peasant movements have often clothed their heroes with the attributes of freedom. The truly free people were considered to be the aristocracy. Thus Robin Hood was really the Earl of Huntington. The Claimant's image as a butcher with an elite secret identity was in line with traditional popular culture and movements of the poor.

The Tichborne cause represented a state of mind as much as a political movement. It expressed an emotion about the unfairness of current society. The Claimant was an ambiguous personality, caught between different stations in society, combining aristocratic airs and lowliness. Such liminal figures in different cultures possess a distinctive charisma.[16] Often revelling in foolishness, they strip off the pretensions of power from holders of high office and so reduce them to the level of a common humanity. As quintes- sential outsiders, they are transformed into representations of universal human values. This may also explain the attractiveness of long lost heir stories in nineteenth-century fiction (of which Tichborne was an example in real life). It would be less interesting if the heirs simply returned and took over their property unhindered. Impeded by greedy relatives or other agents, the struggle to regain wealth created exciting narratives and reduced the holders of wealth to human proportion.

Long lost heirs are different from impostors. For centuries, popular culture has been littered with tales of liars, hoaxers, pretenders, soldiers who turn out to be women and their attendant cast of the gullible and the deceived. Fakery transfixed the popular imagination and had developed a folklore of its own from Perkin Warbeck to Martin Guerre to Anastasia.[17] In the twenty-first century, fakery remains an issue. Identity fraud has become a major problem. Fakes are everywhere from forgers of currency to drag queens. Fakes are actors and transgressors who defy standard forms of categorisation and refuse to accept their allocated social roles. Most societies have their tales of fakery and deception which are specific to time and place.[18] Readers of the Victorian popular press (and most romantic novels) could be forgiven for thinking that no estate in Britain was safe from an alleged long-lost heir turning up with fantastic stories about how their rights had been denied. The Tichborne Claimant was not a wholly unusual figure. The nineteenth century was full of people insisting they were someone else, or the rightful heir to a property whose rights were denied by scheming relatives.

Imposture could be a passport to high society. In 1817, a young woman appeared in Almondsbury, Gloucestershire, wearing what appeared to be Asiatic clothes and speaking a language no one understood. The word spread that she was Princess Caraboo from the island of Javasu and had apparently been abducted by pirates. The exotic figure was taken up and fêted by local high society until it was discovered that Caraboo was really a former nurse called Mary Willcocks, noted for fanciful story-telling, who had adopted the disguise as an alternative to vagrancy. She was later sent to the United States, where her fame preceded her, but eventually returned and devoted the rest of her life to supplying leeches to the Bristol Infirmary.[19] Then there was the notorious case of Tom Provis, who claimed in 1853 to be the son of the late Sir Hugh Smyth by a secret marriage with the daughter of Count Vandenbergh in 1796. He alleged that his mother had died in childbirth and that he had been taken by a butler and given to a carpenter to be reared, whilst his father was told that his son had died. In court, Provis produced a family Bible which contained an entry recording his 'parent's' marriage and his own baptism (obtained from the carpenter who brought him up). It was discovered, however, that the motto on one of the family seals on the documents was misspelt and hence an obvious forgery. He was sent to prison as an impostor.[20]

Unexpected claimants to shares in wealthy estates (some of whom may have been genuine) were not uncommon. From 1872–5, Margaret Robinson pursued her claim to a widow's rights in the Steuart inheritance to the Murthly

and Co. estates. Her allegation was that she had been married to the late
Major Steuart and had had a child by him (though the latter had died). The
marriage, however, was in the 'Scottish manner' when the Major had slipped
a ring on her finger to signify marriage in front of her parents – he, at that
time, having no money or property to allow him to marry her publicly.
Thereafter, they lived together for some time as man and wife, though the
marriage was kept quiet.[21] Judges were divided on the case and it was not
fully settled until 1875 when the Lord Chancellor decided the evidence of
the 'Scotch marriage' was too insubstantial to allow her claim. A similar case
was the Dysart peerage claim before the House of Lords Committee on
Privileges in 1881. The claim was brought by Elizabeth Acford, who said that
she had been seduced by the late Lord Huntingtower, son of Lady Dysart (in
whose service she was then working). In July 1844, they apparently undertook a Scotch marriage in front of a servant. Three children were born but
Huntingtower later deserted her and she was left on the parish. It was
eventually decided that again there was not enough evidence to prove her
story.[22] These cases were of course about disputed marriages, not disputed
identity. They show, however, how systems based on inheritance and succession generated claimants and also how these episodes dragged sordid private
affairs among the elite into the public domain much as divorce cases did.
These cases also addressed the ongoing fascination with the elite as sexual
predators on women who were of lower status. *The Times* disdainfully
argued that, as 'romances of the peerage go', the Dysart case was 'squalid'.[23]

The later Victorian period was characterised by increasing concern with
forms of identification, a phenomenon we associate with the growth of the
modern state. Photographing criminals had become integral to police work
from the 1860s.[24] Fingerprinting came later (in 1901). The mechanisms for
demonstrating identity were becoming more defined. Even in the twenty-
first century, the ways by which we prove we are who we say we are remain
controversial (with the introduction of identification cards raising questions
about protection of civil liberties and privacy). Proving one's identity was
much more difficult in the nineteenth century. This was an age before the
passport or the driving licence. In the nineteenth century, there were six
ways to identify individuals: the evidence of others, who could testify to a
person's identity; the evidence of the face (where photography was useful);
the voice; the marks on a person's body (as well as its shape); the job reference or 'character' (important for servants); and what people said about
themselves. None of these were straightforward. Indeed, we might see the

extreme length of the Tichborne trials as generated by these problems of identification. No form of evidence was unchallengeable; hence the lawyers had to deploy different kinds of evidence and test them out.

There is, of course, another way of identifying people and it is the one most often used in social life: trust. In regular social encounters we trust that people are who they say they are. In most cases we do not ask for proof of identity. Trust is one of the most important forms of social capital available, regulating how we deal with others. The significance of the impostor story is that it represents a breakdown of trust: an individual abuses the trust by taking on an identity not his or her own. The impostor is one who has refused the most basic of human rules – that we hang onto our own identities. For his opponents, the Claimant had noticed that an identity was no longer being used (the late Roger Tichborne) and had simply picked it up and adopted it. The relative ease with which he had done this was one of the most remarkable aspects of the case.

The Claimant inhabited perhaps the most heavily discussed body of the Victorian age, eclipsing Tom Thumb, the Elephant Man and other so-called 'freaks'. How could this lumbering mountain of flesh be the svelte Roger Tichborne? Oddly enough, the lack of resemblance was a source of fascination in itself. Making a contrast of pictures of the undoubted Roger and the Claimant meant that a viewer could actually see the imposture being performed. The fakery was manifest. But Tichbornites insisted that there was a resemblance. Physique changes with age; the Australian diet and climate could actually have reshaped a man. The Claimant's body helped shape the character of the movement. Identifying the Claimant involved comparing the features of Orton and Roger Tichborne, but there was considerable disagreement. It was unclear what colour hair Roger had. When the trial ended, the Claimant's hair was cut as he entered prison and it was found that it had been dyed auburn (perhaps to conform to what he believed was Roger's hair colour). The Claimant's hands were discussed because, for some, they were not working-class hands. Witnesses noted that, when they met the Claimant, one of the first things that made them believe in him was the experience of shaking hands with him and concluding that his hands were the hands of a gentleman who had not had to endure manual labour. This testimony was inconclusive.

There was also the evidence of photography but, as we have seen, this was easy to dispute, especially as photographers had already gained a reputation

The Geometrical Test

for being able to manipulate images. The Chile daguerreotype produced the revelation that Roger Tichborne had ear lobes, whereas the Claimant did not. Given the awkward fact that people don't usually grow ear lobes, supporters had to argue that the photographs had been doctored. Some of the pro-Claimant pamphlets adopted a pseudo-scientific approach. William S. Matthews measured the diameter of the iris in two photographs of the Claimant in 1873 and Sir Roger in 1853 and concluded they represented the same man. He employed geometry to demonstrate that the eyes were at the same distance from each other; thus his scientific test apparently proved that the Claimant was Tichborne.[25] This scientific approach contrasted with other arguments for the Claimant based on intuition (for example, the belief that a mother must know her own son).

The Claimant had several distinguishing marks on his body. There was the brown mark on his side that seemed to correspond to a mark on Roger Tichborne's body, but the mark that occupied most attention was of course the tattoo — or rather, the lack of it. Lord Bellew claimed that he had tattooed Roger at Stonyhurst with his initials, 'R. C. T.'. This was conclusive evidence for opponents that the Claimant was a fake. In contrast, supporters considered it an invention to prevent the trial from going on any longer and costing the Tichborne family more money. The tattoo marks dominated discussion and persisted in memories of the case.[26]

Tattooing enjoyed a peripheral position in British culture. It was usually associated with the working class, particularly sailors, or as a mark on convicts that established their criminal status. When Roger showed off his tattoos, the response of his relatives was shock that he had done something that reeked of low life. Mrs Nangle, on seeing his tattoos, exclaimed, 'Oh, how horrid. It is like a common soldier'. Roger apparently laughed and offered to tattoo her.[27] The tattoo was not, however, an unpopular device amongst the aristocracy. The Prince of Wales allegedly had a tattoo, although it mainly became fashionable only in the 1880s.[28] The Tichborne tattoo itself had an after life in textbooks of medical jurisprudence where it was cited in discussions of distinguishing marks.[29] The tattoo was another area where aristocratic and working-class society met. It was this curious fusion that propelled Tichbornism.

The other anatomical feature of the Claimant that generated discussion was his penis. His supporters had learned of a remarkable medical examination conducted on the Claimant's body by Dr Lipscomb, the Tichbornes' doctor. The Claimant's genitalia had a singular 'malformation', as it was euphemistically described. What this meant was that the Claimant had a retractable penis, which he could withdraw deep within his body. Lipscomb noted that the Claimant's 'penis and testicles are small; the former so much retracted (when not excited) that it rests upon the upper part of the scrotum like a bud'.[30] Lipsomb's findings were later confirmed by the physician, Dr David Wilson, who gave evidence in the Criminal Trial. He supervised a test in which the Claimant urinated and found 'the penis was absolutely out of view, and nothing whatever of it could be seen but the orifice from whence the stream issued'.[31] Wilson put this down to the absence of the 'transversalis perinaea' muscle around the urethra and noted that this condition would not affect the Claimant's ability to have sexual intercourse.[32] All of Orton's surviving siblings insisted that their brother had never had this condition, nor did any evidence emerge that Orton had a 'malformation'. This aspect of the case was to generate a pseudo-pornographic literature in time; one pamphlet entitled *The Tichborne Malformation* insisted on its cover that it was for 'adult males only'. As evidence, the 'malformation' was difficult to employ because it could not be shown whether Roger Tichborne had a retractable penis or not. There was speculation that the Dowager had known about it and would have ascertained that the Claimant had this condition. Supporters claimed that this was why the young Roger was kept in frocks until the age of twelve and that he had been known as 'small cock' both at Stonyhurst and in the army.[33] Was this why his fellow soldiers tied a donkey in Roger's bed as a practical joke? Was the belief that the 'malformation' would prevent Roger having children the reason for Sir Edward Doughty's resistance to his marriage to Kate? This line of inquiry never amounted to much. The 'malformation' tested the limits of Victorian speech. *The Times* could not bring itself to use the word 'penis' when the word was used in court and glossed over this passage in the trial with a brief and mystifying reference to the Claimant's 'peculiar formation'.[34] Tichborne therefore always possessed a slightly obscene dimension, which added to its fascination. The name 'Roger' was also slang for copulation. Although it is difficult to demonstrate, the numerous invocations of 'Roger Tichborne' in popular culture almost certainly played on the double meaning of the name.

The most notable physical characteristic of the Claimant was his fatness. The Claimant's outsize proportions (he was about twenty-six stone) meant that he was easy to identify. Obesity signified a range of things to the Victorians. The Claimant's figure was a representation of wealth. Girth was something that people could admire. It could also signify liberty; not for nothing was John Bull outsize.[35] On the other hand, the fat person was a figure of fun. A street ballad dealt with the Claimant's conviction in the following way:

> They popped him into gaol, but he got so jolly stout,
> The cell it wouldn't hold him; so they had to turn him out,
> They tried to the starving dodge to make his belly thinner,
> When he lived on bread and water and whistled for his dinner.[36]

Arthur Lloyd, a music hall star known for his impersonations of social types that were in vogue, had in his routine a song called 'The Bloated Aristocrat' which both mocked a drunken toff but also rendered him curiously lovable. Significantly, when Lloyd wrote his inevitable song about Tichborne, he interpolated parts of 'The Bloated Aristocrat' into the medley:

> You can see by my walk and all that,
> The shape of my coat and my hat,
> The cut of my hair and my distingué air
> I'm a bloated aristocrat.[37]

Lloyd's aristocrat was significantly fat, an attribute of the elite which the Claimant incarnated. The Claimant was a kind of bloated aristocrat or Champagne Charlie in real life. His image thrived on his addiction to cigars, food and wine. One imagines his top hat perpetually at a tilt.

The Claimant, if he was an impostor, was engaged in an elaborate performance. He resembled an actor putting on the costume of an aristocrat and speaking his lines (though rather badly). The flamboyant theatricality of the Claimant's pursuit of Roger's identity had a larger social meaning. It could suggest that being an aristocrat was simply a matter of play acting. In an age where the aristocracy had resisted the challenges of democracy, where aristocrats still dominated governments and the House of Lords was a vital part of the British constitution, this was not a trivial aspect. The Claimant suggested that the aristocracy were pretty much like anyone else and could be impersonated or even parodied.

The spectacle generated by the Tichborne movement was not just based around the stump campaign but also around the vast amount of ephemera that clogged the market. There was nothing unusual about this. There has always been some sort of souvenir industry from the relics of saints onwards. Monarchy and the major figures of Britain's military glory generated large amounts of paraphernalia but so did religious figures. A huge commemorative industry surrounded Wellington, Nelson and Sir Henry Havelock, who died putting down the Indian Mutiny. From 1871 it became clear that there was a market for Tichborne souvenirs. Any investigation of this ephemera is difficult because of its very nature. Much of it went in the next generation's dustbin. Remnants, however, survive. There were Tichborne cartoons, candle-holders, medallions, ballads, broadsides, tea-cloths, handkerchiefs and a glass plate with a picture of the Claimant and the inscription 'Would you be surprised to hear this man is Roger Tichborne?' It was possible to purchase small plaster figures of the major protagonists in the case (see plate 9) as well as their *cartes de visite* (photographs) which meant that their features were well known to the public. One of the most remarkable products of the case was a set of terracotta figures of Tichborne characters (now in the Brighton Museum) by the artist Randolph Caldecott, presumably not for the mass market. In an act of anthropomorphism, the judges are represented as owls, Hawkins as a hawk, Kenealy as a cock and the Claimant as a turtle.

Also available was a Staffordshire figurine of the Claimant (see plate 11). The figurine was manufactured by Sampson Smith, a leading pottery producer, in 1873 in Longton – one of the Pottery towns that made up the Stoke constituency that went on to elect Kenealy as an MP.[38] 'Staffordshires' like this were popular representations of celebrities of the day, serving the growing world of working-class consumerism. Although beyond the pocket of the poorest Victorians, figurines could be purchased by workers with small disposable incomes, along with commemorative mugs and plates. They were sold as chimney ornaments at street stalls, fairs and seaside resorts. Figurines became adornments of the domestic interior where the mantelpiece became a museum in miniature, a place for the celebration of beauty and repository of memory: vases, mementos of loved ones and rites of passage. The subjects of figurines varied but drew on the whole kaleidoscope of Victorian popular culture. Often the ornaments would represent idealised figures (like the Jack Tar or the fairground musician) or notables from public life: Queen Victoria, the Duke of Wellington, Garibaldi, Napoleon Bonaparte, Moody and Sankey and assorted pugilists. Some depicted scenes from Shakespeare, melodrama or Astley's Circus, whilst others celebrated sportsmen and criminals. Staffordshires (including plates and flatback figures) drew on the mass desire for commemoration and fed off the growth of the popular press, especially illustrated periodicals whose pictures furnished images to be copied.

The Tichborne figure was part of this world of domestic comfort. Sampson Smith clearly believed the figurine was commercially viable because the Claimant was a hero to the kind of people buying pottery. His earthenware figurine depicts the Claimant as a top-hatted, country gentleman devoted to the sporting life. In one hand he holds a rifle and in the other a pigeon. A stylised, crudely coloured ornament about fifteen inches high, it carries the legend, 'Sir R. Tichborne' on the base. In other words, it was a form of propaganda for the Tichborne cause as it did not employ the more neutral title, 'The Tichborne Claimant'. The Claimant's body was shown as only slightly portly, the figure lacking the extreme fatness of other pictures. It presented the Claimant as he wished to be seen, as a country gentleman – the image that was fostered by his appearances at pigeon-shooting contents in 1872/3. We do not know how many copies of the figurine were sold and the reasons why people purchased it must remain a matter of speculation. Supporters may have bought it. Alternatively, some may have seen the Tichborne case as an historical event that should be commemorated. The allusion to country sports and hunting was significant. The object might have aroused the utopian longing for a better place and time that rural images often do. It represented a world of paternalistic wholeness, an object of inchoate yearning which suggest the world of the purchaser is not quite complete.[39] The fact that some people put the Claimant on their mantelpieces demonstrates the hold he exercised over the popular imagination.

Most ephemera took a printed form. Huge numbers of pamphlets were produced by supporters to provide Tichbornites with ammunition for the Claimant's case. Guildford Onslow issued a number of pamphlets with titles such as *200 Facts Proving the Claimant to be Roger Tichborne*, which sold for a penny. Here is one of Onslow's 'facts': 'the Claimant always puts a dot over the "y" in his letters, a fact found to exist in most of young Roger Tichborne's letters.'[40] The repetition and accumulation of detail, which was almost scholarly in form, shows that there were perfectly rational reasons for believing in the Claimant. One of the characteristics of most movements incorporating conspiracy theories is that they devote immense energy to minute details to support their claims. Senator Joe McCarthy, to take the most famous of conspiracy theorists, had 313 footnotes in one of his pamphlets to back up his so-called evidence about Communist infiltration in the United States government.[41] The relentless accretion of detail was intended to provide respectability for the Tichborne cause. Perhaps the most important feature of Onslow's pamphlet was that he could actually itemise 200 pieces of evidence.

The most remarkable piece of Tichborniana was the serialised edition of the Criminal Trial produced by Kenealy between 1875 and 1880. Issued in weekly instalments, it eventually comprised nine volumes. There had been a demand for it for some time and the *Englishman* only promised to go ahead with it if it received 5000 pre-paid subscribers.[42] The paper later questioned 'whether the whole world now possesses in one volume (except, perhaps, in the entire works of SHAKESPEARE) anything so wonderful, so true, so full of interest, as this will be' (the paper optimistically assumed at this stage it would fit into one volume).[43] It was issued from the *Englishman* office and cost 3d. weekly. That the series should have been able to continue up to its conclusion five years later demonstrates the importance within Victorian culture of the trial account as a popular genre and of the continuing interest in Tichborne.

Each issue was extravagantly annotated by Kenealy, although the record of the proceedings was left untouched. Many of the footnotes sniped at the conduct of the trial but others were packed with (sometimes irrelevant) information to aid the reader, including the reprinting of many documents used as evidence. When bound, the volumes were supplemented by one of the most idiosyncratic but thorough achievements in Victorian indexing. This featured such entries as 'Vituperation and foul language of the Attorney-General' under 'V' and 'Unfair distinction made by the tribunals of Justice between the cases of Mr Onslow and Mr Whalley' under 'U'.[44]

Whilst it satisfied the popular taste for trial accounts and the obsession for information about Tichborne, the series was attractive because it was lavishly illustrated. Most of the protagonists in the trial were drawn, usually with great accuracy, from photographs. All pictures of the Claimant described him as 'Sir Roger Tichborne, Bart.'. But, perhaps more significant, were the pictures dealing with earlier episodes in the undoubted Roger Tichborne's life and the myriad representations of the Tichborne estates. The young Sir Roger was shown as a handsome aristocrat, romantically courting Kate Doughty, or as a sporting English gentleman.[45] This suggests a new departure in what had formerly been a largely anti-aristocratic cause. The lifestyle of the aristocracy was shown as desirable. None of the illustrations represented any criticism of the elite. Many pictures legitimated the aristocracy by depicting them caught in a world of Arcadian splendour. Hence the incessant number of pictures lovingly showing the Tichborne estates as a pastoral paradise – barely touched even by rural labourers. One volume includes the following illustrations – 'Scene near Tichborne', 'Interior of Chapel at Tichborne', 'Spring at Tichborne', 'Evening at Tichborne', 'April Showers at Tichborne' and 'Tichborne Waters', in addition to 'Summer at Upton' and 'Winter at Upton.'[46] The same volume featured the Tilborgh portrait of the Tichborne Dole. This legend had already featured in descriptions of the case and could be obtained as a poster in the *Graphic*'s souvenir issue after the end of the trial.[47] In this context, the Dole story and the pastoral imagery of the trial account underline the evocation of feudal paternalism that was introduced by Kenealy. It was the same mood evoked by the Sampson Smith figurine. The Tichborne cause managed to contain within it both a radical anti-aristocratic libertarianism and a feudal yearning that echoed the Young England movement of the 1840s.

The serious tone of this kind of material is in danger of diverting us from the way many Victorians thought about the case. We should not be surprised to hear that many found the whole affair a laughing matter; it was not an event to be taken seriously. The words 'Victorian' and 'comedy' don't often find themselves in the same sentence, but this is an instance of how we misunderstand the period.[48] The trial seemed gloriously pointless, a pantomime of the ridiculous. We learn a great deal about an era through what it considered funny. The Tichborne spectacle revelled in carnivalesque images in which laughter was directed against both sides. There were, for example, comic posters mocking the trial with jokes usually at the expense of the Claimant. A sheet presented the catalogue of an alleged sale of Tichborne

Illustrations from E. V. Kenealy (ed.)
The Trial at Bar of Sir Roger C. D. Tichborne
(1875–80).

Top left: *Contemplation in Tichborne Park*
Top right: *Scene near Tichborne*
Left: *Tichborne Waters*

The Tichborne Jack in the Box (from Fun *26 April 1873)*

relics. Amongst the objects on sale were an 'Egyptian mummy, which it is supposed Lady Tichborne would have recognised as her lost son'. The Attorney-General's speech was offered for sale 'handsomely bound in One Thousand and One Vols'. There was also 'A Lot of Rubbish, among which will be found the oaths of several of the witnesses'. Another poster imagined a drama at the fictitious 'Theatre Royal, Westminster' called 'Ballantine and Orton' in which the character of 'Forlorn Hope' would be played by holders of the Tichborne bonds. Then there was a poster that imagined a play called *Lady Tichborne and her False Hair* which took place at the 'Theatre Royal,

Lies-See-'Em'. Onslow, Whalley and the Claimant appeared as 'three noted spouters'.[49] A common format was the comic alphabet with lines like this:

> B stands for Bogle, a darky what of that,
> He swears he knew Sir Roger before he got so fat.

There was even a fake edition of a paper called the *Tichborne Times*, which parodied the Tichborne press. It recorded Tichborne meetings in which supporters called for an end to trial by jury.[50]

Arthur Sketchley's 'Mrs Brown', a comic Mrs Gamp-like character who featured in a series of comic novels (really music hall turns in print), had several encounters with the Claimant. In one she visits the Tichborne trial hoping to catch a glimpse of the Prince of Wales. Instead she ends up becoming a witness when she is mistaken for someone else.[51]

Punch, the great comic magazine, was another matter. It viewed the Claimant with disdain. The paper's coverage of the cause was somewhat erratic – often it featured the case against its will. On one occasion, the editor until 1874, Shirley Brooks, specifically told his deputy that there should be '*Nothing* about the Tichborne Case' in that week's issue. A friend remembered that:

> If you wanted to get a rise out of S. B. [Shirley Brooks] you had merely to mention the 'Claimant' ... He used to 'snort', literally 'snort' when anything enraged him, and many a 'snort' did the Tichborne case cause him. He was rabid against him.[52]

Brooks's successor, Tom Taylor (author of *The Ticket of Leave Man*), had a similar attitude.

Punch viewed the case as a long-running bore. Early references noted that it was impossible to get away from as everyone was talking about it.[53] The periodical maintained that the only people to do well out of it were lawyers, popular newspapers and the public (not a good thing).[54] When the Claimant was applauded by the audience on a visit to the theatre, *Punch* priggishly riposted:

> What kind of animals 'cheered' a person who, upon oath, has described himself to be utterly despicable, we do not care to ask; but we trust that they were the gentlemen of the pavement, not a theatrical audience.[55]

Not only was the Claimant immoral but he was also a drunkard. His identity as Roger Tichborne was never accepted. Instead he was either Orton, or a monster called (after Lewis Carroll's 'Jabberwocky') the 'Waggawock'. But even worse than the Claimant in *Punch*'s eyes were his supporters. A 'Waggawock Subscription List' of 1872 featured amongst its donors: 'A Hater of Law', 'Fagin and Young Friends', 'A Female Idiot', 'Five Cads' and 'Servants in a Kitchen, after reading the "Penny Dreadful"'. Jonathan Wild and Titus Oates were both credited with giving ten shillings each. In one cartoon, a servant leaves his employer because he cannot stand his 'Master's suckasms [sic] against that poor persecuted Sir Roger'. Supporters at Birmingham were described as the 'baser sort'. Upper-class figures taking part in the agitation, like Onslow, were similarly disowned. The periodical hated the *Englishman* (ironically, Kenealy had been a contributor to *Punch* in the 1840s).[56] In turn, the *Englishman* attacked Tom Taylor when he became editor, referring to him as 'dirt'. It featured a cartoon in which Kenealy is shown as St George, slaying the dragon of Corruption.[57] Underneath the hoofs of his stallion, amidst the dust, lurks a dwarfish man with a long nose and a clown's hat who looks suspiciously like Mr Punch (see p. 209).

The representation of the Claimant as the 'Waggawock' was appropriate because Charles Dodgson (Lewis Carroll) was fascinated by the trial. He went to bed one night during the trial and worked out that the name Edward Vaughan Kenealy could be anagrammed as 'Ah! We dread an ugly knave'.[58] Although he lived in Oxford, he had a home in Guildford and made a point of going down there in 1874 to vote out Guildford Onslow. There is even a theory that his nonsense poem *The Hunting of the Snark* (1876) is actually about the Tichborne case. Certainly, the Barrister in the poem is intended as a parody of Kenealy, who features in several of Henry Holiday's original illustrations (which Dodgson supervised).[59]

The music-hall routines about Tichborne produced uproar. Some of the humour with its comic lawyers looked forward to Gilbert and Sullivan's Savoy operas, particularly *Trial by Jury* and *Iolanthe*. Just after the first trial commenced, the Britannia Theatre in Hoxton featured a sketch in which the Claimant had an india-rubber toe which was stretched across the stage; the Attorney-General called it 'pulling the long bow'. One drunken couple laughed so loud that they had to be thrown out and charged with disturbing the peace.[60] Harry Jackson entranced London audiences with his impersonations of Kenealy complete with wig and umbrella and references to

Kenealy and the Dragon

Cockburn as the 'Lord Chief Injustice'.[61] The Great MacDermott sang about the Claimant:

> If ever there was a damned scamp
> I flatter myself I am he.
> From Cain to the dodger who calls him Roger
> They can't hold a candle to me.[62]

Another theatre presented a diorama of the Claimant's life in Australia accompanied by appropriate melodies whilst, in 1874, showman Randall Williams's 'ghost show' at the Hull Fair featured an image of Tichborne

House with two spooks (the Claimant and Kenealy) popping out of the trees close by.[63]

It was inevitable that the Tichborne case would be taken up by the pantomime and musical theatre, but this created problems. All theatrical performances had to be passed by the Lord Chamberlain (a precondition that existed up to 1968). William Bodham Donne, the Lord Chamberlain's examiner of plays, was determined to suppress all references to the case, in line with his policy of forbidding any mention on stage of contemporary *causes célèbres* or indeed current affairs.[64] All material submitted to him had to have its references to the affair taken out, from the very beginning of the trial. The producers of a comedy-drama called *Sid: or Good out of Evil* at the Graecian Theatre in June 1871, were asked to alter the line 'Here you bring my friend, Paul, and pass him off as another man from Australia. It strikes me he will go there now and you with him at Her Majesty's Expense'. Donne recommended replacing 'Australia' with 'Indiana' or 'Illinois': 'The Drama, though stated to have been written and indeed acted some time ago ... should not permit any real or apparent allusions to the Tichborne case, now pending.'[65]

Donne had his work cut out for him as the Christmas pantomimes were full of references to the case. From the Garrick's *Sinbad the Sailor* in December 1871 he forbade the lines:

and would you be
Surprised to learn Sir Roger Tichborne, he
The heir of all that wealth and property
Yes, but you see the lawyers eat the fat all off me.

From 1871 to 1876, Donne cut Tichborne references from fifteen shows. In some cases, like the Pavilion 1872 pantomime *Harlequin Hop O' My Thumb*, he merely requested that 'the Claimant' be substituted for the name 'Roger Tichborne'. As the case dragged on he became more vigorous in striking out any references. He was not, however, successful in his endeavour to keep the stage free of all mentions of the case. Many clowns frequently extemporised.[66] The stage, although subject to state control, remained an anarchic medium, as shown by the Alhambra's pantomime, *Harlequin Happy Go Lucky*, which delighted the audience with references to the case. Parodying the song 'If ever I cease to love', the Prince in the show protested his passion in the following terms:

May Odger hold fast, and stick to his last;
May Dizzy give a ball at the Hole in the Wall,
May Baxter, Rose and Norton discover Arthur Orton;
May Hawkins QC ask Baigent to tea,
                              If ever I cease to love,
And may Baxter, Rose and Norton discover Arthur Orton
                              If ever I cease to love.

When the fairy Felicia gave the Prince a magic sword that will 'cut down rocks, granite walls or anything else', he asked:

Would it – unless the question's out of place –
cut down the law costs in the Tichborne case?[67]

A popular music hall song was derived from Tichborne: 'Would you be surprised to hear?'[68] A reporter for the *Entr'acte* felt 'The music-hall profession ought to support the Claimant, for he has been quite a god-send to some of our serio-comiques, who have made him a most popular theme for some of their speaking and singing lines'.[69] But music hall did not have a monopoly on Tichborne. It was possible to dance to 'The Tichborne Polka' or 'The Tichborne Schottische', whilst the sheet music of 'The Tichborne Gallop' claimed to have been performed 'with immense success by all the military bands'.[70]

Within the conventional theatre, the affair evinced considerable interest. The Claimant himself had to decline offers to appear in four productions and there were three London theatre managers interested in signing him up.[71] There was at least one performance (by the Astra Dramatic Club) in aid of the Defence Fund.[72] The Claimant disapproved of allusions to him on the stage as much as William Bodham Donne did. Taking a box for the pantomime at the Princess' Theatre, he heard the following lines:

If he's not a Wapping butcher,
He's a whopping baronet.

He promptly walked out and wrote a letter to the manager asking him to delete the lines, following this up with similar requests to the managers of Drury Lane and the Surrey whose shows included Tichborne gags. His request was apparently complied with.[73]

One of the most popular of all music hall comedians named himself after the Claimant. Tiny Harry Relph began his career on the open-air stage in a black face, calling himself 'Young Tichborne; surnamed the Claimant's bootlace' (an earlier music hall performer, J. W. Mann, had used the name 'Tichborne' for a while in 1870). Relph came to his name because he was overweight and it was common at that time to refer to any fat person as 'Tichborne'. His stage name varied. Sometimes it was 'Young Tichborne the Pocket Mackney' (after the popular blackface minstrel E. W. Mackney). On other occasions, it was 'Young Tichborne, Little Black Storm' or 'Tiny Tich'. Performing one evening in Kidderminster, he heard a heckler shout 'wallop up, Little Tich' and thought the abbreviated version was superior because it was easier to remember. Thus Little Tich was born, renowned for his small stature and the enormous boots he wore. Around 1884, he appeared at Foresters Music Hall in London's Mile End Road as 'Little Tich, the Funny Little Nigger' but soon abandoned black face (as well as his puppy fat that had generated the Tichborne comparison). Relph's daughter believed the real reason for the change in the name was because he was confused with the actual Claimant, who was by this time trying to make a living in the halls. The use of the word 'Tich' to describe someone small is derived from Relph but in its origins the term was ironic as it referred to the outsize Claimant.[74]

Anyone who enjoyed the mass culture of the 1870s could not avoid encountering the Claimant. The Wagga Wagga butcher was both a victim of injustice, a villain and an opportunity for vulgarity. There was no one image of the Tichborne Claimant. Historians today often describe popular taste in terms of appropriation.[75] In other words, the interest in Tichborne did not necessarily turn people into partisans one way or the other. People took from these episodes certain things and discarded others. Some bought into the Claimant's case; others opposed it. Many regarded it as a comedy. This was what the Tichborne spectacle involved. But any discussion of the spectacle requires an examination of how the Claimant figured in one of the most important forms of nineteenth-century culture: popular song.

11

Singing the Claimant

Victorian avenues and fairs were noisy places, full of street cries and song. The great social investigator Henry Mayhew commenced his olympian study, *London Labour and the London Poor*, by itemising the street folk one might encounter in the metropolis who he imagined as nomads trying to 'pick up a crust'. He found beggars, cabmen, pedlars, pickpockets, prostitutes, sailors and watermen, as well as costermongers offering every kind of food, and vendors of manufactured household articles and bizarre curiosities. These were people noted for their foul language, impenetrable slang, 'disregard of female honour' and high cheekbones (Mayhew as an anthropologist viewed them as a race apart, characterised by dislike of proper labour). These were noisy enough but there were also the street entertainers: acrobats, black-faced 'Jim Crows', black-profile cutters, comic dancers, conjurers, fire-eaters, fortune tellers, hurdy-gurdy players, jugglers, performing animals, pig-faced ladies, Punch and Judy men, sword-swallowers. Amongst these were the 'chaunters' and long-song sellers who sang on street corners. If a passer-by enjoyed their song, he or she could purchase a copy from the seller in the form of a broadside. There was no music, just the words, so it was important to listen to the tune (many songs offered new lyrics for tunes that were widely known).[1] What has been lost to us are the gestures and inflections that accompanied the songs and helped establish their pathos. The meaning of a serious song could be undercut by a knowing wink; the mood of a comic song transformed by the addition of a doleful expression. London was not alone in its ballad singers. Most places (rural or urban) had some kind of song tradition. For the Irish, their songs were a means of maintaining their national identity and, when in England, sense of exile (although their songs could be sung and enjoyed by English people as well).[2] These street songs were an essential part of everyday life. Up to the mid-Victorian period, the broadside ballad sung at a fair or street corner was a much loved form of popular culture. One of the most popular topics in the 1870s was the Tichborne Claimant.

The 'broadside' can be taken as any piece of literature (but mainly ballads) printed on one sheet of paper and sold in the streets for a penny. It took songs from the oral tradition and fixed them in print. Printed versions of popular songs originated in the sixteenth century and later provided a link between oral and literary culture after the onset of urbanisation and industrialisation.[3] Despite its rural origins, the nineteenth-century ballad produced a distinctive metropolitan voice with songs that expressed the perils and pleasures of city life.

Broadsides present us with problems of interpretation. In many ways they were the cultural form closest to popular experience. Formerly, balladry (or folk song) had concerned itself with the exploits of gallant heroes and romantic love; by the nineteenth century, it had come to embrace the lives of common people and the things that fascinated or entertained them.[4] It can therefore be employed as a mirror of popular mentalities – a valuable source for understanding the world of the working class who leave so few records behind. For all their apparent simplicity, broadsides are complex sources. There was a distinct broadside idiom or view of the world which means they may say more about the views of ballad producers than their audience. It could be argued that broadsides were an early form of mass culture, created by entrepreneurs and foisted onto the working class. Print certainly introduced a commercial element and transformed the songs into a commodity that could be bought and sold rather than passed on from one person to another or from parent to child as in former days.[5] On the other hand, these songs could not have had the audience they did if they failed to engage with popular concerns and speak the language of the street.

The producers of ballads do not seem to have had ambitions to control popular opinion, but to concentrate on the quick profit that could be made. Most commentators allowed that the broadside trade mainly followed the tastes and concerns of the working class.[6] Henry Mayhew noted in his investigation of the trade:

> It must be borne in mind that the street author is closely restricted in the quality of his effusion. It must be such as the patterers approve, as the chaunters can chaunt, the ballad-sellers can chaunt, the ballad-sellers can sing, and – above all – such as the street buyers will buy.[7]

Although capitalist in essence, broadsides remained part of a twilight world between popular culture and capitalism because they were so simple and cheap to produce. The upper classes were almost never involved in the process either as producers or as an audience who might have shaped the content of the songs. We can detect in the form many of the standard themes of popular culture: melodrama, crime, sensation, sex and patriotism. Broadsides illuminate the way the Tichborne affair was experienced by working-class people. The large number of Tichborne broadsides represent a street culture that was at odds with the 'official' world of the courtroom and high society. Too trivial to be termed a form of political resistance, they revelled in a counter-culture based on an exuberant vulgarity, a bloody-minded common-sense, a cheerful disrespect for authority and a dirty laugh. These songs helped constitute the 'public opinion' of the street. The Tichborne cause was sung as well as agitated.

Broadsides produced a form of cultural capital for working-class people, drawing on popular prejudices about the way the world worked and then reinventing them in the form of song or the sensational story. There is no doubt that they were bought and enjoyed by large numbers of people.[8] The publisher James Catnach sold 2,500,000 copies of broadsides on the execution of James Rush, the murderer, in 1849, though this was probably the greatest sale ever achieved by a broadside. Catnach's successor, W. S. Fortey, sold 15,000 copies of sheets on the murderess, Constance Kent, in 1860.[9] Broadsides were parasitic on crime and depended on exciting events, which could make the difference between an income of twenty shillings a week or five shillings. The fortune of Catnach was originally made by the Cato Street Conspiracy and the Queen Caroline affair in 1820.[10] One characteristic of the form was its urgency. A ballad-seller told Henry Mayhew that he never sold a 'last dying speech' (a broadside about a criminal going to the gallows) on any other day except the day of execution – 'all the edge is taken off it after that.'[11] Hence the songs tended to be truly ephemeral; only *The Murder in the Red Barn* surviving in the oral tradition.[12] By the 1850s, the relationship with newspapers was crucial, many broadsides simply copying material from them, but previously broadsides had in effect been the newspapers of their day allowing often illiterate people access to public events, even if usually it was only the description of a terrible murder.[13] They thereby assisted the growth of the public sphere. Moreover, the mid-Victorian popular press (in the form of publications such as *Lloyd's Weekly Newspaper* and *Reynolds's Newspaper*) from the 1850s onwards aped the broadsides when developing the format of popular journalism, offering a steady diet of murder, train-wrecks and romance in order to attract audiences. The broadsides were the seedbed of modern popular journalism.

The audience for broadsides went well beyond the purchaser. In Norfolk, it was not unknown for two poor families to club together to provide the one penny necessary to purchase an execution broadsheet. An informant of Mayhew's once saw eleven people in a cottage listening to an old man reading a broadsheet on the execution of James Rush.[14] They are therefore important evidence for how people thought. Printers and writers were part of the working-class community; their work was rarely patronised by the middle classes.[15] A journalist for the *National Review* claimed 'they are almost all written by persons of the class to which they are addressed'.[16] James Catnach was said to have made over £10,000 by the time he retired, but he was very much the exception.[17] In the 1860s, W. S. Fortey's was a very small-scale oper-ation.[18] It is likely that broadsides were produced in small workshops, a form of penny capitalism. When Charles Hindley called on the prolific Henry Disley, he found both him and his wife in the front shop, working on some cards they were printing. The impression given is that Disley's was a small-scale operation.[19] Broadside printers only required simple presses with a small stock of type and a few decorative blocks. The form was therefore determined by the ease of production.[20] There were only six writers of ballads operating in London in the 1850s. Receiving a mere shilling per song for their rudimentary rhymes, they lived in working-class areas such as St Giles, as did the sellers.[21]

The question of whether this was a distinctively working-class form is a difficult one to answer. Mayhew noted that many street patterers adopted the dress and appearance of the 'gent', wearing moustaches or Henri-Quatre beards.[22] They were actively imitating the fashions and values of another class. Few cultural forms are wholly the preserve of one class (though broad-sides came close to it). The street patterers are best understood in the way that Mayhew tended to see costermongers, as part of the 'dangerous classes', as a people on the margins of society. The image of the 'gent' was therefore a form of fancy dress, emphasising their apartness and signalling their trade. It signalled their sense of being part of neither one social group nor another.

When sold on the streets or in the pub, the broadside reassured the indi-vidual that his or her values were shared with others and so bound people together at an imaginative level (which is why it is significant that Tichborne was a favourite subject). They were not 'individualist' in the sense that a pamphlet, which one read to oneself, was. Song, by its very nature, implies something communal, something to be performed and shared. The places where one could buy them were also communal – the street, the market, the fair, the pub. These were all places where people mixed and where illiteracy was no barrier to enjoyment. As many sheets did not include a tune, they were also dependent upon the relationship between ballad seller and listener, a closer relationship than one simply based on the exchange of cash. The influence of print fixed the songs in a more permanent form and spread London concerns all over the country. There was little resistance to this and local printers often took up songs from the metropolis.[23] In 1861, it was thought that the main circulation of broadsides was outside London.[24]

By the 1860s, broadsides were thought to be on the wane and contemporary commentators believed they were describing a dying cultural form, killed off by songbooks and the emergent popular press.[25] Broadsides were hurt by the abolition of public executions in 1868, which removed one of their main subjects (as well as a location where they were sold). Improved literacy was a factor. The semi-public world of the street ballad may have been less necessary as more private forms of reading took over, although songs continued to remain an integral part of popular culture. The trade certainly slimmed down, but W. S. Fortey and Taylor's of Brick Lane, Spitalfields, were still active in the 1870s.[26] Henry Disley was producing ballads well into the 1880s and H. P. Such only stopped as late as 1917.[27] What is in fact more striking about the broadside is its longevity, lasting well into the 1880s as a popular form.

What was the broadside view of the world? Broadsides were anarchic, resisting the values of 'high culture'. Love (the most common theme) was often expressed through the robust and uncontrolled sexuality of 'free and easy' males. The other great subjects were murder and scandalous details about the home life of the royal family. This was not a world contained by respectable norms prescribed from 'above'; songs had a strong, demotic morality. Crime was usually followed by the inevitable retribution of the hangman's noose and there is no reason to suppose that this was not generated from street morality. The nineteenth century witnessed increasing fears about crime and violence, a concern that underpinned the growth of the police force. Violence, which had once been seen as an unavoidable, if unpleasant, part of everyday life, became something that had to be expunged. There was increasing concentration on the figure of the murderer, a figure demonised and imagined as outside of social norms, from whom society needed protection.[28]

Broadsides took only the vaguest of political stances (which may mirror the vague sense of political matters that many people had) and ignored movements like Chartism. Some were obviously published to serve particular political causes, such as parliamentary reform in 1867, but such items were few. The content of the songs did not imply that the often anonymous producers supported the cause they took up. Printers and writers were concerned with the whole kaleidoscope of popular appetites which could be milked for a profit. Mayhew once found an Irish Catholic patterer delivering a patter against the Pope, even though he did not agree with it.[29]

Over the nineteenth century several themes kept reappearing, suggesting that these were based on working-class perceptions of the world. Not surprisingly, broadsides affirmed the value of the working classes as the motor of society:

Old England's often led the van,
But not without the labouring man.[30]

Their libertarianism promoted a rejection of state intervention, particularly unjust taxation on basic goods and foodstuffs.[31] Instead of class hostility, broadsides emphasised conspiracies of government ministers and the powerful against the people. The rich never came out well. The basis of their wealth was usually not questioned, but the way in which they used it was and they were frequently seen as parasitic on the working class and unprepared to help the very people who were responsible for their wealth:

'Tis said that the labourer's worthy of his hire,
    But where does he get it I beg to enquire,
Not of coal or mill-owner, farmer or squire,
    For they grind down the poor of Old England.
The great landowners are leagued in a band,
    And who will deny it is so?
For game preserves, to monopolise the land,
    That food for the people should grow.
Cries my Lord—'for the starving rabble who cares
    We'll transport poachers, who dare to set snares.
For we think far more of our pheasants and hares
    Than we do for the starving poor of Old England.'[32]

The law made manifest this opposition between rich and poor. A ballad published by H. P. Such (probably in 1868) contrasted the fate of Victor Townley, a gentleman, and Samuel Wright, a bricklayer. Both were convicted of murder but Townley was deemed by doctors to be a lunatic whilst Wright was hanged.[33] Tichborne traded on this kind of injustice. World Turned

Upside Down images were not uncommon – a hangover from an earlier period. In an early nineteenth-century ballad entitled *Past, Present and Future*, the writer complains about the treatment of the poor upon the land:

> For nowadays the gentlemen have brought the labourers low,
> And daily are contriving plans to prove their overthrow.
> So now, my bold companions, the world seems upside down,
> They scorn the poor man as a thief in country and in town.[34]

Broadsides perpetuated a world view based on the carnivalesque.[35] The idea that the world could be turned upside down was not a subversive one. The only social advice dispensed by ballad writers to the working class was the art of remaining merry in the face of life's adversities.[36] In this sense the ballads sustained working-class fatalism – a way of coping with life the best one could given that the rich could not be beaten.[37]

The rare ballads that dealt with the claims of labour employed a language of rights, coupled with a sense of loss at the passing of a traditional way of life:

> In older times the poor could on a common turn a cow,
> The commons all are taken in, the rich have claimed them now,
> If a poor man turns a goose thereon, the rogues will it surround,
> The rich will have the kindness just to pop it in the pound.[38]

The period when such freedom existed was a pre-industrial Golden Age, defined in particular by food and drink imagery:

> Thus MERRY England many a year,
>   (I should have AGES said),
> Renowned for bread, for beef and beer
>   Her freedom bold displayed ...
>
> Of old, our fathers lov'd good Ale,
>   It flowed in Tankard cup and Horn,
> And O'er each plain, and hill, and vale,
>   Made England MERRY night and morn.[39]

This imagery addressed an audience for whom food and drink could not be taken for granted. Beef, however, had become central to the iconography of patriotism in the eighteenth century and British food an emblem of national identity (foreigners ate inferior food, especially if they were French):

Roast Beef! Plum Pudding land of old!
　　What shall I call thee now?
Want, famine in your towns stride bold
　　Your sons half starved that plough.[40]

The image of a 'Plum Pudding land' suggests the Golden Age was defined by an abundance of food. Not for nothing was the *Roast Beef of Old England* a popular song. Food certainly made for chauvinism but it also was a symbol of cultural identity. Edward Kenealy's demand for a free Meat Dinner Table was not an example of his iconoclasm – he was drawing on a popular attitude that can be discerned in the broadsides.

Sometimes the period of the Golden Age was located in the eighteenth century:

In the reign of old George, as you will understand,
Here then was contentment, throughout the whole land,
Each poor man could live and get plenty to eat,
But now he must pine on eight shillings a week.[41]

Sometimes the Golden Age was further back:

In 15 hundred and 72, as you must understand,
There was 10 millions of Britons upon this English Land,
In the time of Queen Elizabeth, the truth I must unfold,
Was work enough for everyone to keep him from the cold.[42]

The broadside evidence therefore suggests that the background to the Tichborne movement in popular culture was an insistence on the dignity of the people (defined as those who worked or who did not have access to power) and by a belief that their rights and freedoms have been eroded by the rich. It was not a language of class and only dealt with economic issues very broadly. Rather, it was a 'moral' language, designed to engender an emotional response. This may well have been how many perceived the world and it explains why the Tichborne cause was presented in the way it was.[43]

The importance that the Tichborne case had in popular culture is expressed emphatically by its constant treatment in ballad form. It was one of the *Standard*'s criticisms of the affair that there had been 'ballads made on him and sung to vulgar tunes'.[44] More than sixty broadsides were produced (including ballads and comic alphabets) and most were in favour of the Claimant. An objection to the use of broadsides as indices of popularity is that the most popular ballads are the least likely to have survived, being well thumbed, leaving only the least read for collectors and hence creating a misleading picture of popular interest.[45] The large number of separate ballads dealing with Tichborne, however, offsets this objection.

Many were produced by Henry Disley, who had started work under James Catnach.[46] By the 1870s, he had almost cornered the market in producing ballads on *causes célèbres*. In 1867, he issued ballads in favour of Reform but otherwise there was no formal political complexion to his work and no evidence of any connection with the Tichborne movement. Most likely, Disley was out to exploit a popular concern. There was an obvious audience for the ballads: crowds outside the courtroom during the trial, people in pubs, even those who attended demonstrations. Tichborne ballads were also produced by his London rivals, H. P. Such and W. S. Fortey, and provincial publishers such as J. Brueton of Birmingham. There is evidence that these ballads were sung at Tichborne events. When the Claimant appeared at the Grand Amalgamated Demonstration of Foresters at Loughborough in August 1872, the procession sang:

> Sir Roger Tichborne is my name,
> I'm seeking now for wealth and fame,
> They say that I was lost at sea,
> But I tell them 'Oh dear, no, not me'.[47]

The recourse to balladry indicates the importance of a song tradition in binding together the movement and reaffirming its popular solidarity. The tone was both joyous and defiant.

The vast majority of broadsides were produced during the second trial or just after, which indicates that ballad writers were reacting to a public interest that had been in existence for some time rather than imposing a concern on their audience. Indeed public interest was often described as part of the song:

But to get up a conviction,
    They had a deal of bother,
Yet the public say, and no mistake,
    He is no other man than Roger.[48]

In a Tichborne alphabet

D stands for Defence Fund, they raised in every Town,
To raise the Claimant up again, when he was broken down.[49]

Another ballad ends by saying that 'He's got the People's verdict and the Nation at his back'.[50] These broadsides were self-aware, recognising their role in the Tichborne spectacle. They painted the public as powerful and able to effect change. The people had made their decisions known in demonstrations up and down the country:

We read of Meetings being held,
    In every Country Town, Sir,
Then don't let London be behind,
    Ne'er see a man cast down, Sir ...[51]

The Tichborne broadsides expressed a yearning for purity in social dealings. This is particularly true in their treatment of the law and manifested the popular hatred of lawyers. It was felt that the trial was one-sided. The Bar was seen as a conspiracy not only against the Claimant but against Kenealy as well:

Now when the big-wigs found that he,
    To them would not be suing,
They knocked their wigs together boys,
    And swore they'd be his ruin;
We dare not do it publicly,
    For fear twould cause a riot,
So we'll get the Gray's Inn Benchers
    To do it on the quiet.

The same song contrasted the Bar with Kenealy's integrity and transformed him into an unlikely hero:

"FAIR PLAY"
FOR
TICHBORNE AND KENEALY.

TUNE:— Better Late Than Never.

Give me the man of honest heart,
  I like no two faced dodger,
But one who nobly speaks his part,
  Like Kenealy did for Roger :
One honest lawyer's found at last,
  Who'll ne'er desert his client,
He knows right well the cause is just,
  He stands up like a giant.

CHORUS:—

Then say men say,
  Be you low or rich born,
And have fair play,
  For Kenealy and for Tichborne.

Upon that trial where honest men,
  Were spurn'd with jeers and laughter,
The witnesses thro' well paid then,
  Will be better paid hereafter;

If Kenealy tried to say a word,
  The bench was in a fury,
How dare he doubt a witness,
  Like the famous mother Jewry.

Now when the big-wigs found that he,
  To them would not be suineg,
They knocked their wigs together boys,
  And swore they'd be his ruin;
We dare not do it publicly,
  For fear twould cause a riot,
So we'll get the Gray's Inn Benchers,
  To do it on the quiet.

Sir Roger bears up like a man,
  His spirit never lacking,
When he gets out there is no doubt,
  He'll give his foes a whacking;
His mother worried to her grave,
  Her son they'd like to settle,
But Roger shows the world he's made,
  Of good old English metal.

We read of Meetings being held,
  In every Country Town, Sir,
Then don't let London be behind,
  Ne'er see a man cast down, Sir,
We ask for justice, and fair play,
  For low as well as rich born,
We'll never cease, till we release,
  Sir Roger Doughty Tichborne.

Fair Play for Tichborne and Kenealy

One honest lawyer's found at last,
    Who'll ne'er desert his client,
He knows right well the cause is just,
    He stands up like a giant.[52]

Praise in *Give a Cheer for Brave Kenealy* also extended to the other supporters:

Stick to him, Mr Whalley, you are a perfect treat,
And you know brave Kenealy, he has never yet been beat,
With Guilford Onslow by your side, show the rum old codger,
That we ain't forgot the Claimant for Kenealy says he's Roger.[53]

The emphasis on loyalty represents the street attitude by which an individual was valued by the extent to which he or she stood by their friends at times of crisis.

The law was perceived as both corrupt and expensive. Not only was there one law for the rich and one for the poor but the people's money was being wasted on funding a trial simply to prosecute an innocent man:

> E stands for Everlasting, the case it might go on
> To feed the hungry lawyers when we are dead and gone.[54]

Furthermore, the trial was rigged and witnesses for the prosecution were bribed:

> Now about the Tichborne case,
>   They say that the trial is not fair,
> Tho I have heard people say that for £5 a day,
>   They'll swear he is not the right heir.[55]

The Claimant's supporters in Sir Roger's old regiment were deemed particularly ill-used:

> The witnesses against poor Roger,
> I think it's a shocking thing,
> Dragged up from the back slums of Wapping.
> To take their words it was a sin,
> While among the friends of Roger,
> Were soldiers who in battle, cool,
> Has nobly fought for England's glories,
> They were put down as rogues or fools.[56]

By criticising the Carabineer evidence, the opposition was presented as unpatriotic. The ballads, however, lack the anti-Catholicism that was a feature of Kenealy's publications, putting in doubt the extent to which anti-Catholicism was part of the movement's appeal.

The tattoo evidence was criticised because it was put forward by an aristocrat of low morals. Lord Bellew was continually mocked for his adultery with Captain Harvey's wife. The Captain's subsidy of five pounds to his wife for travel expenses was particularly sordid. In the ballads we see that people were fascinated by this glimpse into the home lives of the allegedly respectable:

> Now in came stuttering Lord Bellew,
> With a got up yarn about tattoo,
> And Lord Bellew, upon my life,
> You know you tattoo'd the captain's wife,
> Upon that lady you did doat,
> You did it so nice for a £5 note,
> Your character's got such a shock,
> Like Luie, you deserve it hot,
> You are a Lord of noble race,
> But like the rest you're in disgrace,
> Thanks to Dr Kenealy.[57]

Bellew was described in another ballad as 'Lord Tattoo' and compared with the Shah of Persia, then an object of fascination (and the subject of a number of broadsides) because he had visited Britain in 1873 and had many wives.[58]

Katherine Radcliffe's evidence was also considered suspect and an opportunity for mockery about the seduction, which allegedly took place at the old water mill in Tichborne. She received none of the chivalry that middle-class opinion bestowed on her:

> Now his pretty cousin no longer tarried,
> But to Mr Radcliffe she got married,
> She turned up her nose at the Claimant so fat,
> Never saw him before, she told him pat,
> Then the Claimant for spite, he told all about
> His pretty false cousin – let the secret out –
> How they danced the can can down the hill,
> And what they did in the old water mill
> Slap bang before the Jury.[59]

Katherine Radcliffe was also suspicious because of her class background:

> A deal of sympathy and humbug
> Was got up for cousin Kate,
> You may abuse the lower classes
> But mind you do not touch the great,
> That they are angels dropped from heaven
> Divorce courts will prove to you,

But then of course we must excuse them,
Because they've nothing else to do.[60]

Such ballads assumed a high degree of Tichborne 'literacy' on the part of their readership. The cause lent itself to popular interest in the scandalous or illicit sexual behaviour of the aristocracy or the wealthy that appears in broadsides. A Disley sheet entitled *The Naughty Lord and Gay Young Lady* shows an aristocrat caught seducing another man's wife.[61] Broadsides cut the aristocracy down to size. The Tichborne trial took on the character of a Rabelaisian revel. The Claimant was constructed in an almost pornographic way. There was a mildly lewd tone to some of the ballads, which invoked the 'malformation' by way of *double entendre*:

About the marks upon him,
They made a great to do,
They say that he's tattooed upon
His hoop de dooden do.[62]

This is another example (which also reminds us how Victorians were amused by the name 'Wagga Wagga'):

When the Jury said I was not Roger,
Oh! how they made me stagger,
The pretty girls they'll always think
Of poor Roger's wagga wagga.[63]

Because of his alleged breach of the Victorian code against pre-marital sex as well as his malformed penis, the Claimant was an obvious figure to express defiance of imposed sexual custom; a Victorian satyr, challenging order. Pornography had joined forces with radicalism in the early nineteenth century, and Tichborne represents a survival of this tradition.[64]

Even the Claimant's obesity had a curiously obscene feel to it:

They'll melt him down a stone or two,
For the treadmill he will have to do,
His bedstead will be such a topper,
To keep him up, he's such a whopper.[65]

Fatness represented defiance, a symbol of being freeborn. His size represented abundance of food, the pre-industrial world of roast beef for all. He was the modern John Bull. His fatness was a form of resistance, something to be actively celebrated:

> But they knew he was the right man,
>   You may be sure of that.
> Yet they failed to break his spirit,
>   Or pull down an ounce of fat.[66]

Fatness together with the Claimant's sexual indiscretions (the alleged seduction of Kate Doughty) made him a representative of the 'other' in Victorian culture: an inversion of respectability (the essence of carnival). His cause questioned the boundaries of respectable culture. Ballads defended the Claimant against charges that he was an 'artful dodger' ('dodger' of course rhymes with 'Roger'). The term 'dodger' captures the broadside mentality. It refers to characters who are slippery and indirect while recognising that life demands a lot of 'dodging'. The Claimant was imagined as someone who was streetwise, rule breaking, a ladies' man, roguish but lovable. *The Tichborne Budget* informs us his 'heart is as big as his belly'.[67] A song even compared him to Falstaff.[68]

There was also a sporting dimension to his appeal and he was imagined as a sporting hero. One ballad described the case as a 'race for the Tichbourne [sic] sweepstakes'[69] Popular cartoons sometimes presented him as a boxer. The case was linked to the mass pleasure in gambling (the Tichborne Bond scheme was a form of gambling). Commercialised sport had become integral to popular culture during the nineteenth century.[70]

The Claimant in popular culture was often represented as a dangerous character, able to bend the law in his own direction, living on the edge of respectability, not part of the underworld but not honest either. This image was similar to two of the most popular fictional characters of the Victorian period, Ally Sloper and Mr Punch, enemies of Victorian respectability.[71] Ally Sloper's adventures originally appeared as cartoons in the paper *Judy* in 1867. He was a lovable rogue, a lower-class confidence trickster with an eye for the ladies. He was dressed as a costermonger, a 'rough' costume aping genteel society but never respectable. Not caring when his wife and daughter were carted off to the workhouse, he often indulged in drunken, loutish behaviour. He was the embodiment of a rough, low-life world but he became enormously popular. There were various kinds of Sloper memorabilia including Sloper walking sticks; one of the earliest British films in the 1890s even shows a man laughing at an Ally Sloper comic. Mr Punch's roots go back to the fairs and festivals of the eighteenth century. The Punch myth celebrates not only wife-beating but also uncontrolled masculinity. Both figures emerged from the rough culture of the common people but were domesticated: Punch became an innocuous entertainment for children by the seaside and Sloper in the 1880s was to lose his working-class background in favour of a vaguer identity as 'man of the people', though he retained a delinquent air.

The Claimant's image was similar to the earlier incarnations of these two. These figures mocked social conventions and celebrated low desires and dishonesty. Significantly, *Judy* featured an imagined encounter between the Claimant and Ally Sloper. In the cartoon, Sloper eats some oysters and swells to Tichborne proportions. Deciding to capitalise on this, he goes on tour and attracts much sympathy from men in rural labourer's clothing, until he has the misfortune to meet the real Claimant.[72] The Tichborne affair was Punch and Judy for real. Figures like Punch, Sloper and the Claimant offered a carnivalesque world and, like early modern carnivals, by questioning the social order and turning it upside down, served to release tension and perpetuate the social system.

The Claimant was not simply a fashionable topic of the moment but remained an enduring subject for the broadsides. In 1880 H. Such produced a broadside lamenting that he had been in prison for six years and promising that, if he were freed, 'Many a working man will shake him by the hand'. The actual release of the Claimant in 1884 was celebrated by a broadside that defiantly insisted he was he was the right man.[73] Such longevity as a broadside issue demonstrates the way the Tichborne cause became an integral part of working-class culture.

In the Tichborne broadsides we encounter a world view that was patriotic, exuberant, aggressively manly and disrespectful, particularly of elites. When the Prince of Wales attended the Tichborne trial, a ballad asked if he was looking for Lady Mordaunt (with whom he had been linked in the notorious divorce action of 1870).[74] Ballads related to the world through sex and sport (hence the employment of sporting metaphors and the revelations about the private lives of the privileged). In the broadsides can be found not just the origins of modern mass journalism but the way we live now.

DOWNFALL
OF POOR
OLD ROGER

Fourteen years penal servitude.

The Tichborne trial is now done,
    Doodah, doodah,
We hear that Hawkins' side has won,
    Doodah. doodah day.
Kenealey now deserves a rest,
    Doodah, doodah,
For the big fat man he's done his best,
    Doodah, doodah day.

CHORUS.

But poor old Roger's done.
They have settled him at last,
They may prove he was the rightful
    heir,
When we are gone and past.

Now Hawkins he does feel so jolly,
He's banished care and melancholy,
He went home on —— night,
Jumped into bed and cuddled his wife.

And Mother Jury's got her tin,
She can go and spend it all in gin,
She saw young Orton stripped I'm sure
And danced with him the perfect cure.

The claimant has to prison gone,
I think he'll find it rather warm,
For oakum he will have to pick,
And his skilly won't be very thick.

When he did to prison go,
They made of him a perfect show,
They cropped his hair so very thin,
And then his troubles did begin.

To see him strip and have a bath,
I am sure would make the people laugh
To dress him they did begin,
A knickerbocker suit they put him in.

They'll melt him down a stone or two,
For the treadmill he will have to do,
His bedstead will be such a topper,
To keep him up, he's such a whopper.

The claimant now can't blow his bacca,
He'll wish he'd stop'd in Wagga Wagga
Oh that he will. I know full well,
When he is in his prison cell.

The Tichborne trial is now o'er,
Of trials like that we want no more,
The cost the country lots of money,
And make some people feel so funny.

    But never mind old boy,
In fourteen years you'll be free,
And if you do return again,
We'll welcome you with glee.

Disley, Printer, High-street, St Giles.

Downfall of Poor Old Roger

12

The Freeborn Briton

An 1875 cartoon in *Judy*, a comic periodical, showed Disraeli, dressed as a policeman, defending the Lord Chief Justice from a mob of braying donkeys and anthropomorphised animals including a toad named 'Filth'. The mob attempts to present petitions labelled 'slander', 'abuse', 'lies'. 'Sir Roger forever and Millbank for the judges', 'calumny', 'Englishman' and 'K-N—LY and Magna Charta'. Disraeli sternly announces 'Mud-throwing – and quite time to stop it, too'. The following week's issue featured a cartoon in which Disraeli asks his gardener (John Bull) to clear away poisonous fungus in the shape of Doctor Kenealy.[1]

Judy found the politics of the Tichborne movement easy to dismiss and so might we. Contemporaries often viewed it as a ragbag of nostalgia, idiocy and irrelevant posturing, an ignoble lost cause that suggested the working class could not be trusted with the vote. *Judy* merely expressed prevailing middle-class opinion. At first sight, the notion that Tichborne counts as a radical – or even a political movement – seems to be stretching things a little. Historians have often failed to discuss the Tichbornites as part of the development of nineteenth-century politics.[2] Yet Jack Williams, a stalwart of the Marxist Social Democratic Federation in the 1880s, looked back on the Magna Charta Association as a major radical organisation prepared to denounce the 'cheap and nasty Manchester School' and its association with laissez faire.[3] The Tichborne Claimant inspired one of the largest political movements of the mid-Victorian era. But it is not enough to reinstate Tichborne in Victorian history. The Claimant forces us to view the development of modern mass politics and the movement towards democracy in new ways.

The politics of the Tichborne movement raises plenty of questions that require explanation. It was a radical movement at a time when radicalism was apparently in decline. It was a working-class and largely anti-aristocratic movement, to assist a man become a member of the aristocracy. It was an anti-Catholic movement to support a man who claimed to come from a Roman Catholic family. It supported the monarchy at a time when republicanism had briefly been in the ascendant in popular politics. It was led by Kenealy, surely one of the most bizarre and unlikely platform agitators of the nineteenth century. The Tichborne movement, in fact, runs counter to everything we have been told about social class and the politics it generates. Or does it? While not downgrading the eccentric or exotic aspects of Tichbornism, it had far more in common with popular politics in the nineteenth century than might at first appear.

The orthodoxy used to hold that working-class and radical politics had flourished in the early years of the nineteenth century, propelled by the social cleavages of industrialisation and the poverty and exploitation that came in its wake.[4] Demands for reform were made by agitators from 'Orator' Hunt in the years after the Napoleonic Wars to Feargus O'Connor and the Chartists in the 1840s, when the 'Condition of England question' was in the ascendant. These were the years of the mass platform when the poor demanded social and political reform; in particular, universal manhood suffrage. Democracy was seen as the solution to social ills; Westminster had to be made accountable. Chartism was terrifying because it appeared to be a harbinger of class warfare and revolution. Many leading Chartists thus spent much of the 1840s in jail. Three petitions demanding political reform were presented to Parliament by Chartists (the last in the year of European revolutions, 1848) but Westminster rejected change and the demands expressed by the People's Charter went unheard for a generation. Instead, the Great Exhibition of 1851 was seen as the symbol of a new, more confident capitalism. The mid-Victorian economic boom improved living standards during the 1850s and fears of revolution abated until the economic problems of the 1880s produced the spread of socialist and class-based ideas, leading to the foundation of the Labour Party in 1900. There was a brief upsurge in radical protest in 1866 when the Reform League demanded the expansion of the franchise and took over Hyde Park to protest (the skilled urban working class got the vote the following year in 1867). Otherwise, radicalism found itself in a cold climate. Indeed the transition to partial mass democracy in 1867 showed that the working class was no longer considered the threatening presence it had been in the Chartist era. The popular liberalism associated with William Gladstone set the political weather for the generation of the 1870s (even though Gladstone was defeated by Disraeli in 1874).

What does Tichborne have to teach us about the politics of the period? The Tichborne agitation demonstrates that there was in fact a considerable continuity of radicalism from the early Victorian generation into the 1870s and beyond.[5] Radical arguments, language and strategy were maintained in the difficult years when the hopes of Chartism had become a distant dream.

In many ways radicalism proved more successful in this period than it had been in the 1840s. The property qualification for MPs was abolished in 1858, some workers got the vote in 1867, and the secret ballot was introduced in 1872 – all demands of the People's Charter, although reforms fell far short of the Chartist requirement of universal manhood suffrage. Many former Chartists, such as Ernest Jones, found their way into the radical wing of the Liberal Party – a formidable coalition in the mid-Victorian years which embraced the old Whig aristocracy and businessmen, Anglicans and non-conformists, the middle classes and the labour aristocracy.[6] Liberals believed in the slogan, 'Liberty, Retrenchment and Reform', holding that free trade and cheap government expanded the sum of human happiness. Although Liberals countenanced state intervention on a case by case basis, by and large they supported the workings of laissez-faire economics, holding that state interference in the economy reduced the sum of liberty. The Liberal Party in the country was always more radical than the party in parliament and it was a diverse coalition prone to fissure but which was usually united in its admiration for the moral rectitude of its heroes, William Gladstone and John Bright. Radical liberalism with its openness to labour representation and limited state intervention had a powerful appeal.

We can detect strains of radical liberalism in the Tichborne movement. George Whalley and Guildford Onslow were Liberal MPs. Whalley may have been a fanatical anti-Catholic, but he had also been connected with the reformer Edwin Chadwick in efforts to obtain greater central control over local administration. He was also a supporter of the Freehold Land Society movement, whose liberal philosophy of self-help and self-improvement with temperance connections was similar to his own.[7] Some 'advanced' liberals supported the movement at a local level.[8] There were traces of radical liberalism in Kenealy's demands for a 'free breakfast table', meaning the abolition of duties on basic foodstuffs because they were a form of indirect taxation. Similarly, his hostility to income tax (which most workers did not pay) was one shared by many radical liberals, as they believed an undemocratic state had no right to extract revenue in this way: there should be no taxation without representation. But Kenealy, as we have seen, did not support extending the franchise to create a more representative state. Tichbornism was never confined to liberalism. Indeed, like some contemporary republicans in the period, it operated in an area outside the most powerful ideology of the Victorian age.[9]

Kenealy had links with both liberalism and conservatism. His movement borrowed from different sets of ideas (although many Tichbornites were probably more concerned about the fate of the Claimant than the proposals of the Magna Charta Association). The movement also drew on the more unpleasant elements of popular politics, courting the mentality that was named as 'jingoism' in 1877 and developing ever more fantastic conspiracy theories to explain how the Claimant had failed to win his case.

Tichborne demonstrates how little we really understand of how popular politics works. The vocabulary of 'left' and 'right' is of little help here. Although these terms date from the French Revolution, they are primarily twentieth-century in usage. In any case, they are part of a parliamentary language, which often has little application at the level of the common people. Many people had world views that were complex, no doubt incoherent and con-tradictory, and that did not fit neatly into the left or right scheme of things; they did not identify with the political process, viewing politicians as crooks spouting words that have nothing to do with their lives.[10] The Tichborne movement allows us to catch a glimpse of these demotic mentalities.

In what way were the Tichbornites radicals? To understand the world of nineteenth century radicalism, we must forget about the coming of socialism (even though, as we have seen, there were links between the Magna Charta Association and the new generation of socialists in the 1880s). Radicalism was a dynamic set of ideas in itself. The Tichbornites were part of a history of radical activity that went back to the eighteenth century. Conscious of its radical heritage, one column was written for the *Englishman* by an author employing the name 'Junius', echoing the author of the scurrilous letters (1769–72) that attacked George III and his ministers.[11] Although Tichbornites did not agitate for the key demand of democracy, they elaborated on the basic radical themes of the freeborn Englishman, the Norman Yoke and the balanced constitution.[12]

Tichbornism spoke with ease to a politics and culture that was essentially libertarian. The Magna Charta Association proclaimed that its purpose was to 'win back Rights which every free-born Briton may claim'.[13] British radicalism was based on an idea of civic virtue that needed to be protected against encroachment from above. There should be no interference in the life of the working man by an unjust, unrepresentative and oligarchic state. Although Thomas Paine had contemplated a kind of welfare state in the 1790s, most radicals believed that state intervention was a bad thing. They celebrated the fact that Britain did not have absolutist rulers like some continental states and resisted any possible moves towards despotism.

If radicalism had a theory, it was that of the Norman Yoke. Many radicals believed that the nation had been essentially democratic in the age of Alfred the Great. The arrival of William the Conqueror in 1066 had destroyed these English freedoms. The land had been divided amongst his Norman barons and the common people disenfranchised. The result was the enduring domination of power by the aristocracy and the subordination of the working classes. The Norman Yoke explained the collusion of monarchy and aristocracy in creating the combination of patronage, bribery and unrepresentative interests that constituted British government and became known as 'Old Corruption' or what Cobbett called 'the Thing'. The belief in the Norman Yoke served as the political theory of radicalism for generations.[14] Thomas Paine, though critical of the obsession with the English constitution, nevertheless subscribed to the idea. His pamphlet *Common Sense* (1776), which helped stimulate the American Revolution, attacked the whole basis of the constitution and monarchy by lambasting the figure of William the Conqueror:

A French bastard landing with an armed banditti and establishing himself King of England, against the consent of the natives, is, in plain terms, a very paltry, rascally original. It certainly hath no divinity in it ... The plain truth is that the antiquity of English monarchy will not bear looking into.[15]

Radicals in the nineteenth century spoke in terms of lost rights that needed to be restored (which is why they often appear backward looking). Their target was the oligarchic state, run as a racket for the aristocracy. Oliver Cromwell and the heroes of the English Revolution were rehabilitated as figures who had stood against tyranny (George Whalley was one of the parliamentarians who supported the building of a statue of Cromwell at Westminster). We hear the distinctive radical assumptions about the Norman Conquest in the Tichbornite John De Morgan's defence of the common lands as the source of English virtue:

The Common has been seized and 'enclosed' by act of the Landlord Parliament ... It is this tyranny shod with iron that has trampled down the peasant from the yeoman to a pauper; that, under Norman tyranny, took the manure from the peasant, now takes his sheep, then his cows, then his common land, till he is left with nothing but precarious wages.[16]

The *Englishman* spoke in the same terms:

> The holders have not title to the land; they never had a title except that
> of theft and spoliation. WILLIAM the Conqueror stole the land and
> gave it among the followers.[17]

The choice of the name 'Magna Charta Association' was not casual. Radicals
had long appealed to both Magna Carta and the 1689 Bill of Rights as
guarantees of the freeborn Englishman and the nearest things that Britain
possessed to a written constitution.[18] A few years prior to the foundation of
Kenealy's association, Josephine Butler appealed to Magna Carta in her
struggle against the Contagious Diseases Acts, which, she maintained, were
unconstitutional. In her notorious pamphlet, *The Constitution Violated*
(1871), she quoted the aphorism, 'Magna Charta is in everybody's lips but
in nobody's hands' and embarked on a scholarly appraisal of the Charter to
demonstrate that the forced inspection of prostitutes was a violation of the
most basic English legal principles.[19] E. G. Smith, of the Finsbury branch of
the Magna Charta Association, articulated his hostility to the Irish Coercion
Bill by using the following medievalist imagery that epitomised the cause:

> [he] drew parallels between the time when Englishman were serfs and
> slaves, with iron collars round their necks, and the present time, when
> they were threatened with serfdom and slavery, with invisible collars and
> chains. In the days when King JOHN was forced to sign Magna Charta
> there were but two appeals to be made – to petition or to the sword.
> And so it was today. Englishmen were seeing their Constitutional
> Rights, one by one, taken from them, and it was their duty to protest
> against such an invasion. (Cheers.)[20]

The recourse to charters of liberties (as in the Chartist movement) or to
arguments about a balanced constitution were the stock in trade of politics
after the Glorious Revolution of 1688.[21] Freedom in constitutionalist terms
came from maintaining a balance between the monarchy, the aristocracy
(in the form of the House of Lords) and the people (the House of Commons).
Kenealy's desire to restore the Bill of Rights and support the House of Lords
made sense within the assumptions of constitutionalism. The *Englishman*
focused on 'Old Corruption' demanding that the crown and government
'cease that atrocious system of patronage, which has made us abject slaves

under a subtle despotism'.[22] It condemned the telephone company as an example of 'jobbery and monopoly on the part of a government department'.[23] Any kind of state control was offensive to the rights of freeborn Englishmen.

In this sense the Tichborne movement represents the last phase of a radical argument that was becoming increasingly anachronistic. Socialists and New Liberals in the early twentieth century came to argue from different premises (focusing on class and the economy), although constitutionalism never completely disappeared from oppositional arguments and enjoyed a brief revival in the 1980s. Defining freedom through the separation of parliamentary powers (an idea enshrined in the American constitution) was still a relatively conventional idea in the 1870s, which was why Kenealy deployed it.

Radical movements spoke of democracy and the welfare of the poor, but they were often led by men who were not poor. The history of radicalism is full of leaders who came from the middle or even the upper classes: Sir Francis Burdett, Admiral Cochrane, Henry Hunt, Feargus O'Connor, Ernest Jones. They presented themselves as champions of the people despite their lack of proletarian credentials. Embracing the worlds of high and low, they became emblems of romance.[24] They were articulate and prone to self-dramatisation, although they were often dismissed as demagogues by middle-class opinion. Crucially, they had the time and money to travel, to write and to organise, things that local working-class leaders lacked, which enabled them to achieve national recognition. Viewed in this light, Kenealy and Guildford Onslow (who was a seasoned platform performer) simply adopted the mantle of the gentleman leader that was part of the repertoire of radicalism. Since that time, there has been a strand in politics of gentleman leaders who have employed the platform in an attempt to lead the 'people': Charles Bradlaugh, Victor Grayson, James Maxton, Oswald Mosley, Tony Benn, George Galloway. Even the Claimant (despite his lack of interest in political questions) must have appeared as a kind of gentleman leader when he toured the country in 1872/3. His stump oratory, however, was not so much the mutation of a tradition (he was not a gifted speaker) but a parody of it. His campaign borrowed from the rough and tumble associated with elections where the candidates could be treated as popular heroes but also jeered and derided.[25] The *Standard* compared him to 'a favourite candidate at a contested election'.[26] A reporter, observing the Claimant addressing a Nottingham crowd from a hotel room balcony, fancied he had 'heard other "Claimants" on the ... balcony – claimants to the representation of the borough in Parliament'.[27]

The Claimant adopted the persona of the candidate on the hustings but his purpose was not to secure votes but money. He was a different kind of gentleman leader.

Kenealy's denunciation of political parties was not unusual either. There has always been some resistance at a popular level to the idea of political parties. In the eighteenth century, there were frequent demands for 'measures not men'. This mentality, which never came to terms with the idea of an Opposition opposing just for the sake of it, had not died out (and still has not completely gone away). In any case, mass democracy was relatively new and existed only partially. Mass parties were still in the process of what proved a long and haphazard formation.[28] Parties had a difficult time organising the new electorate. The idea that people could be neatly divided into Liberals and Conservatives was a relatively new idea with which many felt uncomfortable. Tichborne expressed this kind of unease. Kenealy's self-presentation at Stoke as an independent, free from the constraints of party, may have assisted in his victory in the 1875 by-election.

The themes of Magna Charta had some echoes of Chartism, although without its commitment to universal manhood suffrage. On one occasion, the *Englishman* inquired after the existence of O'Connorville (one of the egalitarian communities the Chartists attempted to create) with regard to creating its own Building and Insurance Society. Edward Hornsey, a seventy-nine-year old former Chartist from Wellingborough, was inspired to send in verse from the Chartist *Northern Star* to the *Englishman*. On another occasion, the Barnoldswick Magna Charta Association heard a talk comparing the trial of the Claimant to that of the Chartist Ernest Jones, who had been imprisoned in 1848.[29]

This continuity of radicalism was evident in the political career of John De Morgan. His movement for the preservation of common lands represented the continuation of earlier struggles against enclosure and he developed the idea that the Claimant's plight was essentially one of civil liberties. De Morgan presented himself as a gentleman leader and his lecture topics were a collage of the radical tradition. He devoted a whole series of lectures to the English Interregnum: 'Men of the Commonwealth'. These included 'Cromwell, Citizen, Soldier and Monarch', 'Hampden, Pym and Eliot, a Republican Trinity' and 'The Regicides, a Plea and Vindication'. Some of his other lecture topics reveal different radical influences: 'Shelley, Humanitarian, Sceptic and Politician', 'John Wilkes', 'William Cobbett', 'Garibaldi, Soldier, Patriot and Hermit', 'Junius and his Writings'.[30] On political questions, he lectured on 'The

Game Laws', 'The Labourer's Right to the Soil', 'Why I Oppose the State Church', 'Why Ireland Should Have a Native Parliament', 'Vaccination, Unsound in Theory, Unsafe in Practice' and 'Internationalism, the Only Remedy for Present Evils'. He was a strong critic of imperialism, denouncing Disraeli as 'the empress maker', and of the royal family, who, he characterised as 'these royal drones'.[31] He admitted that he was basically a 'Chartist of the old school'.[32] His periodical *De Morgan's Monthly* embraced the Chartist platform as well as votes for women.

The Tichborne agitation reinvented platform politics. The 'platform' represented both the location of popular protest (the place from which speeches could be delivered) and the programme of reform that captured the political imagination from 1815 onwards. It was the device through which radicals could draw crowds together and was associated with a diagnosis of social ills that blamed the aristocracy and prescribed democracy as the solution. This was the world of Orator Hunt, whose platform of democratic reform at St Peter's Field in Manchester led to the Peterloo massacre in 1819. This was also the world of the Chartists who sometimes employed the threat of the crowds assembled before the platform in their attempt to make the government adopt their Six Points. Tichborne rhetoric was always backward-looking, evoking the ancient constitutionalism that had serviced popular orators from the time that the platform had been born. But the Tichbornites lived in a different era. Theirs was an age in which large crowd activities were increasingly policed and regimented. Where the Chartists sometimes held meetings on the edges of great cities free from control by local authorities, the Claimant's lectures were usually located indoors, in town halls or music halls, and required entrance by ticket (although subversive remarks were still made).

The Tichborne movement draws attention to an area of popular politics that was not wholly defined by the assumptions of liberalism and also to the tensions within liberalism. It reworked the culture of constitutionalism and maintained old radical forms: the defence fund, the petition, the platform agitation, the use of pressure group tactics. The language of patriotism and equality before the law drew on the belief in the rights of the freeborn Englishman. But clearly it was different from other forms of radicalism. It derived from Chartism a commitment to a programme of demands but did not support universal manhood suffrage (or the other points of the People's Charter). On the other hand, the framework established by Kenealy provided a basis for cooperation with other radical groups. Its allusion to Magna

Carta places it within the radical tradition but this does not mean it was identical to earlier movements that had invoked the document. Kenealy's use of Magna Carta was as much an example of his antiquarian interests as a radical argument. The whole basis of politics had changed since the Chartist years.

Tichborne, like many agitations of the period, was cross-class, but there is no getting away from the fact that it was largely working-class in composition. Whereas some radicals employed the language of class and even class struggle in the nineteenth century, it was more common to talk about 'the people' and their rights.[33] 'The people' is an ambiguous term, which was used by different people in different ways throughout the nineteenth century. Its ambiguity, however, may have been part of its strength as a term and account for its durability. It is impossible to be against 'the people'.

Tichbornites certainly employed the language of 'the people' rather than 'class'. When, like Onslow in the stump campaign, they did talk in class terms, it was in the form of a traditional alliance between the working and middle classes against the aristocracy. This kind of rhetoric is often called 'populism', a word with many meanings, which has increasingly come into use because of the poverty of our political vocabulary.[34] It describes a politics that cannot be fully defined by the language of 'left' and 'right' but which venerates the good sense and virtue of the 'people'. 'Populism' has been linked to a variety of movements all over the world. The US agrarian and Russian socialist movements of the late nineteenth century both described themselves as 'populist'.[35] During the twentieth century, 'populism' has become more widespread all over the world but attempts to define it have remained so vague that any form of popular politics can be said to be populist (in which case, the word means nothing). It has sometimes been taken to mean ideas of moderate reformism, rather than those which desired revolutionary change. The term has not always had a positive meaning. Populism became associated with reactionary movements that thrived on paranoia and sustained themselves through conspiracy theories, which suggested unknown forces were threatening the rights of the people (such as McCarthyism in the United States).[36] 'Populism' has also been used to describe the political theory of English radicalism.[37] Tichbornism is better seen as a specific form of political expression (that needs to be looked at in its own terms) rather than simply as part of a broader populist syndrome.[38] The virtue of the term 'populism' was to draw attention to the untheorised and emotional, even sentimental, nature of much plebeian political thinking. Voters for a political party often do not agree with, or are often not aware of, much of their chosen party's political beliefs. As important as its political programme is the feeling that a party generates.

Tichbornites were certainly paranoid and given to conspiracy theories. They were prone to fantastical claims about lawyers, politicians and Jesuits. Such a belief in sinister figures opposed to the people often creates the mentality of the crank and contributes to the darker side of popular culture. One embarrassing feature of British radicalism has been its occasional bouts of anti-Semitism.[39] Kenealy was prepared to denounce Disraeli as a Jew, part of a wave of anti-Semitic abuse against the Prime Minister that became marked in the 1870s.[40] Mostly, however, the Tichbornites were neither irrational nor malign. The Pittendreigh episode was highly suspicious and concerns about the inequality of the law was a fact of life for many people. Tichborne therefore refuses most of the standard political categories.

A key term that ran through the movement and represents its mentality was 'fair play'. This may appear to be an odd term which hardly amounts to an ideology but it demonstrates Tichborne's linkages to popular culture. It was a demand for straight dealing in social behaviour that was widely employed in the nineteenth century. 'Fair play' was a moralistic and commonsensical term that appealed to working-class people, no doubt because of its connections to the world of sport. The term 'fair play' was common in broadsides. In the East Anglian song, 'Pity Poor Labourers', the complaint is that:

Fair play is a stranger these many years past,
And Pity's bunged up in an old oaken cask,
But the time's fast approaching, it's very near come,
When we'll all have the farmers under our thumb.[41]

A comic ballad attacking food adulteration was entitled New Intended Act of Parliament, Agreed to by Sir John Fairplay, and Seconded by Mr Steady, for the Public Good.[42] These terms – 'Fair Play' and 'Steady' – express a belief in a coming social harmony if only purity of behaviour can be restored to public life. The term 'fair play' extended well beyond the broadsides. In 1831, when an orator denounced the Established Church before a crowd in Huddersfield, there were shouts of 'fair play for the people' as well as 'end of all monopolies' and 'roast beef of old England'.[43] In 1849, William John Evelyn, the protectionist candidate in the West Surrey by-election, won, promising 'fair play in competition' for English farmers.[44] It was the flexibility and ambiguity of the term which made it so useful. Evelyn at the time was trying to modify his own protectionist views because of the challenge of the Free Trade interest. In 1870, a correspondent of the Plymouth *Western Daily Mercury* calling him or herself 'Fair Play' complained about the one-sided nature of the Contagious Diseases Acts in that only women were inspected.[45] In the early 1890s the drink trade responded to temperance vans that toured racecourses and fairs promoting prohibition of alcohol by sending out their own 'Fair Play' vans with lecturers who attacked regulation of alcohol by local government.[46]

The term 'fair play' constantly flitted in and out of the Tichborne movement. The subtitle of the *Tichborne News and Anti-Oppression Journal* was *A Weekly Newspaper Advocating Fair Play for Every Man*. Supporters would often call themselves 'lovers of fair play'. One Tichborne ballad was actually called *'Fair Play' for Tichborne and Kenealy*. Here are some of the numerous examples of its use in broadsides:

Whoever the Claimant is,
    Through the country they say,
From first to last, in this great case,
    He has not had fair play.[47]

Then Judge and Jury rattle away,
    But let the fat man have fair play,
And everywhere the people say
    O what will be the verdict.[48]

F stands for Fair Play, right throughout the nation,
And every man should have it too, no matter what his station.[49]

Keep up your blooming pecker, you're sure to win the day,
If judge and jury see it out and let him have fair play.[50]

'Fair play' was not just a handy slogan; there was more at stake. It represented the popular view that the law should equal morality and justice. This was not, however, how the legal system developed in the nineteenth century. The Judicature Acts, which were enacted during the Tichborne trials, not only remodelled the court system but were premised on the belief that jurisprudence should exist as a science in itself separate from morality. Equity principles were to prevail over common law precedents where there was a conflict. Things had been different in the eighteenth century. In the age of Blackstone, it was understood that the law should be linked to virtue and manners. This was usurped by the rise of a separate discipline of social science and legal positivism. The law appeared increasingly alien to politics, popular culture and even to human nature itself. 'Fair play' was a demand that the law should remember what its primary purpose was. It represented an assertion that there was such a thing as natural law; it was a demand that the law must have social as well as merely civic responsibilities.[51] This was a different doctrine from what liberalism had become in the Gladstonian age. Tichbornism harnessed the older argument that the law needed to relate to human nature.[52]

What many people complained about was not so much the rule of law as the kind of law. A utopian idea of 'fairness' was opposed in popular culture to the current state of the law, hence the language of 'fair play' for the Tichborne Claimant. The Victorian legal system, with its emphasis on the rigid classification of lives and experience, was in effect put on trial by the Claimant's supporters.

By the recurring employment of 'fair play', the idea of the trial as a jolly sporting gamble was intensified. The presence of two noted sporting gentlemen, Lord Rivers and Guildford Onslow, around the Claimant no doubt helped. Sport has often been employed as a metaphor for society. In the Tichborne cause, the Tichborne family and the legal profession were not considered to be playing by the rules. 'Fair play' therefore captured the incoherent but profoundly moralistic sense that drew working-class people to the Tichborne cause.

The spectacle of working-class people supporting an aristocrat (as opposed to a gentleman leader) was not as unusual as it might appear. In 1820–21, Queen Caroline obtained enormous support from workers as well as from radicals. Caroline and the Tichborne Claimant both had an ambivalent relationship to political radicalism. Whilst enjoying a productive alliance with radicals such as John Gast and William Cobbett, Caroline's cause never represented more than a case of 'Us' against 'Them'. The movement had little to say about social injustice yet there is no doubt that it was the most elaborate popular cause of its time and united radicals disorientated in the wake of the 1820 Cato Street Conspiracy (the attempted assassination of the Cabinet).[53]

Princess Caroline, whose marriage to the Prince of Wales had never been happy, left England in 1814 for the Continent, where she was alleged to have taken an Italian lover. On the death of George III in 1820, the new King determined to divorce her. Caroline then decided to return home on the advice of Alderman Matthew Wood, the Radical MP, and was welcomed as a popular heroine. As she would accept no settlement, the ministry was compelled to initiate a Bill of Pains and Penalties to deprive her of her title as Queen. She was effectively to be put on trial as a woman whose morals made her unfit to be a monarch. To the crowds who delivered loyal addresses to her, hers was a matter of injured innocence. Demonstrations, ballads and pamphlets all attested to the extraordinary support she enjoyed from the people. Radicals, silenced by the Six Acts, were able to challenge and mock authority under the banner of the Queen. In print and on the streets, George IV was held up to popular ridicule and the Queen received support from all over the country.

The Bill passed its third reading with a majority that had shrunk from twenty-eight to nine. Fearful of the popular reaction, the government dropped it, resulting in triumph for Caroline and her supporters. All across the country, celebrations took place including bell-ringing and demonstrations.[54] Interest in the Queen soon declined, especially as the ministry did not resign and Caroline went on to accept a pension of £50,000 – a blow to her followers. But support revived as the Coronation Day (19 July 1821) drew closer. The Queen arrived at Westminster Abbey and was refused entry. After attempting to enter by several doors, she gave up and left. A few weeks later (on August 7), she died. It was not, however, the end of her cause.

The government wanted to move Caroline's body abroad to Brunswick as soon as possible and planned for the coffin to bypass the centre of the metropolis and be taken across North London to Harwich. Their plans were frustrated as a crowd blocked the route and demanded that the dead Queen be taken through the city. Again the authorities gave in. Two men were killed when Guards opened fire on the crowd at Cumberland Gate. Their funerals were also turned into great public occasions, attended by over 70,000 people. The affair ended there, as it no longer had a figurehead alive to sustain it.

Tichborne was in many ways a revival of the language and ethos of the Queen Caroline affair. In 1820, radicals had complained about a government conspiracy against the Queen, then elaborated into a conspiracy against the people. People showed their support using traditional means, many of which would later be used in support of the Claimant. There were bands, banners and placards at demonstrations. Petitions were signed and loyal addresses delivered. Numerous jugs and plates declaring loyalty to the Queen were made.[55] The radical William Benbow published a broadsheet using familiar radical language: 'Englishmen! You who love Fair Play and Open Trial, now open your eyes and read! Green Bags, SEALED UP, were sent to the Parliament about the Queen.'[56] The 'green bag' in which the evidence for the prosecution was delivered to Parliament was a much used metaphor for the secret and conspiratorial behaviour of the government. These criticisms of 'Behind Closed Doors' politics as opposed to 'Open' political behaviour were a constant thread in constitutionalist radicalism.

The suffering Queen seemed to epitomise the oppression of the people, just as the Claimant later would. Whatever radical content the cause had was effaced by the simple melodrama of the wronged woman. Women themselves featured prominently in the cause.[57] The Queen's lost rights became the people's lost rights, generating a language of radical patriotism. A broadside issued in Northallerton warned:

The times are awful – the rights of the PEOPLE are in danger – and the Patriots of Old England must continue to be firm, or the Land of our Nativity will be a land of slaves.[58]

Like Tichborne, this provoked a recourse to Magna Carta. One pamphlet celebrated:

THE BARONS
of Runnymede Field,
Who once made a Tyrant's ambition to yield
By guarding OLD ENGLAND
With Liberty's Shield,
And demanding THE THING
that John sign'd.[59]

Foreign witnesses who gave evidence of the Queen's philandering abroad were attacked by the crowd at Dover. Thomas Majocci, who said that the Queen had had an affair with her Italian companion, Bartolomeo Bergami, became a particular figure of fun. His constant answer to Brougham's questions during the trial, 'Non mi ricordo' ('I do not recall'), became a popular catchphrase (much like Coleridge's 'Would you be surprised to hear?').[60] Indeed a poster mocking the Claimant in 1874 announced that 'Since the days of Majocci ... there has never been such a confirmed instance of *non mi ricordo* as in the cross-examination of the Claimant'.[61] Tichbornites were aware of the comparisons with the Queen Caroline case. Kenealy complained during the trial: 'One of the most fatal blotches in the case against QUEEN CAROLINE, was the enormous sums of money paid to Witnesses; and I say this is also one of the worst blotches on the present Prosecution.'[62]

A decade later, another bizarre and colourful elite figure became an emblem of the people's aspirations. This was John Nicholls Tom, alias Sir William Courtenay.[63] He tapped the millenarian culture of rural labourers in Kent during the 1830s, but combined it with a tradition of aristocratic radicalism that the Tichborne cause would draw on as well. He was a gentleman leader who posed as tribune of the people. Tom (sometimes spelled 'Thom') was a wine merchant from Truro with a history of mental illness. Doctors diagnosed him with a form of obsessional behaviour they termed 'monomania'. In 1832, he disappeared on a trip to Liverpool to sell malt and failed to contact his wife. He emerged in London during the struggle over the Reform Bill, employing the name 'Squire Thompson', and may have been exposed to the numerous currents of radical thought in circulation.[64] In 1832, he arrived in Canterbury, dressed in Oriental clothes, giving his name as Count Rothschild and then, cashing in even more flamboyantly on the mystique of aristocracy, calling himself Sir William Percy Honeywood Courtenay, Knight of Malta, rightful heir to the Earldom of Devon and the Kentish estates of Sir Edward Hales, King of the Gypsies and King of Jerusalem. (The real Sir William Courtenay was in France at the time.) Through his titles, fabulous clothes and great generosity, the false Sir William attracted interest and support from all sectors of the community and was encouraged to stand for Canterbury as an Independent candidate in the election of December 1832.

He claimed to be uncorrupted by party – a concept which he held in disdain and which accounts for the popularity of figures of his sort. In his opening address, he told electors that 'any man, who belongs to a party, whether Tory or Whig, cannot serve the Public'.[65] Instead, he staked his claim for support on a general sense of opposition to the rotten state of things. He emphasised patriotism and liberty and attempted to embody the free-born Englishman. Typically, he said in the significantly titled 'Magna Charta',

> Purity is my object. To go into your Legislature the undeviating friend of ENGLAND'S LIBERTY ... I shall remain True Blue – to the National Faith, and to the engagements I have entered into between this city and the brave Englishmen[66]

His programme urged the abolition of tithes, placemen and taxation on all productive classes as well as universal suffrage. He opposed flogging in the army and supported the raising of wages. According to the *Kentish Observer*, 'He further promised a return to the good old days of roast beef and mutton, and plenty of prime, nut-brown ale'.[67]

This mysterious figure emerging from nowhere, promising purity and a return to the uncorrupt values of a mythical England may have appealed to the majority of locals in Canterbury but he made little impact on the actual voters. He only achieved 379 votes and, even worse, polled a mere four votes in the East Kent election shortly afterwards. But even though he lost, he was treated as a popular hero (some children were even named in his honour).[68]

Courtenay viewed the enemy as corrupt administration, which oppressed of the people. Good government, responsible to the people (he advocated annual parliaments), was the only remedy. In 1833 he edited a short-lived publication called the *Lion* in which he developed his Romantic and aristocratic form of radicalism: 'we shall always be found the foremost in supporting our king and country, according to the faith of our forefathers, the heroes of Magna Charta.'[69] For all his libertarianism, there was an unmistakable feudal tone – the characteristic contradiction which links him to the Tichbornites: a belief in 'noblesse oblige' (the good aristocrat who can connect with ordinary people).

He was subsequently sent to prison after perjuring himself during a smuggling trial, but the charge was changed to detention in a lunatic asylum (where his identity as Tom was established). Apparently sane, he was released in 1837, whereupon he found new support amongst small farmers and labourers outside Canterbury in the parishes around Hernhill and the Ville of Dunkirk, areas that had been the site of agrarian revolt during the Captain Swing disturbances of 1830 and which had resisted the New Poor Law of 1834. He announced he was Jesus Christ and that the Second Coming had arrived. Gathering an 'army' of followers around him, he marched through the countryside with a loaf of bread on a pole (a traditional symbol often employed in protest movements). Courtenay promised to end the oppression of the poor by the rich and claimed that the biblical time of Jubilee was at hand when land would be redistributed. This belief in the millen-nium (the Second Coming of Jesus Christ) flourished in early Victorian Britain. The presence of an army of labourers disturbed local authorities in Sittingbourne and prompted a warrant for Courtenay's arrest. When an agent attempted to serve the warrant, Courtenay shot him. Soldiers were immediately dispatched to put down this

apparent revolt. The farmers retreated to Bossenden Wood where they fought
a brave but unsuccessful battle against the military. Eight (including Courtenay)
were killed and seven wounded. Bossenden Wood became a scandal. Radicals
compared it to Peter-loo and claimed that Courtenay and his supporters had
been murdered because they opposed the New Poor Law. It was the last battle
involving   soldiers on English soil (later conflicts involved the police) and was
possibly an attempt at a larger agrarian rebellion.

Courtenay's career showed how an impostor could become a popular
leader. His exoticism was crucial in establishing support. By not being part
of the party machine, he articulated 'Them' and 'Us' politics. Public corporations were made up of 'turtle-soup gentry and public wine-bibbers, who
feeling their present situation but weak and feeble, use every unmanly and
grovelling method to support their failing dynasty'.[70] The people, by contrast,
were 'The Voice of God'.[71] The episode also revealed how the adoption of an
aristocratic personality could be combined with demotic, radical politics.
Tichborne's popularity had precedents. Kenealy and the Claimant were part
of a longer history of bizarre celebrities whose stories and charisma transformed them into tribunes of the people.

Tichborne also derived from something that was often at odds with radicalism: popular Toryism. At one time historians used not to acknowledge that
this even existed. Deference and identification with the prevailing social
order, the monarchy and the House of Lords were, however, part of popular
culture. The role of pubs in propagating the Tichborne cause meant that the
movement had some affinities with the kind of Toryism that adored sport
and the beer-barrel, and cheered the Queen and national triumphs, whilst
disdaining metropolitan elites for being out of touch with the people. Working-
class Toryism in Lancashire helped Disraeli into power in the General Election
of 1874. There was a strong tradition of factory paternalism where workers
identified with their employers and with the institutions of the state.[72] The
presence of Irish labourers in Lancashire also pushed many English workers
into an aggressive ultra-Protestantism. The Conservative Party employed
anti-Catholicism, the nation, the monarchy and the empire as constituent
parts of its appeal. We should not, however, assume that Conservatism was
entirely distinct from radicalism. Both stressed the rights of the people and
supported the constitution. Conservatives identified with working-class
pleasure, which meant the right to drink. Tichborne employed the same
language of drink, popular rights and national identity.

Kenealy courted popular monarchism. He chose to dedicate his edition of the Tichborne trial account to the Queen and the first issue contained two full-page portraits of Kenealy and Victoria. Within the four page dedication, Kenealy outlined his own conception of the constitution, which drew on radical arguments about the Norman Yoke. For Kenealy, the Ancient Constitution, which was 'the work of the wisest of men', had been destroyed and had been replaced by 'an Oligarchy which governs in the interests only of a few Great Families'. The times required that the monarchy should be restored to the people.[73] But Kenealy also blamed the distance between monarch and people on past kings who did not care about the constitution and allowed the oligarchy to develop. Thus under George II, 'WALPOLE was in reality Master of England: the great Families who surrounded him and supported him were everything. The SOVEREIGN was nothing'. The worst example of this tendency was George IV: 'God preserve this country from a Prince and a reign like his; for if we had such a second voluptuary, the Vatican could buy him with its unlimited millions; and for the gratification of his sensualism could win him to almost any meanness in its interest.' But all was not lost. As Kenealy claimed, Victoria

> *is* our QUEEN, and represents our ancient Kings; and the blood of ALFRED and the PLANTAGENETS is in her veins, and we are loyal to our old and heroic traditions. And what care we for such people as GLADSTONE, or that apostate Jew DISRAELI, when compared with this true and noble Lady, who ought to be our QUEEN, but is not.

Kenealy asked that she 're-assume the crown of ALFRED, and EDWARD and ELIZABETH, and makes herself again a power in the State'.[74]

This was an intriguing political strategy at a time usually considered as the high-tide of English republicanism, with the Queen still in mourning and distant from the people.[75] It has been held that the modern cult of monarchy did not commence until the Golden Jubilee of 1887.[76] The relative success of the Kenealyite Tichborne movement in attracting support suggests a need to reassess this view.[77] Republicanism certainly did not account for the whole of popular culture. When Gladstone organised the service of thanksgiving in St Paul's Cathedral for the recovery of the Prince of Wales from typhoid, an enormous crowd came to watch. Disraeli was cheered and Gladstone ignored, thus cementing the connection with the monarchy in popular Toryism.[78] Kenealy's advocacy of monarchy suggests that, whilst individual monarchs might be attacked, the actual institution of monarchy remained sacred for many. Chartist meetings would often start with a toast to the Queen in the 1840s.

Radicalism since the eighteenth century had employed the language of patriotism. The great claim of radicals was that it was the elite that was unpatriotic whilst patriotism involved standing up for the rights of ordinary people. John Bull, one of the great nationalist emblems, was as often as not a radical figure until the mid-nineteenth century.[79] It was only in the later nineteenth century that patriotism became the preserve of the political right. Disraeli successfully annexed it for the Conservative Party in the 1870s, linking it to monarchy and empire.[80] This was never uncontested, however, and there is a long history of patriotism and strong national feelings amongst radicals and the left.[81] Tichborne demonstrates that radical uses of patriotism were still alive in the 1870s. Kenealy's celebration of monarchism was not necessarily at odds with radicalism, although the Tichborne movement became more obviously republican in the 1880s.

Given that Tichborne has affinities with both radicalism and Toryism, the best way to think of it is as a form of pastiche. Kenealy and the Tichbornites drew on the whole repertoire of Victorian thought, borrowing omnivorously from all parts of the political spectrum. Ideas and political philosophy had few fixed frontiers. Gladstone commenced his career as a Conservative and ended it as a Liberal. Kenealy made something of the same political journey, enjoying old-fashioned Toryism but later standing for Parliament as a Liberal and as a kind of radical. His Tichborne leadership was an elaborate performance in which he was concerned as much with the style of politics as with the content, employing the identity of the gentleman leader.

One aspect of the Tichborne movement was certainly in line with British radicalism. It was largely (but not entirely) masculine. Some women participated but they were relatively few. We know that they attended meetings and there was a demonstration of the Ladies' Branch of the Magna Charta Association at Gunter's Hall, Fulham.[82] The *Englishman* emphasised the support of women for the Claimant, on one occasion claiming their support was caused by being more receptive to the word of God.[83] The prominent Tichbornites were, however, all men (apart from Georgina Weldon). In many ways, popular politics had become increasingly masculine since the early years of the nineteenth century.[84] Radicalism focused increasingly on male citizenship from the early 1840s onwards. The Magna Charta Association was distinctive in that it advocated votes for women, but this was not pushed very strongly. Within the history of the struggle for the female franchise, Tichborne barely warrants a footnote.

The Tichborne movement was in many ways an eccentric movement led by one of the most bizarre political leaders of the nineteenth century. Yet it articulated many of the traditional concerns of popular politics: a belief in civic virtue and the rights of the people, suspicion of metropolitan elites, demands for equality before the law, robust patriotism and support for gentleman leaders. There is also the possibility (though we cannot be sure) that Tichborne expressed a form of politics for people who were not otherwise attracted to politics. It is easy to assume that the 1867 Reform Act naturally led to the two party system and the spread of democratic values. The popularity of Tichborne stands as a reminder of how complex this process was. The Magna Charta Association resisted full democracy and opposed the party system. Perhaps the Tichbornites were foolish and ridiculous, but they also produced a politics based on utopian feelings about society and a belief in a better world. Theirs was a politics of desire.

13

Melodrama

In 1877, as the Claimant languished in prison, the Duke's Theatre reopened with a new 'grand sensational drama' called *The Two Mothers*. The play by two forgotten writers deals with the extraordinary resemblance between the main characters, Sir Lionel Ravenswood and a labourer called Alfred Burton (both played by the same actor). Frustrated in his desire to marry his cousin Blanche, Sir Lionel heads for exile in the goldfields of Australia. He is followed by Burton, also in love with Blanche though a married man, who murders him on the voyage. The ship is wrecked and Burton is the only survivor. In Australia, Burton determines to pass himself off as his victim. Returning to Ravenswood Hall, he convinces Sir Lionel's mother that he is her son. At the same time, Burton's mother arrives searching for information about his whereabouts. She recognises her son but he silences her by saying that, if discovered, he will be hanged. Burton's wife, Ellen, opposes his scheme to bigamously marry Blanche and sets out to expose him. The impostor attempts to kill her at a railway cutting but is prevented by his mother. In a struggle, Burton falls across the tracks, just as a train appears and is killed.[1] *The Times* reviewer complained that the events with the railway at the end were 'not very intelligible', though scenes with trains on stage were part of the spectacle that audiences had come to expect from theatre in this period. There were no doubts about the inspiration for the story which *The Times* described as 'a paraphrase of the story of a Millbank prisoner, whose name the country seems to be at last sick of hearing'.[2] The Tichborne case had become a source for melodramatic theatre. It had found its natural home.

Tichborne-inspired melodramas were nothing new.[3] During the civil trial a play was submitted to a manager in which the Claimant committed three murders in the first act.[4] Shortly afterwards, the Theatre Royal, Hanley near Stoke (part of the constituency that elected Kenealy as an MP) presented a drama titled *The Lost Heir and the Wreck of the Bella* which proved very popu-lar. The same actor played both Robert (sic) Tichborne and the Claimant. The play ends at the Tichborne trial, where Arthur Orton arrives in time to testify he is not the Claimant and save the day. The Attorney-General abandons his brief and the jury finds for the Claimant.

The *Era* complained about the play's 'disregard of facts' and sniffed, 'This is the sort of stuff provided for the intelligent playgoers of the potteries?'[5] The following month, the Surrey Theatre in London presented *The Claimant; or, The Lost One Found* by H. P. Grattan, an in-house playwright. The management played safe, not wishing to fall foul of the law, and the title was the closest thing in the play to the events at Westminster Hall. The play concerned a female claimant who had been previously abducted by a wicked uncle. She proves her identity not by a tattoo but by a scar on her wrist. The play was a huge success at the Surrey, despite dialogue such as: 'John Smith! I think I have heard that name before!'[6] An East End theatre offered *The Wreck of the Bella* with a character based on Jean Luie.[7] In 1875, the Ambigu Comique in Paris proposed a play called *L'Affaire Tichborne*. The censor objected and it ended up being called *L'Affaire Coverly*. The play did, however, feature a character called Arthur Gordon, who committed murder, robbery and bigamy. According to one account, *The Two Mothers* was an Anglicisation of this play. This was not unusual; there was a lively cross-channel traffic between the popular theatres of London and Paris.[8]

Melodrama is the connecting thread in the Tichborne affair. The world of moustache-twirling seducers, old retainers, swaggering bandits, patriotic Jack Tars, long-lost children, talented horses and distressed damsels helped determine the way the cause was perceived. The language employed to talk about the case and the sometimes hysterical feelings it generated were wrought from fictional conventions that were second nature to Victorians brought up on the culture of sensation. Melodrama was more than just a theatrical genre; it was a form that invested the world with meaning. The invocation of melodramatic vocabulary was intended to move listeners and to generate humanitarian and sympathetic feelings. The melodramatic language of Tichbornites was intended to make people identify with the Claimant's plight and promote action (or at least send money for the defence fund). Even the Claimant's original 'Appeal to the Public' described his cause in melodramatic terms. He maintained he was a victim of 'might against right', a lone figure up against the purse of the government, 'the strings of which will, no doubt, be freely pulled for the purpose of proving me to be a perjurer and a forger'.[9] This is very different from the satirical mode of the street ballads (though they could invoke melodrama at times). The Tichborne cause had pathos.

In cultural terms, the distance between the law courts, the political platform and the theatre was not great. Each depended on particular kinds of performance and thus provided a stage (of an unconventional kind) for melodrama.

There were suggestions that the Tichborne case should be moved from the law courts to the theatre where it really belonged. It was also not unusual for contemporaries to refer to the case as the 'Tichborne romance'. Literary conventions and references shaped the way in which the case was perceived. For example, Andrew Bogle was likened by Kenealy during the trial to a character in the early melodrama, *Paul and Virginia* (based on the 1785 novel), a true friend who remained 'faithful to the death, true as gold itself'.[10] Opening his summing up at the end of the trial, the Lord Chief Justice invoked the two Dromios in Shakespeare's *Comedy of Errors* as an example of mistaken identity (also a stock melodramatic plot point).[11] Contemporaries encountered the trial every morning in dramatic form when they read trial accounts in newspapers, where they were laid out as theatrical scripts with the name of a speaker followed by his or her dialogue. When the Claimant was sentenced in 1874, some newspapers responded with theatrical metaphors: 'Virtue is rewarded, vice is punished and the villain of the piece sinks through the proper trap-door into his place of punishment.'[12]

The stump agitation managed to combine the framework of a political agitation with show business. As the *Nottingham Daily Guardian* put it, 'There is a novelty about the whole thing that would delight the heart of a Barnum'.[13] The Claimant became an object of display, a great Victorian curiosity. Melodrama helps account for the rich theatricality of the Tichborne cause.

Today, the words 'melodrama' and 'melodramatic' have become terms of derision. They are associated with a theatre of grand gestures and ham-acting and, in everyday life, with hysterical behaviour. But melodrama's meanings in the nineteenth century were more complex and far reaching. The Victorians were the heirs to the Romantic movement, which helps account for the era's sentimentality.[14] The theatre and melodramatic conventions provided Victorians with an emotional vocabulary and a way of interpreting the world in which they lived. Dramatic conventions, including melodrama, pervaded politics, the media, street life and popular culture. Morality was always clearcut. Melodrama could never cope with irony, which explains its mixed fortunes in the twentieth century.

Melodrama was the first great popular literature of the modern world.[15] It derived from the stage but came to shape fiction, storytelling and much else. Melodrama was a moralistic and sentimental kind of play that dramatised the struggle of Good and Evil and expressed it through the representation of heightened and excessive emotions. Stories could be comic or tragic but all were intricately plotted and stressed the role of chance and coincidence. The concerns of melodrama were dominated by conflicts between rich and poor, town and country, right and wrong. The simplicities of village life were preferred to the city, where order was overturned and custom was replaced by lawlessness. Plots frequently involved the oppression of the poor by the rich, which appealed to the mass audiences of the nineteenth century. There were moments of hysteria and terror but also comedy and opportunities for music, dance and song. The modern 'Bollywood' epic today is probably the truest inheritor of nineteenth-century melodramatic spectacle, though melodrama has shaped much of popular culture from Hollywood cinema to the Mills and Boon novel. Victorian melodrama also sponged off other dramatic and popular forms such as fairy stories, morality plays, newspapers, ballads, sermons and contemporary *causes-célèbres*.

In the nineteenth century, melodrama was a theatre of utopian longing that expressed alarm at the challenge to traditional forms of morality brought about by a changing society. It could be conservative by assuming that only traditional hierarchies could maintain order, or it could be radical in its representation of virtue based in the common people. Either way, it gave voice to the fear and disorientation brought about by the rise of a market economy that disregarded traditional morality, in which the poor were allowed to suffer and traditional order was uprooted. The one position that melodrama did not take up was classical liberalism, and it never celebrated the operation of the market.

Victorian Britain was a haunted house. Inside the head of every Victorian reformer there were voices or whispers: a young seamstress was becoming a ghost through overwork, a child was being beaten by a brutal parent, a black slave's humanity was denied by an overseer's whip. These whispers were put there by newspaper reportage and parliamentary inquiries but they were reassembled by the melodramatic imagination. However, melodrama's didacticism was reserved for its promotion of virtue and distinction between right and wrong. There was no overt political purpose behind it and in that sense it was conservative. Nevertheless, the themes and topics dramatised on stage raised issues that were political and spoke to a variety of political agendas. This explains why melodrama shaped the language of popular radicalism and why politics and fiction so frequently overlapped. The Chartist Ernest Jones not only promoted democracy but also wrote melodramatic novels, including *Woman's Wrongs* (1855), which dealt with the exploitation of the poor by the rich. Literature, theatre and the political platform were linked in complex ways. For example, the most distinctive element in nineteenth-century melodrama was its emphasis on domesticity and the threat to the working-class home from the evil aristocracy which was also the chief concern of popular radicalism. The melodramatic imagination helped not only to colour but to construct radical thought.

Melodrama emerged towards the end of the eighteenth century. It was shaped by the values of Romanticism which swept through the arts and popular culture. Strictly speaking, melodrama originated in France and emerged from both high and low culture. Jean-Jacques Rousseau coined the term 'mélo-drame' (meaning a drama with music) to describe his play *Pygmalion* (1770), but it was also fostered by the pantomime tradition which was of Italian origin.[16] Melodrama could also claim indigenous British roots. We can detect the influence of the Gothic novel such as Anne Radcliffe's *The Mysteries of Udolpho* (there were Gothic stage melodramas involving ruined castles, brigands and sinister monks) and earlier plays such as John Gay's *The Beggar's Opera* (1728). Melodrama, as we would recognise it today, only took shape during the French Revolution. René Charles Gilbert de Pixeré-court penned a series of popular plays that were staged in Paris on the Boulevard du Temple – or the 'Boulevard du Crime' as it came to be known, because the entertainments specialised in tales of outlaws, danger and deception. These melodramas represented the democratisation of feeling. Earlier plays were essentially about the lives of the elite. The new sensation revealed that drama could now be found in the lives of the common people. The revolutionary stage abounded with depictions of their goodness and virtue which was under threat from the corruption of the rich. Although conservative, melodrama always contained these radical and democratic strains. De Pixerécourt was widely imitated. His *Coelina: ou, l'enfant de la mystère* (1800) was a major international success. Its plot, appropriately enough for present purposes, involved the return of a man who visits his old haunts after a long absence.

The play marked the introduction of melodrama into England (although London theatre was already evolving in its direction). Thomas Holcroft, the dramatist and political radical, saw *Coelina* at the Ambigu in Paris and, in an act of plagiarism not unusual in the period, presented his own version in English at Covent Garden under the title *A Tale of Mystery* in 1802. The play was not only a huge hit but changed British theatre. Such was melodrama's ubiquity on the nineteenth-century stage that it spawned its own sub-genres including outlaw melodramas, domestic melodramas or nautical melodramas

which chronicled the heroic exploits of the Jack Tar and presented naval
battles and shipwrecks on stage.[17] Producers vied with each other to offer
the most spectacular and realistic effects. Many circus entertainments in the
early nineteenth century were composed of melodramas which showed off
performing animals, a perennial crowd pleaser.[18] Quite simply, nineteenth-
century theatre was melodrama and would remain so until the theatre of
naturalism (the plays of Ibsen and Shaw) came along in the late Victorian
era. Melodrama began to decline because it faced competition from music
hall but, at the beginning of the twentieth century, it gained a new lease of
life in the silent cinema.

Although some middle-class elements disapproved of the alleged
immorality of theatre, large numbers of people attended melodramatic
entertainments. The East End of London had theatres such as the Britannia,
Hoxton, which drew in large working-class audiences. Even the poorest could
watch melodramas, performed in penny gaffes (cheap theatres where actors
would take over a small shop and present primitive, brief entertainments
for a small entry fee). Few Victorians were unfamiliar with the conventions
of the popular stage such as the heartless squire or the lovable yokel.

During the nineteenth century, melodrama became such a powerful
form of expression that it could not be confined by the proscenium arch. Its
conventions began to infect art, literature, music, journalism, law and the
way in which people saw the world.[19] It became a form of cultural capital for
working-class people. Paintings and fiction employed melodrama to express
psychological states (melodrama's elaborate gestures and manual semaphore
were not just a style of acting but an elaborate attempt to represent emotion
and interior experience).[20] As the art of pleading developed in Victorian law
courts, barristers used the techniques of melodrama to sway juries on behalf
of their clients by employing a moving or melodramatic style.[21] Many
Victorians first encountered the stories of Charles Dickens (who notoriously
loved the stage) not in his own works but through the melodramatic adap-
tations of novels that were popular favourites. Popular fiction from Dickens's
own novels to the boys' story paper were influenced by melodrama's unlikely
dramatic plots and passionate structure of feeling.[22]

In the mid-Victorian years, the Sensation Novel of Wilkie Collins, Mrs
Henry Wood and Mary Elizabeth Braddon reworked many of the themes of
traditional melodrama for a middle-class audience by allowing for a greater
complexity of motivation in its characters. Crime was no longer something
that happened among the dangerous classes of London's East End (the usual

setting in early Victorian fiction). Now it stalked the parlours of polite society. As we have seen, the Tichborne Claimant may have been inspired in his quest by Braddon's novel, *Aurora Floyd* (1863). The eponymous character is an impetuous, fiery, horseriding, black-eyed woman who marries a young squire but carries a terrible secret which is eventually revealed. She once foolishly married a stable groom (whom she thought had later died) but suddenly discovers herself a bigamist when he turns up out of the blue and threatens to blackmail her. The Claimant was sufficiently moved to write down a passage from the book in his pocket book at Wagga Wagga. Mrs Braddon sent the Lord Chief Justice a copy of the novel which Cockburn admitted he read from beginning to end with great interest during the trial.[23] The Tichborne case was made from fictions in every sense.

Melodrama provided nineteenth-century popular culture with a form of expression that placed ordinary people, including women, on stage, allowing the nineteenth-century audience to view itself in a romanticised form. Indeed, the melodramatic stage actually helped create a working-class public sphere – a place where popular issues could be at least articulated in some form. Its unlikely or escapist plots, however, implied that it was possible to live other lives. Popular culture contained a utopian dimension.

One of the mysteries of Tichborne is why it was an anti-aristocratic move-ment assisting a *soi-disant* aristocrat. If we remember that the Victorians were raised on melodrama, this is less of a problem. Melodrama managed to combine deference and populism, two qualities that should in theory be antithetical. The numerous tales in which poor families were threatened with eviction by unscrupulous landlords struck a chord with the people hugging the theatre ceiling in the gods. Domestic melodramas depicted threats to the family. Aristocratic seducers who smarmed their way through many dramas became objects of fear.[24] Indeed, the deployment of landlords and aristocrats as villains in melodrama was possibly one reason for the continuing appeal of land nationalisation as an issue up to 1914.[25] The plight of Queen Caroline in 1820 was perceived through the conventions of melo-drama, which explains why many women were able to identify with her and come to her aid.[26] Melodrama opened up spaces that allowed for women's concerns to be expressed. Yet, ironically, melodrama was a conservative form. Whilst it appeared to side with the common people, it rarely challenged social hierarchies and, whilst it featured evil aristocrats, the preferred solution to their machinations was a more benevolent aristocracy. Melodramatic writers were also often far from radical. Charles Reade, for example, in his play, *Free Labour* (adapted from his novel *Put Yourself in His Place*), dealt with trade union violence during the 1866 Sheffield Outrages and sided against the workers.

The wider dimensions of melodrama were complex. Melodramatic language created an opportunity for popular concerns to be addressed; it provided ordinary people with a voice and a way of understanding the world. At the same time, melodrama trivialised many issues and failed to allow for a more political analysis of the situation. We can see all this in the Tichborne movement.

The Tichborne story echoed popular fiction in numerous ways. The Claimant was allegedly an innocent man unjustly kept from his inheritance. The sealed packet containing the secrets of ancient families was a familiar device from the stage. The young Roger Tichborne's military career, adventurous explorations in South America and history of thwarted love made him a natural figure for romance, as did his handsome features. The pictures in Kenealy's trial account represent Sir Roger as a dashing hero. Even the Claimant of the 1870s could be fitted into this mould. Although not a debonair figure by any stretch of the imagination, he claimed to be an aristocrat who had descended amongst the common people by becoming a butcher in Wagga Wagga, whilst his ability to address crowds of working-class people showed that he retained the common touch. As a man returning from the past, he was a Victorian Count of Monte Cristo (Alexandre Dumas' 1844 novel was much dramatised during the century). The Claimant's suggestion that he had a dark secret in his past (that he had been an outlaw, and that he or Arthur Orton had participated in the murder of 'Ballarat Harry') cast him as a Romantic robber or Robin Hood figure. Robbers had been favourite characters in melodrama going back to Schiller's *The Robbers*. They were heroes as in penny dreadful portrayals of Dick Turpin or also villains as in the popular play, *The Miller and His Men* by Isaac Pocock, first staged in 1813.

Whilst melodrama sustained the Claimant's cause in some respects, its opponents engaged in a form of what we might call 'counter melodrama'. Sexual danger was an ongoing theme in the cultural politics of melodrama. In this version, the Claimant was a blackguard because of his allegations concerning the seduction of Katherine Doughty (the future Lady Radcliffe). The prosecution lawyers were determined to rescue her reputation. Coleridge told the jury in the Civil Trial (allegedly with tears in his eyes), 'It is not for me to sing her praises; but I know that all my life long when I want to point to an example of how a woman can be modest and courageous, and can mingle gentleness with firmness, I shall point to the conduct of Mrs Radcliffe in the Sessions House at Westminster'.[27] Domestic melodrama was full of maidens trying to protect their virtue from unscrupulous cads who were gentlemen only in name. There was a powerful interlinking of sexuality and property that ran through the Tichborne saga. The Claimant had invaded the Tichbornes' domestic space and made outrageous allegations of a sexual nature. Female virtue was therefore central to the story.

We might also see the Claimant as a kind of blackmailer, a stock character in Victorian fiction. The blackmailer was terrifying because he made private matters public, including false allegations about women. If his allegations were true, the Claimant had exposed the private conduct of the aristocracy but was himself guilty of bigamy because of the secret marriage. His description of Sir Roger's past painted a terrible portrait of aristocratic life (which Kenealy pursued during the criminal trial). If the Claimant was a liar, then Lady Radcliffe was a classic melodramatic 'wronged woman'. The popularity of bigamy in Victorian fiction (for example, Mary Elizabeth Braddon's fiction) was a way of turning illicit sex into a crime for which the offender could actually be jailed. It had the advantage that it was a sexual offence that was not so outrageous that it could not be spoken about.[28]

The other wronged woman in the story was, of course, the Dowager, who was largely interpreted through melodrama. Tichbornites alleged that her reunion with her long lost son had been betrayed by the Tichborne family. A supporter proclaimed at a meeting in Leicester (which had a large spiritualist community):

> The public see the cloud of doubt hovering around the verdict still, and while Roger Tichborne is pining away in a prison hospital, there speaks from that cloud a mother's voice, and her words, like a message from the spirit world, go right home to the English heart and vibrate the tenderest chord in the parental breast, 'I am as certain as I am of my own existence, and do distinctly and positively swear that this man is my firstborn son, the issue of my marriage with Sir James Francis Doughty Tichborne'.

The argument that a mother must know her own child was one of the most potent. Onslow at the same meeting claimed that 'It was impossible ... for a mother to forget her child', and, against suggestions that the Dowager was senile, remarked 'a shrewder and more talented woman he never knew'. It was only because of 'the persecutions and miseries which she endured that she died at length of a broken heart'.[29] In the counter-melodrama of the Tichborne family, the Dowager was an obsessive whose foolish 'recognition' unleashed havoc on all around.

The core of melodrama was domesticity with all of its profound symbolic importance. During the trial and long afterwards, there were rumours that the Claimant was really an illegitimate Tichborne who had returned to claim the wealth from which his bastardy had excluded him. Had Orton's mother been seduced by Sir James Tichborne and was this claim the consequence? Melodrama made these kinds of fantasy possible. Familial imagery has often been used to represent the social order.[30] The case was founded on a threat to the family unit and an attempt to recreate it through establishing a bond between a mother and her son (Roger's father having died in 1862). Melodramas often dealt with the quest by a son for his parents. The wanderings of Sir Roger (and the Claimant) from South America to Australia did not just provide the narrative with exoticism. The geographical separation of the Claimant from his family spoke to a fear that melodrama historically expressed. A sentimental verse about the case went as follows:

> Oh! Mother, I come, ye have called me long,
> In the plaintive voice of the lonesome song,
> Now borne on the waves as they rose and fell,
> Now breathed o'er the gale like a fairy spell;
> Surrounding me ever where'er I might roam,
> Was that sweet low murmuring voice from home,
>
> Oh! Roger, my son! I am lone, I am lone!
> Oh! Roger, my son! Come home! Come home![31]

One 'J. R.' of Colne in Hampshire wrote to the *Englishman* about how he had been away from his home for fourteen years. On his return, he was recognised immediately by his mother. For him, the mother's instinct was crucial.[32]

Melodrama's audiences were often made up of people who were far from home. The nineteenth century witnessed unparalleled amounts of mobility both within Britain and through emigration. Families were constantly split up and mothers separated from their sons.[33] The pathos of Tichborne was based on homecoming. It was a story rooted in homesickness.

Part of the poignance of melodrama is this sense of absence. In Tom Taylor's *The Ticket of Leave Man* (1863), the return of a long lost son is integral to the plot. In Moncrieff's *The Scamps of London* (1843), a young man returns from the colonies in time to rescue his brother from scheming relatives. But the Claimant's return to a mother gave the story an Oedipal charge. The Dowager Lady Tichborne was symbolically central to the narrative. The Claimant's opponents were acting in a way that went against the laws of nature by trying to break the umbilical link between a mother and her son. In melodrama, the parent – child relationship was vital. Not for nothing is the most famous line in melodrama, 'Dead, dead, and never called me mother'.[34] Many plays were family dramas, representing threats to the family that had to be negotiated or tales in which mothers sacrificed themselves for their children. The Tichborne melodrama was based on a conservative view of motherhood as a product of natural forces that no woman can control.[35] The central argument of the movement was that, by the light of nature, a mother must know her own son. Supporters of the Tichborne Defence Fund made it clear that it was the mother's recognition that made people believe in the Claimant.[36]

Homecomings were also important because they represented a search for identity. The hero in melodrama is often one searching for his parents or attempting to find out what his true name is. Many French melodramas employed the hero or heroine's first name (such as *Victor: ou l'enfant du forêt*) with the implication that they were trying to complete themselves through finding a surname. By the same token, many villains were often only referred to by their surnames, suggesting they were incomplete.[37] A clichéd sequence in melodrama was the recognition scene, particularly encounters between parents and children, where an identity in crisis became complete. The Tichborne story was made up of a series of deeply moving recognition scenes. These ranged from the Dowager's recognition of her 'son' to that of many of the army officers who had served with Sir Roger and who maintained this was their former comrade. Supporters were not only moved but wished to see the Tichborne family complete once more. No wonder that women at the Claimant's meetings would shout 'poor thing'.[38] There is no reason to believe they were insincere.

The domestic nature of the Tichborne plot can also be linked to another feature of the melodramatic imagination: the concern with duality, which Romanticism had fostered.[39] The Claimant's two identities (Roger Tichborne and Arthur Orton) gave the story a fascination familiar to readers of contemporary fiction, which abounded with doubles or double lives. The opening story in G. W. M. Reynolds's *The Mysteries of London* (1844–55), one of the most popular novels of its time, concerns two brothers who follow different paths in life, one good and one bad. In Wilkie Collins's *The Woman in White* (1860), the narrative hangs around two women who are mistaken for one another, with terrible results. In Mrs Henry Wood's *East Lynne* (1861), Lady Isabel Carlyle is forced to work in her own home, disguised as a governess, whilst her husband lives there with another woman. This kind of strangeness and displacement was echoed by the possibility that the Claimant was a butcher living among the aristocracy. The concern with duality also expressed the polarity of public versus private – a form of culture that would eventually produce Robert Louis Stevenson's *The Strange Case of Dr Jekyll and Mr Hyde* in 1886. Although the comparison is ahistorical, the Claimant was a kind of Mr Hyde figure. He represented the dark, unrespectable side of the aristocracy. Even for believers, the Claimant was a sexual libertine. The function of plots based on doubling is often to make public what society represses. The case confirmed the radical image of the aristocracy as lazy and immoral.

The Victorians lived double lives, divided between public and private. Well before Freud uncovered the subconscious, they were aware of hidden depths to the mind, the preserve of the mesmerist or the animal magnetist who exposed alternate selves.[40] Doubles featured in melodrama. One of the most popular nineteenth-century plays was Dion Boucicault's dramatisation of Dumas' *The Corsican Brothers* (1852), the swashbuckling story of twins who live parallel lives. Tichborne ephemera constantly matched up pictures of the undoubted Sir Roger and the Claimant, unlikely doubles who reminded viewers that the body was subject to change and that identity itself was unstable. Tichborne challenged the protocols of melodrama in one sense. Melodrama as a form was based on certainty: there was a clear division between right and wrong. Nineteenth-century popular culture valued transparency. It was essentially a public form that insisted the essentials of character should be made visible. The duality of Roger Tichborne and the Claimant was, in contrast, based on uncertainty. The elusiveness of the Claimant's identity (and the different and conflicting tales he told about himself) meant that he never quite fitted the melodramatic mode of transparent behaviour that signifies essential goodness.

Melodrama was crucial to the development of the Tichborne movement because it also dealt in conspiracy theories.[41] The typical melodramatic plot involved some kind of conspiracy against goodness. Stock villains included the nobility but also their stewards, which made Vincent Gosford's evidence immediately suspect. The delivery of the 'sealed packet' by Sir Roger Tichborne to his steward was in itself a familiar device of the stage. Other villains included lawyers who were presented as henchmen of the squirearchy in their attempts to pursue riches; their function was to frustrate justice. The conspiratorial melodrama of Tichborne also associated it with another popular anxiety: the fear of identifiable groups whose purpose was to sabotage decent humanity. The Tichborne movement was against Roman Catholicism, the lunacy laws, compulsory vaccination and the Contagious Diseases Acts. All of these movements can be linked to a dread of intrusion, whether by priests, doctors or the state.

Anti-Catholicism was an enduring aspect of Victorian life up to the early twentieth century (and in areas such as Glasgow and Liverpool, right up to the present). The Conservative Party in the 1870s established its identity as the ultra-Protestant party, which enabled it to make considerable inroads in Lancashire. To some extent, anti-Catholicism really meant hostility to the Irish but in its wake, it introduced a range of moral panics, particularly about the role of the confessional and the fear that young women were being incarcerated in convents against their will. The *Englishman* complained:

> the unreasoning echo sounds 'Every man's house is his castle'. What then? May every man, therefore, corrupt, seduce, flog, or imprison his female servant? May every man, therefore, lock up his wife with or without attendance and food? May every man, therefore, ensnare his neighbour's daughter and lock her up in a cell inaccessible to all the world but himself? No, ten thousand times, NO.[42]

In the 1860s, William Murphy stormed the country with his lectures and inflammatory pamphlet, *The Confessional Unmasked*. He claimed the Confessional was employed by degenerate Catholic priests to obtain access to the secrets of young women and to convince them to give their money to the Church. Murphy's meetings were usually accompanied by riots and he was finally beaten to death by outraged Catholics. Anti-Catholicism was one of the ethnic factors that divided the working classes.[43] Tichborne, however, had no Irish dimension to it. Although prominent supporters like George Whalley were vocal ultra-Protestants, Tichborne itself was one stage removed from the world of Victorian anti-Catholicism. In any case, the Claimant, if Tichborne, was a Catholic (and even the young Arthur Orton had apparently been received into the Catholic Church in Melipilla). The movement was really more anti-Jesuit than it was anti-Catholic, a phobia that flourished more in continental Europe than it did in Britain.[44] Whalley's political crusade was to drive Jesuits from Britain. The Jesuit order featured as villains in melodramatic fiction, the best example being the character of the evil Rodin in Eugène Sue's *The Wandering Jew* (1844). Jesuits were believed to be in the vanguard of a conspiracy to re-Catholicise Britain and the Confessional was seen as an attempt to subvert the minds of the nation. Opening the speech for the defence, Kenealy drew on Sue by claiming that 'many persons regard the indictment brought against the Defendant as a sort of representation in actual life of the "Wandering Jew", where a powerful religious confraternity under the guidance and leadership of the Jesuit RODIN entered into a conspiracy to deprive the descendants of the real owner of millions of money'.[45] Walter Bagehot later compared support for the Claimant with the passion for Sue's *Wandering Jew* of Parisian artisans.[46]

The phobias generated by the Confessional were curiously matched by the concern with the Lunacy Laws expressed by the Magna Chartist Georgina Weldon. Mad doctors replaced priests. Concern that rich young women were being placed against their will in asylums had already been the subject of Wilkie Collins's *The Woman In White* (1860) and Charles Reade's *Hard Cash* (1863). The crusades against the Contagious Diseases Acts and Compulsory Vaccination were promoted using melodramatic language. Typically, they were supported by the Tichbornites. What united these disparate movements was a fear of surveillance. They expressed the fear that the home and the body were under threat. Mad doctors could drag sane women from their homes (or so Georgina Weldon claimed). The Contagious Diseases Acts permitted the medical inspection of prostitutes and sometimes of respectable women mistaken for prostitutes.[47] Tichbornites attacked what they claimed was an unjust state which not only imprisoned the Claimant but attacked civil liberties.

Melodrama flourished also in journalism. One of the few national newspapers to support the Claimant was *Reynolds's Newspaper*, one of the most popular newspapers of its day with a circulation of 350,000, largely in manufacturing districts.[48] Published cheaply at one penny, it appeared on Sundays in the 1870s, the one day when the working class had the leisure to read a newspaper.[49] Whereas papers like *Lloyd's Weekly Newspaper* and the *Weekly Times* claimed to have a mass readership in this period but were mainly read by the lower middle class, *Reynolds's* managed to penetrate deep into the working class itself. Amongst its readers were members of the building and clothing trades, miners and railway workers, small farmers, factory operatives and privates in the army (in addition to a lower middle-class readership). *Reynolds's* was the first great mass market newspaper. Whilst the Liberal *Lloyd's* patronised the working class, *Reynolds's* offered full-blooded support for all causes of the 'people' (the construction it tended to use instead of 'class'). It became a crucial vehicle for the Tichborne cause because the trial at Westminster fitted with the conspiracy-ridden way that it saw the world.

The 'Reynolds' of the title was George W. M. Reynolds.[50] Today, he is largely forgotten, but in his time he was one of the leading figures of the Chartist movement, he helped launch mass-market journalism (pioneering the kind of approach that is still employed by the tabloid press), and he was possibly the most popular novelist of the nineteenth century. Reynolds had acquired fame in the 1840s when he cashed in on the popularity of Eugène Sue's *The Mysteries of Paris* (1842) with his epic serial *The Mysteries of London*. This ran from 1844 to 1855 and dramatised the horrors of the Victorian under-world and working-class life. Reynolds combined these with sensational, melodramatic plots about contested inheritances, cross-dressing women, gypsies and body-snatchers. He often interrupted his novel to provide statistical evidence about the conditions of the poor, which he blamed on the heartless aristocracy. Apparently radicalised by his own narrative, this led him onto the Chartist platform in 1848, the year of revolutions. His most enduring achievement, however, was the foundation of *Reynolds's Newspaper* in 1850. It lasted for over a century until 1967. The paper combined radical critique, republicanism and a relentless assault on the aristocracy with sensational stories about train wrecks, divorces and urban danger. In other words, there was no serious division between Reynolds's reportage, politics and fiction. These worlds were linked through melodrama. In *Reynolds's Newspaper*, the news was melodrama.

Reynolds's melodramatic approach derived from the early nineteenth-century tradition of 'unrespectable radicalism' that was influenced by Thomas Paine and employed pornography and scurrilous sexual satire to deflate its opponents.[51] Reynolds's publications were tamer than those that flourished during the bawdy years of Regency radicalism but he was often accused of being a pornographer. He loathed the spirit of 'flunkeyism' that was abroad in Britain (meaning deference to the elite) and he was particularly concerned with aristocratic men preying on working-class women for sexual purposes.[52] Melodrama allowed a radical analysis of the condition of

Britain to emerge in his pages. As has been seen, there was a relationship between the new mass newspapers and the street broadsides. Reynolds copied the sensationalist account of crime that the broadside had pioneered and fixed it in an enduring form as the basic formula of mass journalism. Tichbornism was based on this intersection between popular, street culture and the forms of mass culture, which employed melodrama and sensation to attract a wide audience.

Up to 1874 the paper remained ambivalent about the Claimant, reporting the trial and criticising the administration of justice. It treated Tichborne initially as a vehicle for critiquing lawyers, focusing on the extreme cost of the case and hence on the cost of law itself: 'There is no reason why law should not be cheap, except it be to fill the voracious maw of greedy counsel, and the no less greedy attorneys from whom they receive instructions.'[53] The paper did not leap immediately to the Claimant's defence, and one correspondent noted that the editor was not disposed to believe in the Claimant's identity.[54] What changed this stance was the popular support that the Claimant excited. The paper concluded that 'The British Public does not like to see any man persecuted, and that English love of fair play resents the act of trampling upon a downfallen man.'[55] During the criminal trial, it criticised the government for undertaking to defray the expenses of one side and not the other. After the Claimant's conviction it came out in his favour partly because it perceived the majority of 'the people' to believe in him. It assisted with the defence fund and Kenealy even hoped that Reynolds would join him as a Magna Charta member of Parliament.[56] Although this never happened, the paper continued to support and publicise the movement up to the end, despite Reynolds's death in 1879.[57] Its main reason for doing this can be summed up in the phrase 'Vox Populi Vox Dei'. Reynolds's Newspaper's use of melodramatic journalism helped add to the radicalism of the Tichborne cause.

The Claimant also inspired novelists to write more orthodox melodramas. Charles Reade based his novel The Wandering Heir on the case and persuaded Ellen Terry out of retirement in 1874 to appear in the dramatic version on stage.[58] Anthony Trollope later used it as the basis for Is He Popinjoy? (1878), an attempt to cash in on the trial. Today the novel is principally remembered for its satire of the early women's rights movement. The plot had nothing to do with the Tichborne case but the tale of a disputed inheritance in an old aristocratic family was bound to have resonance for the original readers.[59] At street level, the cause generated a serialised penny dreadful,

Young Tichbourne of Wapping Old Stairs: His Astounding Adventures by Land and Sea. Only a few issues have been traced which suggests it was not popular and was discontinued.

In Australia, the Tichborne case influenced one of the classics of Anti-podean literature, Marcus Clarke's *His Natural Life* (sometimes titled *For the Term of His Natural Life*) (1874) which involved a rethinking of the Tichborne story. In Clarke's version a British aristocrat is wrongly accused of a crime and transported to Australia. The novel became an indictment of the terrible conditions suffered by convicts (another example of how melodrama could be combined with reportage). Clarke's interest in the Tichbornes led to a lesser known novel about Chidiock Tichborne.[60] Rolf Boldrewood, author of the celebrated novel *Robbery Under Arms* about the Australian goldfields, was also inspired by Tichborne when writing *Nevermore* (1892).[61]

Melodrama slowly faded as a popular form of entertainment, but many of its techniques were inherited by the early cinema. The radical aspects of melodrama found their counterpart in the social dramas of the silent screen, where the evils of society were presented in a melodramatic way.[62] Melo-drama's influence on the cinema was enormous. For example, its stress on domesticity meant that women's concerns were often centre stage, feeding into the Hollywood 'woman's picture'.[63] Nevertheless, melodrama was indelibly rooted in the nineteenth century, which may explain why radicals in the twentieth century have not employed it as part of their vocabulary. Unlike G. W. M. Reynolds, twentieth-century radicals have had an ambivalent rela-tionship with popular culture.[64] The Tichborne case is an example of a radical cause that was unembarrassed about either melodrama or popular culture. Like the broadside ballad, melodrama recognised the existence of class society but it had very little idea about what to do about it. Ultimately, it failed to address the mature industrial society of late Victorian Britain. When nineteenth-century melodrama has been revived, it has therefore usually been in an ironic way, for the purposes of nostalgia or to provide a kind of entertainment that can be laughed at.[65]

Melodrama at its most radical never had a specific programme to deal with social ills. For the most part it really represented only a feeling of distress at the corrupt and disorderly nature of society. Tichborne was similarly incoherent, an example of how it had settled into melodrama's cosmology. What melodrama did have was a colourful language and repertoire of themes that were appropriated by the Tichbornites. Ultimately, the Tich-borne case was melodramatic in that it was a form of street theatre. The crowds that emerged in support of the Claimant saw themselves as locked in combat with authority and in terms derived from melodrama.[66] In a sense, the people were the real heroes of the Tichborne movement, just as melodrama with all its limitations was the theatre of democracy.

14

Epilogue

For Tichbornites, the Claimant's cause effectively ended in 1886 but, for the Claimant, it never came to an end. He continued to insist that he was Sir Roger Tichborne, a message that he proclaimed in music halls and circuses. The stump campaign of 1872/3 began once more but in a minor key. His theatrical career after leaving prison in 1884 did not advance his cause or bring him much money. In 1886, he sailed for New York, but his expectations of finding a new audience were soon dashed. John De Morgan apparently played a role in helping him obtain a lecturing date, but his first lecture on 27 June drew barely a hundred people. Remarkably, another man now came forward claiming to be Sir Roger Tichborne. The two Claimants confronted each other in an office in Brooklyn and denounced each other as impostors.[1] By the following year, the Claimant was reduced to becoming an attraction in various saloons and then eventually a bartender – a natural occupation for him. He returned to London at the end of 1887.

In England, his stage career had one important personal consequence – he met Lily Enever, a music hall singer. Mary Ann Bryant, his wife, had left him whilst he was in prison and around 1880 gave birth to another man's child. Although apparently not divorced, the Claimant married Enever and settled in the Paddington area of north London. Four children were born in this relationship but, sadly, none lived beyond infancy. Theirs was a happy marriage but they were soon reduced to destitution. The Claimant paraded himself around north London pubs vainly trying to sell his autograph. His hard poverty compelled the Claimant to accept an offer from the *People*. In 1895, he agreed to write a series of articles for the paper in which he admitted he was Arthur Orton. He described how the imposture had commenced as a practical joke on a friend in Wagga Wagga called Dick Slade (to whom he had boasted of his illustrious ancestry). It was Slade who had initially shown him the Dowager's advertisement. Events then took on a life of their own, once William Gibbes and his wife connected him to Roger Tichborne. He admitted that Bogle had been a key source for information about the Tichbornes. The articles were published as the 'Confession of the Tichborne Claimant'.[2]

Old Tichbornites were amazed. There were criticisms of inaccuracies in the text and suggestions that it had been ghost-written. The story in the *People* might have galvanised some activity. H. B. Harding, who had once edited the *Tichborne Gazette*, wrote to Biddulph to suggest that a reply be written. Harding, by this stage, was in a bad state, as destitute as the Claimant, and paranoid. He maintained that he needed police protection against other surviving Tichbornites. Harding then persuaded William Alfred Frost, formerly a journalist on the *Englishman*, to write a response. Frost knew the case inside out and had been close to Kenealy. He had written detailed articles in Kenealy's Tichborne trial account and was able to demonstrate that there were a large number of factual errors in the so-called 'Confession'. Frost, however, could not sell his refutation to a newspaper and publication had to wait until 1913.[3] Nothing happened about Harding's other idea, which would have been the ultimate absurdity. He wanted to prosecute the Claimant for perjury in claiming he was Arthur Orton.[4]

The Claimant penned his confession expecting to receive thousands of pounds from the *People*. He later commented about this episode, 'Money bought me – and that is the only thing in my life that I wish I could undo'.[5] In the event, he received only a few hundred pounds but employed the money to establish a tobacconist shop in Islington. He also reverted to claiming he was Sir Roger Tichborne and disowned the confession by writing articles for the *Weekly Dispatch* and *Tit-Bits* signed as Tichborne. One day his shop was robbed and he enjoyed the remarkable experience of being believed in a court of law when he identified the robber.[6] The tobacconist's business soon failed, as did an attempt to sell ham and beef. He then exhibited himself as a peep-show in hotels and was a familiar sight in local pubs. A benefit was held for him at the Laurie Arms and he could often be found in the Pontefract Castle where people would buy him drinks.

In 1897, John Churton Collins, the literary critic, sought the Claimant out and found him living with his wife in great poverty in Bayswater. The Claimant (to Collins's disbelief) maintained that he was Tichborne and that William Cresswell, the insane man in the Australian asylum, was really Arthur Orton. He did, however, admit to embarrassment about the Lady Radcliffe allegation. The leading Tichbornites, such as Anthony Biddulph (who died in 1895), were no longer available to provide him with funds. The Claimant subsequently wrote Collins begging letters and asked the scholar if he could place articles for him in the press. In December he informed Collins that he was twenty-five shillings behind on the rent and was threatened with eviction. The Claimant was indeed thrown out by his landlord in January 1898. His wife went to stay with her mother, as they had nowhere to live, whilst he was forced to seek out a cheap bed.[7] His final lodging was at 21 Shouldham Street, near Baker Street. He was riddled with gout and had had no food for days when he died of heart failure on 1 April 1898. His wife found the body.

In death, the Claimant proved to be a great public attraction once more. Cranks and curiosity mongers queued up at the mortuary to catch a last sight of the body and sketch or make a wax model of his face. Collins visited the corpse in the undertaker's premises (which exhibited pictures of the Tichborne trial) and found the Claimant laid out by the body of a well-known costermonger called King Coffee.[8] About five thousand people attended the funeral in Paddington Cemetery (now Willesden Lane Cemetery). Local publicans paid for the burial – the final tribute of the drink interest that had so sustained the Claimant during his life. Copies of a pamphlet titled *True Confessions of Arthur Orton* (probably a reprint of his articles in the *People*) were hawked round the crowds. Pubs in the vicinity did a roaring trade and the procession ended with a drunken woman being led away to the local police station.[9] In an act of extraordinary generosity, the Tichbornes gave permission for the name 'Sir Roger Charles Doughty Tichborne' (with Roger Tichborne's date of birth) to be placed on his coffin. As it was a pauper burial, the grave was unmarked, but the Claimant was identified as Tichborne in the cemetery's records. The service was presided over by a Protestant minister. The Claimant shares his plot with a number of other souls too poor to afford a proper funeral.

The Tichborne Claimant destroyed many of the people who came into contact with him. Guildford Onslow lost his seat in Parliament through his advocacy of the Claimant's cause. John Helsby (who looked after the Claimant's family whilst he was in prison) was financially ruined by his efforts in the cause and his family was reduced to poverty.[10] Kenealy lost his career. Harding ended up destitute. Lord Rivers feared at the end of his life that he had made a mistake in believing the man from Wagga Wagga.[11] The Claimant's first wife ended up working as a member of staff in the Southampton workhouse, where she insisted on being called Lady Tichborne (or sometimes, 'Mrs T'). She worked in the casual ward, assisting female tramps take a bath, and once said she would prefer the life of a vagrant to living with her former husband, who was a terrible drunk. Her eldest daughter disowned her for her life on the road.[12] She remained in the workhouse until her death in 1926. She never learned to read. The other Lady Tichborne (the Claimant's second wife) ended more happily. She married an Islington fish salesman and escaped from the poverty that had engulfed her during her connection with the Claimant.

The Tichborne cause did, however, go into the next generation. Whilst the Claimant was in prison, the leading Tichbornites had his children put through school. The Claimant's sons (by Mary Ann Bryant) eventually enlisted in the army but their subsequent story has proved impossible to trace as they changed their names. Of the two daughters, one took no interest in the case and died just after the First World War. Not so the other daughter, Teresa Mary Agnes. She insisted on her rights as a Tichborne. Brought up in gentility, she had never really known her father. On the Claimant's release from prison, she was appalled by his poor manners. Accompanying him on the lecture circuit, she also objected to his frequent womanising. She later maintained that her father had confessed to her that he had actually killed Arthur Orton, which explained his unwillingness to talk in detail about his past.[13] Desperate for money, Teresa eventually took to the stage herself using the name 'Alexander', and became a barmaid for a while, although she appears to have avoided becoming a prostitute, a not unusual fate for single women facing destitution in Victorian Britain. She was friendly for a while with a man whom she called 'Goldie'. Sitting in a cab with him, she realised that 'Goldie' was actually Henry Tichborne, once the infant baronet in the first Tichborne trial. She claimed that, some years later, he sent her some money via the family solicitor who said that, whilst Sir Henry acknowledged her, she would never get anyone else in the family to so do.[14] As the new century dawned, she decided to insist on her rights and demanded that the Tichbornes assist her financially. She pestered Joseph Tichborne (the son of Henry Tichborne), sold flowers outside his flat with a notice explaining who she was and, in 1912, actually attempted to assassinate him on his wedding day at the church. This led to a spell in jail (where she found herself in the company of the Pankhursts and joined them on hunger strike). She later established a dress-making business which collapsed. In 1924, she began to hang around the Tichborne estate and poisoned herself in a Winchester police station, possibly to draw attention to herself. The Tichbornes agreed to channel some funds to her through a priest in Tunbridge Wells, where she died in September 1939.

The other person to continue the fight was Maurice Kenealy. From before the age of sixteen, his life had been subordinated to the cause of the

Claimant, first by assisting his father in court, next by editing the *Englishman* and then by leading the movement. After the demise of the paper he spent the next thirteen years in America working as a journalist. He returned to England and, in 1913, published *The Tichborne Tragedy*, a major study of the case, which continued to argue that the Claimant was genuine. It was dedicated to the president of the Protestant Truth Society. Maurice died in 1921 when he fell off the cliffs at Rottingdean. He never got away from the case. In *The Tichborne Tragedy*, he said 'Life, indeed, seems to date for me from that morning, early in March 1873, when Lord Rivers called upon my father'.[15] For him, the Tichborne case was not just a tragedy; it was also a curse.

Many of Kenealy's twelve children went on to live remarkable lives.[16] Ahmed, the eldest, fell out with his father during the 1870s; the elder Kenealy considering that his son had wasted his time and money. He abandoned any parliamentary ambitions, although his association with his father's news-papers came in useful. He left for the United States where he appears to have prospered as a journalist specialising in articles about yachting. Another son, Alex, also became a reporter in the United States, where he learned the techniques of the sensationalist 'New Journalism'. He returned to Britain and worked for Lord Northcliffe's *Daily Mirror*, where, as assistant editor, he was crucial to its success. Charlemagne Kenealy became a magistrate in South Africa. The two most notable daughters were Annesley and Arabella. Annesley became a nurse and then subsequently a novelist, journalist and supporter of votes for women. Her writings were not distinguished. In later life, she became extremely litigious. In 1915 she sued W. H. Smith for labelling her novel *A 'Water-Fly's' Wooing: A Drama in Black and White Marriages* (an attack on half-breeds and miscegenation) immoral. When the judge (the son of John Duke Coleridge) decided there was no case, Annesley informed the court she had just taken poison. She was later charged with attempted suicide (but was released after a brother paid a bond for good behaviour). More talented was her elder sister, Arabella Madonna Kenealy, who was one of the first female doctors as well as a midwife. She went on to become an enthusiast for eugenics and racial development, an opponent of vivisection and an advocate of mystical femininity. Arabella wrote over twenty novels, many of which were concerned with social themes such as marriage, mother-hood and sexuality. She was, however, appalled by the militancy of the Suffragettes and distanced herself from feminism, a cause that, in her eyes, ignored the essential differences between men and women. In 1908,

Arabella edited her father's memoirs. Amongst her other works were *Feminism and Sex-Extinction* (1920) and *The Human Gyroscope* (1934). This generation of Kenealys embodied the vast range of interests (as well as the eccentricities) that had marked out their father.

The Tichborne case remained part of the folklore of London's East End up to the Second World War.[17] 'Datas' the Memory Man, for example, could astonish music hall audiences with his ability to recall obscure details of the case. In his youth, 'Datas' had sought out the Claimant in his tobacconist's shop and impressed him with his memory of all the dates in the case.[18] Rumours circulated as late as the 1920s that Arthur Orton's mother had been made pregnant by a Tichborne and that the Claimant was the illegitimate offspring.[19] The Tichborne case, however, declined in popular memory, although there has continued to be more interest in the case in Australia. The Claimant's waxwork at Madame Tussaud's was removed in 1891 (a useful index of contemporary fame). Novelists on the other hand were inspired by the case. Jorge Luis Borges, Leonard Merrick, Mat Schulz, Julian Symons, Patrick White and Robin Maugham (whose father Lord Maugham, brother of W. Somerset Maugham, wrote an important study of the trials) penned stories that were based in some form on the Claimant.[20] John Young even wrote two epic poems inspired by Tichborne.[21] David Yates's film *The Tichborne Claimant* appeared on the anniversary of the Claimant's death in 1998. It presented the events largely through the eyes of Andrew Bogle and became essentially a remake of *Kind Hearts and Coronets*.

The Claimant was written up in the literature of great trials, Victorian sensation and true-life crime. Douglas Woodruff wrote a magisterial treatment of the trials in 1957 based on almost twenty years of research (he regretted not commencing work on it earlier and thus losing the opportunity to interview the Claimant's daughter).[22] With the exception of Michael Roe's important study of Kenealy, professional historians have avoided Tichborne.[23] Few have chosen to analyse the politics of the Tichborne movement. They were allegedly an example of the irrational dimension of working-class life and in any case out of place after the rise of Socialism and the Labour Party. Few were nostalgic about this most eccentric of lost causes.

This book has sought to challenge the separation between sensationalism and the more conventional topics of history. History nowadays is about far more than the records of monarchs and statesmen; it is concerned with all aspects of human life and behaviour. It is easy to dismiss Tichborne as an example of the peripheral or ephemeral – something that does not merit serious consideration. Yet, as the historian Robert Darnton reminds us, it is the apparently peripheral that can help illuminate a way of life.[24] We need to take seriously the role of the Claimant as a figure of wish-fulfilment for thousands of people in the mid- to late-Victorian years.

The bulk of the evidence suggests that the Claimant was Arthur Orton, and that he was guilty as charged. We can only speculate on what went inside his head – the desire for money, the longing for the kind of aristocratic life that he discovered in Sensation fiction. The Claimant was a chancer and a gambler who kept rolling the dice in the hope of finding fortune. He was a confidence trickster in an age that valued transparency. He was a villain, but also an object of longing. He was an actor who had stumbled on a secret – that social life is dependent on performance: to be an aristocrat you only have to pretend to be one.

And what of the Tichborne movement? It would be dishonest to deny that it was peopled by cranks and obsessives, but to leave it at that belittles its significance and complexity. The movement was conservative and jingoistic but also part of the history of radicalism. Tichbornism demonstrates that radicals and conservatives frequently contended over similar territory: nation, empire, the constitution. This does not mean radicalism and Toryism were the same, although it is true that the left has its own history of patriotism and a complex relationship with national identity.[25] There were negative aspects of the Tichborne movement. It was led by a fanatic (Kenealy) and its combination of jingoism with paranoia and conspiracy theories appears to anticipate some of the darker moments of twentieth-century history. But it was also a movement that believed in fair play and justice, that expressed some of the frustrations of working-class life, that attacked the workhouse and unjust taxation. Determining whether the Claimant could get justice in a court of law turned Tichborne into a test of civil liberties. It will not do to dismiss the case as an example of the irrational or eccentric or even bloody-minded dimension of popular culture. This was also a story of resistance. Working-class people struggled to help a working-class man become an aristocrat. The movement both attacked but also confirmed the existing order of things. The ambivalence of the Tichborne cause made it significant as a mirror of popular mentalities. Tichbornism was a movement that was sustained more by images and symbols than by any ideology. Its invocations of fair play, patriotism and justice spoke to the emotions of British people. For over a decade, it managed to rouse workers to defend both the Claimant's rights and what they thought of as their own rights.

The Victorians loved their heroes and adorned their mantelpieces with their images: Gladstone, Prince Albert, Grace Darling, the Duke of Wellington, Dickens, Garibaldi. Although an unlikely figure to do so, there is no doubt that the Tichborne Claimant stands among them.

APPENDIX 1
Tichborne Family Tree

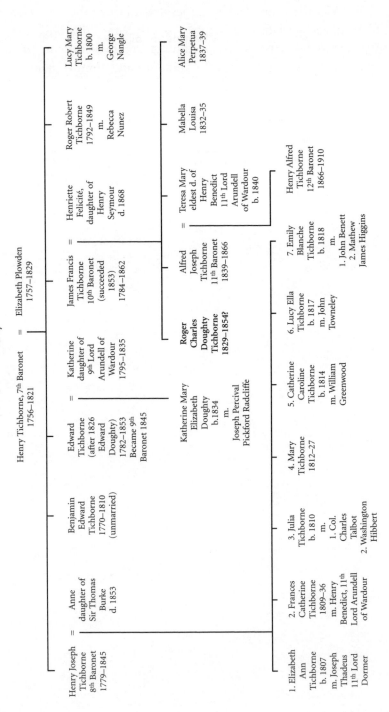

Henry Tichborne, 7th Baronet 1756–1821 = Elizabeth Plowden 1757–1829

Henry Joseph Tichborne 8th Baronet 1779–1845 = Anne daughter of Sir Thomas Burke d. 1853

Benjamin Edward Tichborne 1770–1810 (unmarried)

Edward Tichborne (after 1826 Edward Doughty) 1782–1853 Became 9th Baronet 1845 = Katherine daughter of 9th Lord Arundell of Wardour 1795–1835

James Francis Tichborne 10th Baronet (succeeded 1853) 1784–1862 = Henriette Felicité, daughter of Henry Seymour d. 1868

Roger Robert Tichborne 1792–1849 m. Rebecca Nunez

Lucy Mary Tichborne b. 1800 m. George Nangle

Katherine Mary Elizabeth Doughty b.1834 m. Joseph Percival Pickford Radcliffe

Roger Charles Doughty Tichborne 1829–1854?

Alfred Joseph Tichborne 11th Baronet 1839–1866 = Teresa Mary eldest d. of Henry Benedict 11th Lord Arundell of Wardour b. 1840

Mabella Louisa 1832–35

Alice Mary Perpetua 1837–39

Henry Alfred Tichborne 12th Baronet 1866–1910

1. Elizabeth Ann Tichborne b. 1807 m. Joseph Thadeus 11th Lord Dormer

2. Frances Catherine Tichborne 1809–36 m. Henry Benedict, 11th Lord Arundell of Wardour

3. Julia Tichborne b. 1810 m. 1. Col. Charles Talbot 2. Washington Hibbert

4. Mary Tichborne 1812–27

5. Catherine Caroline Tichborne b. 1814 m. William Greenwood

6. Lucy Ella Tichborne b. 1817 m. John Towneley

7. Emily Blanche Tichborne b. 1818 m. 1. John Benett 2. Mathew James Higgins

The Claimant's Family Tree

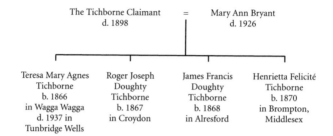

The Tichborne Claimant d. 1898	=	Mary Ann Bryant d. 1926

| Teresa Mary Agnes
Tichborne
b. 1866
in Wagga Wagga
d. 1937 in
Tunbridge Wells | Roger Joseph
Doughty
Tichborne
b. 1867
in Croydon | James Francis
Doughty
Tichborne
b. 1868
in Alresford | Henrietta Felicité
Tichborne
b. 1870
in Brompton,
Middlesex |

APPENDIX 2

Dramatis Personae

Abraham Anidjah Helped organise Tichborne meetings in 1872–3.

William Ballantine Led the Claimant's 'defence' in the Civil Trial.

Maltman Barry Journalist and Tory Marxist: supported the Claimant.

Lord Bellew School Friend of Roger Tichborne's; alleged to have tattooed him.

Anthony Biddulph Cousin of the Tichbornes: supported the Claimant.

Francis Baigent Antiquarian and friend of the Tichbornes: supported the Claimant.

Andrew Bogle Former servant of Edward Doughty (key witness for the Claimant).

William Bovill Judge in the Civil Trial.

Mary Ann Bryant (later Castro, later Tichborne) The Claimant's first wife.

Tomas Castro Resident of Melipilla, Chile, whose name was adopted by the Claimant.

The Claimant Also known as Tomas Castro, Roger Tichborne and Arthur Orton.

William Cobbett Barrister and supporter of the Claimant (son of the great reformer).

Alexander Cockburn Lord Chief Justice and Judge in the Criminal Trial.

John Duke Coleridge Solicitor General: Led the Claimant's 'prosecution' in the Civil Trial.

William Cresswell Lunatic (alleged to be Arthur Orton).

Arthur Cubbitt Owner of the Missing Friends Agency of Sydney.

John De Morgan Radical and Tichbornite.

Benjamin Disraeli Conservative Prime Minister 1868, 1874-80 (Earl of Beaconsfield from 1876).

Edward Doughty Ninth Baronet and father of Katherine Doughty.

Katherine Doughty (later Lady Radcliffe) Cousin of Roger Tichborne and daughter of Edward Doughty (later married Joseph Radcliffe).

Lady Katherine Doughty Wife of Edward Doughty.

Lily Enever The Claimant's second wife.

T. M. Evans Editor of the *Leicester Evening News* and supporter of the Claimant.

William Foster Australian cattle rancher who employed the Claimant.

Henry Hawkins Served on 'prosecuting' team in the Civil Trial and led the Prosecution in the Criminal Trial.

William Gibbes Wagga Wagga lawyer (identified the Claimant).

Hardinge Giffard Served on Claimant's 'defence' team in Civil Trial.

William Gladstone Liberal Prime Minister 1868–74, 1880–85, 1886, 1892–3.

Vincent Gosford Steward to Edward Doughty.

Henry Beckett Harding Tichbornite.

John Holmes The Claimant's first solicitor.

Mrs. Jewry Sister of Arthur Orton.

Mina Jury Cousin of the Ortons; witness against the Claimant.

Edward Kenealy The Claimant's barrister in the Criminal Trial (subsequently led the Magna Charta Association).

Maurice Kenealy Son of Edward Kenealy and editor of the *Englishman*.

J. P. Lipscomb Tichborne family doctor.

Jean Luie Alleged he was the steward on the *Osprey*.

Mary Ann Loder Arthur Orton's teenage sweetheart.

Colonel Franklin Lushington Lessee of Tichborne House.

Sara Macalister Widow of William Foster; witness against the Claimant.

John Mackenzie Agent of the Tichbornes (investigated Australian evidence).

Sergeant-Major Marks Served with Roger Tichborne in the army and supporter of the Claimant.

John Moore Roger Tichborne's servant in South America.

Guildford Onslow Liberal MP for Guildford and leading supporter of the Claimant.

Arthur Orton Last definitive sighting 1852.

Charles Orton Brother of Arthur Orton.

George Orton Father of Arthur Orton.

Mrs Pittendreigh Wife of clerk in Tichbornes' solicitors office; alleged to have offered to provide the Claimant with information.

George W. M. Reynolds Reformer, novelist and pro-Claimant journalist.

Lord Rivers Supporter of the Claimant.

Alfred Seymour Roger Tichborne's uncle.

Henry Seymour Roger Tichborne's uncle.

G. B. Skipworth Justice of the Peace and supporter of the Claimant.

Alfred Tichborne brother of Roger Tichborne and eleventh Baronet.

Henriette-Felicité Tichborne Roger Tichborne's mother (the Dowager Lady Tichborne).

Henry Tichborne Eighth Baronet and grandfather of Roger Tichborne.

Henry Alfred Joseph Tichborne Son of Alfred Tichborne and twelfth Baronet (the infant Baronet in the Civil Trial).

James Tichborne Tenth Baronet and Roger Tichborne's father.

Teresa Tichborne Widow of Alfred Tichborne.

Roger Tichborne Last definitive sighting 1854

Mary Ann Tredgett Sister of Arthur Orton.

Alfred Walton Architect and Liberal candidate in the Stoke by-election.

Georgina Weldon Spiritualist, musician and Tichbornite.

George Whalley Liberal MP and anti-Catholic: supported the Claimant.

Jonathan Whicher Detective employed by the Tichbornes.

APPENDIX 3

An Uncontested Chronology

1827   James Francis Tichborne marries Henriette Felicité Seymour (later the Dowager Lady Tichborne).

1829   *29 January* Birth of their son, Roger Charles Doughty Tichborne.

1834   *20 March* Birth of Arthur Orton.

1839   *4 September* Birth of Alfred Tichborne.

1845   Sir Edward Doughty (né Tichborne) becomes ninth Baronet on death of Henry Tichborne.

1845–8   Roger Tichborne educated at Stonyhurst.

1848–52   Roger Tichborne serves in 6th Dragoon Guards (Carabineers).

1849   *June* Orton in Valparaiso.

1851   *June* Orton back in Wapping.

1852   *11 January* Sir Edward Doughty forbids Roger to see his daughter, Katherine.

         27 November Orton sails for Hobart Town, Tasmania.

1853   *1 March* Roger sails from Havre, bound for Valparaiso.

         May Orton arrives in Hobart.

         19 June Roger arrives in Valparaiso and hears that his father has become tenth Baronet on the death of Sir Edward Doughty.

1854   *12 April* Roger sets sail on the *Bella*.

1862   *11 June* James Tichborne dies and Roger's younger brother, Alfred, becomes eleventh Baronet.

1865   *January* Tomas Castro marries Mary Ann Bryant.

         13 April Castro writes to James Richardson of Wapping requesting information about Arthur Orton.

         May Dowager writes to Cubitt's Missing Friends Agency in Australia to secure its services in her search for her son.

         July Advertisements placed in Australian press asking for news of Roger.

         Autumn William Gibbes of Wagga Wagga confronts Castro with the allegation that he is Roger Tichborne.

         21 December Cubbitt writes to Dowager with news of discovery.

1866   *January* Claimant writes to Dowager.

22 February Death of Sir Alfred Tichborne; his son, Henry Alfred Joseph Tichborne, becomes twelfth Baronet.

2 June Claimant leaves Wagga Wagga for Sydney.

9 July Claimant remarries in the Catholic Church, Goulburn.

2 September Claimant leaves Sydney for England.

25 December Claimant arrives in London with his family and Bogle and goes to Ford's hotel. He then pays a visit to Wapping.

28 December Claimant goes incognito to Alresford.

1867   *1 January* Claimant returns to London.

10 January Claimant goes to Paris and is recognised by the Dowager.

21 January Claimant returns to London and, soon after, moves to Croydon.

18 May Biddulph recognises the Claimant as Roger.

27 June Bills filed in Chancery on the Claimant's affidavits.

July Guildford Onslow recognises the Claimant.

31 July–2 August Examination at Law Society Building.

28 August Claimant writes to Tomas Castro of Melipilla, Chile (whose name he had taken).

28 October Pedro Castro replies on behalf of his father who is insane.

1868   *12 March* Death of Dowager.

April Claimant moves to Alresford.

September Claimant sails for Chile to help with Commission.

1869   *29 January* Claimant returns to Alresford.

7 February Claimant meets supporters in the 'Swan' Hotel, Alresford, to explain his sudden return.

15 February Dr Lipscomb informs Onslow of the Claimant's 'malformation'.

March The Claimant moves to Kensington to be in London for the court case.

4 May Australian Commission examines witnesses.

1870   *14 April* Tichborne Bond scheme launched.

1871   *10 May Tichborne* v *Lushington* opens.

5 June Cross-examination of the Claimant by Coleridge commences.

7 July Adjournment until 7 November.

7 November–mid-January Ballantine cross-examines 100 witnesses.

1872   *15 January–4 March* Coleridge makes a one month long address and calls witnesses.

4 March Jury intervenes to say that it has heard enough evidence.

6 March Claimant non-suited and arrested.

7 March–26 April Claimant in Newgate.

25 March Claimant's 'Appeal to the Country'.

9 April Claimant indicted for perjury and forgery.

14 May Tichborne demonstration in Alresford.

May–March (1873)The 'Stump' campaign.

11–12 December Onslow and Whalley make inflammatory remarks at St James' Hall, Piccadilly.

1873   *25 January* Onslow and Whalley fined for contempt of court.

29 January Skipworth fined for contempt of court.

23 April Criminal Trial begins.

23 April–20 May Evidence from the Civil trial read out.

20 May–10 July 215 witnesses for the Crown.

11 July–21 July Adjournment to allow Kenealy time to prepare Defence.

22 July–21 August Kenealy's speech for the Defence.

21 August–27 October Kenealy calls witnesses including Jean Luie on 14 Oct.

31 October–27 November Trial ceases whilst evidence about Jean Luie is checked.

11 December Jean Luie sentenced for perjury.

1874   *15 January–28 January* Hawkins replies for the Crown.

29 January–28 February Cockburn's summing-up.

28 February Claimant sentenced to fourteen years' penal servitude.

11 April The *Englishman* appears for the first time.

July False Personations Act and Tichborne Estates Act passed.

1 August Kenealy disbenched by Gray's Inn.

2 December Kenealy loses patent as Queen's Counsel.

1875   *16 February* Kenealy elected as MP for Stoke-upon-Trent.

23 April Debate in Commons on Tichborne trial.

1876   *September/October* Schism in Magna Charta Association leads to formation of E.W. Bailey's National Magna Charta Association.

1880   *3 April* General Election. Kenealy loses his seat.

16 April Kenealy dies.

1882   *August* Onslow dies.

1884   *11 October* Claimant released from prison.

1886   *22 May* Last issue of the *Englishman*.

11 June Claimant arrives in New York.

1887   *(late 1887)* Claimant back in England.
1895   *19 May–30 June* Claimant's confession in the *People* serialised.
1898   *1 April* Death of the Claimant.

Notes

Notes to Chapter 1: Enter the claimant

1   Chapters 1 and 2 rely on the standard authorities on the Tichborne case: J. B. Atlay, *Famous Trials of the Century* (London: Grant Richards, 1899); Frederick Herbert (Lord) Maugham, *The Tichborne Case* (London: Hodder and Stoughton, 1936); Douglas Woodruff, *The Tichborne Claimant: A Victorian Mystery* (London: Hollis and Carter, 1957); Geddes MacGregor, *The Tichborne Imposter* (Philadelphia: Lippincott, 1957); Martin Gilbert, *The Claimant* (London: Constable, 1957); Michael Roe, *Kenealy and the Tichborne Cause: A Study in Mid-Victorian Populism* (Melbourne: University of Melbourne Press, 1974); Robyn Annear, *The Man Who Lost Himself: The Unbelievable Story of the Tichborne Claimant* (London: Robinson, 2003). Referenced material is derived from my own research.

2   Isaac D'Israeli, *Curiosities of Literature* (London: Routledge, 1867 [1834]), p.241. Chidiock Tichborne may not have been entirely accurate. The earliest evidence for the association of the Tichborne family with the area dates from *c.*1135 when the Bishop of Winchester granted the land that is now Tichborne Park to a Walter de Tichborne: see E. Roberts and E. Crockford, *A History of Tichborne* (n.d.), p.3.

3   Sir Walter Besant, *London North of the Thames* (London: Adam and Charles Black, 1911), p.621.

4   The Doughty estate was subsequently disentailed in 1850 and the provision requiring Roger Tichborne to take the surname of Doughty and to adopt the Doughty arms was removed: Noel Hughes, 'The Tichbornes, the Doughtys and Douglas Woodruff', *Recusant History*, 23 (1997), pp.602–19.

5   Rory Miller, *Britain and Latin America in the Nineteenth and Twentieth Centuries* (London: Longman, 1993), p.9, 94.

6   John M. MacKenzie, *The Empire of Nature: Hunting, Conservation and British Imperialism* (Manchester: Manchester University Press, 1988).

7   Charles Waterton, *Wanderings in South America* (London: J. Mawman, 1825), pp.307–26. On Waterton's possible influence, see Lord Maugham, *The Tichborne Case*, p.39.

8   *The Tichborne Romance* (London: Simpkin, Marshall, 1871), p.53.

9   Keith Swan, *A History of Wagga Wagga* (Wagga Wagga: City of Wagga Wagga, 1970).

10 *The Times*, 10 November 1871, p.10.

Notes to Chapter 2: Going to Law

1   Rous to R.C. Tichborne, 24 January 1867: Manuscripts Miscellaneous 782, p.167, Lincoln's Inn Library.
2   *The Tichborne Romance* (London: Simpkin, Marshall, 1871), pp.44–7.
3   Cullington to P. Radcliffe, 31 October 1866: Radcliffe Papers I, 659, box F, Leeds Record Office.
4   *The Tichborne Romance*, p.80.
5   Ibid., p.148.
6   Ernest Hartley Coleridge (ed.), *Life and Correspondence of John Duke Lord Coleridge, Lord Chief Justice of England* (London: William Heinemann, 1904), ii, p.187.
7   Frederick Herbert (Lord) Maugham, *The Tichborne Case* (London: Hodder and Stoughton, 1936), p.11.
8   Richard Harris (ed.), *The Reminiscences of Sir Henry Hawkins, Baron Brampton* (London: Edward Arnold, 1904), i, pp.310–11.
9   Douglas Woodruff, *The Tichborne Claimant: A Victorian Mystery* (London: Hollis and Carter 1957), p.113.
10 *The Times*, 16 March 1868, p.7.
11 Hubert Dormer to Lady Dormer, 20 March 1868: Dormer of Grove Park Papers, CR 895/100, Warwickshire County Record Office.
12 Wilfred Scawen Blunt, *My Diaries: Being a Personal Narrative of Events, 1888–1914* (London: Martin Secker, 1919), i, pp.359–60; ii, pp.134–5.
13 Sir Pyers Mostyn to P. Radcliffe, 31 January 1869: Radcliffe Papers, I, 659, box F, Leeds Record Office.
14 Holmes to R.C. Tichborne, 16 December 1868: Manuscripts Miscellaneous 776, pp.193–4, Lincoln's Inn Library.
15 Onslow to Holmes, 31 January 1869: Manuscripts Miscellaneous 781, p.107, Lincoln's Inn Library.
16 Henry Bruce to his wife, 14 March 1872, in Henry Austin Bruce, *Letters of the Rt Hon. Henry Austin Bruce, a.c.b. Lord Abedave of Duffyn* (privately printed, 1902), i, p.337.
17 Woodruff, *Tichborne Claimant*, p.165.
18 *The Times*, 16 November 1871, p.5.

Notes to Chapter 3: The Courtroom

1   Some of Henry Hawkins's advocacy in the Tichborne case was later reprinted to serve as an example of the lawyer's art: Richard Harris, *Illustrations in Advocacy* (London: Waterlow, 1884), pp. 227–39. Subsequent editions expanded this material.
2   J. R. Lewis, *The Victorian Bar* (London: Robert Hale, 1982), p.13.

3   The classic work on the public sphere is Jürgen Habermas, *The Structural Trans-formation of the Public Sphere: An Inquiry into a Category of Bourgeois Society* (Cambridge: Polity, 1989). See also Craig Calhoun (ed.), *Habermas and the Public Sphere* (Cambridge, Massachusetts: MIT Press, 1999).

4   *Era*, 9 July 1871, p.9.

5   In 1845 the Oxford and Western Circuit actually ejected a member for provid-ing the press with shorthand notes of trial proceedings: Jan-Melissa Schramm, *Testimony and Advocacy in Victorian Law, Literature and Theology* (Cambridge: Cambridge University Press, 2000), p.14.

6   Patrick Brantlinger, 'What is "Sensational" about the "Sensation Novel"?', *Nineteenth-Century Fiction*, 37 (1982), pp.1–28.

7   Richard D. Altick, *Victorian Studies in Scarlet* (London: Dent, 1972) and *Evil Encounters: Two Victorian Sensations* (London: John Murray, 1987); Mary S. Hartman, *Victorian Murderesses: A True History of Thirteen Women Accused of Unspeakable Crimes* (London: Robson, 1977); Thomas Boyle, *Black Swine in the Sewers of Hampstead: Beneath the Surface of Victorian Sensationalism* (London: Hodder and Stoughton, 1990); Judith Knelman, *Twisting in the Wind: The Murderess and the English Press* (Toronto: University of Toronto Press, 1998); L. Perry Curtis, Jr, *Jack the Ripper and the London Press* (New Haven, Connecticut: Yale University Press, 2001).

8   On the Yelverton case, see Rebecca Gill, 'The Imperial Anxieties of a Nineteenth-Century Bigamy Case', *History Workshop Journal*, 57 (2004), pp.58–78; on the Mordaunt case, see Elizabeth Hamilton, *The Warwickshire Scandal* (London: Pan, 2000 [1999]).

9   John Sutherland, 'Writing *The Woman in White*', in his *Victorian Fiction: Writers, Publishers, Readers* (London: Macmillan, 1995), pp.28–54.

10 *The Times*, 11 November 1870, p.9.

11 The fiction of the action of ejectment was developed in the sixteenth century: see A. W. B. Simpson, *An Introduction to the History of Land Law* (Oxford: Oxford University Press, 1961), ch. 7; On legal fictions, see Oliver R. Mitchell, 'The Fictions of the Law: Have They Proved Useful or Detrimental to its Growth?', *Harvard Law Review*, 7 (1893-94), pp.249–65; Sir Henry Maine, *Ancient Law* (London: John Murray, 1930 [1906]), ch. 2; Lon L. Fuller, *Legal Fictions* (Stanford, California: Stanford University Press, 1967); John H. Baker, *The Law's Two Bodies: Some Evidential Problems in English Legal History* (Oxford: Oxford University Press, 2001), ch. 2.

12 Avner Offer, *Property and Politics, 1870-1914: Landownership, Law, Ideology and Urban Development in England* (Cambridge: Cambridge University Press, 1981), p.11.

13 John R. Reed, *Victorian Conventions* (Athens, Ohio: Ohio University Press, 1976) ch. 12.

14 Richard A. Cosgrave, 'The Reception of Analytical Jurisprudence: The Victorian Debate on the Separation of Law and Morality, 1860-1900', *Durham University Journal*, 74 (1981), pp.47–56; David Sugarman and G.R. Rubin, 'Introduction' in Rubin and Sugarman (eds), *Law, Economy and Society, 1750–1914: Essays in the History of English Law* (Abingdon: Professional Books, 1984), p.78.

15 Raymond Cocks, *Foundations of the Modern Bar* (London: Sweet and Maxwell, 1983); Daniel Duman, 'The Creation and Diffusion of a Professional Ideology in Nineteenth-Century England', *Sociological Review*, 37 (1979), pp.113–38.

16 Lewis, *The Victorian Bar*, p.62.

17 John Beattie, 'Scales of Justice: Defence Counsel and the English Criminal Trial in the Eighteenth and Nineteenth Centuries', *Law and History Review*, 9 (1991), pp.221–67; David J.A. Cairns, *Advocacy and the Making of the Adversarial Criminal Trial, 1800-1865* (Oxford: Clarendon Press, 1998); John H. Langbein, *The Origins of Adversary Criminal Trial* (Oxford: Oxford University Press, 2003); Allyson N. May, *The Bar and the Old Bailey, 1750–1850* (Chapel Hill, North Carolina: University of North Carolina Press, 2003).

18 Christopher Allen, *The Victorian Law of Evidence* (Cambridge: Cambridge University Press, 1997).

19 Allyson N. May, *The Bar and the Old Bailey*, pp.124–32.

20 Ibid., pp. 48–9 for Charles Phillips' reputation; ch. 8 for the Courvoisier case.

21 A collection of ballads, songs and other verses, British Library, callmark 11661. dd.20, p.7.

22 John Ashton, *Modern Street Ballads* (London: Chatto and Windus, 1888), pp.346–8.

23 Martha Vicinus, *Broadsides of the Industrial North* (Newcastle-upon-Tyne: Frank Graham, 1975), p.53.

24 Prince Leopold of Belgium to Dr Poore, n.d. [1871?], Poore Papers, 39 M85/PC/F32, Hampshire Record Office.

25 Ray Geary, '"Born Pious, Literary and Legal": Lord Coleridge's Criticisms in Law and Literature' in Michael Freeman and Andrew D. E. Lewis (ed.), *Law and Literature*, (Oxford: Oxford University Press, 1999), pp.463–80.

26 Walter L. Arnstein, *Protestant versus Catholic in Mid-Victorian England: Mr Newdegate and the Nuns* (Columbia, Missouri: University of Missouri Press, 1982).

27 A.W.B. Simpson, *Cannibalism and the Common Law: The Story of the Tragic Last Voyage of the Mignonette and the Strange Legal Proceedings to Which it Gave Rise* (Chicago: Chicago University Press, 1984).

28 Richard Harris (ed.), *The Reminiscences of Sir Henry Hawkins, Baron Brampton* (London: Edward Arnold, 1904), i, pp.3–4.

29 He died soon after, in 1873: J.G. Witt, *Life in the Law* (London: T. Werner Laurie, 1906), pp. 110–11; Evelyn Burnaby, *Memories of Famous Trials* (London: Sisley's, 1907), p.140.

30 William Ballantine, *Some Experiences of a Barrister's Life* (London: Richard Bentley, 1882), ii, p.173.

31 Ernest Hartley Coleridge (ed.), *Life and Correspondence of John Duke, Lord Coleridge, Lord Chief Justice of England* (London: William Heinemann, 1904), ii, p.199.

32 Gordon S. Haight (ed.), *The George Eliot Letters* (New Haven, Connecticut: Yale University Press, 1955), v, p.243.

33 On testimony and circumstantial evidence, see Alexander Welsh, *Strong Representations: Narrative and Circumstantial Evidence in England* (Baltimore: Johns Hopkins University Press, 1992); Schramm, *Testimony and Advocacy in Victorian Law, Literature and Theology.*

34 Ballantine, *Some Experiences of a Barrister's Life*, ii, p.172.

35 *The Times*, 2 December 1871, p.10.

36 This reconstruction is based on three different sets of reports: *The Tichborne Romance* (London: Simpin, Marshall and Co., 1871); *Tichborne* v. *Lushington* (London: n.d.) and the accounts in *The Times*.

37 *The Tichborne Romance*, p.12.

38 Ibid., p.17.

39 Ibid., p.22.

40 Coleridge (ed.), *Life and Correspondence of ... Lord Coleridge*, ii, p.414, 423.

41 *The Tichborne Romance*, p.45.

42 Ibid., p.73.

43 Ibid., p.48.

44 Ibid., p.60.

45 Ibid., p.66.

46 Ibid., pp.94–5.

47 *The Times*, 21 November 1871, p.8.

48 *Tichborne* v. *Lushington*, iv, p.4225.

49 Coleridge (ed.), *Life and Correspondence of ... Lord Coleridge*, ii, p.205.

50 *The Tichborne Romance*, p.79.

51 Ibid., p.76.

52 Ibid., p.130.

53 Ibid., pp.140–1.

54 Coleridge (ed.) *Life and Correspondence of ... Lord Coleridge*, ii, p.418.

55 Ibid., ii, p.415.

56 Ibid., ii, p.417.

57 Ballantine, *Some Experiences of a Barrister's Life*, i, p.175.

58 E.g. *Punch* 15 July 1871, p.11.

59 *The Times*, 13 June 1871, p.11.

60 Both exchanges from *The Tichborne Romance*, p.205.

61 Ibid., p.165.

62 Ibid., pp. 160–1.

63 Coleridge (ed.), *Life and Correspondence of ... Lord Coleridge*, ii, p. 416.

64 *The Tichborne Romance*, p.264.

65 *Tichborne* v. *Lushington*, iii, p. 3501.

66 Ibid., iii, p.3513.

67 Ibid., iii, pp.4109–10.

68 George Augustus Sala, *The Life and Adventures of George Augustus Sala* (London: Cassell, 1896), pp.580–81.

69 *The Times*, 7 March 1872, p.12.

Notes to Chapter 4: Stumping the Country

1   *Reynolds's Newspaper*, 31 December 1871, pp.4–5. See also the *Era*, 17 December 1871, p.8; 31 December 1871 p.4. The 1872 pantomime at the Britannia Theatre, Hoxton, featured a sketch about the Claimant: Tichborne Case scrapbook, Manuscripts Miscellaneous, 788, p.2 (my pagination), Lincoln's Inn Library. For the Alhambra, see Raymond Mander and Joe Mitchenson, *Lost Theatres of London* (London: New English Library, 1976), ch.1.

2   *Era*, 9 July 1871, p.9.

3   John Theodore Tussaud, *The Romance of Madame Tussaud's* (London: Odhams, 1920), pp.141–4.

4   Thomas Wright, *Our New Masters* (London: Strahan, 1873), p.330. On Wright, see Alastair Reid, 'Intelligent Artisans and Aristocrats of Labour: The Essays of Thomas Wright' in Jay Winter (ed.), *The Working Class in Modern British History: Essays in Honour of Henry Pelling* (Cambridge: Cambridge University Press, 1983), pp.171–86.

5   Edward Vaughan Kenealy, *The Trial at Bar of Sir Roger C.D. Tichborne, Bart* (London: *Englishman*, 1875), [hereafter Kenealy, *Trial*], Introduction, p.223.

6   Derek Beales, 'Garibaldi in England: The Politics of Italian Enthusiasm', in John A. Davis and Paul Ginsborg (eds), *Society and Politics in the Age of the Risorgimento: Essays in Honour of Denis Mack Smith* (Cambridge: Cambridge University Press, 1991), pp.184–216.

7   *The Times*, 27 March 1872, p.5.

8   3 *Hansard*, 210, cols 888–89, (8 April 1872).

9   Coleridge to Gladstone, 1 June 1872: Add. MSS. 44138, fos 134–7, British Library.

10 *Daily Telegraph*, 23 March 1872, p.3.

11 *Newcastle Weekly Chronicle*, 13 July 1872, p.4.

12 W. E. Adams, *Memoirs of a Social Atom* (London: Hutchinson, 1903), p.149.

13 *Southampton Observer and Winchester News*, 1 June 1872, p.7.

14 'Blondin Interviewed' (19 September 1873): Newspaper Cuttings, Local Studies

department, Birmingham Central Reference Library. I am grateful to Brenda Assael for this reference.

15 *Morning Advertiser*, 26 April 1872, p.5.

16 *Reynolds's Newspaper*, 21 April 1872, p.2.

17 Ibid., 28 April 1872, p.6.

18 *Nottingham Daily Guardian*, 19 July 1872, p.4.

19 Minutes of the Sunday Evening Debating Society, i, p.851, 857, Birmingham Central Library. On the Hope and Anchor Debating Society, see Vivien Hart, *Distrust and Democracy: Political Distrust in Britain and America* (Cambridge: Cambridge University Press, 1978), ch.4.

20 *Tichborne Comicalities* (nd).

21 *South Durham Herald*, 20 July 1872, p.2.

22 *Morning Advertiser*, 8 April 1872, p.7.

23 Charles R. Warren (ed.), *Sixty Years on the Turf: The Life and Times of George Hodgman, 1840–1900* (London: Grant Richards 1903), p.113.

24 *Loughborough Advertiser*, 15 August 1872, p.5.

25 Cited in Mark Girouard, *Victorian Pubs* (London: Studio Vista, 1975), p.12.

26 David W. Gutzke, *Protecting the Pub: Brewers and Publicans against Temperance* (Woodbridge, Suffolk: Royal Historical Society/Boydell Press, 1989), p.33.

27 Brian Harrison, *Drink and the Victorians: The Temperance Question in England, 1815–1872* (London: Faber and Faber, 1971). See also A.E. Dingle, *The Campaign for Prohibition in Victorian England: The United Kingdom Alliance, 1872–1895* (London: Croom Helm, 1980); Lilian Lewis Shiman, *Crusade against Drink in Victorian England* (Basingstoke: Macmillan, 1988).

28 Ian A. Burney, *Bodies of Evidence: Medicine and the Politics of the English Inquest, 1830–1926* (Baltimore: Johns Hopkins University Press, 2000), pp.80–7.

29 John Belchem, 'Ribbonism, Nationalism and the Irish Pub', in his *Merseypride: Essays in Liverpool Exceptionalism* (Liverpool: Liverpool University Press, 2000), pp.60–100.

30 Peter Bailey, 'The Victorian Barmaid as Cultural Prototype', in his *Popular Culture and Performance in the Victorian City* (Cambridge: Cambridge University Press, 1998), pp.151–74.

31 John Greenaway, *Drink and British Politics since 1830: A Study in Policy-Making* (Basingstoke: Palgrave Macmillan, 2003), p.8.

32 Gutzke, *Protecting the Pub*.

33 Patrick Joyce, *Work, Society and Politics: The Culture of the Factory in Later Victorian England* (Brighton: Harvester Press, 1980), pp.292–301; see also Martin Pugh, *The Tories and the People, 1880–1935* (Oxford: Basil Blackwell, 1985); Jon Lawrence, 'Class and Gender in the Making of Urban Toryism, 1880–1914', *English Historical Review* 31 (1993), pp.163–86.

34 Warren (ed.), *Sixty Years on the Turf*, pp. 112–3; on horse racing, see Wray Vamplew,

The Turf: A Social and Economic History of Horse Racing (London: Allen Lane, 1976).

35 *Daily Telegraph*, 27 March 1872, p.3.

36 *Reynolds's Newspaper*, 18 August 1872, p.1; *Morning Advertiser*, 9 August 1872, p.6.

37 *Morning Advertiser*, 11 April 1872, p.2.

38 *Hampshire Chronicle*, 13 April 1872, p.7.

39 *Western Gazette and Flying Post*, 12 April 1872, p.7; *Hampshire Chronicle*, 20 April 1872, p.3.

40 *Tichborne News and Anti-Oppression Journal* (hereafter *Tichborne News*), 3 August 1872, p.1.

41 *Hampshire Chronicle*, 18 May 1872, p.3.

42 The following evidence is based on the lists in *Tichborne Gazette*, 28 May 1872, p.1; 18 June 1872, p.1; 2 July 1872, p.1.

43 *Tichborne Gazette*, 2 July 1872, p.1.

44 *Hampshire Chronicle*, 16 November 1872, p.7.

45 Ibid., 23 November 1872, p.7; 30 November 1872, p.7; 4 January 1873, p.6.

46 *The Times*, 7 March 1872, p.9.

47 *Saturday Review*, 9 March 1872, p.298.

48 *Nottingham Daily Guardian*, 22 July 1872, p.4.

49 *Morning Advertiser*, 8 March 1872, pp.4–5; 22 March 1872, p.5; 4 April 1872, p.4.

50 Basil L. Crapster, 'The London *Morning Advertiser*: Two Notes on its Editorial History', *Victorian Periodicals Review* 7 (1974), pp.3–10; idem, 'Thomas Humber, 1828–1902: Tory Journalist', *Victorians Periodicals Review*, 8 (1975), pp.115–25; Alvar Ellegard, 'The Readership of the Periodical Press in Mid-Victorian Britain: II. Directory' *Victorian Periodicals Review*, 4 (1971), p.4.

51 *Tichborne Gazette*, 28 May 1872, p.3.

52 Ibid., 28 May 1872, p.3.

53 Ibid., 28 May 1872, p.3.

54 *Portsmouth Times and Naval Gazette*, 26 June 1872, p.4.

55 *Tichborne News*, 15 June 1872, p.1.

56 Ibid., 15 June 1872, p.1.

57 Brian Harrison, 'The Sunday Trading Riots of 1855', *Historical Journal*, 8 (1965), pp.219–95.

58 *Tichborne News*, 22 June 1872, p.3.

59 *South Durham Herald*, 13 July 1872, p.2.

60 H. C. G. Matthew, 'Rhetoric and Politics in Great Britain, 1860–1950', in P. J. Waller (ed.), *Politics and Social Change in Modern Britain: Essays Presented to A. F. Thompson* (Brighton: Harvester, 1987), p.39.

61 This paragraph relies heavily on Joseph S. Meisel, *Public Speech and the Culture of Public Life in the Age of Gladstone* (New York: Columbia University Press, 2001).

62 John Coffey, 'Democracy and Popular Religion: Moody and Sankey's Mission to Britain, 1873-1875', in Eugenio Biagini (ed.), *Citizenship and Community: Liberals, Radicals and Collective Identities in the British Isles, 1865–1931* (Cambridge: Cambridge University Press, 1996), pp.93–119.

63 Thomas Carlyle, 'Stump-Orator' (1850), in his *Latter-Day Pamphlets* (London: Chapman and Hall, 1858), pp.160–1.

64 The account of the Alresford meeting is taken from *Hampshire Chronicle*, 18 May 1872, p.3, and *Morning Advertiser*, 15 May 1872, p.6.

65 *The Times*, 24 May 1872, p.5; 4 June 1872, p.10.

66 Ibid., 25 May 1872, p.12.

67 *Bristol Mercury and Western Counties Advertiser*, 25 May 1872, p.8.

68 Quoted in Kenealy, *Trial*, Introduction, p.110.

69 Kenealy, *Trial*, Introduction, pp.110–12; *Bristol Mercury and Western Counties Advertiser*, 25 May 1872, p.8.

70 *Morning Advertiser*, 27 May 1872, p.3; *Bristol Mercury and Western Counties Advertiser*, 1 June 1872, p.7.

71 *Morning Advertiser*, 14 June 1872, p.5.

72 *Tichborne Gazette*, 18 June 1872, p.1.

73 Kenealy, *Trial*, Introduction, pp.104–7.

74 *Hampshire Chronicle*, 10 August 1872, p.7.

75 3 *Hansard*, 213, col. 848 (9 August 1872).

76 Walter L. Arnstein, *Protestant versus Catholic in Mid-Victorian England: Mr Newdegate and the Nuns* (Columbia, Missouri: University of Missouri Press, 1982), p.67, 124.

77 E.g. *Punch*, 10 June 1865, p.238; 5 September 1868, p.99; 24 October 1868, p.171; 5 December 1868, p.212; 3 June 1871, p.230; 31 January 1874, p.43; 19 June 1875, p.259, 260; 8 September 1877, p.102; 26 October 1878, p.191. The *Nottingham Daily Guardian* noted that Whalley was familiar to readers because of his appearances in *Punch* and other comic periodicals (18 July 1872, p.2).

78 Henry W. Lucy, *A Diary of the Salisbury Parliament, 1886–1892* (London: Cassell, 1892), p.179; L.W. Dundas, Marquis of Zetland (ed.), *The Letters of Disraeli to Lady Bradford and Lady Chesterfield* (London: Ernest Benn, 1929), i, p.65.

79 G. H.Whalley, *Early British History* (Hove: Combridges, 1922), p.28.

80 Kenealy, *Trial*, Introduction, p.119.

81 *Hampshire Chronicle*, 27 July 1872, p.1.

82 *Tichborne Gazette*, 2 July 1872, p.3.

83 Sir Arthur Underhill, *Change and Decay: The Recollections and Reflections of an Octogenarian Bencher* (London: Butterworth, 1938), pp.63–4. For similar memories see William Edwin Adams, *Memoirs of a Social Atom* (London: Hutchinson, 1903), pp.149–50.

84 *Batley Reporter and Guardian*, 17 August 1872, p.7.

85 *Newcastle Weekly Chronicle*, 13 July 1872, p.5.

86 *Birmingham Daily Post*, 28 August 1872, p.4.

87 *Grimsby Advertiser*, 7 September 1872, p.2.

88 *Daily Courier* (Liverpool), 28 March 1873, pp.4–5.

89 *Market Rasen Weekly Mail*, 14 September 1872, p.5.

90 *Grimsby Advertiser*, 7 September 1872, p.2.

91 *Daily Courier* (Liverpool), 20 September 1872, p.5.

92 *Nottingham Daily Guardian*, 20 July 1872, p.8.

93 *Newcastle Weekly Chronicle*, 13 July 1872, p.4.

94 *South Durham Herald*, 13 July 1872, p.2.

95 *Nottingham Daily Guardian*, 20 July 1872, p.5.

96 *Birmingham Daily Post*, 27 August 1872, p.5; *South Durham Herald*, 13 July 1872, p.2. See also *Daily Post* (Liverpool), 19 September 1872, supplement, p.1.

97 *Birkenhead and Cheshire Advertiser*, 1 March 1873, p.3.

98 *Bristol Mercury and Western Counties Advertiser*, 25 May 1872, p.8; *Southampton Observer and Winchester News*, 15 June 1872, p.3.

99 *Bristol Mercury and Western Counties Advertiser*, 25 May 1872, p. 8.

100 *Weekly Mail* (Cardiff), 21 December 1872, p.6.

101 *Southampton Observer and Winchester News*, 2 November 1872, p.5.

102 *Darlington and Stockton Telegraph*, 18 January 1873, p.5.

103 *Eastern Post*, 14 July 1872, p.7.

104 *Tichborne News*, 13 July 1872, p.1, 3; 20 July 1872, p.3; *Morning Advertiser*, 8 July 1872, p.3, 4; *Hampshire Chronicle*, 13 July 1872, p.3.

105 *Reynolds's Newspaper*, 18 August 1872, p.1.

106 *The Times*, 8 August 1872, p.12.

107 *Tichborne News*, 31 August 1872, p.2.

108 Ibid., 31 August 1872, p.3.

109 *Morning Advertiser*, 7 September 1872, p.7.

110 Ibid., 9 August 1872, p.6.

111 *The Times*, 10 August 1872, p.10.

112 *Hampshire Chronicle*, 21 September 1872, p.3; on Anderson, see Ex-Chief Inspector Cavanagh, *Scotland Yard Past and Present: Experiences of Thirty-Seven Years* (London: Chatto and Windus, 1893), pp.183–6.

113 *Southampton Chronicle and Winchester News*, 25 May 1872, p.5.

114 *Western Gazette and Flying Post*, 30 August 1872, p.5.

115 Coleridge to Gladstone, 1 June 1872: Gladstone Papers, Add. MSS. 43, 138 fos 134–7, British Library.

116 Kenealy, *Trial*, Introduction, p.227. The Tichbornes were related by marriage to the Arundells.

117 Kenealy, *Trial*, Introduction, p.232.

118 Ibid., p.236.

119 Ibid., p.239.

120 *Brighton Examiner*, 21 January 1873, p.3.

121 Sir John Charles Fox, *The History of Contempt of Court: The Form of Trial and Mode of Punishment* (Oxford: Oxford University Press, 1927) p.114. See p.44 for a definition of 'stranger'.

122 G. B. Skipworth, *To True and Honest-Hearted Englishmen* (1873) in Legal Scrapbook, L. Gen. A. 1361, Bodleian Library, Oxford.

123 Kenealy, *Trial*, Introduction, p.242.

124 Ibid., p.243.

125 Ibid., p.244; Sir John Charles Fox, *Contempt of Court*, pp. 31–2, has the full exchange.

126 G. B. Skipworth, *To True and Honest-Hearted Englishmen*.

127 G. B.Skipworth, *G.B.Skipworth on his Imprisonment* (Caistor: George Parker, 1873), p.5, 13.

128 Anthony Arlidge and David Eady, *The Law of Contempt* (London: Sweet and Maxwell, 1982), pp.vii, 17; William S. Holdsworth, *A History of English Law* (London: Methuen, 1956), i, p.393; Fox, *Contempt of Court*, p.2.

129 Christopher J. Miller, *Contempt of Court* (London: Paul Elek, 1976), p.69.

130 Fox, *Contempt of Court*, p.30.

131 [Later Sir] John Charles Fox, 'The King v. Almon' *Law Quarterly Review* 24 (1908), p.192; see *Law Journal*, 19 April 1873, p.229, for a contemporary statement of this assumption.

132 W. F. Finlason, 'Contempt of Court'

133 William S. Holdsworth, *History of English Law* (London: Methuen, 1965), xv, p. 120.

134 [Later Sir] John Charles Fox, 'Eccentricities of the Law of Contempt', *Law Quaerterly Review*, 274 (1920), p. 395.

135 Arlidge and Eady, *Law of Contempt*, p. 174, 177; Nigel Lowe and Sir Gordon Borrie, *Borrie and Lowe's Law of Contempt* (London: Butterworths, 1983), p. 103.

136 Miller, *Contempt of Court*, p.90, 156–60.

137 Fox, *Contempt of Court*, p.223.

138 *Oswestry Advertizer and Mongomeryshire Mercury*, 12 March 1873, p.3.

139 *Chester Guardian and Record*, 1 March 1873, p.8.

140 *Hampshire Chronicle*, 1 March 1873, p.6.

141 George Foster, *The Spice of Life: Sixty-Five Years in the Glamour World* (London: Hurst and Blackett, 1939), pp.143–44.

Notes to Chapter 5: The Great Trial at Bar

1   *Report of the Prosecution of Dr Kenealy for Cruelty to a Child* (London: n.p. 1850?).

2   Reprinted in George H. Knott and Eric R. Watson, *The Trial of William Palmer* (London: William Hodge, 1952), pp.317–42.

3   Arabella Kenealy, *Memoirs of Edward Vaughan Kenealy, LLD* (London: John Long, 1908), p.75.

4   Ibid., p.236.

5   Edward Kenealy, *The Inaugural Address to the Members of the Temperance Institute* (Cork: George Nash, 1845), p.11; Edward Kenealy, 'Lines on Lord Ashley's Motion', *Bentley's Miscellany* xii (1842), pp.31–2.

6   Paul Anderton, 'The Liberal Party of Stoke-on-Trent and Parliamentary Elections, 1862–1880: A Case Study in Liberal-Labour Relations' (University of Keele MA thesis, 1976), pp.22–3; David Christie Murray, *Recollections* (London: John Long, 1908), pp.67–8; Maurice Edward Kenealy, *The Tichborne Tragedy* (London: Francis Griffiths, 1913), p.367.

7   Arabella Kenealy, *Memoirs*, pp. 84–5.

8   See Richard Faber, *Young England* (London: Faber and Faber, 1987).

9   Edward Kenealy, *Edward Wortley Montagu: An Autobiography* (London: T. Cautley Newby, 1869), i, pp.16–17.

10 Arabella Kenealy, *Memoirs*, p.234.

11 Edward Kenealy, *Edward Wortley Montagu*, i, pp.61–2.

12 Arabella Kenealy, *Memoirs*, p.173.

13 As late as 1845, he was prepared to describe himself as a Catholic in the Cork Temperance Institute, though this could well have been to appease his audience: Edward Kenealy, *The Inaugural Address to the Members of the Temperance Institute* (Cork: George Nash, 1845). His autobiography states that he abandoned the faith at university: Arabella Kenealy, *Memoirs*, pp.84–5.

14 *The Medium and Daybreak*, 19 March 1875, p.184; 7 January 1876, p.7. See also Edward Kenealy, 'A Venetian Romance', *Ainsworth's Magazine*, 2 (1842), p.519; George Pember, *Theosophy, Buddhism and the Signs of the End* (London: Hodder and Stoughton, 1891), pp.45–7.

15 Edward Kenealy, *The Prayers, Meditations and Visions of Kenealy (Imaum Mahidi): The Twelfth Messenger of God* (Watford: C.W. Hillyear, 1909), pp.197–8.

16 Edward Kenealy, *The Book of God: An Introduction to the Apocalypse* (London: Trübner and Co., 1868?), p. 4; Arabella Kenealy, *Memoirs*, p.216, 178.

17 Edward Kenealy, *The Book of God: A Commentary on the Apocalypse* (London: Trübner and Co., 1870) p. 654; idem (ed.), *Trial at the Bar of Sir R. C. D. Tichborne* (London: *Englishman*, 1875), [hereafter Kenealy, *Trial*], Introduction, p.5.

18 Edward Kenealy, *The Book of God: A Commentary*, p.216.

19 Edward Kenealy, *The Book of God: An Introduction*, p.3; *The Book of God: A Commentary*, p. 604, 666.

20 Charles Wells Hillyear, *Kenealy: The Twelfth Messenger of God* (Watford: C. W. Hillyear, 1915), p.38.

21 Edward Kenealy, *The Book of God: An Introduction*, p.4.

22 Charles Wells Hillyear, *Kenealy*, p.40.

23 Ibid., p.4, 12.

24 Edward Kenealy, *The Prayers, Meditations and Visions of Kenealy*, pp.197–8.

25 *The Times*, 18 April 1873, p.10.

26 Quoted in Kenealy, *Trial*, vii, p.341.

27 John H. Langbein, *The Origins of Adversary Criminal Trial* (Oxford: Oxford University Press, 2003), esp. p.272; see also John Beattie, 'Scales of Justice: Defence Counsel and the English Criminal Trial in the Eighteenth and Nineteenth Centuries', *Law and History Review*, 9 (1991), pp.221–67; David J. A. Cairns, *Advocacy and the Making of the Adversarial Criminal Trial, 1800–1865* (Oxford: Clarendon Press, 1998).

28 Graham Parker, 'The Prisoner in the Box: The Making of the Criminal Evidence Act, 1898', in J. A. Guy and H. G. Beale (eds), *Law and Social Change in British History* (London: Royal Historical Society, 1984), pp.156–75.

29 Mark Twain, *Following the Equator: A Journey around the World* (New York: Hartford, 1897), pp.157–8.

30 'Cockburn, Alexander James Edmund (1802–1880)', *Oxford Dictionary of National Biography* (Oxford: Oxford University Press, 2004), xii, pp.328–332; William Ballantine, *Some Experiences of a Barrister's Life* (London: Richard Bentley, 1882), pp.113–19.

31 Kenealy, *Trial*, i, pp.82–6; Arabella Kenealy, *Memoirs*, pp.250–1.

32 *The Times*, 28 December 1881, p.3; 28 April 1887, p.5.

33 Kenealy, *Trial*, i, p.1.

34 *The Times*, 24 April 1873, p.14.

35 George Lansbury, *Looking Backwards – and Forwards* (London: Blackie and Sons, 1935), p.138.

36 *The Tichborne Romance* (London: George Routledge, 1872); *The Times* 17 April 1873, p.11.

37 *The Times*, 20 September 1873, p.9.

38 Ibid., 23 September 1873, p.7, 9.

39 Ibid., 16 June 1873, p.14; Kenealy, *Trial*, ii, pp.93–4.

40 *Morning Advertiser*, 18 August 1873, p.4; Kenealy, *Trial*, iv, p.243 and v, pp.254–6.

41 *The Times*, 25 October 1873, p.9; Return relating to Joint Stock Companies, 27 April 1874, *Parliamentary Papers*, 1874 (124), 62, 457, p.77.

42 William Powell Frith, *My Autobiography and Reminiscences* (London: R. Bentley, 1887), ii, pp.41–5.

43 *Daily News*, 18 September 1873, p.3.

44 This reconstruction is based on five different accounts of the criminal trial: Kenealy, *Trial*; Alexander Cockburn, *The Tichborne Trial: The Summing-Up of the Lord Chief Justice* (London: J.R. Maxwell, n.d.); *The Queen v. Thomas Castro, Otherwise Arthur Orton, Otherwise, Sir Roger Charles Doughty Tichborne*

(London: Vacher and Sons, 1873–4); *Charge of the Lord Chief Justice* (London: Vacher and Sons, 1874); and the reports in the *The Times*.

45 Ballantine, *Some Experiences of a Barrister's Life*, ii, p.182.

46 Kenealy, *Trial*, iii, p.106.

47 Henry Brougham, *Speeches of Henry Lord Brougham* (Edinburgh: Adam and Charles Black, 1838), i, p.105.

48 *The Times*, 9 November 1864, p. 9; *Law Times*, 12 November 1864, pp. 16-18.

49 James Fitzjames Stephen and Albert Venn Dicey both noted how uncertain the professional morality of the Bar was: James Fitzjames Stephen,'The Morality of Advocacy', *Cornhill Magazine*, 3 (1861), p. 453; Albert Venn Dicey, 'Legal Etiquette', *Fortnightly Review*, new series, 2 (1867), p.171. See also Allyson N. May, *The Bar and the Old Bailey, 1750–1850* (Chapel Hill, North Carolina: University of North Carolina Press, 2003), ch.8.

50 R. E. Francillon, *Mid-Victorian Memories* (London: Hodder and Stoughton, n.d.), p.122; Thomas Edward Crispe, *Reminiscences of a KC* (London: Methuen, 1909), p.71.

51 Arabella Kenealy, *Memoirs*, p.253, 259.

52 *The Times*, 29 April 1873, p.10.

53 Ibid., 30 April 1873, p.12.

54 Ibid., 1 May 1873, p.14.

55 Kenealy, *Trial*, i, p.47.

56 Ibid., iii, p.249.

57 Ibid., i, pp.19, 27, 375.

58 *The Times*, 1 July 1873, p.11.

59 Ibid., 23 July 1873, p.7.

60 Kenealy, *Trial*, iii, p.106. Henry (later Cardinal) Manning had been Roman Catholic Archbishop of Westminster since 1865. Robert Lowe was Chancellor of the Exchequer 1868–73.

61 Ibid., iii, pp.90–118.

62 *The Times*, 25 September 1873, p.11; *Reynolds's Newspaper*, 28 September 1873, p.4.

63 *Pall Mall Gazette*, 17 January 1874, p.6.

64 Kenealy, *Trial*, vii, p.196.

65 Ibid., vii, p.61 (emphasis in original).

66 *Annual Register*, 1874, part two, p.183.

67 Herbert Henry Asquith, Earl of Oxford and Asquith, *Memories and Reflections, 1852–1927* (Cassell, 1928), i, p.63.

68 Peter Brooks and Paul Gewirtz (eds.), *Law's Stories: Narrative and Rhetoric in the Law* (New Haven: Yale University Press, 1996); Michael Freeman and Andrew D. E. Lewis (eds), *Law and Literature* (Oxford: Oxford University Press, 1999); Jan-Melissa Schramm, *Testimony and Advocacy in Victorian Law, Literature*

and Theology (Cambridge: Cambridge University Press, 2000); Alexander Welsh, *Strong Rep-resentations: Narrative and Circumstantial Evidence in England* (Baltimore: John Hopkins University Press, 1992).

69 Cockburn, *The Tichborne Trial*, p.101.

70 Ibid., pp.7–8.

71 Ibid., p.87.

72 Ibid., p.284.

73 Ibid., p.282.

74 Ibid., p.282.

75 Ibid., p.283.

76 Ibid., p.284.

77 *Charge of the Lord Chief Justice*, p.4832.

78 Ibid., p.4833.

79 *Daily News*, 2 March 1874, p.6.

80 *Standard*, 2 March 1874, p.6.

81 *Pall Mall Gazette*, 2 March 1874, p.1. See also *Daily News*, 3 March 1874, p.5. On the Martin Guerre case, see Natalie Zemon Davis, *The Return of Martin Guerre* (Cambridge, Massachusetts: Harvard University Press, 1983).

82 *Morning Advertiser*, 2 March 1874, p.4.

83 *Standard*, 3 March 1874, p.4; *Times*, 2 March 1874, pp.8–9.

84 *Pall Mall Gazette*, 17 March 1874, pp.4–5; 24 March 1874, pp.3–4.

85 *Morning Post*, 2 March 1874, p.3.

86 *Huddersfield Daily Chronicle*, 7 April 1875, p.3. Robert Lowe to P. Radcliffe, 20 October 1872; P. Radcliffe to Robert Lowe, 18 February 1873: Radcliffe Papers I 659, box F, Leeds Record Office.

87 Arthur Griffiths, *Fifty Years of Public Service* (London: Cassell, 1904), p.215; 'A Ticket-of-Leave Man', *Convict Life; Or, Revelations Concerning Convicts and Convict Prisons* (London: Wyman, 1879), pp.121–4.

88 *Pall Mall Gazette*, 2 March 1874, p.2; *Solicitor's Journal and Reporter*, 11 April 1874, p.439.

89 *Law Times*, 7 March 1874, p.321.

90 The *Law Times* cited the case of Edwin James as a precedent: *ibid* 7 March 1874, p.321; on James, see J.R. Lewis, *Certain Private Incidents: The Rise and Fall of Edwin James, QC, MP* (Newcastle-upon-Tyne: Templar North, 1980).

91 *Solicitor's Journal and Reporter*, 7 March 1874, p. 337.

92 *Law Times*, 8 August 1874, p. 261; *Solicitor's Journal and Reporter*, 21 March 1874, p. 373.

93 This decision has been defended by Justice Megarry basing his argument on Kenealy's editorship of the Englishman: 'R. E. M.', 'Dispatented, Disbenched and Disbarred'. *Law Quarterly Review*, 90 (1974), pp. 463–65. Megarry underrates the determination of the legal profession to expel Kenealy.

Notes to Chapter 6: The Magna Charta Association

1 J. F. C. Harrison, 'Chartism in Leicester', in Asa Briggs (ed.), *Chartist Studies* (London: Macmillan, 1959), pp.99–146; Bill Lancaster, *Radicalism, Cooperation and Socialism: Leicester Working-Class Politics, 1860–1906* (Leicester: Leicester University Press, 1987).

2 *Englishman*, 11 April 1874, p.10.

3 Accounts of the Leicester meeting can be found in ibid., 11 April 1874, p.12; 18 April 1874, pp.21–2.

4 Thomas Cooper, *The Life of Thomas Cooper* (Leicester: Leicester University Press, 1971 [1872]), pp.175–6.

5 *Englishman*, 18 April 1874, p.18.

6 Ibid., 11 April 1874, p.11.

7 Ibid., 11 April 1874, p.14; 25 April 1874, p.38.

8 It was possible to break even with a sale of about 4000: Edward Royle, *Radicals, Secularists and Republicans: Popular Freethought in Britain, 1866–1915* (Manchester: Manchester University Press, 1980), p.157.

9 *The Times*, 25 September 1875, p.8.

10 *Englishman*, 29 August 1874, p.332; 26 December 1874, p.603.

11 Ibid., 23 May 1874, p.110.

12 Ibid., 11 July 1874, p.215. W.H. Smith also refused to handle the Secularist press and, for a while, Joseph Cowen's radical *Newcastle Weekly Chronicle*: Edward Royle, *Radicals, Secularists and Republicans*, p.262; Nigel Todd, *The Militant Democracy: Joseph Cowen and Victorian Radicalism* (Tyne and Wear: Bewick Press, 1991) p.56, 125.

13 Ibid., 2 May 1874, p.61.

14 Ibid., 23 May 1874, p.110.

15 Maurice Edward Kenealy, *The Tichborne Tragedy* (London: Francis Griffiths, 1913), p.4.

16 'W. A. F.' (William Alfred Frost), *An Exposure of the Orton Confession of the Tichborne Claimant* (London: Lynwood 1913), p.13.

17 Nadja Durbach, '"They Might As Well Brand Us": Working-Class Resistance to Compulsory Vaccination in Victorian England', *Social History of Medicine*, 13 (2000), pp.45–62 (quotation on p. 46). See also Logie Barrow, '"In the Beginning Was the Lymph": The Hollowing of Stational Vaccination in England and Wales, 1840–98' in Steve Sturdy (ed.), *Medicine, Health and the Public Sphere in Britain, 1600–2000* (London: Routledge, 2002) pp. 205–23; idem, 'Clashing Knowledge-Claims in Nineteenth-Century English Vaccination', in Willem de Blécourt and Cornelie Usborne (eds), *Cultural Approaches to the History of Medicine: Mediating Medicine in Early Modern and Modern Europe* (Basingstoke: Palgrave, 2004), pp.171–91; Nadja Durbach, *Bodily Matters: The*

Anti-Vaccination Movement in England 1853–1907 (Durham, North Carolina: Duke University Press, 2005).

18 *Englishman*, 11 April 1874, p.10; 2 May 1874, p.62.

19 Ibid., 25 April 1874, p.45; 23 May 1874, p.110; 19 September 1874, p.381.

20 Ibid., 11 April 1874, p.10.

21 Ibid., 15 August 1874, p.300.

22 Ibid., 9 May 1874, p.77.

23 Ibid., 9 May 1874, p.78.

24 Ibid., 20 February 1875, p.725.

25 Ibid., 21 November 1874, p.522; 19 December 1874, p.581, 587.

26 Ibid., 11 July 1874, p.213. On the Eleusis Club, see Edward Royle, *Radicals, Secularists and Republicans*, p.199, 202, 203.

27 Ibid., 25 September 1874, p.397.

28 Ibid., 10 October 1874, pp.418–23, for an account of the Leicester meeting.

29 Ibid., 10 October 1874, p.424.

30 Ibid., 24 October 1874, pp.449–50.

31 Ibid., 24 October 1874, p.451.

32 Ibid., 31 October 1874, p.467.

33 This echoed the celebration of foolishness in early modern Europe: Natalie Zemon Davis, *Society and Culture in Early Modern France* (London: Duckworth, 1975), ch.4.

34 *Englishman*, 31 October 1874, p.467.

35 Ibid., 5 December 1874, p.555.

36 *National Independent and People's Advocate*, 17 June 1876, p.4.

37 *Englishman*, 21 November 1874, p.513.

38 Report of the Select Committee of the House of Commons on Public Petitions, 1872–1882 (British Library callmark B.S. 91/6). For more information on the Tichborne petitions, see Rohan McWilliam, 'The Tichborne Claimant and the People: Investigations into Popular Culture, 1867–1886' (University of Sussex D.Phil. thesis, 1990), appendix 5.

39 See Colin Leys, 'Petitioning in the mid–Nineteenth and Twentieth Centuries', *Political Studies* 3 (1955), pp.45–64.

40 Report of the Select Committee ... on Public Petitions, 1875, p.44; appendix p.99.

41 This account is based on *Englishman*, 12 December 1874, pp.560–64.

42 T. W. Mason, 'Nineteenth-Century Cromwell', *Past and Present*, no.40 (1968), pp.187–91; Raphael Samuel, 'The Discovery of Puritanism, 1820–1914: A Preliminary Sketch', in his *Island Stories: Unravelling Britain* (London: Verso, 1998), pp.276–322.

43 *Englishman*, 16 October 1875, p.496.

44 *Times*, 6 November 1868, p.5

45 *Englishman*, 6 March 1875, p.762.

46 Ibid., 30 January 1875, p.677.

47 *Englishman's Magazine*, March 1875, p.132.

48 Ibid., January 1875, p.11.

Notes to Chapter 7: The People's Candidate

1 *Essays on Reform* (London: Macmillan, 1867); see also Christopher Harvie, *The Lights of Liberalism: University Liberals and the Challenge of Democracy* (London: Allen Lane, 1976).

2 H. J. Hanham, *Elections and Party Management: Politics in the time of Disraeli and Gladstone* (London: Longmans, 1959).

3 Jon Lawrence, *Speaking for the People: Party, Language and Popular Politics in England, 1867–1914* (Cambridge: Cambridge University Press, 1998), ch. 7.

4 Paul Anderton, 'The Liberal Party of Stoke-upon-Trent and Parliamentary Elections, 1862–80: A Case Study of Liberal-Labour Relations' (University of Keele, unpublished MA Thesis, 1974).

5 On Owen, see Aled Jones, 'Workmen's Advocates: Ideology and Class in a Mid-Victorian Labour Newspaper System' in Joanne Shattock and Michael Wolff (eds), *The Victorian Periodical Press: Samplings and Soundings* (Leicester: Leicester University Press, 1982), pp.297–316.

6 Detlev Mares, 'Walton, Alfred Armstrong', in Joyce M. Bellamy and John Saville (eds), *Dictionary of Labour Biography*, x (London: Macmillan, 2000), pp.213–18.

7 Anderton, 'The Liberal Party of Stoke-upon-Trent', p.99.

8 Terence A. Lockett, *Davenport Pottery and Porcelain, 1794–1887* (Newton Abbot: David and Charles, 1972), p.24, 30–31.

9 *Staffordshire Daily Sentinel*, 7 January 1875, p.3; 12 January 1875, p.3; *Staffordshire Sentinel* 16 January 1875, p.5.

10 *Staffordshire Sentinel*, 9 January 1875, p.5; *Englishman*, 16 January 1875, p.674.

11 *Staffordshire Daily Sentinel*, 19 January 1875, p.3.

12 *Staffordshire Sentinel*, 16 January 1875, p.7.

13 Ibid., 23 January 1875, p.7.

14 Ibid., 23 January 1875, p.7.

15 Ibid., 9 January 1875, p.4.

16 Ibid., 23 January 1875, p.5.

17 *Potteries Examiner*, 16 January 1875, p.5.

18 *Staffordshire Sentinel*, 13 February 1875, p.5.

19 Hanham, *Elections and Party Management*, pp.26–27.

20 *Staffordshire Sentinel*, 13 February 1875, p.7.

21 Ibid., 13 February 1875, p.7.

22 Ibid., 23 January 1875, p.7.

23 Ibid., 23 January 1875, p.7.

24 Ibid., 23 January 1875, p.7; 30 January 1875, p.7.

25 Ibid., 16 January 1875, p.1.

26 *Potteries Examiner*, 30 January 1875, p.7.

27 Ibid., 30 January 1875, p.7.

28 Ibid., 30 January 1875, p.8.

29 *Staffordshire Sentinel*, 23 January 1875, p.8; 30 January 1875, p.7.

30 Ibid., 30 January 1875, p.8.

31 Ibid., 23 January 1875, p.8; 30 January 1875, p.7; 6 February 1875, p.7.

32 Ibid., 23 January 1875, p.6.

33 Ibid., 30 January 1875, p.7.

34 Ibid., 30 January 1875, p.5.

35 *Potteries Examiner*, 13 February 1875, p.7.

36 *Englishman*, 13 February 1875, p.708; *How I Became a Socialist* (London: Twentieth-Century Press, 1894), pp.37–38. On Jack Williams see Kenneth D. Brown, 'Williams, John (Jack) Edward', in Joyce M. Bellamy and John Saville (eds), *Dictionary of Labour Biography*, vi (London: Macmillan, 1982) pp.269–272.

37 *Englishman*, 13 February 1875, p.708.

38 *Staffordshire Daily Sentinel*, 27 January 1875, p.3.

39 Ibid., 30 January 1875, p.7.

40 Fanny Allen to Emma Darwin, 27 April 1875: Henrietta E. Litchfield, *Emma Darwin: A Century of Family Letters* (Cambridge: privately printed, 1904), ii, pp.273–74.

41 Josiah C. Wedgwood, *A History of the Wedgwood Family* (London: St Catherine's Press, 1909), p.195.

42 *Englishman*, 13 February 1875, p.709.

43 *Staffordshire Daily Sentinel*, 3 February 1875, p.3.

44 *Staffordshire Sentinel*, 30 January 1875, p.7.

45 Frederick Boase (ed.), *Modern English Biography* (London: Frank Cass, 1965 [1901]), cols 924–25.

46 *Englishman*, 30 January 1875, p.7.

47 *Staffordshire Sentinel*, 30 January 1875, p.7.

48 *Potteries Examiner*, 30 January 1875, pp.7–8; *Staffordshire Daily Sentinel*, 1 February 1875, p.3.

49 *Staffordshire Sentinel*, 30 January 1875, p.7.

50 Poster in Radcliffe Papers I 659, box E, Leeds Record Office.

51 *Staffordshire Sentinel*, 30 January 1875, p.7.

52 Ibid., 30 January 1875, p.7; see also *Potteries Examiner*, 23 January 1875, p.4.

53 *Staffordshire Sentinel*, 30 January 1875, p.7.

54 Ibid., 30 January 1875, p.7.

55 Ibid., 30 January 1875, p.7.

56 *Staffordshire Daily Sentinel*, 29 January 1875, p.2.

57 *Potteries Examiner*, 23 January 1875, p.4.

58 *Staffordshire Sentinel*, 30 January 1875, p.8.

59 Ibid., 16 April 1923, p.7.

60 Ibid., 13 February 1875, p.5; *Potteries Examiner*, 6 February 1875, pp.4–5.

61 *Staffordshire Sentinel*, 30 January 1875, p.7.

62 Ibid., 30 January 1875, p.3, 7.

63 *Potteries Examiner*, 6 February 1875, p.7; *Englishman*, 13 February 1875, p.708.

64 *Potteries Examiner*, 6 February 1875, p.7.

65 *Stoke Election: Hurrah for Kenealy*, Hanley Central Library.

66 *Englishman*, 13 February 1857, p.708.

67 Henry Broadhurst, *Henry Broadhurst MP: The Story of his Life from a Stone-mason's Bench to a Treasury Bench* (London: Hutchinson, 1901), p.98.

68 *Staffordshire Sentinel*, 30 January 1875, p.7.

69 *Nation* (Dublin), 31 August 1872, p.550; John Archer Jackson, *The Irish in Britain* (London: Routledge and Kegan Paul, 1966), p.87.

70 *Staffordshire Sentinel*, 23 January 1875, p.7.

71 'An Old Potter' [C. Shaw], *When I Was a Child* (Wakefield: S.R. Publishers, 1969 [1903]), pp.177–79.

72 Home Office Papers, 45/7991 fos 9, 11–13, National Archives.

73 Louis T. Stanley, *Collecting Staffordshire Pottery* (London: W.H. Allen, 1963), pp.43–46, 53–56.

74 *Englishman*, 13 February 1875, pp.706–77.

75 Ibid., 13 February 1875, p.706.

76 3 *Hansard*, 220, cols 1354–55 (9 July 1874); 221, cols 554–55 (23 July 1874).

77 *Staffordshire Sentinel* 20 February 1875, p.7.

78 *Englishman*, 13 February 1875, p.706.

79 *Staffordshire Sentinel*, 20 February 1875, p.7

80 *Englishman*, 13 February 1875, p. 706.

81 *The Times*, 17 February 1875, p. 9.

82 *Blackwood's Magazine*, 117 (1875), pp. 526–8.

83 *Derby and Chesterfield Reporter*, 19 February 1875, p. 4.

84 *Potteries Examiner*, 20 February 1875, p. 4.

85 *Staffordshire Sentinel*, 20 February 1875, p. 5.

86 Quoted in ibid., 20 February 1875, p. 7.

87 *The Times*, 17 February 1875, p. 9.

88 *Staffordshire Sentinel*, 20 February 1875, p. 5.

89 Ibid., 20 February 1875, p. 5.

Notes to Chapter 8: Tichborne Radicalism

1 Andrew Rothstein, *A House on Clerkenwell Green* (London: Lawrence and Wishart, 1966); Stan Shipley, *Club Life and Socialism in Mid-Victorian London* (London: History Workshop, 1983 [1971]); Watson Eugene Lincoln Jr., 'Popular Radicalism and the Beginnings of the New Socialist Movement in Britain, 1870–1885' (University of London, unpublished D.Phil thesis, 1977); John Davis, 'Radical Clubs and London Politics, 1870–1900', in David Feldman and Gareth Stedman Jones (eds), *Metropolis London: Histories and Representations since 1800* (London: Routledge, 1989), pp.103–28; Antony Taylor, 'Modes of Political Expression and Working-Class Radicalism: The London and Manchester Examples' (University of Manchester, unpublished D.Phil. thesis, 1992).

2 Charles Bradlaugh, *Letter to E.V. Kenealy* (London: C. Watts, 1875); *Bee–Hive*, 27 February 1875, p.11; 9 October 1875, p.3.

3 3 *Hansard*, 222, cols 486–90 (18 February 1875); Henry W. Lucy, *A Diary of Two Parliaments: The Disraeli Parliament* (London: Cassell, 1885), pp.51–52.

4 Ibid., 223, (23 April 1875), cols 1513–1613.

5 Ibid., 228, cols 246–50 (17 March 1876).

6 *Battersea and Wandsworth Observer*, 4 September 1875, p.3.

7 3 *Hansard*, 224, cols 1955–56 (15 June 1875); 225, cols 138–39 (17 June 1875); 240, cols 621–22 (24 May 1878); 243, col. 1840 (27 February 1879).

8 Ibid., 232, cols 414–17 (15 February 1877); 234, cols 1328–29 (5 June 1877); cols 1447, 1449, 1457, 1463 (7 June 1877); 243, col. 1519 (20 February 1879).

9 Ibid., 244, cols 692–96 (11 March 1879).

10 Ibid., 238, cols 384–90 (26 February 1878); 239, cols 575–77 (4 April 1878); 251, cols 198–99 (2 March 1880).

11 Ibid., 227, col. 1759 (9 March 1876); 229, col. 433 (11 May 1876).

12 Ibid., 225, cols 1521–22 (15 July 1875); see also 264, col. 1311 (20 March 1879); 264, col. 1435 (21 March 1879). Kenealy's attacks on the Prince of Wales and on the Prince's friend, Valentine Baker (who attempted to sexually assault a young woman on a train), were one of the reasons for his break with Whalley: see *Battersea and Wandsworth Observer*, 4 September 1875, p.3; 11 September 1875, p.3.

13 *The Times*, 30 March 1875, p.6.

14 *Pall Mall Gazette*, 30 March 1872, p.10.

15 Norman St John Stevas (ed.), *The Collected Works of Walter Bagehot* (London: The Economist, 1974), vii, pp.241–4.

16 *Bristol Observer*, 3 April 1875, p.3; *The Times*, 31 March 1875, p.9.

17 Rohan McWilliam, 'The Tichborne Claimant and the People: Investigations into Popular Culture, 1867–1886' (University of Sussex D.Phil. thesis, 1990), appendix 4.

18 William Collison, *The Apostle of Free Labour* (London: Hurst and Blackett, 1913), pp.6–9.

19 *The Times*, 11 August 1875, p.12.

20 *East Essex and Halstead Times*, 22 April 1876, p.5. I owe this reference to the late Arthur Brown. On Rushbrooke (a tailor who was active in promoting the co-operative movement and agricultural trade unionism), see A. F. J. Brown, *Chartism in Essex and Suffolk* (Chelmsford: Essex Record Office, 1982) p.40, 79, 100, 111–13, 120–21.

21 *National Independent and People's Advocate*, 29 July 1876, p.4.

22 *Englishman*, 17 March 1877, p.380; 21 April 1877, p.43; 28 April 1877, p.61; 1 September 1877, p.346; 26 July 1879, p.269; 24 April 1886, p.167. The Magna Charta Congress had considered setting up a Sick Benefit, Life Assurance and Burial Society in 1876 though nothing came of it: *Report of the Magna Charta Congress, August, 1876* (London: *Englishman* Office, 1876), p.13.

23 *The Times*, 14 May 1875, p.5.

24 Ibid., 25 September 1875, p.8.

25 *Englishman*, 29 May 1875, p.115; 31 July 1875, p.257, 263; 5 February 1876, p.693; 12 February 1876, p.714; 4 August 1877, pp.284–85; F.W.S. Craig (ed.), *British Parliamentary Election Results, 1832–1885* (London: Macmillan, 1977), p.143.

26 Ibid., 13 September 1879, pp.377–8 (Ahmed Kenealy); election poster in Tichborne Case Folder (John Johnson Collection, Bodleian library) (Skipworth); *Englishman*, 20 December 1884, p.793 (Atkinson); *Little John's Tichborne Text Book and Tichborne for Nottingham!! An Apology* (Birmingham: n.p., 1879?) (Claimant).

27 *True Briton*, 30 May 1874, p.2.

28 *The Times*, 24 May 1875, p.13; 25 May 1875, p.8.

29 *Tichborne Gazette*, 6 November 1875, pp.3–4.

30 *Englishman*, 29 January 1876, pp.680–81; 4 September 1875, p.340.

31 *Report of the Magna Charta Congress, November, 1876* (London: *Englishman* Office, 1876), pp.1–6.

32 It is unclear but this may have become the People's Social and Political Reform Association of which Bailey was president in 1877: *National Anti-Compulsory Vaccination Reporter*, 1 September 1877, p.12.

33 *The Times*, 2 April 1875, p.5.

34 Ibid., 16 October 1875, p.9; 3 December 1875, p.8. See also *Croydon Advertiser and East Surrey Reporter*, 4 December 1875, p.5.

35 Ibid., 19 May 1875, p.7; 25 May 1875, p.8.

36 Ibid., 24 January 1877, p.9; 25 January 1877, p.7; 27 January 1877, p.6.

37 Ibid., 4 September 1877, p.7; 8 September 1877, p.9; 15 September 1877, p.10.

38 Ibid., 29 September 1877, p.10; 9 January 1878, p.12; *Englishman* 23 June 1877, p.186.

39 *The Times*, 29 July 1875, p.8.

40 Ibid., 17 December 1879, p.9; 25 December 1879, p.9; 13 January 1880, p.10; 24 June 1880, p.11; 25 June 1880, p.4; 26 June 1880, pp.11–12, 15–16; *Battersea and Wandsworth Observer*, 4 September 1875, p.3; Memorandum of H.B. Harding, 5 June 1876, Douglas Woodruff Papers, series 7, box 32, folder 1, Georgetown University.

41 *The Times*, 1 December 1875, p.11. Tom Sayers was a famous boxer.

42 Arthur Griffiths, *Fifty Years of Public Service* (London: Cassell, 1904), pp.213–15.

43 *The Times* 10 January 1878, p.10; 17 June 1879, p.7.

44 *National Anti–Compulsory Vaccination Reporter*, 1 March 1880, p.104. I have been unable to trace copies of the *Ventilator*. On Longman and Anti–Vaccination, see his *Fifteen Years Fight against Compulsory Vaccination* (London: n.d., 1900).

45 *Englishman*, 9 January 1875, pp.626–27; 26 February 1876, p.746.

46 Ibid., 2 January 1875, pp.608–11; 1 January 1876, p.619.

47 Ibid., 9 January 1875, p.608; 27 April 1878, pp.56–57.

48 Miranda Wolpert, 'Butler, Josephine Elizabeth', in Joseph O. Baylen and Norbert J. Gossman (eds), *Biographical Dictionary of Modern British Radicals* (Hassocks: Harvester, 1988), iii, p.155; Judith Walkowitz, *Prostitution and Victorian Society: Women, Class and the State* (Cambridge: Cambridge University Press, 1980), p.108. On one occasion, Josephine Butler actually corresponded with the *Englishman* (on the subject of the 'White Slave Trade'): *Englishman*, 10 July 1880, p.219. See also Anne Summers, '*The Constitution Violated*: The Female Body and the Female Subject in the Campaigns of Josephine Butler', *History Workshop Journal*, 48 (1999), pp.1–15.

49 *Englishman*, 27 March 1875, pp.812–13; 10 April 1875, p.9; 29 July 1876, p.259; 15 June 1878, pp.116–17. On the Percy case, see Judith R. Walkowitz, *Prostitution and Victorian Society*, p.110.

50 Ibid., 2 September 1876, pp.340–41; 25 August 1877, p.326; 9 March 1878, p.362; *Report of the Magna Charta Congress, August, 1875* (London: *Englishman* Office, 1876), p.14. The Manchester Magna Charta Association heard a talk on Anti–Vaccination: *Englishman*, 26 June 1880, p.190.

51 *Englishman*, 1 April 1876, p.821.

52 Ibid., 6 April 1878, p.7; 27 May 1876, p.116; 10 June 1876, p.153; 27 May 1876, p.123; 7 October 1876, p.10; 12 May 1877, p.93.

53 Ibid., 5 February 1876, p.689; 9 March 1878, p.358; 13 September 1879, pp.373–74; 20 March 1880, p.392; Bradlaugh, *Letter to E. V. Kenealy*; *Englishman*, 17 January 1880, p.252.

54 *Englishman*, 6 May 1876, p.67.

55 Ibid., 8 January 1876, p.630.

56 Ibid., 23 January 1875, p.655.

57 Ibid., 8 January 1875, p.628; 20 May 1875, p.102.

58 *The Times*, 9 February 1876, p.10, 12.

59 *Englishman*, 18 April 1876, p.8.

60 Saunders also spoke at an open–air demonstration in Canning Town, when he described himself as a working-class Liberal: *Tichborne Gazette*, 8 July 1874, p.4.

61 Charles Maurice Davies, *Mystic London: or Phases of Occult Life in the Metropolis* (London: Tinsley Brothers, 1875), ch. 12; *Tichborne Gazette*, 22 July 1875, p.2.

62 *Morning Advertiser*, 18 May 1875, p.5.

63 *The Lavington Case: Affidavits of the Rev. Edward Randall ... of Mr H.B. Harding ... and Mr H.L. Buck* (Brighton: Curtis, 1859).

64 *Tichborne Gazette*, 14 July 1875, p.2.

65 Ibid., 23 June 1875, p.1.

66 Ibid., 6 November 1875, p.1.

67 *Circular of the Great National Tichborne Release Association*: Douglas Woodruff Papers, series 7, box 32, folder 1, Georgetown University.

68 *Report of the Magna Charta Congress, August, 1875*, p.2, 11.

69 G. E. Gray to A.J.W. Biddulph, 12 January 1876; 22 January 1876; G. E. Gray to T. M. Evans, 26 January 1876; G. E. Gray to A. J. W. Biddulph, 26 January 1876, 1 June 1876; memorandum of H. B. Harding, 5 June 1876; H. B. Harding to A. J. W. Biddulph, 16 June 1876, 18 June 1876, 4 July 1876; Resolutions ... for consideration at the proposed special meeting of the Provincial Friends of Sir Roger Tichborne (draft manuscript): Douglas Woodruff Papers series 7, box 32, folder 1, Georgetown University.

70 Contained in Douglas Woodruff Papers, series 7, box 32, folder 1, Georgetown University.

71 It is unclear whether the Provincial Friends was the same organisation as the National Tichborne Release Association: Douglas Woodruff Papers, series 7, box 32, folder 1, Georgetown University.

72 *Englishman*, 21 August 1880, p.316.

73 Resolution ... for consideration at the proposed special meeting of the Provincial Friends of Sir Roger Tichborne: Douglas Woodruff Papers, series 7, box 32, folder 1, Georgetown University.

74 *Englishman*, 11 March 1876, p.783.

75 There are two contemporary biographical accounts written by sympathisers: 'A Free and Independent Elector of Leicester', *Who Is John De Morgan?* (London: George Howe, 1877); Silvester St Clair, *Sketch of the Life and labours of Jno. De Morgan, Orator, Elocutionist, and Tribune of the People* (Leeds: De Morgan, 1880). The latter alludes on page 5 to a work by De Morgan entitled *Five Years Auto-biography* which I have been unable to trace.

76 'A Free and Independent Elector', *Who Is John De Morgan?*, pp.2–3; St Clair, *Jno. De Morgan*, pp.3–6; Institute of Marxism–Leninism, *The General Council of the*

First International, 1871–72: Minutes (Moscow: Progress Publishers, 1968), v, p.141, 148, 213.

77 Malcolm Chase, 'Republicanism: Movement or Moment?' in David Nash and Antony Taylor (eds), *Republicanism in Victorian Society* (Stroud: Sutton, 2000), pp.42–3; *National Reformer*, 8 December 1872, p.361; *Newcastle Daily Journal*, 18 September 1873, p.2; 'A Free and Independent Elector', *Who Is John de Morgan?*, p.5; Joseph Howes, *Twenty-Five Years Fight with the Tories* (Leeds: Petty and Sons, 1907), pp.7–12; Edward Royle, *Radicals, Secularists and Republicans: Popular Free Thought in Britain, 1866–1915* (Manchester: Manchester University Press, 1980), p.202. De Morgan's understanding of religion was decidedly unorthodox. He later claimed in a lecture that 'Christ's doctrines referred solely to this world and man's temporal interests': Charles Maurice Davies, *Unorthodox London: or Phases of Religious Life in the Metropolis* series 2 (London: Tinsley Brothers, 1875), p.217. This apparent 'secularism' did not prevent De Morgan from later using hymns: see John De Morgan (ed.), *Hymns, Songs and Chants: Specially Compiled for Use at John De Morgan's Meetings* (2nd edn. Leeds: De Morgan and Co., 1880). Many of these tended to stress the duty to love one's neighbour rather than the supernatural aspects of Christianity.

78 Henry Collins and Chimen Abramsky, *Karl Marx and the British Labour Movement: Years of the First International* (London: MacMillan, 1965), p.278.

79 *National Reformer*, 17 November 1872, pp.315–16; St Clair, *Jno. De Morgan*, p.6.

80 St Clair, *Jno. De Morgan*, p.10.

81 Home Office Papers 45/9413/56640, f. 47, National Archives.

82 On the Plumstead Common riots, see also Rob Allen, 'The Battle for Plumstead Common', *South London Record*, 1 (1985), pp.16–20'; idem, 'The Battle for the Common: Politics and Populism in Mid-Victorian Kentish London', *Social History*, 22 (1997), pp.61–77.

83 Howes, *Twenty–Five Years*, pp.16–19.

84 'A Free and Independent Elector', *Who Is John De Morgan?*, pp.6–7; *De Morgan's Monthly*, 15 January 1877, p.40; on Richmond see *The Times*, 5 July 1877, p.12. These disturbances were not unusual in this period: see John Field, '"When the Riot Act was Read": A Pub Mural of the Battle of Southsea, 1874', *History Workshop Journal*, 10 (1980), pp.152–63; H.L. Malchow, 'Public Gardens and Social Action in Late Victorian London', *Victorian Studies*, 29 (1985), pp.97–124.

85 *People's Advocate and National Vindicator of Right versus Wrong*, 19 June 1875, p.4.

86 *De Morgan's Monthly*, 1 May 1877, p.61.

87 W. T. Vincent, *The Records of the Woolwich District* (London: J. S. Virtue, 1888–90), ii, p.588.

88 *Tichborne Gazette*, 3 June 1874, p.3.

89 *People's Advocate*, 19 June 1875, p.4.

90 Ibid., 26 June 1875, p.7; 24 July 1875, p.7.

91 [John De Morgan], *The Tichborne Scandal* (n.d.). p.4, 6.

92 *People's Advocate*, 24 July 1875, p.7; 7 August 1875, p.1; *Times*, 3 August 1875, p.11.

93 See, for example, *Englishman*, 10 February 1877, p.292, 299; 11 January 1879, p.235.

94 E.g. *People's Advocate*, 24 July 1875, p.7; 21 August 1875, p.1. De Morgan in fact promised to lecture on Magna Charta topics.

95 *People's Advocate*, 31 July 1875, p.7.

96 Ibid., 21 August 1875, p.7; 28 August 1875, p.6. *Report of the Magna Charta Congress, August, 1875* makes no reference to this incident. It lists only eleven metropolitan representatives as being present, however, when there should have been twelve (p.2).

97 *Tichbornite*, 15 November 1877, pp.4–5 (my pagination).

98 *The Times*, 17 April 1877, p.10.

99 Silvester St Clair places the numbers at between 40,000 and 90,000, but the figures are almost undoubtedly inflated (*Jno. De Morgan*, p.14).

100 *The Times*, 17 April 1877, p.10; 18 April 1877, p.8; Lucy, *A Diary of Two Parliaments*, pp.208–13; John Bailey (ed.), *The Diary of Lady Frederick Cavendish* (John Murray, 1927), ii, p.202.

101 *The Times*, 19 April 1877, p.10.

102 Ibid., 19 June 1877, p.11.

103 Ibid., 16 July 1877, p.9.

104 St Clair, *Jno. de Morgan*, p.14.

105 This information is derived from De Morgan's edition of Dion Boucicault, *Ireland's Story* (New York: Metropolitan Publishing Company, 1881), p.1, 16.

106 Richard Shannon, *Gladstone and the Bulgarian Agitation, 1876* (London: Thomas Nelson, 1963), p.67; see also Ann Pottinger Saab, *Reluctant Icon: Gladstone, Bulgaria and the Working Classes, 1856–1878* (Cambridge, Massachusetts: Harvard Uni-versity Press, 1991).

107 On Barry, see Richard Condon, 'The Political Career of Michael Maltman Barry, 1871–1909' (Oxford University, unpublished B.Litt. thesis, 1972); Rohan McWilliam, 'Barry, Michael Maltman', in Joseph O. Baylen and Norbert E. Gossman (eds), *Biographical Dictionary of Modern British Radicals*, iii, pp.72–8.

108 *People's Advocate*, 15 April 1876, p.1.

109 Paul Martinez, 'The "People's Charter" and the Enigmatic Mr Maltman Barry', *Bulletin of the Society for the Study of Labour History* no.41 (Autumn 1980), pp.34–45.

110 3 *Hansard*, 226, col. 501 (3 August 1875); 230, cols 882–83 (3 July 1876); 233, cols 1131–36 (13 April 1877); 234, cols 818–26 (11 May 1877); 236, cols 699–703 (9 August 1877).

111 *Englishman*, 15 July 1876, p.233; 5 August 1876, p.275.

112 Ibid., 30 September 1876, p.411.

113 Ibid., 5 January 1878, p.219; Hugh Cunningham, 'British Public Opinion and the Eastern Question, 1877–81' (University of Sussex D.Phil. thesis, 1969), p.128, 148.

114 *Englishman*, 21 February 1880, p.334.

115 Paul Anderton, 'The Liberal Party of Stoke-upon-Trent and Parliamentary Elections, 1862–80: A Case Study of Liberal-Labour Relations' (University of Keele, unpublished MA thesis), p.194.

116 *Englishman*, 20 March 1880, pp.389, 392.

117 Ibid., 3 April 1880, p.427.

118 Ibid., 1 May 1880, p.62.

119 George Sexton, *The Late Dr Kenealy and the Lessons to be Learned from his Life: A Sermon* (London: The London Publishing Company, 1880).

120 Ibid., p. 13.

Notes to Chapter 9: After Kenealy

1   J. B. Atlay, *Famous Trials of the Century* (London: Grant Richards, 1899), p.391.

2   *Englishman*, 29 May 1880, p.125.

3   Ibid., 17 January 1880, pp.255–6; 21 February 1880, p.334; 28 February 1880, p.351, 352; 8 May 1880, p.78.

4   Ibid., 24 July 1880, p.248.

5   Ibid., 16 October 1880, p.440.

6   *Report of the Magna Charta Congress, November, 1876* (London: *Englishman* Office, 1876), p.7.

7   Harold Perkin, 'Land Reform and Class Conflict in Victorian Britain', in his *The Structured Crowd: Essays in English Social History* (Brighton: Harvester, 1981), p.120.

8   *Englishman*, 26 June 1880, p.184.

9   Ibid., 9 April 1881, p.392.

10   Ibid., 23 April 1881, p.16.

11   Ibid., 22 April 1882, p.408.

12   Ibid., 11 June 1881, p.123; 19 January 1884, pp.25–6; 29 March 1884, pp.181–2; 24 January 1885, pp.53–4. It regularly publicised the Land Nationalisation Society: 7 October 1882, p.799.

13   Ibid., 19 February 1881, pp.274–5.

14   Thomas William Heyck, *The Dimensions of British Radicalism: The Case of Ireland, 1874–95* (Urbana, Illinois: University of Illinois Press, 1974), ch. 3.

15   *Englishman*, 12 February 1881, p.271.

16   Ibid., 19 February 1881, p.287. It is likely that Mr Williams was Jack Williams, later

of the Social Democratic Federation, who was a supporter of Anti–Coercion.

17 *Englishman*, 19 February 1881, p.288.

18 Ibid., 19 February 1881, pp.285, 287–8; 26 February 1881, p.304; *Times*, 14 February 1881, p.11.

19 *Englishman*, 9 April 1881, p.399.

20 Ibid., 11 June 1881, p.125.

21 Ibid., 17 January 1880, p.252.

22 Ibid., 11 December 1880, pp.124–5 (emphasis in original).

23 Ibid., 23 April 1881, pp.8–9; see also ibid, 2 October 1880, p.411.

24 Ibid., 23 April 1881, p.16.

25 Ibid., 21 August 1880, pp.312–13; 10 July 1880, p.220; 17 July 1880, p.236.

26 Ibid., 4 June 1881, pp.107–8; 11 June 1881, pp.124–5; 18 June 1881, pp.137–8.

27 M. S. Wilkins, 'The Non–Socialist Origins of England's First Important Socialist Organisation', *International Review of Social History*, 4 (1959), pp.199–207.

28 *Englishman*, 26 March 1881, p.366.

29 Ibid., 9 April 1881, p.388; 7 May 1881, p.40.

30 *Pall Mall Gazette* 8 September 1881, p.4; E. P. Thompson, review of C. Tsuzuki's *H. M. Hyndman and British Socialism*, *Bulletin of the Society for the Study of Labour History*, 3 (1961), p.68.

31 Henry Mayers Hyndman, *The Record of an Adventurous Life* (London: Macmillan, 1911), pp.237–45.

32 *Englishman*, 18 June 1881, pp.139–40.

33 Ibid., 11 June 1881, p.123; 7 May 1881, p.40.

34 Ibid., 18 June 1881, p.142.

35 Ibid., 18 June 1881 p.142.

36 Ibid., 7 February 1885, p.82.

37 The series started in ibid., 29 October 1881, pp.10–11; the reference to Marx came in the issue for 14 January 1882, p.186.

38 Ibid., 23 April 1881, pp.8–9.

39 Ibid., 27 October 1883, p.437.

40 The serialisation began in ibid., 17 May 1884, p.293.

41 Ibid., 23 September 1883, p.762.

42 Ibid., 30 June 1883, p.168; 20 October 1887, pp.420–22; 27 October 1883, pp.436–7; 3 November 1883, pp.452–4; 24 November 1883, pp.501–53; 1 December 1883, pp.522–3; 7 February 1885, p.88; 9 January 1886, p.23.

43 Alex Owen, *The Darkened Room: Women, Power, and Spiritualism in Late Nineteenth-Century England* (London: Virago, 1989) esp. ch. 6.

44 The most substantial biographies are Edward Grierson, *Storm Bird: The Strange Life of Georgina Weldon* (London: Chatto and Windus, 1959) and Brian Thompson, *A Monkey Among Crocodiles: The Life, Loves and Lawsuits of Mrs Georgina Weldon* (London: Harper Collins, 2000). See also the biography by her

nephew, Philip Treherne, *A Plaintiff in Person: Life of Mrs Weldon* (William Heinemann, 1923), and her own autobiography, *Mémoires Weldon: Justice (?) Anglaise* (Gisors, France: privately printed, 1902). Important work has been done on Mrs Weldon by women's historians: Judith R. Walkowitz, *City of Dreadful Delight: Narratives of Sexual Danger in Late-Victorian London* (London: Virago, 1992), ch. 6; Helen Nicholson, '"Not Alone": Georgina Weldon's Dramatic Protest Against the Lunacy Laws', *Women and Theatre Occasional Papers*, 3 (1996), pp.70–94.

45 Kathleen Jones, *Mental Health and Social Policy, 1845–1959* (London: Routledge and Kegan Paul, 1960), ch. 2.

46 Georgina Weldon, *How I Escaped the Mad Doctors* (Mrs Weldon [London: privately printed], 1882).

47 Grierson, *Storm Bird*, p.204.

48 *Englishman*, 29 May 1880, p.124; 5 June 1880, p.131; 19 June 1880, p.171; 24 July 1880, p.252.

49 Ibid., 25 March 1876, pp.803–4.

50 E.g., ibid., 17 June 1876, pp.165–6; 30 September 1876, p.411; 4 May 1878, p.75; 31 July 1880, p.265.

51 Ibid., 4 February 1882, p.234; 30 June 1883, p.171.

52 Ibid., 29 December 1883, p.590.

53 Ibid., 28 January 1882, p.219.

54 *The Times*, 21 February 1884, p.7; *Englishman*, 3 January 1885, p.14.

55 *Englishman*, 27 May 1882, p.491.

56 Ibid., 27 May 1882, p.488.

57 Ibid., 30 June 1883, p.168.

58 Ibid., 23 September 1882, pp.760–3.

59 Ibid., 1 November 1884, pp.680–1.

60 E.g., ibid., 22 May 1880, p.105.

61 Ibid., 26 May 1883, p.84.

62 *The Times* 3 June 1884, p.9.

63 Ibid., 22 October 1877, p.7; 11 September, 1878, p.11.

64 Ibid., 19 November 1883, p.7.

65 John Theodore Tussaud, *The Romance of Madame Tussaud's* (London: Odhams, 1920) p.144.

66 Hugh Cunningham, 'British Public Opinion and the Eastern Question' (University of Sussex D.Phil. thesis, 1969), pp.286–7.

67 *The Times* 30 October 1884, p.10; 31 October 1884, p.10; 11 November 1884, p.10; *Englishman* 8 November 1884, pp.693–5.

68 *Englishman*, 15 November 1884, pp.713–6; 29 November 1884, pp.746–7. Handbill for Moss's Theatre of Varieties (Michael Diamond collection). I am grateful to Michael Diamond for this reference.

69 See his list of engagements in *Englishman*, 20 December 1884, p. 795.

70 Ibid., 22 May 1886, p. 175; 15 May 1886, p. 179.

71 Ibid., 22 May 1886, p. 183.

72 Ibid., 22 May 1886, p. 183.

73 Ibid., 22 May 1886, p. 183.

Notes to Chapter 10: Spectacle

1 George Bernard Shaw, *Androcles and the Lion* (London: Longmans, 1963 [1914]), p.16.

2 E. T. Cook and A. Wedderburn (eds), *The Works of John Ruskin* (London: George Allen, 1907), xxix, p.480.

3 Antony Taylor, *Lords of Misrule: Hostility to Aristocracy in Late Nineteenth and Early Twentieth-Century Britain* (Basingstoke: Palgrave Macmillan, 2004).

4 Peter Bailey, 'Champagne Charlie and the Music Hall Swell Song' in his *Popular Culture and Performance in the Victorian City* (Cambridge: Cambridge University Press, 1998), pp.101–27.

5 The most influential treatment of the carnivalesque has been Mikhail Bakhtin, *Rabelais and his World* (Cambridge, Massachusetts: MIT Press, 1968). On the carn-ivalesque, see also Peter Burke, *Popular Culture in Early Modern Europe* (London: Temple Smith, 1978); Peter Stallybrass and Allon White, *The Politics and Poetics of Transgression* (London: Methuen, 1986).

6 Iain McCalman, *Radical Underworld: Prophets, Revolutionaries and Pornographers in London, 1795–1840* (Cambridge: Cambridge University Press, 1988); see also Anna Clark, *Scandal: The Sexual Politics of the British Constitution* (Princeton, New Jersey: Princeton University Press, 2004).

7 V. A. C. Gatrell, *The Hanging Tree: Execution and the English People, 1770–1868* (Oxford: Oxford University Press, 1994).

8 We now know these attempts at cultural elevation by the elite had only limited success: Peter Bailey, *Leisure and Class in Victorian England: Rational Recreation and the Contest for Control, 1830–1885* (London: Methuen, 1987 [1978]).

9 This passage is heavily influenced by Gareth Stedman Jones, 'Working-Class Culture and Working-Class Politics in London, 1870–1900: Notes on the Remaking of a Working Class' in his *Languages of Class: Studies in English Working-Class History, 1832–1982* (Cambridge: Cambridge University Press, 1983), pp.179–38. This remains one of the most stimulating discussions of its theme. The historical literature on the coming of mass culture in Victorian Britain has been heavily influenced by the writings of the interwar Frankfurt School of Marxist critics. Key works on Victorian leisure include: Bailey, *Leisure and Class in Victorian England*; idem, *Popular Culture and Performance in the Victorian City*; Hugh Cunningham *Leisure in the Industrial Revolution*,

c.1780–c.1880 (London: Croom Helm, 1980); Eileen and Stephen Yeo (eds), *Popular Culture and Class Conflict, 1590–1914: Explorations in the History of Labour and Leisure* (Brighton: Harvester, 1981); John K. Walton and James Walvin (eds), *Leisure in Britain, 1780–1939* (Manchester: Manchester University Press, 1983); Martin Hewitt (ed.), *Unrespectable Recreations* (Leeds: Leeds Centre for Victorian Studies, 2001). For important discussions of trends in the historiography of nineteenth-century leisure, see Peter Bailey, 'The Politics and Poetics of Modern British Leisure: A Late Twentieth-Century Review', *Rethinking History*, 3 (1999), pp.131–75; Emma Griffin, 'Popular Culture in Industr-ializing England', *Historical Journal*, 45 (2002), pp.619–35. See also Stuart Hall, 'Notes on Deconstructing "the Popular"', in Raphael Samuel (ed.), *People's History and Socialist Theory* (London: Routledge and Kegan Paul, 1981), pp.227–40.

10 Gareth Stedman Jones, 'The "Cockney" and the Nation, 1780–1988', in David Feldman and Gareth Stedman Jones (eds), *Metropolis London: Histories and Repres-entations since 1800* (London: Routledge, 1989), pp.272–324.

11 Peter Bailey 'Music Hall and the Knowingness of Popular Culture', in his *Popular Culture and Performance in the Victorian City*. On music hall, see also Peter Bailey (ed.), *Music Hall: The Business of Pleasure* (Milton Keynes: Open University Press, 1986); Jacqueline Bratton, *Music Hall: Performance and Style* (Milton Keynes: Open University Press, 1986); Dagmar Kift, *The Victorian Music Hall: Culture, Class and Conflict* (Cambridge: Cambridge University Press, 1996); Paul Maloney, *Scotland and the Music Hall, 1850–1914* (Manchester: Manchester University Press, 2003). On up–to–dateness in popular culture, see Andrew Horrall, *Popular Culture in London, c.1890–1918: The Transformation of Entertainment* (Manchester: Manchester University Press, 2001).

12 F. M. L. Thompson, *The Rise of Respectable Society: A Social History of Victorian Britain, 1830–1900* (London: Fontana, 1988). On the labour aristocracy, see Eric J. Hobsbawm, 'The Labour Aristocracy in Nineteenth-Century Britain', in his *Labouring Men: Studies in the History of Labour* (London: Weidenfeld and Nicolson, 1964) pp.272–315; Robert Q. Gray, *The Labour Aristocracy in Victorian Edinburgh* (Oxford: Clarendon Press, 1976); Geoffrey Crossick, *An Artisan Elite in Victorian Society: Kentish London, 1840–1880* (London: Croom Helm, 1978).

13 My approach here follows Peter Bailey's path-breaking article, 'Will the Real Bill Banks Please Stand Up?', recently reprinted under the title 'A Role Analysis of Working-Class Respectability', in his *Popular Culture and Performance in the Victorian City*, pp.30–46.

14 Jones, 'Working-Class Culture and Working-Class Politics in London', pp.227–28.

15 Eric J. Hobsbawm, *Bandits* (London: Weidenfeld and Nicolson, 1969); Gillian Spraggs, *Outlaws and Highwaymen: The Cult of the Robber in England from the Middle Ages to the Nineteenth Century* (London: Pimlico, 2001).

16 This point is influenced by the anthropologist Victor Turner who has explored the idea of 'liminality'. The liminal figure is a vital archetype in many cultures that attempt to ritualize transitional states. The liminal personality is ambiguous, caught between different stations in society, combining aristocratic airs and lowliness. Turner argues that 'Liminality implies that the high could not be high unless the low existed, and he who is high must experience what it is like to be low'. Liminal people are threshold people who move between different worlds and Turner reveals how the movement of liminal figures from high to low and back again generated an unstructured yearning for a different kind of society that is more integrated than the present one. Turner uses as examples holy beggars, third sons and simpletons who revel in their foolishness in contrast to the alleged sagacity of elites. They usher in what Turner calls 'Communitas', a communion of equal individuals who submit to the general authority of ritual elders. See his *The Ritual Process: Structure and Anti-structure* (London: Routledge and Kegan Paul, 1969), p.95, 97, 106–7, 110.

17 Clive Cheesman and Jonathan Williams, *Rebels, Pretenders and Impostors* (London: British Museum, 2000). I discuss the cultural role of impostors further in 'Unauthor-ised Identities: The Impostor, the Fake and the Secret History in Nineteenth- Century Britain' in Margot Finn, Michael Lobban and Jenny Bourne Taylor (eds.), *Spurious Issues* (forthcoming).

18 Natalie Zemon Davis, *Remaking Impostors: From Martin Guerre to Sommersby* (London: Royal Holloway, University of London, 1997).

19 John Wells, *Princess Caraboo: Her True Story* (London: Pan Books, 1994). See also Margaret Russett, 'The Caraboo Hoax: Romantic Woman as Mirror and Mirage', *Discourse* 17 (1994–5) pp.26–47; Anne Janowitz, 'Caraboo: A Singular Impositon' (unpublished typescript, 1999). My thanks to Anne Janowitz for allowing me to see her work on the Caraboo case.

20 *The Heath House and Ashton Cause* (Bristol: J. Hewitt, 1853).

21 Unidentified press clipping in 'Causes-Célèbres' (scrapbook in private collection), iv, p.104; see also *Times*, 8 June 1875, p.11.

22 'Causes-Célèbres', iv, pp.128–36; see also *Times*, 8 March 1881, p.4.

23 *The Times*, 9 February 1881, p.9.

24 John Tagg, *The Burden of Representation: Essays on Photographies and Histories* (Basingstoke: Macmillan Education, 1988) p.7; see also Jane Caplan and John Torpey (eds), *Documenting Individual Identity: The Development of State Practices in the Mod-ern World* (Princeton: Princeton University Press, 2001). Christopher Kent discusses problems of identity in the Tichborne case in 'Victorian Self-Making, or Self-Unmaking? The Tichborne Claimant Revisited', *Victorian Review*, 17 (1991), pp.1–17.

25 William S. Matthews, *Admeasurement of Photographs, as Applied to the Case of Sir Roger Tichborne* (n.p., 1873?); idem, *From Chile to Piccadilly with Sir Roger*

Tichborne: Identity Demonstrated Geometrically with Photo-Type Illustrations (Bristol: J. Wright, 1876).

26 In the stream of consciousness narrative of James Joyce's *Ulysses*, Tichborne was invoked with reference to Bellew and the tattoo marks: James Joyce, *Ulysses* (Oxford: Oxford University Press, 1993 [1922]), p.604.

27 Edward Kenealy (ed.), *The Trial at Bar of Sir Roger C. D. Tichborne* (London: Englishman, 1875–80), [hereafter Kenealy, *Trial*], ii, p.327.

28 James Bradley, 'Body Communication?: Class and Tattoos in Victorian Britain', in Jane Caplan (ed.), *Written on the Body: The Tattoo in European and American History* (London: Reaktion, 2000), pp.136–55.

29 Arnold Swaine Taylor, *The Principles and Practice of Medical Jurisprudence* (London: R & A Churchill, 1873), i, p.604; Charles Meymott Tidy, *Legal Medicine* (London: Smith, Elder and Co., 1882), i, p.190, 256–7.

30 (W. A. Frost?), *The Tichborne Malformation* (n.d.), p.11.

31 Ibid., p.3.

32 Ibid., pp.7–9.

33 Ibid., pp.16, 18.

34 *The Times*, 25 October 1873, p.11.

35 On John Bull, see Jeanine Surel, 'John Bull', in Raphael Samuel (ed.), *Patriotism: The Making and Unmaking of British National Identity* (London: Routledge, 1989), iii, pp.3–25; Miles Taylor, 'John Bull and the Iconography of Public Opinion in England, *c.* 1712–1929', *Past and Present*, 134 (1992), pp.93–128.

36 *The Great Tichborne Trial*: Tichborne Case Folder, John Johnson Collection, Bodleian Library, Oxford University.

37 Arthur Lloyd, *The Tichborne Case: A Comic Medley* (London: W. Dalcorn, 1873).

38 Information from Mrs D.S.Skinner, Potteries Museum and Art Gallery. Sampson Smith's firm lasted until 1963: Anthony Oliver, *The Victorian Staffordshire Figure: A Guide for Collectors* (London: Heinemann, 1971), pp.147–8. On Staffordshire pottery, see also Reginald Haggar, *Staffordshire Chimney Ornaments* (London: Phoenix House, 1955); Louis T. Stanley, *Collecting Staffordshire Pottery* (London: W. H. Allen, 1963); Anthony Oliver, *Staffordshire Pottery: The Tribal Art of England* (London: Heinemann, 1981); P.D. Gordon Pugh, *Staffordshire Portrait Figures and Allied Subjects of the Victorian Era* (Woodbridge: Antique Collectors Club, 1987 [1970]); Lincoln Hallinan, *British Commemoratives: Royalty, Politics, War and Sport* (Woodbridge, Suffolk: Antique Collector's Club, 1995); Asa Briggs, *Victorian Things* (Stroud: Sutton, 2003 [1988]), ch. 4.

39 Susan Stewart, *On Longing: Narratives of the Miniature, the Gigantic, the Souvenir, the Collection* (Baltimore: John Hopkins University Press, 1984). For the significance of collecting and popular memory, see Marius Kwint, Christopher Breward and Jeremy Aynsley (eds), *Material Memories* (Oxford: Berg, 1999),

esp. Kwint's 'Introduction: The Physical Past' (pp.1–16) but also passim. For further discussion of the Tichborne figure, see Rohan McWilliam, 'The Theatricality of the Staffordshire Figurine', *Journal of Victorian Culture*, 10 (2005), pp.107–14.

40 Guildford Onslow, *200 Facts Proving the Claimant to be Roger Tichborne* (London: George Howe, n.d.), p.23.

41 Richard Hofstadter, *The Paranoid Style in American Politics and Other Essays* (London: Cape, 1966), pp.36–7.

42 *Englishman*, 11 July 1874, p.215.

43 Ibid., 9 January 1875, p.624.

44 Kenealy, *Trial*, Introduction, p.335.

45 See, for example, ibid., 'Roger Fly-Fishing', ii, p.319; 'In the Wood', ii, p.385; 'The Lovers', iii, p.377.

46 Ibid., iv, p.19, 33, 57, 153, 169, 137, 121. See John Berger, *Ways of Seeing* (London: BBC, 1972), pp.106–8, for a deconstruction of this kind of pastoral imagery.

47 *Pictorial Souvenir of the Great Tichborne Case*.

48 Donald Gray, 'The Uses of Victorian Laughter', *Victorian Studies*, 10 (1966), pp.145–76.

49 These are all in an untitled collection of ephemera in the British Library: call-mark: 1881 c. 3.

50 Both the alphabet and *The Tichborne Times* are in 'A collection of pamphlets, posters, caricatures, etc., relating to the Tichborne trial', British Library call-mark: 1888 c.20.

51 Arthur Sketchley, *Mrs Brown on the Tichborne Case* (London: George Routledge, 1872); idem, *Mrs Brown on the Tichborne Defence* (London: George Routledge, 1873?). See also 'Mr Brown', *The Goings On of Mrs Brown at the Tichborne Trial* (London: Ward Lock, n.d.).

52 G. S. Layard, *A Great 'Punch' Editor* (London: Pitman, 1907), pp.456–7.

53 *Punch*, 1 July 1871, p.266; 3 February 1872, p.47.

54 Ibid., 8 July 1871, p.9.

55 Ibid., 29 July 1871, p.30.

56 Ibid., 1 July 1871, p.266; 16 March 1872, pp.115–7; 27 April 1872, p.171; 10 July 1875, p.5; 25 April 1874, p.180.

57 *Englishman*, 13 June 1874, p.151; 25 July 1874, p.241.

58 Charles Dodgson to Francis Paget, 21 February 1874, in Morton N. Cohen (ed.), *The Letters of Lewis Carroll* (London: Macmillan, 1979), i, p.208.

59 Martin Gardner (ed.), *The Annotated Snark* (London: Penguin, 1973 [1962]), pp.83–4. I am grateful to Kali Israel for alerting me to this possible link between the Claimant and Carroll's poem.

60 Unidentified clipping in Tichborne Scrapbook, Manuscripts Misc. 788, Lincoln's Inn Library.

61 *Entr'acte*, 11 December 1875, p.4.

62 Quoted in Louis Bamberger, *Bow Bell Memories* (London: Sampson Low, Marston and Co., 1931), p.155.

63 *Entr'Acte*, 24 August 1872, p.3; Vanessa Toulmin, *Randall Williams, King of Showmen: From Ghost Show to Bioscope* (London: The Projection Box, 1998), pp.14–5.

64 J. F. Stottlar, 'A Victorian Stage Censor: The Theory and Practice of William Bodham Donne', *Victorian Studies*, 13 (1970), p.273.

65 Daybooks indexing the Lord Chamberlain's Plays, Add. MSS 53704, p.124, British Library.

66 *Pall Mall Gazette*, 5 March 1872, p.4.

67 *Reynolds's Newspaper*, 31 December 1871, pp.4–5. Baxter, Rose and Norton were the Claimant's solicitors during the Civil Trial. It numbered the Conservative Party amongst its other clients. The 1872 pantomime at the Britannia Theatre, Hoxton, featured a sketch about the Claimant: Manuscripts Miscellaneous 788, Tichborne Case scrapbook, p.2 (my pagination), Lincoln's Inn Library.

68 H. Chance Newton, *Crime and the Drama: Or Dark Deeds Dramatized* (London: Stanley Paul, 1927), p.115.

69 *Entr'acte*, 7 September 1872, p.4.

70 M. C. Barter, *The Tichborne Gallop* (London: John Blockley, 1872); W. Denzel Moore, *The Tichborne Polka* (London: Frank Griffiths, 1873); W. Archer, *The Tichborne Schottische* (London: J. McDowell, n.d.).

71 *Hampshire Chronicle*, 18 May 1872, p.5.

72 *Tichborne Gazette*, 18 June 1872, p.3.

73 *Eastern Post*, 20 January 1872, p.4.

74 'Little Tich' [Harry Relph], *Little Tich* (London: Greening, 1911), p.28, 32; Mary Tich and Richard Findlater, *Little Tich: Giant of the Music Hall* (london: Elm Tree Books, 1979), esp. pp. 24–32.

75 Roger Chartier, 'Culture as Appropriation: Popular Cultural Uses in Early Modern France' in Steven L. Kaplan (ed.), *Understanding Popular Culture: Europe from the Middle Ages to the Nineteenth Century* (Berlin: Mouton Publishers, 1984), pp. 229–53.

Notes to Chapter 11: Singing the Claimant

1   Henry Mayhew, *London Labour and the London Poor* (London: Griffin, Bohn, 1861), i, pp.3–4. On London street culture, see James Winter, *London's Teeming Streets, 1830–1914* (London: Routledge, 1993). On street entertainers, see John Benson, *The Penny Capitalists: A Study of Nineteenth-Century Working-Class Entrepreneurs* (Dublin: Gill and Macmillan, 1983), pp.65–72; Brenda Assael, 'Music in the Air: Noise, Performers and the Contest over the Streets of the Mid-Nineteenth-Century Metropolis' in Tim Hitchcock and Heather Shore (eds), *The*

Streets of London: From the Great Fire to the Great Exhibition (London: Rivers Oram, 2003) pp.183–97.

2 Phil Eva, 'Home Sweet Home? The "Culture of Exile" in Mid-Victorian Popular Song', *Popular Music*, 16 (1997), pp.131–50.

3 Martha Vicinus, *The Industrial Muse: A Study of Nineteenth-Century British Working-Class Literature* (London: Croom Helm, 1974), p.26.

4 Vivian de Sola Pinto and Allan Edwin Rodway (eds.), *The Common Muse: An Anthology of Popular British Ballad Poetry, XVth–XXth Century* (London: Chatto and Windus, 1957), p.3; Vicinus, *Industrial Muse*, p.9; Louis James, *Print and the People, 1819–1851* (London: Allen Lane, 1976), p.39. We will observe a similar development in the theatre in Chapter Thirteen, below.

5 Ian Watson, *Song and Democratic Culture in Britain: An Approach to Popular Culture in Social Movements* (London: Croom Helm, 1983), p.15.

6 Vic Gammon comments about broadsides that they are 'in a sense too redundant, too unmotivated, too useless to lie' about the culture from which they emerged: Victor A. F. Gammon, 'Popular Music in Rural Society: Sussex, 1815–1914' (University of Sussex D.Phil. thesis, 1985), p.209. See also Vicinus, *Industrial Muse*, p.3, 15, 19–21; Martha Vicinus, *Broadsides of the Industrial North* (Newcastle-upon-Tyne: Frank Graham, 1975), p.7; Roy Palmer (ed.), *Birmingham Ballads* (Birmingham: City of Birmingham Education Department, 1979), p.4; Dave Harker, *One for the Money: Politics and Popular Song* (London: Hutchinson, 1980), p.196.

7 Mayhew, *London Labour and the London Poor*, i, p.220.

8 Ibid., i, p.220.

9 Charles Hindley, *Curiosities of Street Literature* (London: The Broadsheet King, 1966 [1871]), ii, p.159.

10 Charles Hindley, *Curiosities of the Catnach Press* (London: privately printed, 1886), pp.47–50; Mayhew, *London Labour*, i, p.220.

11 Mayhew, *London Labour*, i, p.234. On execution ballads, see V.A.C. Gatrell, *The Hanging Tree: Execution and the English People, 1770–1868* (Oxford: Oxford University Press, 1994), chs 4–5.

12 Alun Howkins, 'The Voice of the People: The Social Meaning and Context of Country Songs', *Oral History*, 3 (1975), p.62.

13 Mayhew, *London Labour*, i, p.283.

14 Ibid., i, pp.280–81; Vicinus, *Broadsides*, p.9.

15 Vicinus, *Industrial Muse*, p.255. V. A. C. Gatrell argues that tradespeople and the provincial middle classes sometimes read broadsides: *The Hanging Tree*, p.169.

16 'Street Ballads', *National Review*, 13 (1861), pp.399–400.

17 Mayhew, *London Labour*, i, p.220.

18 Leslie Shepard, *John Pitts: Ballad Printer of Seven Dials, London, 1765–1844* (Pinner: Private Libraries Association, 1969), pp.87–91.

19 Hindley, *Catnach Press*, p.xvi.

20 E. D. MacKerness, *A Social History of English Music* (London: Routledge and Kegan Paul, 1966), p.133.

21 Mayhew, *London Labour*, i, p.222, 252, 279–80.

22 Ibid., i, p.214.

23 Gammon, 'Popular Music', p.217; Vicinus, *Broadsides*, p.7.

24 'Street Ballads', p.400.

25 Ibid., p.397.

26 William Henderson, *Victorian Street Ballads* (London: Country Life, 1937), p.16.

27 Shepard, *John Pitts*, p.84; Pinto and Rodway (eds), *Common Muse*, p.27, 92–3.

28 V. A. C. Gatrell, 'Crime, Authority and the Policeman–State', in F. M. L. Thompson (ed.), *The Cambridge Social History of Britain* (Cambridge: Cambridge University Press, 1990) iii, pp.249–54; John Carter Wood, 'A Useful Savagery: The Invention of Violence in Nineteenth–Century England', *Journal of Victorian Culture*, 9 (2004), pp.22–42.

29 Mayhew, *London Labour*, i, p.237.

30 *The Labouring Man*, 'A collection of ballads ... collected by the Rev. Sabine Baring Gould', British Library callmark L.R.271.a.2, ii, p.141.

31 'A collection of ballads ... collected by the Rev. Sabine Baring Gould', British Library callmark L.R.271.a.2, v, p.234; *Old Merry England*, 'A collection of songs', British Library callmark 1876.d.41, i, p.189.

32 *Poor of Old England*, 'A collection of ballads ... collected by the Rev. Sabine Baring Gould', British Library callmark L.R.271.a.2, v, p.240.

33 'A collection of ballads ... collected by the Rev. Sabine Baring Gould', British Library callmark L.R.271.a.2, v, p.196.

34 'A collection of ballads ... collected by the Rev. Sabine Baring Gould', British Library callmark L.R.271.a.2, i, p.48.

35 David Kunzle, 'World Upside Down: The Iconography of a European Broadsheet Type' in Barbara A. Babcock (ed.) *The Reversible World: Symbolic Inversion in Art and Society* (Ithaca: Cornell University Press, 1978), pp.39–94.

36 'Street Ballads', pp.412–13; George Johns Bennett, 'The Poetry of the Seven Dials', *Quarterly Review*, 244 (1867), p.406.

37 Gareth Stedman Jones calls this the 'culture of consolation', *Languages of Class: Studies in English Working-Class History, 1832–1982* (Cambridge: Cambridge University Press, 1983), p.237.

38 *Past, Present and Future*, 'A collection of ballads ... collected by the Rev. Sabine Baring Gould', British Library callmark L.R.271.a.2, i, p.48.

39 *Old Merry England*, 'A collection of songs', British Library callmark 1876.d.41, i, p.189.

40 *Old Merry England*, 'A collection of songs', British Library callmark 1876.d.41,

i, p.189. On the cultural politics of beef, see Ben Rogers, *Beef and Liberty* (London: Chatto and Windus, 2003).

41 *Present Times: or Eight Shillings a Week*, 'A collection of songs', British Library callmark 1876.d.41, ii, p.1331.

42 *Britons United*, 'A collection of ballads ... collected by the Rev. Sabine Baring Gould', British Library callmark L.R.271.a.2, viii, p.222.

43 See also Patrick Joyce, *Visions of the People: Industrial England and the Question of Class, 1840–1914* (Cambridge: Cambridge University Press, 1991), ch. 10.

44 *Standard*, 8 March 1872, pp.4–5.

45 Victor Neuberg, 'The Literature of the Streets', in H. J. Dyos and Michael Wolff (eds), *The Victorian City: Images and Realities* (London: Routledge and Kegan Paul, 1973), i, p.193.

46 Hindley, *Catnach Press*, p.xvi.

47 *Leicester Chronicle and Leicestershire Mercury*, 17 August, 1872, p.3.

48 *Conviction of the Claimant* (Disley), Radcliffe Papers I, 659, box F, Leeds Record Office.

49 *The Tichborne ABC*, Bodleian Library, Oxford, callmark: 2803.d.3.

50 *The Great Tichborne Trial*, broadside scrap book, p.5, Birmingham Central Library, callmark F A082.2 L.

51 *'Fair Play' for Tichborne and Kenealy*, private collection.

52 Ibid.

53 *Give a Cheer for Brave Kenealy*, private collection.

54 *The Tichborne ABC*, Bodleian Library, Oxford, callmark 2803.d.3, p.14; see also *Downfall of Poor Old Roger*, Tichborne Case Folder, John Johnson Collection, Oxford University.

55 *The Scamp*, private collection.

56 *We'll Not Forget Poor Roger Now*, Tichborne Case Folder, John Johnson collection, Oxford University.

57 *The Tichborne Belief*, Tichborne Case Folder, John Johnson collection, Oxford University.

58 *The Defence of Sir Roger*, Lilly Library, Indiana University.

59 *The Tichborne Belief*.

60 *We'll Not Forget Poor Roger Now*.

61 Hindley, *Curiosities*, ii, p.134.

62 *Jolly Old Sir Roger*, British Library callmark 1888.c.20.

63 *Poor Roger Tichborne's Lamentation*, private collection.

64 Iain McCalman, *Radical Underworld: Prophets, Revolutionaries and Pornographers in London, 1795–1840* (Cambridge: Cambridge University Press, 1987).

65 *Downfall of Poor Old Roger*, Tichborne Case Folder, John Johnson collection, Oxford University.

66 *Conviction of the Claimant*, Radcliffe Papers I, 659 box E, Leeds Record Office.

67 *The Tichborne Budget*, Lilly Library, Indiana University.

68 *He's Right, Sir Roger Tichborne*, Lilly Library, Indiana University.

69 *Roger or Not Roger: or the Race for the Tichbourne Sweepstakes*, Lilly Library, Indiana University.

70 Adrian Harvey, *The Beginnings of a Commercial Sporting Culture in Britain, 1793–1850* (Aldershot: Ashgate, 2004).

71 See Peter Bailey, '*Ally Sloper's Half Holiday*: Comic Art in the 1880s', in his *Popular Culture and Performance in the Victorian City*, pp. 47–79; Robert Leach, *The Punch and Judy Show: History, Tradition and Meaning* (London: Batsford, 1985).

72 *Judy*, 12 June 1872, p. 82.

73 'Copy of Verses on the Expected release of Sir Roger Tichborne', private collection; 'Tichborne Released', private collection.

74 *Would You Be Surprised to Hear? I am Sir Roger Tichborne* (sic), Lilly Library, Indiana University.

Notes to Chapter 12: The Freeborn Briton

1 *Judy*, 21 April 1875, p.4; 28 April 1875, p.14.

2 The great exception to this is Michael Roe, *Kenealy and the Tichborne Cause: A Study in Mid-Victorian Populism* (Melbourne: Melbourne University Press, 1974). See the critical remarks about Tichborne in John Saville, 'The Background to the Revival of Socialism in England', *Bulletin of the Society for the Study of Labour History*, 11 (1965), pp.13–19.

3 *How I Became a Socialist* (London: Twentieth-Century Press, 1894), pp.37–8.

4 See Rohan McWilliam, *Popular Politics in Nineteenth-Century England* (London: Routledge, 1998) for a discussion of the very large historiography on this subject.

5 The great statement of the 'continuity of radicalism' thesis is Eugenio Biagini and Alastair J. Reid (eds), *Currents of Radicalism: Popular Radicalism, Organised Labour and Party Politics in Britain, 1850–1914* (Cambridge: Cambridge University Press, 1991). See also Eugenio Biagini, *Liberty, Retrenchment and Reform: Popular Liberalism in the Age of Gladstone, 1860–1880* (Cambridge: Cambridge University Press, 1992); Margot C. Finn, *After Chartism: Class and Nation in English Radical Politics, 1848–1874* (Cambridge: Cambridge University Press, 1993); Miles Taylor, *The Decline of British Radicalism, 1847–1860* (Oxford: Clarendon Press, 1995).

6 On the mid-Victorian Liberal party, see John R. Vincent, *The Formation of the British Liberal Party, 1857–1868* (Hassocks: Harvester, 1976 [1966]); Biagini, *Liberty, Retrenchment and Reform*; Jonathan Parry, *The Rise and Fall of Liberal Government in Victorian Britain* (New Haven, Connecticut: Yale University

Press, 1993); H. C. G. Matthew, *Gladstone, 1809–98* (Oxford: Clarendon Press, 1997).

7 Whalley to Chadwick, 5 April 1848, 18 March 1874, 12 July 1874: Edwin Chadwick Papers 2093, University College, London; Malcolm Chase, 'Out of Radicalism: The Mid-Victorian Freehold Land Society Movement', *English Historical Review*,106 (1991), pp.333–4.

8 Geoffrey Crossick, *An Artisan Elite in Victorian Society: Kentish London, 1840–1880* (London: Croom Helm, 1978), pp.232–3.

9 Antony Taylor, *'Down with the Crown': British Anti-Monarchism and Debates about Royalty since 1790* (London: Reaktion, 1999), pp.71–2, 76, 78, 94–5.

10 Richard Hoggart, *The Uses of Literacy: Aspects of Working-Class Life, with Special Reference to Publications and Entertainments* (London: Chatto and Windus, 1957), esp. ch. 3; Stephen Yeo, 'On the Uses of Apathy', *European Journal of Sociology*, 15 (1974), pp.279–311; Stephen Fielding, Peter Thompson and Nick Tiratsoo, *England Arise!: The Labour Party and Popular Politics in 1940s Britain* (Manchester: Manchester University Press, 1995).

11 E.g. *Englishman*, 8 January 1876, pp.632–3.

12 E. P. Thompson, *The Making of the English Working Class* (London: Pelican, 1988 [1963]), ch. 4.

13 *Englishman*, 17 January 1880, p.252.

14 Christopher Hill, 'The Norman Yoke', in John Saville (ed.), *Democracy and the Labour Movement: Essays in Honour of Dona Torr* (London: Lawrence and Wishart, 1954), pp.11–66; see also Asa Briggs, 'Saxons, Normans and Victorians', in Asa Briggs (ed.), *The Collected Essays of Asa Briggs* (Brighton: Harvester, 1985), ii, pp.215–35.

15 Thomas Paine, *Common Sense* (London: Penguin, 1976 [1776]), pp.78–9.

16 *De Morgan's Monthly*, 1 May 1877, p.39.

17 *Englishman*, 9 April 1881, p.392.

18 On the uses of Magna Carta, see Anne Pallister, *Magna Charta: The Heritage of Liberty* (Oxford: Clarendon Press, 1971).

19 Reprinted in Jane Jordan and Ingrid Sharp (eds), *Josephine Butler and the Prostitution Campaigns: Diseases of the Body Politic* (London: Routledge, 2003), ii, pp.211–303 (quotation from p.212).

20 *Englishman*, 26 February 1881, p.302.

21 Richard Price, *British Society, 1680–1880: Dynamism, Containment and Change* (Cambridge: Cambridge University Press, 1999), chs 7–8. On constitutionalism, see in particular John Belchem, 'Republicanism, Popular Constitutionalism and the Radical Platform in Early Nineteenth-Century England', *Social History*, 6 (1991), pp.1–32; James Epstein, 'The Constitutional Idiom', in his *Radical Expression: Political Language, Ritual, and Symbol in England, 1790–1850* (New York: Oxford University Press, 1994) pp.3–28; James Vernon (ed.), *Re–Reading*

the Constitution: New Narratives in the Political History of England's Long Nineteenth Century (Cambridge: Cambridge University Press, 1996).

22 *Englishman*, 25 December 1880, p.157.

23 Ibid., 1 January 1881, p.169.

24 Patrick Joyce, *Visions of the People: Industrial England and the Question of Class* (Cambridge: Cambridge University Press, 1991), pp.39, 44–71; on the 'gentleman leader', see James Vernon, *Politics and the People: A Study in English Political Culture, c.1815–1867* (Cambridge: Cambridge University Press, 1993), ch. 7; John Belchem and James Epstein, 'The Nineteenth–Century Gentleman Leader Revisited', *Social History*, 22 (1997), pp.174–93.

25 Frank O'Gorman, 'Campaign Rituals and Ceremonies: The Social Meaning of Elections in England, 1780–1860', *Past and Present*, 135 (1992), pp.79–115; Vernon, *Politics and the People*.

26 *Standard*, 27 April 1872, p.5.

27 *Nottingham Daily Guardian*, 19 July 1872, p.4.

28 H. J. Hanham, *Elections and Party Management: Politics in the Age of Disraeli and Gladstone* (Hassocks: Harvester, 1978); Jon Lawrence, *Speaking for the People: Party, Language and Popular Politics in England, 1867–1914* (Cambridge: Cambridge University Press, 1998).

29 *Englishman*, 16 October 1875, p.446; 20 September 1879, p.412; 26 February 1881, p.303.

30 Most of these lectures do not seem to have been published so it is unclear what De Morgan actually felt about these subjects. It is, however, clear from the titles of the lectures on Shelley and Garibaldi that he was an admirer of them.

31 John De Morgan, *India and How We Obtained It* (n.p., 1876); idem, *A Letter to the Right Hon. Earl Beaconsfield* (n.p., 1878), p.4; idem, *Royal Knavery!* (London: George Howe, 1878).

32 *De Morgan's Monthly*, 2 April 1877, p.53. The paper constantly referred to Chartism. Pages 54–55 of the latter issue reprinted a speech of Ernest Jones from 1850. The issue for September 1876 included an article on 'Chartist Oratory' (p.7) and the periodical also reprinted some of the Chartist Thomas Cooper's poetry: 1 March 1877, p.47.

33 Joyce, *Visions of the People*.

34 For Patrick Joyce, 'populism' better expresses the nature of nineteenth-century popular political culture than the language of class: see his *Visions of the People*.

35 Ghitta Ionescu and Ernest Gellner (eds), *Populism: Its Meaning and National Character* (London: Weidenfeld and Nicolson, 1969); J.B. Alcock, '"Populism": A Brief Biography', *Sociology*, 5 (1971), pp.371–87; Margaret Canovan, *Populism* (London: Junction Books, 1981).

36 Richard Hofstadter, *The Paranoid Style in American Politics* (London: Cape, 1966), p.98

37 E. P. Thompson, *The Making of the English Working Class* (London: Pelican, 1968 [1963]), p.888; see also Craig Calhoun, *The Question of Class Struggle: Social Foundations of Popular Radicalism during the Industrial Revolution* (Chicago: University of Chicago Press, 1982).

38 This is where I part company to some extent with Michael Roe's pioneering work. See his *Kenealy and the Tichborne Cause*, ch. 7, which relates Tichborne to a broader populist tendency within mass politics. This was a remarkable and important thing to discuss at a time when social historians were mainly interested in issues around class consciousness and class struggle. Patrick Joyce's *Visions of the People* develops this kind of approach to interrogate the way working-class people employed non-class based categories (such as religion, melodrama and national identity) in making sense of society. Joyce labels this form of subjectivity 'populism'.

39 W. D. Rubinstein, 'British Radicalism and the "Dark Side" of Populism', in his *Elites and the Wealthy in Modern Britain: Essays in Social and Economic History* (Brighton: Harvester, 1987), pp.339–373.

40 Anthony Wohl, '"Dizzi-Ben-Dizzi: Disraeli as Alien', *Journal of British Studies*, 34 (1995), pp.375–411; see also Todd Endelman and Tony Kushner (eds), *Disraeli's Jewishness* (London: Valentine Mitchell, 2002).

41 'A collection of songs', British Library callmark 1876.d.41, ii, p.1330.

42 Martha Vicinus, *The Industrial Muse: A Study of Nineteenth-Century British Working-Class Literature* (London: Croom Helm, 1974), p.30.

43 Robert D. Storch, 'Please to Remember the Fifth of November: Conflict, Solidarity and Public Order in Southern England, 1815–1900', in Storch (ed.), *Popular Culture and Custom in Nineteenth-Century England* (London: Croom Helm, 1982), p.79.

44 Robert Sykes, 'Politics and Electoral Behaviour in Guildford and West Surrey, 1790–1868' (University of Surrey, D.Phil. thesis, 1977), p.288.

45 Judith R. Walkowitz, *Prostitution and Victorian Society: Women, Class and the State* (Cambridge: Cambridge University Press, 1980), p.177.

46 David W. Gutzke, *Protecting the Pub: Brewers and Publicans against Temperance* (Woodbridge: Boydell, 1989), pp.219–20.

47 *Conviction of the Claimant*: Radcliffe papers I, 659, box E, Leeds Record Office.

48 *Waiting for the Verdict*, Bodleian Library, Oxford, callmark 2803.d.3.

49 *The Tichborne ABC*, Bodleian Library, Oxford, callmark 2803.d.3.

50 *The Great Tichborne Trial*, broadside scrap book, p.5, Birmingham Central Library, callmark F A082.2 L.

51 J. G. A. Pocock, *Virtue, Commerce and History: Essays on Political Thought, Chiefly in the Eighteenth Century* (Cambridge: Cambridge University Press, 1985), p.49.

52 See also David Wayne Thomas's discussion of the Tichborne case in his

Cultivating Victorians: Liberal Culture and the Aesthetic (Philadelphia: University of Phila-delphia Press, 2004), ch. 3.

53 I. J. Prothero, *Artisans and Politics in Early Nineteenth-Century London: John Gast and his Times* (Folkestone: Dawson, 1979), p.133.

54 Home Office Papers, 40/15, fos 65, 114, 115, 120, 129, 147, 148, 149, 154, 175, 176, 177, 186, 187, 196, 222, National Archives.

55 Louis T. Stanley, *Collecting Staffordshire Pottery* (London: W. H. Allen, 1963), p.95.

56 *Bill of Pains and Penalties*, in Home Office Papers, 40/14 fol. 49, National Archives.

57 Thomas W. Laqueur, 'The Queen Caroline Affair: Politics as Art in the Reign of George IV', *Journal of Modern History* 54 (1982), pp.417–66. See also Anna Clark, *The Struggle for the Breeches: Gender and the Making of the British Working Classes* (London: Rivers Oram, 1995), pp.164–74; idem, *Scandal: The Sexual Politics of the British Constitution* (Princeton, New Jersey: Princeton University Press, 2004), ch. 8.

58 Home Office Papers, 40/16 fol. 77, National Archives.

59 *The Queen and Magna Charta: or The Thing that John Sign'd* (London: T.Dolby, 1820), p.4.

60 Thomas W. Laqueur, 'The Queen Caroline Affair', p.448, 452–4.

61 'Police News': *Mammoth Sheet of the Great Tichborne Trial* (n.d.): Douglas Wood-ruff Papers, series 7, box 41, Georgetown University.

62 Edward Kenealy, *The Trial at Bar of Sir Roger C.D. Tichborne* (London: *English-man*, 1875–80) [hereafter, Kenealy, *Trial*], vii, p.221.

63 *The Eccentric and Singular Productions of Sir William Courtenay ... to which are Added his Weekly Publication 'The Lion'* (Canterbury: Henry Wood, 1833); 'Canter-buriensis', *The Life and Extraordinary Adventures of Sir William Courtenay* (Canterbury: James Hunt, 1838); 'Old Stories Re-Told: John Thom, Alias Sir William Courtenay, Knight of Malta and King of Jerusalem', *All the Year Round*, 4 May 1867, pp.441–6; and *A Canterbury Tale of 50 Years Ago* (n.d. 1888). The standard work on 'Sir William Courtenay' is Barry Reay, *The Last Rising of the Agricult-ural Labourers: Rural Life and Protest in Nineteenth-Century England* (Oxford: Clarendon Press, 1990). See also P.G. Rogers, *Battle in Bossenden Wood: The Strange Story of Sir William Courtenay* (London 1961); E. P.Thompson, *The Making of the English Working Class* (London: Pelican, 1968 [1963]) pp.880–81; J. F. C. Harrison, *The Second Coming: Popular Millenarianism, 1780–1850* (London 1979), pp.213–15.

64 Reay, *The Last Rising of the Agricultural Labourers*, p.112.

65 *Eccentric and Singular Productions ...*, p.5.

66 Ibid., p.6. Courtenay used 'Magna Charta' on at least two other occasions: ibid., p.7, 13.

67 Rogers, *Battle in Bossenden Wood*, p.24.

68 Reay, *The Last Rising of the Agricultural Labourers*, p.114.

69 *Eccentric and Singular Productions ...*, p.13.

70 Rogers, *Battle in Bossenden Wood*, p.49.

71 *Eccentric and Singular Productions ...*, p.19.

72 Patrick Joyce, *Work, Society and Politics: The Culture of the Factory in Later Victorian England* (Brighton: Harvester, 1980); Martin Pugh, *The Tories and the People, 1880– 1935* (Oxford: Blackwell, 1985); Jon Lawrence, 'Class and Gender in the Making of Urban Toryism, 1880–1914', *English Historical Review*, 108 (1993), pp.629–52.

73 Kenealy, *Trial*, Introduction, pp.3–6.

74 Ibid., pp.3–6.

75 Norbert J. Gossman, 'Republicanism in Nineteenth-Century England', *International Review of Social History*, 7 (1962), pp.47–60; Edward Royle, *Radicals, Secularists and Republicans: Popular Free Thought in Britain, 1866–1915* (Manchester: Manchester University Press, 1980); Feargus D'Arcy, 'Charles Bradlaugh and the English Republican Movement, 1868–1878', *Historical Journal*, 25 (1982), pp.367– 383; Taylor, *'Down with the Crown'*; David Nash and Antony Taylor (eds), *Republicanism in Victorian Society* (Stroud: Sutton, 2000).

76 David Cannadine, 'The Context, Performance and Meaning of Ritual: The British Monarchy and the 'Invention of Tradition', *c.* 1820–1977', in E. J. Hobsbawm and Terence Ranger (eds), *The Invention of Tradition* (Cambridge: Cambridge University Press, 1983), pp.101–64.

77 In *Queen Victoria: First Media Monarch* (Oxford: Oxford University Press, 2003), John Plunkett argues that there was a strong monarchist presence in early Victorian popular culture. See also Paul Pickering, '"The Hearts of the Millions": Chartism and Popular Monarchism in the 1840s', *History*, 88 (2003), pp.227–48.

78 William M. Kuhn, 'Ceremony and Politics: The British Monarchy, 1871–2', *Journal of British Studies*, 26 (1987), pp.133–62; Robert Blake, *Disraeli* (London: Eyre and Spottiswoode, 1966), pp.521–22.

79 Miles Taylor, 'John Bull and the Iconography of Public Opinion in England, *c.*1712–1929', *Past and Present*, 134 (1992), pp.93–128.

80 Hugh Cunningham, 'The Language of Patriotism, 1750–1914', *History Workshop Journal*, 12 (1981), pp.8–33.

81 Paul Ward, *Red Flag and Union Jack: Englishness, Patriotism and the British Left, 1881–1924* (Woodbridge: Boydell, 1988).

82 *Englishman*, 6 May 1876, p.69.

83 Ibid., 8 January 1876, p.630.

84 Keith McClelland, 'Masculinity and the "Representative Artisan" in Britain, 1850–1880' in Michael Roper and John Tosh (eds), *Manful Assertions: Masculinities in Britain since 1800* (London: Routledge, 1991), pp. 74–91; idem,

'Rational and Respectable Men: Gender, the Working Class and Citizenship in Britain, 1850–1867' in Laura Frader and Sonya O. Rose (eds), *Gender and Class in Modern Europe* (Ithaca, New York: Cornell University Press, 1996), pp. 280–93.

Notes to Chapter 13: Melodrama

1 M. J. Mayer and J. E. Child, *The Two Mothers* (1877): Lord Chamberlain's collection of plays (British Library). I am grateful to Michael Diamond for informing me about this play.
2 *The Times*, 3 April 1877, p.5. On tableaux, see Martin Meisel, *Realizations: Narrative, Pictorial and Theatrical Arts in Nineteenth-Century England* (Princeton, New Jersey: Princeton University Press, 1983).
3 H. Chance Newton, *Crime and the Drama: or Dark Deeds Dramatized* (London: Stanley Paul, 1927), pp.111–19.
4 *Morning Advertiser*, 5 October 1872, p.4.
5 *Era*, 3 March 1872, pp.5–6; see also *Pall Mall Gazette*, 5 March 1872, p.4. The Alexandra Opera Theatre in Sheffield also presented a play called *The Lost Heir* based on Tichborne: *Entr'Acte*, 24 August 1872, p.4.
6 *Era*, 7 April 1872, p.11.
7 Newton, *Crime and the Drama*, p.115. Newton was unable to identify the location of this production, which he had seen as a child.
8 *Era*, 8 April 1877, p.5.
9 *Daily Telegraph*, 27 March 1872, p.3.
10 Edward Kenealy (ed.), *The Trial at Bar of Sir Roger C. D. Tichborne* (London: Englishman, 1875–80) [hereafter Kenealy, *Trial*], iii, p.278.
11 Alexander Cockburn, *The Tichborne Trial: The Summing-Up of the Lord Chief Justice of England* (London: Ward, Lock and Tyler, 1874), p.5.
12 *Pall Mall Gazette*, 2 March 1874, p.1; see also *Daily News*, 3 March 1874, p.5.
13 *Nottingham Daily Guardian*, 18 July 1872, p.2.
14 George Kitson Clark, 'The Romantic Element, 1830–1850', in J.H. Plumb (ed.), *Studies in Social History* (London: Longmans, 1955), pp.209–39.
15 On melodrama, see Michael R. Booth, *English Melodrama* (London: Herbert Jenkins, 1965); Louis James, 'Taking Melodrama Seriously: Theatre and Nineteenth-Century Studies', *History Workshop Journal*, 3 (1977), pp.151–8; Jane Moody, *Illegiti-mate Theatre in London, 1770–1840* (Cambridge: Cambridge University Press, 2000); Frank Rahill, *The World of Melodrama* (University Park, Pennsylvania: Pennsylvania State University Press, 1967); James L. Smith, *Melodrama* (London: Methuen, 1973).
16 Imported from Italy, pantomime was a theatre of silence, as Louis XIV banned the use of speech in all Parisian theatres except the Comédie Française. Melo-

drama, a theatre of elaborate gestures, originated partially in mime. See Frederick Brown, *Theater and Revolution: The Culture of the French Stage* (New York: Viking Press, 1980), p.ix.

17 Gillian Russell, *The Theatres of War: Performance, Politics and Society, 1793–1815* (Oxford: Clarendon Press, 1995).

18 Marius Kwint, 'The Legitimization of the Circus in Late Georgian England', *Past and Present*, 174 (2002), pp.72–115; Brenda Assael, *The Circus and Victorian Society* (Charlottesville, Virginia: University of Virginia Press, 2005).

19 Peter Brooks, *The Melodramatic Imagination: Balzac, Henry James, and the Mode of Excess* (New Haven, Connecticut: Yale University Press, 1976); Elaine Hadley, *Melodramatic Tactics: Theatricalized Dissent in the English Marketplace, 1800–1885* (Stanford: Stanford University Press, 1995). See also Rohan McWilliam, 'Melodrama and the Historians', *Radical History Review*, 78 (2000), pp.57–84.

20 Meisel, *Realizations*. See also Louis James, 'Was Jerrold's Black Ey'd Susan More Popular than Wordsworth's Lucy?', in David Bradby, Louis James and Bernard Sharratt (eds), *Performance and Politics in Popular Drama* (Cambridge: Cambridge University Press, 1980), p.8.

21 J. R. Lewis, *The Victorian Bar* (London: Robert Hale, 1982), p.13, 120.

22 Kelly Boyd, *Manliness and the Boys' Story Paper in Britain: A Cultural History, 1855–1940* (London: Palgrave, 2003).

23 Cockburn, *The Tichborne Trial*, p.101.

24 Martha Vicinus, '"Helpless and Unfriended": Nineteenth-Century Domestic Melodrama', *New Literary History*, 13 (1981), pp.127–43; Anna Clark, 'The Politics of Seduction in English Popular Culture, 1748–1848', in Jean Radford (ed.), *The Progress of Romance: The Politics of Popular Fiction* (London: Routledge and Kegan Paul, 1988) pp.47–72; Judith R. Walkowitz, *City of Dreadful Delight: Narratives of Sexual Danger in Late-Victorian London* (London: Virago, 1992), ch. 7.

25 Raphael Samuel, Ewan McColl and Stuart Cosgrave (eds), *Theatres of the Left, 1880–1935: Workers' Theatre Movements in Britain and America* (London: Routledge and Kegan Paul, 1985), pp.x–xi, xvi.

26 Thomas W. Laqueur, 'The Queen Caroline Affair: Politics as Art in the Reign of George IV', *Journal of Modern History*, 54 (1982), pp.417–66; Anna Clark, *The Struggle for the Breeches: Gender and the Making of the British Working Class* (London: Rivers Oram, 1995), ch. 9.

27 Ernest Hartley Coleridge (ed.), *Life and Correspondence of John Duke Coleridge, Lord Chief Justice of England* (London: William Heinemann, 1904), ii, pp.192–93.

28 Winifred Hughes, *The Maniac in the Cellar: Sensation Novels of the 1860s* (Princeton, New Jersey: Princeton University Press, 1980), p.31. See also Jeanne

Fahnestock, 'Bigamy: The Rise and Fall of a Convention', *Nineteenth-Century Fiction*, 36 (1981), pp.47–71.

29 *Englishman*, 19 October 1874, pp.418–23.

30 E.g. Lynn Hunt, *The Family Romance of the French Revolution* (London: Routledge, 1992).

31 Unidentified newspaper clipping in Local Collection Cuttings Album (General): St Marylebone Public Library.

32 *Englishman*, 5 December 1874 p.555.

33 David Vincent links the rise in literacy to family mobility in *Literacy and Popular Culture: England, 1750–1914* (Cambridge: Cambridge University Press, 1989). See also John Reid, *Victorian Conventions* (Athens, Ohio: Ohio University Press, 1975), ch. 10.

34 The actual line is 'dead, dead, dead! and he never knew me, never called me mother'. It comes from the dramatisation of Mrs Henry Wood's *East Lynne*: T. A. Palmer, *East Lynne* (London: Samuel French, 1874), p.38.

35 E. Ann Kaplan, *Motherhood and Representation: The Mother in Popular Culture and Melodrama* (London: Routledge, 1992), ch. 1.

36 *Tichborne Gazette*, 28 May 1872, p.1; 18 June 1872, p.1; 2 July 1872, p.1.

37 Julia Przybos, *L'entreprise mélodramatique* (Paris: Librarie José Corti, 1987), p.87.

38 *Nottingham Daily Guardian*, 20 July 1872, p.8.

39 Karl Miller, *Doubles: Studies in Literary History* (Oxford: Oxford University Press, 1985).

40 Alison Winter, *Mesmerized: Powers of Mind in Victorian Britain* (Chicago: University of Chicago Press, 1998).

41 On conspiracy theories, see Michael Billig, *Fascists: A Social Psychological View of the National Front* (London: Academic Press, 1978), ch. 9.

42 *Englishman*, 16 May 1874, p.91.

43 On Anti-Catholicism, see Geoffrey Best, 'Popular Protestantism in Victorian Britain', in R. Robson (ed.), *Ideas and Institutions of Victorian Britain* (London: G. Bell, 1967), pp.115–42; Edward Norman, *Anti-Catholicism in Victorian England* (London: George Allen and Unwin, 1968); Walter L. Arnstein, *Protestant versus Catholic in Mid-Victorian England: Mr. Newdegate and the Nuns* (Columbia, Missouri: University of Missouri Press, 1982); Denis G. Paz, *Popular Anti-Catholicism in Mid-Victorian England* (Stanford, California: Stanford University Press, 1992); Frank H. Wallis, *Popular Anti-Catholicism in Mid-Victorian Britain* (Lampeter: Edwin Mellen Press, 1993). See also Patrick Joyce, *Work, Society and Politics: The Culture of the Factory in Later Victorian England* (Brighton: Harvester, 1980), pp.255–61; Neville Kirk, *The Growth of Working-Class Reformism in Mid-Victorian England* (London: Croom Helm, 1985).

44 Geoffrey Cubitt, *The Jesuit Myth: Conspiracy Theory and Politics in Nineteenth-Century France* (Oxford: Clarendon Press, 1993).

45 Kenealy, *Trial*, iii, p.249.

46 Norman St John Stevas (ed.), *The Complete Works of Walter Bagehot* (London: *Economist* 1975), vii, pp.242–43.

47 Judith R. Walkowitz, *City of Dreadful Delight: Narratives of Sexual Danger in Late-Victorian London* (London: Virago: 1992) is an important treatment of these aspects of the melodramatic imagination.

48 James Grant, *The Newspaper Press: Its Origin, Progress and Present Position* (London: George Routledge, 1872), iii, p.97.

49 Raymond Williams, 'Radical and/or Respectable', in Richard Boston (ed.), *The Press We Deserve* (London: Routledge and Kegan Paul, 1970), p.20; Virginia S. Berridge, 'Popular Journalism and Working-Class Attitudes, 1854–1886: A Study of *Reynolds's Newspaper*, *Lloyd's Weekly Newspaper* and the *Weekly Times*' (University of London D.Phil. thesis, 1976), p.34.

50 On Reynolds, see Rohan McWilliam 'The Mysteries of G. W. M. Reynolds: Radicalism and Melodrama in Victorian Britain' in Malcolm Chase and Ian Dyck (eds), *Living and Learning: Essays in Honour of J. F. C. Harrison* (London: Scolar, 1996), pp.182–98; see also Ian Haywood, *The Revolution in Popular Literature: Print, Politics and the People* (Cambridge: Cambridge University Press, 2004), chs 6, 8.

51 Iain MacCalman, *Radical Underworld: Prophets, Revolutionaries and Pornographers in London, 1795–1840* (Cambridge: Cambridge University Press, 1988), ch. 10.

52 E.g. *Reynolds's Newspaper*, 1 January 1860, p.1; 29 September 1872, p.1.

53 Ibid., 10 March 1872, p.4.

54 Ibid., 14 April 1872, p.1.

55 Ibid., 21 April 1872, p.4.

56 Virginia Berridge, 'Popular Sunday Papers and Mid-Victorian Society' in George Boyce et al. (eds), *Newspaper History* (London: Constable, 1978), pp.384–45.

57 E.g, *Reynolds's Newspaper*, 26 October 1884, p.1.

58 Wayne Burns, *Charles Reade: A Study in Victorian Authorship* (New York: Bookman Associates, 1961), p.290, 296.

59 See John Sutherland, 'Was he Popenjoy?', in his *Is Heathcliff a Murderer?: Puzzles in Nineteenth-Century Fiction* (Oxford: Oxford University Press, 1996), pp.168–75 for the linkage between Trollope's novel and the Tichborne case.

60 Marcus Clarke (with Andrew Hislop), *Chidiock Tichborne: or, the Catholic Conspiracy* (London: Eden Remington and Co., 1893).

61 For Boldrewood's indebtedness to Tichborne when writing *Nevermore*, see Paul de Serville, *Rolf Boldrewood* (Melbourne: Melbourne University Press, 2000), pp.236–37.

62 Kevin Brownlow, *Behind the Mask of Innocence: Films of Social Conscience in the Silent Era* (London: Jonathan Cape, 1990).

63 Christine Gledhill, *Home is Where the Heart is: Studies in Melodrama and the Woman's Film* (London: British Film Institute, 1987).

64 Chris Waters, *British Socialists and the Politics of Popular Culture, 1884–1914* (Manchester: Manchester University Press, 1990).

65 An exception to this was Mike Alfred's 1987 production of *The Wandering Jew* at the National Theatre, which succeeded in recreating nineteenth-century melodrama in its own terms.

66 Patrick Joyce, *Visions of the People: Industrial England and the Question of Class, 1848–1914* (Cambridge: Cambridge University Press, 1991).

Notes to Chapter 14: Epilogue

1 Douglas Woodruff, *The Tichborne Claimant: A Victorian Mystery* (London: Hollis and Carter, 1957), p.436.

2 *People*, 19 May to 30 June 1895.

3 'W. A. F.' (William Alfred Frost), *An Exposure of the Orton Confession of the Tichborne Claimant* (London: Lynwood, 1913).

4 H. B. Harding to A. J. W. Biddulph, 22 June 1895, Douglas Woodruff Papers, series 7, box 32, folder 1, Georgetown University.

5 Datas, *Datas: The Memory Man* (London: Wright and Brown, 1932), p.12.

6 Woodruff, *The Tichborne Claimant*, p.439.

7 L. C. Collins (ed.), *Life and Memoirs of John Churton Collins* (London: The Bodley Head, 1912), pp.191–8.

8 Collins (ed.), *Life and Memoirs*, p.198.

9 Unidentified newspaper clipping in Local Collection Cuttings Album (General), St Marylebone Public Library).

10 Letter of Esther Ruth Brown (friend of the Helsby family) to Douglas Woodruff, 3 January 1953, Douglas Woodruff Papers, series 7, box 34, folder 10, Georgetown University.

11 William Day, *Turf Celebrities I Have Known* (London: F.V. White, 1891) p.44.

12 Amelia Eckett correspondence with Douglas Woodruff, 1954–6: Douglas Woodruff Papers, series 7, box 35, folder 11, Georgetown University.

13 Woodruff, *The Tichborne Claimant*, p.443.

14 Theresa Tichborne, 'Consequences: Some of the Inner History of the Doughty Family', manuscript in Douglas Woodruff Papers, series 7, box 35, folder 24, Georgetown University.

15 Maurice Kenealy, *The Tichborne Tragedy* (London: Griffiths, 1913), p.4.

16 Most of the material on the next generation of Kenealys is derived from Michael Roe, *Kenealy and the Tichborne Cause: A Study in Mid-Victorian Populism* (Melbourne: Melbourne University Press, 1974), ch. 8.

17 Robert Barltrop and Jim Wolveridge, *The Muvver Tongue* (London: The Journeyman Press, 1980), p.52.

18 Datas, *Datas*, pp.9–15.

19 H. Chance Newton, *Crime and the Drama: or, Dark Deeds Dramatized* (London: Stanley Paul, 1927), p.113; 'The True History of the Tichborne Case', *Cornhill Magazine*, 67 (1929), pp.19–24.

20 Leonard Merrick, *The Worldlings* (London: John Murray, 1900); Jorge Luis Borges, *A Universal History of Infamy* (London: Allen Lane, 1973 [1954]); Julian Symons, *The Belting Inheritance* (London: Collins, 1965); Robin Maugham, *The Link: A Victorian Mystery* (London: Heinemann, 1969); Patrick White, *The Twyborn Affair* (London: Cape, 1979); Mat Schulz, *Claim* (Sydney: Flamingo, 1996).

21 John Young, *Sir Roger Tichborne Up-to-Date: or the Whirligig of Fate* (London: Bernard Quaritch, 1901); *The Lost Sir Roger* (Edinburgh: McFarlane and Erskine, 1908).

22 Woodruff, *The Tichborne Claimant*.

23 Roe, *Kenealy and the Tichborne Cause*.

24 Robert Darnton, *The Great Cat Massacre and Other Episodes in French Cultural History* (London: Allen Lane, 1984), esp. pp.4–5, 77–8.

25 Paul Ward, *Red Flag and Union Jack: Englishness, Patriotism and the British Left, 1881–1924*

Bibliography

This is a brief guide to the main primary and secondary works. Further references can be found in the notes and in Rohan McWilliam, 'The Tichborne Claimant and the People: Investigations into Popular Culture, 1867–1886' (University of Sussex D.Phil. thesis, 1990) which contains a fuller bibliography. The latter also contains a more detailed guide to the newspapers and Tichborne ephemera that were employed in the writing of this book. The section on secondary sources below lists the main studies of the Tichborne case and some of the works that have informed my thinking about the subject.

PRIMARY SOURCES
Manuscripts
Birmingham Central Library:
   Broadside scrap book
Minutes of the Sunday Evening Debating Society.
Bishopsgate Institute, London: George Howell Papers.
Bodleian Library, Oxford: John Johnson Collection, Tichborne Case Folder.
British Library. Department of Additional Manuscripts:
   Daybooks indexing the Lord Chamberlain's Plays. Add. MS 53702-708.
   William Ewart Gladstone Papers.
Georgetown University Library, Special Collections Division, Washington, DC: Douglas Woodruff Papers.
Hampshire Record Office:
Miscellaneous Papers 39M85/PC/F32; 70M75-M-21; Photocopy 57 (Tichborne Dole); 138-M84-W/ 10; 37-M48/132/35; 37-M48/67; 37-M48/67; 37-M48/37; 37-M48/74.
Leeds Archives Department: Radcliffe Papers.
Lincoln's Inn, London: John Holmes Papers.
National Archives, Kew: Home Office Papers.
University College London: Edwin Chadwick Papers.
Warwickshire County Record Office: Dormer of Grove Park MSS.

Tichborne Ephemera
The following libraries and museums have important collections of Tichborne ephemera including ballads, broadsides, cartoons, music,

posters and other forms of Tichborniana. Private collections are not
listed here.

Birmingham Central Library: broadside scrap book, callmark F AO82.2 LL]).

Bodleian Library, Oxford: the C.H. Firth collection of broadsides and the
John Johnson Collection.

Brighton Museum.

British Library (listed under Orton, Arthur, in the catalogue).

Georgetown University, Washington DC: Douglas Woodruff Papers.

Hanley Central Library, Hanley.

Leeds Record Office: Radcliffe Papers.

Library of Congress, Washington DC.

Lilly Library, Indiana University, Bloomington, Indiana.

London Library: Tichborne case scrapbook.

London University: Senate House Library.

St Bride's Printing Library, London.

St Marylebone Public Libraries Local Collection: cuttings album – general
(scrapbook).

University of Southampton Library: Cope Collection.

SECONDARY SOURCES
Books

Altick, Richard D., *Victorian Studies in Scarlet* (London: Dent, 1970).

Annear, Robyn, *The Man Who Lost Himself: The Unbelievable Story of the
Tichborne Claimant* (London: Robinson, 2003).

Arnstein, Walter L., *Protestant versus Catholic in Mid-Victorian England: Mr
Newdegate and the Nuns* (Columbia, Missouri: University of Missouri
Press, 1982).

Atlay, J. B., *Famous Trials of the Century* (London: Grant Richards, 1899).

Atlay, J. B., *The Tichborne Case* (London: W. Hodge, 1917).

Bailey, Peter, *Leisure and Class in Victorian England: Rational Recreation and
the Contest for Control, 1830–1885* (London: Methuen, 1987 [1978]).

Bailey, Peter, *Popular Culture and Performance in the Victorian City*
(Cambridge: Cambridge University Press, 1998).

Biagini, Eugenio, *Liberty, Retrenchment and Reform: Popular Liberalism in
the Age of Gladstone, 1860–1880* (Cambridge: Cambridge University
Press, 1992).

Biagini, Eugenio and Alastair J. Reid (eds), *Currents of Radicalism: Popular*

Radicalism, Organised Labour and Party Politics in Britain, 1850-1914 (Cambridge: Cambridge University Press, 1991).

Bratton, Jacqueline S., *The Victorian Popular Ballad* (London: Macmillan, 1975).

Briggs, Asa, *Victorian Things* (London: Batsford, 1988).

Brooks, Peter, *The Melodramatic Imagination: Balzac, Henry James and the Mode of Excess* (New Haven: Yale University Press, 1976).

Burton, Sarah, *Impostors: Six Kinds of Liar* (London: Viking, 2000).

Canavon, Margaret, *Populism* (London: Junction Books, 1981).

Cocks, Raymond, *Foundations of the Modern Bar* (London: Sweet and Maxwell, 1983).

Colley, Linda, *Britons: Forging the Nation, 1707–1837* (New Haven, Connecticut: Yale University Press, 1992).

Collins, Henry and Chimen Abramsky, *Karl Marx and the British Labour Movement: Years of the First International* (London: Macmillan, 1965).

Colls, Robert and Philip Dodd (eds), *Englishness: Politics and Culture, 1880–1920* (London: Croom Helm, 1986).

Crossick, Geoffrey, *An Artisan Elite in Victorian Society: Kentish London, 1840-1880* (London: Croom Helm, 1978).

Cunningham, Hugh, *Leisure in the Industrial Revolution, c.1780–1880* (London: Croom Helm, 1980).

Darnton, Robert, *The Great Cat Massacre and Other Episodes in French Cultural History* (London: Allen Lane, 1984).

Daumas, Georges, *L'affaire Tichborne* (Paris: Les Oeuvres Libres, 1933).

Davis, Natalie Zemon, *The Return of Martin Guerre* (Cambridge, Massachusetts: Harvard University Press, 1983).

Diamond, Michael, *Victorian Sensation: or The Spectacular, the Shocking, and the Scandalous in Nineteenth-Century Britain* (London: Anthem Press, 2003).

Epstein, James, *Radical Expression: Political Language, Ritual, and Symbol in England, 1790–1850* (New York: Oxford University Press, 1994).

Epstein, James, *In Practice: Studies in the Language and Culture of Popular Politics in Modern Britain* (Stanford, California: Stanford University Press, 2003).

Falk, Bernard, *The Naughty Seymours* (London: Hutchinson, 1940).

Finn, Margot, *After Chartism: Class and Nation in English Radical Politics, 1848–1874* (Cambridge: Cambridge University Press, 1993).

Fox, John C., *The History of Contempt of Court: The Form of Trial and the Mode of Punishment* (Oxford: Oxford University Press, 1927).

'W. A. F.' [Frost, William Alfred], *An Exposure of the Orton Confession of the Tichborne Claimant* (London: Lynwood, 1913).

Geertz, Clifford, *The Interpretation of Cultures* (London: Hutchinson, 1975).

Gilbert, Michael, *The Claimant* (London: Constable, 1957).

Girouard, Mark. *The Return to Camelot: Chivalry and the English Gentleman* (New Haven: Yale University Press, 1981).

Golby, J. M. and A. W. Purdue, *The Civilisation of the Crowd: Popular Culture in Britain, 1750–1900* (London: Batsford Academic and Educational, l984).

Hanham, H. J., *Elections and Party Management: Politics in the Time of Disraeli and Gladstone* (Brighton: Harvester, 1978 [1959]).

Harrison, Brian, *Drink and the Victorians: The Temperance Question in England, 1815–1872* (London: Faber and Faber, 1971).

Harrison, J. F. C., *The Common People: A History from the Norman Conquest to the Present* (London: Fontana, 1984).

Harrison, Royden, *Before the Socialists: Studies in Labour and Politics, 1861–1881* (London: Routledge and Kegan Paul, 1965).

Hart, Viven, *Distrust and Democracy: Political Distrust in Britain and America* (Cambridge: Cambridge University Press, 1978).

Hartman, Mary S., *Victorian Murderesses: A True History of Thirteen Respectable Women Accused of Unspeakable Crimes* (London: Robson, 1977).

Hobsbawm, Eric J., *Bandits* (London: Weidenfeld and Nicolson, 1969).

Hobsbawm, Eric J., *Labouring Men* (London: Weidenfeld and Nicolson, 1964).

Hobsbawm, Eric J., *Worlds of Labour* (London: Weidenfeld and Nicolson, 1984).

Hobsbawm, Eric, and Terence Ranger (eds), *The Invention of Tradition* (Cambridge: Cambridge University Press, 1983).

Hofstadter, Richard, *The Paranoid Style in American Politics and Other Essays* (London: Cape, 1966).

Hoggart, Richard, *The Uses of Literacy* (London: Pelican, 1958 [1957]).

Hollis, Patricia, *The Pauper Press* (Oxford: Oxford University Press, 1970).

Hoppen, K. Theodore, *The Mid-Victorian Generation, 1846-1886* (Oxford: Clarendon Press, 1998).

Ionescu, G., and E. Gellner (eds), *Populism: Its Meaning and National Character* (London: Weidenfeld and Nicolson, 1969).

James, Louis, *Fiction for the Working Man, 1830–1850: A Study of the Literature Produced for the Working Classes in Early Victorian Urban England* (Oxford: Oxford University Press, 1963).

James, Louis, *Print and the People, 1819–1951* (London: Allen Lane, 1976).

Jones, Gareth Stedman, *Languages of Class: Studies in English Working-Class History, 1832–1982* (Cambridge: Cambridge University Press, 1983).

Jones, Gareth Stedman, *Outcast London: A Study in the Relationship between Classes in Victorian Society* (London: Penguin, 1984 [1971]).

Joyce, Patrick, *Democratic Subjects: The Self and the Social in Nineteenth-Century England* (Cambridge: Cambridge University Press, 1994).

Joyce, Patrick, *Visions of the People: Industrial England and the Question of Class, 1848–1914* (Cambridge: Cambridge University Press, 1991).

Joyce, Patrick, *Work, Society and Politics: The Culture of the Factory in Late Victorian England* (Brighton: Harvester, 1980).

Kenealy, Maurice, *The Tichborne Tragedy* (London: Francis Griffiths, 1913).

Kirk, Neville, *The Growth of Working Class Reformism in Mid-Victorian England* (London: Croom Helm, 1985).

Lancaster, Bill, *Radicalism, Co-operation and Socialism: Leicester Working-Class Politics, 1860-1906* (Leicester: Leicester University Press, 1987).

Lawrence, Jon, *Speaking for the People: Party, Language, and Popular Politics in England, 1867–1914* (Cambridge: Cambridge University Press, 1998).

Leach, Robert, *The Punch and Judy Show: History, Tradition and Meaning* (London: Batsford Academic and Educational, 1985).

Lewis, J. R., *The Victorian Bar* (London: Robert Hale, 1982).

MacGregor, Geddes, *The Tichborne Impostor* (New York: Lippincott, 1957).

McWilliam, Rohan, *Popular Politics in Nineteenth-Century England* (London: Routledge, 1998).

Maugham, Frederic Herbert (Lord), *The Tichborne Case* (London: Hodder and Stoughton, 1936).

Offer, Avner, *Property and Politics, 1870–1914: Landownership, Law, Ideology and Urban Development in England* (Cambridge: Cambridge University Press, 1981).

Pelling, Henry M, *Popular Politics and Society in Late Victorian Britain* (London: Macmillan, 1968).

Perkin, Harold, *The Origins of Modern English Society, 1780–1880* (London: Routledge and Kegan Paul, 1969).

Pocock, J. G. A. *Virtue, Commerce and History: Essays on Political Thought and History, Chiefly in the Eighteenth Century* (Cambridge: Cambridge University Press, 1985).

Price, Richard, *British Society, 1680–1880: Dynamism, Containment, and Change* (Cambridge: Cambridge University Press, 1999)

Reed, John R., *Victorian Conventions* (Ohio: Ohio University Press, 1975).

Richter, Donald C., *Riotous Victorians* (Ohio: Ohio University Press, 1981).

Roe, Michael, *Kenealy and the Tichborne Cause: A Study in Mid-Victorian Populism* (Melbourne: University of Melbourne Press, 1974).

Rothstein, Arthur, *A House on Clerkenwell Green* (London: Lawrence and Wishart, 1966).

Royle, Edward, *Radicals, Secularists and Republicans: Popular Free Thought in Britain, 1866-1915* (Manchester: Manchester University Press, 1980).

Rubin, G. R., and David Sugarman (eds), *Law, Economy and Society, 1750–1914: Essays in the History of English Law* (Oxford: Professional Books, 1984).

Rubinstein, W. D., *Elites and the Wealthy in Modern British History: Essays in Social and Economic History* (Brighton: Harvester, 1987).

Schwartz, Hillel, *The Culture of the Copy: Striking Likenesses, Unreasonable Facsimiles* (New York: Zone Books, 1996).

Sennett, Richard, *The Fall of Public Man* (New York: Alfred A. Knopf, 1977).

Shannon, Richard T., *Gladstone and the Bulgarian Agitation, 1876* (London: Thomas Nelson, 1963).

Shepard, Leslie, *The Broadside Ballad: A Study in Origins and Meaning* (London: Herbert Jenkins, 1962).

Shipley, Stan, *Club Life and Socialism in Mid-Victorian London* (Oxford: Journeyman Press/History Workshop Centre, 1983 [1971]).

Simpson, A. W. B., *Cannibalism and the Common Law: The Story of the Tragic Last Voyage of the 'Mignonette' and the Strange Legal Proceedings to which it Gave Rise* (Chicago: Chicago University Press, 1984).

Stallybrass, Peter and Allon White, *The Politics and Poetics of Transgression* (London: Methuen, 1986).

Stoker, Bram, *Famous Impostors* (London: Sidgwick and Jackson, 1910).

Storch, Robert D. (ed.), *Popular Culture and Custom in Nineteenth-Century England* (London: Croom Helm, 1982).

Taylor, Antony, *'Down with the Crown': British Anti-monarchism and Debates about Royalty since 1790* (London: Reaktion, 1999).

Taylor, Miles, *Ernest Jones, Chartism, and the Romance of Politics, 1819–1869* (Oxford: Oxford University Press, 2003).

Tholfson, Trygve R., *Working Class Radicalism in Mid-Victorian England* (London: Croom Helm, 1976).

Thomas, David Wayne, *Cultivating Victorians: Liberal Culture and the Aesthetic* (Philadelphia, Pennsylvania: University of Pennsylvania Press 2004).

Thompson, E. P., *The Making of the English Working Class* (London: Pelican, 1968 [1963]).

Thompson, F. M. L., *English Landed Society in the Nineteenth Century* (London: Routledge and Kegan Paul, 1963).

Turner, Victor W., *Dramas, Fields and Metaphors: Symbolic Action in Human Society* (Ithaca: Cornell University Press, 1974).

Vernon, James, *Politics and the People: A Study in English Political Culture, c.1815–1867* (Cambridge: Cambridge University Press, 1993).

Vicinus, Martha, *The Industrial Muse: A Study of Nineteenth Century British Working-Class Literature* (London: Croom Helm, 1974).

Vincent, John, *The Formation of the British Liberal Party, 1857–1868* (Hassocks: Harvester, 1976 [1966]).

Walkowitz, Judith R., *City of Dreadful Delight: Narratives of Sexual Danger in Late-Victorian London* (London: Virago, 1992).

Walkowitz, Judith R. *Prostitution and Victorian Society: Women, Class and the State*. Cambridge: Cambridge University Press, 1980.

Warner, Marina, *Monuments and Maidens: The Allegory of the Female Form* (London: Weidenfeld and Nicolson, 1985).

Wiener, Martin J., *English Culture and the Decline of the Industrial Spirit, 1850-1980* (Cambridge: Cambridge University Press, 1981).

Williams, Raymond, *Culture and Society, 1780-1950* (London: Pelican, 1982 [1958]).

Williams, Raymond, *The Long Revolution* (London: Chatto and Windus, 1961).

Woodruff, Douglas, *The Tichborne Claimant* (London: Hollis and Carter, 1957).

Articles and Essays

Allcock, J. B., 'Populism: A Brief Biography', *Sociology*, 5 (1971), pp.371–87.

Anderson, Perry, 'Origins of the Present Crisis', *New Left Review*, no. 23 (1964), pp.26–53.

Belchem, John, 'Republicanism, Popular Constitutionalism and the Radical Platform in Early Nineteenth-Century England', *Social History*, 6 (1981), pp.1–32.

Belchem, John, and James Epstein, 'The Nineteenth-Century Gentleman Leader Revisited', *Social History*, 22 (1997), pp.174–93.

Bennett, Tony, 'The Politics of "the Popular" and Popular Culture', in Bennett et al (eds), *Popular Culture and Social Relations* (Milton Keynes: Open University Press, 1986), pp.6–21.

Berridge, Virginia, 'Popular Sunday Papers and Mid-Victorian Society', in George Boyce et al (eds), *Newspaper History* (London: Constable, 1978), pp.247–64.

Chartier, Roger, 'Culture as Appropriation: Popular Cultural Uses in Early Modern France', in Steven L. Kaplan (ed.), *Understanding Popular Culture: Europe from the Middle Ages to the Nineteenth Century* (Berlin: Mouton, 1984), pp.229–53.

Cunningham, Hugh, 'Jingoism in 1877–78', *Victorian Studies*, 14 (1971), pp.429–53.

Cunningham, Hugh, 'The Language of Patriotism, 1750-1914' *History Workshop Journal*, no.12 (1981), pp.8–33.

D'Arcy, Feargus, 'Charles Bradlaugh and the English Republican Movement, 1868–1878', *Historical Journal*, 25 (1982), pp.367–83.

Duman, Daniel, 'The Creation and Diffusion of a Professional Ideology in Nineteenth-Century England', *Sociological Review*, 27 (1979), pp.113–38.

Eley, Geoff, 'Re-Thinking the Political: Social History and Political Culture in Eighteenth and Nineteenth-Century Britain', *Archiv für Sozialgeschichte*, 21 (1981), pp.427–57.

Gossman, Norbert J., 'Republicanism in Nineteenth Century England', *International Review of Social History*, 7 (1962), pp.47–60.

Hall, Stuart, 'Notes on Deconstructing "the Popular"', in Raphael Samuel (ed.), *People's History and Socialist Theory* (London: Routledge and Kegan Paul, 1981), pp.227–40.

Hill, Christopher, 'The Norman Yoke', in John Saville (ed.), *Democracy and the Labour Movement* (London: Lawrence and Wishart, 1954), pp.11–66.

Howkins, Alun, and C. Ian Dyck, 'The Time's Alteration: Popular Ballads, Rural Radicalism and William Cobbett', *History Workshop Journal*, no. 23 (1987), pp.20–38.

Hughes, Noel, 'The Tichbornes, the Doughtys and Douglas Woodruff', *Recusant History*, 23 (1997), pp.602–19.

James, Louis, 'Taking Melodrama Seriously: Theatre and Nineteenth-Century Studies', *History Workshop Journal*, no. 3. (1977), pp.151–8.

Jones, Gareth Stedman, 'Some Notes on Karl Marx and the English Labour Movement', *History Workshop Journal*, no. 18 (1984), pp.124–137.

Kent, Christopher, 'Victorian Self-Making, or Self-Unmaking?: The Tichborne Claimant Revisited', *Victorian Review*, 17 (1991), pp.1–16.

Laqueur, Thomas W., 'The Queen Caroline Affair: Politics as Art in the Reign of George IV', *Journal of Modern History*, 54 (1982), pp.417– 66.

McKibbin, Ross, 'Why Was There No Marxism in Great Britain?', *English Historical Review*, 99 (1984), pp.297–331.

McWilliam, Rohan, 'Radicalism and Popular Culture: The Tichborne Case and the Politics of "Fair Play", 1867–1886', in Eugenio Biagini and Alastair J. Reid (eds), *Currents of Radicalism: Popular Radicalism, Organised Labour and Party Politics in Britain, 1850–1914* (Cambridge: Cambridge University Press, 1991), pp.44–6.

McWilliam, Rohan, 'The Theatricality of the Staffordshire Figurine', *Journal of Victorian Culture*, 10 (2005), pp.107–14.

Neuberg, V. E., 'The Literature of the Streets', in H. J. Dyos and Michael Wolff (eds), *The Victorian City: Images and Realities* (London: Routledge and Kegan Paul, 1973), i, pp.191–209.

Roberts, Edward, 'Tichborne: An Historical Introduction', *Hatcher Review*, 4 (1992), pp.40–49.

Saville, John, 'The Background to the Revival of Socialism in England', *Bulletin of the Society for the Study of Labour History*, no.11 (1965), pp.13–19.

Senelick, Lawrence, 'Politics as Entertainment: Victorian Music Hall Songs', *Victorian Studies*, 19 (1975), pp.149–80.

Thompson, F. M. L., 'Social Control in Victorian Britain', *Economic History Review*, 2nd series, 34 (1981), pp.189–208.

Whitehead, Andrew, 'Dan Chatterton and his "Atheistic Communistic Scorcher"', *History Workshop Journal*, no. 25 (1988), pp.83–99.

Wilkins, M. S., 'The Non-Socialist Origins of England's First Important Socialist Organization', *International Review of Social History*, 4 (1959), pp.199–207.

Yeo, Stephen, 'A New Life: The Religion of Socialism in Britain, 1883-1896', *History Workshop Journal*, no. 4 (1977), pp.5–56.

Yeo, Stephen, 'On the Uses of Apathy', *European Journal of Sociology*, 15 (1974), pp.279–311.

Theses

Anderton, Paul, 'The Liberal Party of Stoke-on-Trent and Parliamentary Elections 1862–1880: A Case Study in Liberal-Labour Relations'. University of Keele MA thesis, 1974.

Berridge, Virginia S., 'Popular Journalism and Working-Class Attitudes, 1854–1886: A Study of *Reynolds's Newspaper*, *Lloyd's Weekly Newspaper* and *The Weekly Times*'. University of London Ph.D. thesis, 1976.

Condon, Richard, 'The Political Career of Michael Maltman Barry, 1871–1909'. University of Oxford B.Litt thesis, 1972.

Cunningham, Hugh St C., 'British Public Opinion and the Eastern Question, 1877–8'. University of Sussex D.Phil thesis, 1969.

Gammon, Victor A. F., 'Popular Music in Rural Society: Sussex 1815–1914'. University of Sussex D.Phil thesis, 1985.

Joyce, Patrick, 'Popular Toryism in Lancashire, 1860–1890'. University of Oxford D.Phil thesis, 1975.

Lincoln Jr, Watson Eugene, 'Popular Radicalism and the Beginnings of the New Socialist Movement in Britain, 1870–1885'. University of London D.Phil. thesis, 1977.

McWilliam, Rohan, 'The Tichborne Claimant and the People: Investigations into Popular Culture, 1867–1886'. University of Sussex D.Phil. thesis, 1990.

Sykes, Robert, 'Politics and Electoral Behaviour in Guildford and West Surrey, 1790–1868'. University of Surrey D.Phil. thesis, 1977.

Taylor, Antony, 'Modes of Political Expression and Working-Class Radicalism: The London and Manchester Examples'. University of Manchester D.Phil. thesis, 1992.

Thomson, Robert S., 'The Development of the Broadside Ballad Trade and its Influence upon the Transmission of English Folksongs'. Cambridge University D.Phil. thesis, 1974.

Index

Illustrations in the text are rendered in **bold**.